MAN AND HIS WORK
Conflict and Change

MAN AND HIS WORK
Conflict and Change

GEORGE RITZER

University of Kansas

APPLETON-CENTURY-CROFTS

Educational Division

New York   MEREDITH CORPORATION

To my parents

Copyright © 1972 by MEREDITH CORPORATION

72 73 74 75 76 / 10 9 8 7 6 5 4 3 2 1

Library of Congress Card Number: 76–181822

PRINTED IN THE UNITED STATES OF AMERICA

390–74315–1

Contents

Foreword

Writing the foreword to another's book is much like being invited to dinner. One reaction is to be critical of the meal, although happily such is not the case here. Another reaction is to be a self-centered guest who seeks to convert the occasion to his own ends. In this way, the foreword becomes a convenient vehicle for its author to develop his own ideas within the general subject of the book; the intent is to try to make the appetizer the entire meal. Fortunately, there are very few, if any, such introductions that have become well known in their own right aside from the books whose company they share. George Bernard Shaw, of course, elevated the introductions to his plays to the level of independent essays, but the plays after all were all his own. Finally, the foreword can be treated as a polite duty, as if the guest really had other things to do and very little time to spare for the invitation. In those instances, the foreword looks like the tray of hors d'oeuvres at a cocktail party, with variety but with little substance. Perhaps it is very fortunate that most readers never read the foreword but go on at once to the main body of the book.

In this case, I feel that I am much more than a guest who has been invited to dinner. I have read the book in its earliest draft and subsequent revisions so that I have been able to develop a better understanding of what Ritzer has attempted than the reader will be able to obtain immediately. This is not to claim that I have made any distinct mark either on the writing or on Ritzer's main intentions. Rather, I know that I have learned more from him about the subject than he could have learned from me. In this very important sense I have found it rewarding to be allowed the association with someone who obviously knows his subject and enjoys writing about it. I can think of no better reason for writing a book.

For the person who has studied some sociology but who is just beginning the study of occupations, there will be some material that is familiar from other contexts and some material that is entirely new. Undoubtedly, he will recognize some features in the sociology of occupations that link it with a more general sociology, for example, the use of occupations as a basis for social stratification. On the other hand, he will very likely learn either about new occupations or about some features of occupations that he did know. For instance, we know that there are taxi drivers, but not many people know the stresses and satisfactions which these drivers experience. In these and other aspects, Ritzer has succeeded in weaving together occupational descriptions with a deeper analysis of the occupation and its place in the broader structure.

For sheer variety, ingenuity, and complexity there probably is no better example of man's social inventiveness than the occupational structures he has created in industrial societies. To comprehend the difference between a small agricultural society in which very few occupations are necessary and a large industrial society in which thousands of different occupations are found is to appreciate the enormous intricacy of social organization that is required to make a functioning unity of such diversity. Aside from meeting the apparent instrumental demands of a detailed division of labor to carry out the tasks required in an industrial society, the occupational structure also carries added functions of equal, if not greater, social importance: as a basis for social prestige, as a criterion of social class, as an organized means for allocating the products and services produced by the economy, as a set of incentives that direct a significant part of the individual's energies and aspirations, and as a focus for self-interest that can color the person's political and social ideologies. It is little wonder, therefore, that probably the single most important insight into an individual is the work that he does.

In view of these critical functions served by the occupational structure, it is both reasonable and scientifically sound to find that sociologists have devoted a good deal of their attention to the study of this subject. Even a glance at the lengthy bibliography that Ritzer has drawn upon in writing this book should prove this point. Perhaps what is equally striking in that bibliography is the number and variety of studies of specific occupations that sociologists have sought to describe. In this, Ritzer properly acknowledges the work of Everett Hughes and his students in developing a coherent body of literature that must be considered as outstanding in American sociology.

Yet, Ritzer has aimed at more than a listing of this literature or a summary of descriptive studies of a number of occupations. He has sought to analyze the links that exist between the occupational structure and the social structure. Although the first can be analytically distinguished, as Ritzer does in his several discussions of occupations as corporate entities, he maintains a constant awareness of the interrelationships between developments in the occupational structure and those occurring in the broader society. For example, his specific consideration of the occupational conflicts encountered by blacks and by females necessarily includes the consideration of conflicts endured by both of these groups in other, broader, social dimensions. From this perspective, it is not at all accidental that many of the aims of blacks and of women's liberationists point specifically at the lack of opportunities and the discriminatory treatment which are encountered within the occupational structure. Notice, however, that these aims are not alone a demand for the economic opportunities and economic security that are associated with the higher-status occupations. Included with these materialistic demands is the desire to share in the prestige and recognition that such occupations can confer upon individuals. Herein lie the added functions of the occupational structure that I listed above.

Ritzer's awareness of the interplay between occupations and society also includes attention to change and conflict as social processes that enhance that interplay. For example, the efforts by members of an occupation to elevate themselves to a professional status are stimulated originally by the higher status and greater rewards that society places upon the professions as compared with other occupational groups. This drive toward professionalization in its turn serves to alter the recruitment patterns, to tighten the process of certification, and even to alter the self-conceptions that members of an occupation have about themselves. Quite obviously, we have become a society that seems to be dedicated to professionals, even in sports.

The attention that Ritzer gives to conflict situations and the means of their solution within the occupational structure is another noteworthy feature of his analysis. Aside from the so-called "free" professionals, most people work for others. In this situation of occupational interface, where different occupations must work together, there are many surfaces where frictions can and do arise. Union jurisdictional disputes are probably the most obvious instances of such frictions. Yet, there are also work situations where several professions are involved and where there are conflicts as to lines of authority and responsibility. The university in the last few years is one example of challenge and modification of traditional lines of authority. The point is that such conflicts, depending upon their severity, can create crisis situations that interfere with the expected functioning of an organization or of society as a whole. The means to contain and to resolve such conflicts in an institutional manner, therefore, are required. I believe that by addressing himself to such problems, Ritzer has contributed importantly to our knowledge of occupations and occupational structure.

A final feature of Ritzer's book is his concentrated effort to develop testable propositions as a result of his prior analysis. I believe that this is both unique and noteworthy in a book that is intended primarily for students. All too often, we remain content with condensing and shaping a considerable body of literature so as to present a palatable product to students, instead of also trying to encourage them to use the knowledge they have gained. Ritzer has sought to involve students in the subject by suggesting hypotheses that are on the edge of our present knowledge and that represent ideas worthy of further pursuit. I interpret this as encouragement to all readers of this book to consider the next steps in the development of the sociology of occupations. Clearly, as I have implied throughout, and as Ritzer specifies at many points, the new knowledge that can be gained about the occupational structure very likely will have significance for the nature of social structure as well.

In writing this foreword I have attempted to steer between some of the alternatives that I described at the outset. I could not begin to discuss or even to enumerate all of the ideas that are contained in this book. Nor have I tried to establish a single orientation in the mind of the reader. Rather, like a willing guest, I have wanted only to suggest to him some of the broad dimensions that he will discover in this encounter with the sociology of occupations. Above all, I have desired to whet his appetite for an intellectual experience that will be complex and intriguing, as it will be rewarding.

Leonard Reissman

Preface

In any book such as this there are a number of people to thank. Two people have had an enormous effect on me as a sociologist as well as on this book. The first, chronologically, is Professor Harrison M. Trice of Cornell University. He managed the almost impossible feat of changing an ex-businessman into an ardent lover of sociology and the sociological perspective. Further, his interest in occupational sociology had a great impact on me and many of the points discussed in this book rely heavily on his insights into occupational life. The second is Leonard Reissman, my ex-colleague at Tulane University, and editor of this book. His honesty in tearing apart an earlier draft will always be appreciated. In addition, his helpful comments as the final draft developed have made this a far better book than it otherwise would have been. The failings in this book are mine and whatever I have contributed could not have been accomplished without the love and understanding of my wife, Sue. Thanks must also go to my sons, David and Jeremy, whose shining faces at the end of a hard day at the typewriter have made it all worthwhile. I must also thank the members of my classes in occupational sociology for the insights they offered after reading earlier drafts of the manuscript. Barry Billings, my assistant at Kansas, helped with the bibliography, and Jack Harris, a student assistant at Tulane, must also be thanked for his help in preparing the footnotes as well as for his critical reading of the manuscript. Mrs. Elizabeth Greene, secretary of the sociology department at Tulane, really deserves coauthorship for translating random thoughts into meaningful sentences and chapters. Gratitude must also be expressed to Mary Margaret Smith, Freda Faber, Deborah Huff, and Barbara Johnson for their ability to type the final draft of this manuscript from unintelligible jottings.

Ithaca, N.Y., June 1971

MAN AND HIS WORK
Conflict and Change

1

Introduction: The Sociological Study of Occupations

ASPECTS OF OCCUPATIONAL SOCIOLOGY

The study of occupational life constitutes one of the important subareas within sociology, but it is frequently confused with other sociological fields which are also related to the workworld. A useful first step in defining the sociology of occupations (and the concerns of this book) is to demonstrate how it differs from related areas of sociological concern. One such area is the sociological study of formal or complex organizations.[1] The focus in this area is on the formal structure of organizations and the informal structures inevitably spawned within them. Some, but certainly not all, of occupational sociology is concerned with the question of the structure of the organizations in which many occupations are found. Rather, the focus in occupational sociology is on the reciprocal effects of organizational structure on occupational life. Thus, when a doctor is employed in a hospital, his occupational behavior is affected by the organization and, conversely, his presence in the hospital affects its structure. Further, when the occupational sociologist studies occupations in organizations, he is also concerned with the impact of the various occupations on each other. Thus in the hospital setting he may focus on the conflict and cooperation between doctors, nurses, and administrators. When the occupational sociologist focuses on occupations in organizations, he is concerned with a series of different questions than the sociologist who focuses on studying organizations. More important, a number of occupations are not found in formal organizations, or, if they are, their worklife is not affected significantly by them. Examples of individuals in such "free" occupations are the independent merchant, the independent taxi driver, the doctor in private practice, and the poolroom hustler. Other occupations such as the janitor and the night watchman exist in formal organizations, but because of

[1] For a good, recent review of theories of complex organizations see Nicos P. Mouzelis, *Organisation and Bureaucracy: An Analysis of Modern Theories* (London: Routledge and Kegan Paul, 1967).

the nature of their work their behavior is not determined to a great extent by the organization. These two groups of occupations, in particular those that do not exist within formal organizations, have been almost the exclusive domain of occupational sociology. Occupational sociology and the sociological study of organizations, while related, are thus clearly not coterminous.

Industrial sociology is another subarea within sociology which, while related to occupational sociology, is not coterminous with it.[2] The study of occupations is only one aspect of industrial sociology; others are work organizations, unionization, industrialization, and the relationship between management and unions as well as that between industry and the community. While the occupational sociologist may touch upon these questions in the course of studying occupations, he does not give them a place of central concern as does the industrial sociologist. Industrial sociology is thus in one sense broader than occupational sociology, while in another it remains narrower. The occupational sociologist studies a wide array of occupations, many of which are not found in an industrial setting. Some examples of persons in these occupations, to be discussed later in this book, include physicians, store owners, strip teasers, jazz musicians, and migrant farm workers.

Since occupational sociology clearly differs in a number of respects from related subfields within sociology, what are the major topics studied by the sociologist who investigates occupations? Perhaps the best summary of the

TABLE 1-1

Major Topics in Occupational Sociology and Percentage of Articles
in the Period 1953–1959 Dealing with Each Topic

Topic	% of Articles 1953–1959
Career	12.9
Occupational status and mobility	21.0
Ethnic group and occupations	8.2
Workforce	8.2
Occupational role and personality	16.4
Occupational images	5.1
Occupational comparisons	5.1
Methodology	7.7
Client-professional relations	1.0
Occupational culture and ethics	9.8
Miscellaneous	4.6
	100.0

Adapted from Erwin Smigel et al., "Occupational Sociology: A Re-examination," *Sociology and Social Research* 47 (1963), 475.

[2] The major textbook in this field is Delbert C. Miller and William H. Form, *Industrial Sociology: The Sociology of Work Organizations*, 2nd ed. (New York: Harper & Row, 1964).

topics dealt with by occupational sociologists may be found in a 1963 examination by Smigel et al.[3] of the status of the field from 1953–1959 (see Table 1-1).

THE FOCUS OF THE BOOK

Although this book concentrates on many of these topics, some omissions should be noted. Specifically, little attention is paid to questions of occupational status and mobility, the workforce, and methodology. Since these three topics, taken together, account for 36.9 percent of the occupational studies between 1953 and 1959, some explanation of their omission here is necessary.

The explanation lies in this book's basic focus: the vast number of ethnographic studies of occupations. By ethnographic studies we mean studies that are primarily descriptive. Studies of occupational mobility, status, and the workforce actually contain little data that is descriptive, and these studies comprise a separate but related body of knowledge. Another reason for omitting these studies is merely the problem of space limitations. But more important, studies of occupational status and mobility are more frequently and adequately summarized and reviewed than other topics in occupational sociology.[4] Such studies often use occupations as indices for social class; however, this book is concerned with occupational characteristics as such rather than as social indices. Workforce analysis is valuable, but it is primarily of economic importance and tangential to the main point of trying to learn more about occupations themselves. The question of methodology in occupational sociology is omitted because it is even more tangential to the analysis of occupations per se. Further, it is perhaps better dealt with as a topic in a book on methodology than in a book on occupations.

This book, then, constitutes an attempt to summarize and categorize the vast number of ethnographic studies of occupations. That such an effort is needed is shown by the following critique of a recent textbook in occupational sociology:

The book will be of less value to the teacher who views occupations as corporate structures that are of interest both of themselves and for what they tell us about general social processes in the traditions of Everett Hughes or Talcott Parsons. Characteristically, the rich ethnographic detail of specific occupations-in-process is eschewed in favor of more global and *ad hoc* statements about types of occupations in general.[5]

[3] Erwin Smigel et al., "Occupational Sociology: A Re-examination," *Sociology and Social Research* 47 (1963), 472–477.

[4] See, for example, Seymour Martin Lipset and Reinhard Bendix, *Social Mobility in Industrial Society* (Berkeley: University of California Press, 1959).

[5] Richard A. Peterson, Review of *Occupational Sociology* by Lee Taylor, *American Sociological Review* 34 (1969), 777.

By focusing on these ethnographic studies, this book moves toward an analysis of the internal processes of occupational life. Such a choice excludes another area of occupational sociology—the relationship between the occupational system and the various other social systems in society—which might well have been included. Omission of this topic is not to be construed as a denial of its importance, for the relationships among subsystems are central to all areas of sociology. However, the relationship between occupations and other social systems has been dealt with in another recent text in occupational sociology.[6]

No systematic study has yet focused adequately on the internal processes of occupational life. In sum, then, this book seeks to review the ethnographic studies of occupations and in the process to examine carefully the internal processes in occupational life. Returning to Table 1-1, all the topics except occupational status and mobility, the workforce, and methodology constitute the major themes of this book, and all but occupational comparisons may be included under the heading of internal processes of occupational life.

In focusing on internal *processes,* this book clearly adopts a *dynamic* view of occupational life. If the reader is looking for static descriptions of various occupations, he must look elsewhere. Individuals in occupations are not faced with static structure, but with dynamic systems. Occupational life, like life in general, is characterized by constant conflict and change, in spite of occasional and long periods of relative quiescence. So far, these periods of quiescence have not been studied to any great extent by occupational sociologists. Perhaps the growth of ethnomethodology, with its interest in everyday life, will rectify this imbalance. Although periods of calm in occupational life have as worthy a claim to sociological study as periods of turmoil, this book reflects the current state of occupational sociology and focuses on conflict and change. By concentrating on periods of conflict and change, the occupational sociologist has been able to learn much about occupational life.

There is also an historical reason for the study of process in occupational life. Occupational sociology had its origins at the University of Chicago, which is generally noted for its interest in social processes.[7] (In contrast, the Ivy League universities are much more noted for their adherence to the more static functionalist approach to the study of social phenomena.) The father of occupational sociology, Everett Hughes, is a product of the Chicago School. Hughes occupies this position because of his contributions as both teacher and theorist. Virtually all of the major figures in occupational sociology were either his students or were influenced by his ideas about occupational life. According to Hughes, "Oswald Hall, Howard S. Becker, Harvey Smith,

---

[6] Richard H. Hall, *Occupations and the Social Structure* (Englewood Cliffs, N.J.: Prentice-Hall, 1969).

[7] R. James McCorkel, "Chicago and Ivy League Sociologies of Occupations: A Comparative Analysis of Assumptions, Theories, and Methods" (Paper presented at meeting of the Southern Sociological Society, New Orleans, La., April 11, 1969).

Edward Gross and Julius Roth would certainly consider themselves my students."[8] Other occupational sociologists who were influenced by Hughes while students at Chicago include William Kornhauser, Nelson Foote, Anselm Strauss, and Kirson Weinberg. That these men are indeed some of the central figures in occupational sociology is reflected in the number of times their work is cited in ensuing chapters. Every other sociologist who considers himself an occupational sociologist, if not directly influenced by Hughes, has certainly been influenced by his ideas on occupational life. Throughout the course of this chapter, and the bulk of the book, many of Hughes' basic notions are cited.

We have come this far in the introductory chapter without defining an occupation. There are many definitions, but a very recent one seems to be the best: "An occupation is the social role performed by adult members of society that directly and/or indirectly yields social and financial consequences and that constitutes a major focus in the life of an adult."[9] Clearly, no book can deal with the approximately 30,000 occupations in the United States, but all of them can be included under the headings of a small number of occupational categories. The Smigel et al. study already referred to lists occupational categories along with the percentage of published articles devoted to each in the period 1953–1959 (see Table 1-2).

TABLE 1-2

*Major Occupational Categories and Percentage of Articles
in the Period 1953–1959 Devoted to Each*

Occupational Categories	% of Articles 1953–1959
Professions	47.5
Proprietors, managers, and officials	22.2
Clerks and kindred workers	2.0
Skilled workers and foremen	2.0
Semiskilled workers	7.1
Unskilled workers	10.1
Military	9.1
	100.0

Adapted from Erwin Smigel et al., "Occupational Sociology: A Re-examination," *Sociology and Social Research* 47 (1963), 474.

Although Table 1-2 gives the reader some idea of where occupational sociologists have focused their attention, it proved not to be a useful scheme for organizing this book and has therefore been radically altered. The following is the categorization system employed in this book:

[8] Everett Hughes, personal communication to the author.
[9] Hall, *Occupations and Social Structure*, pp. 5–6.

Chapter 2:   Professions.
   a)   Professionals employed in organizations (e.g., industrial scientists).
   b)   Professionals not employed in organizations ("free" professionals).
        The major examples are the physician and lawyer in private prac-
        tice.
Chapter 3:   Managers, officials, proprietors (e.g., business managers, prison
             camp officials, and pharmacists).
Chapter 4:   Middle-level occupations.
   a)   First-line supervisors (e.g., foremen).
   b)   Skilled craftsmen (e.g., printers).
   c)   Semiprofessionals (e.g., schoolteachers, social workers, nurses).
   d)   White-collar workers (e.g., clerks and salesmen).
Chapter 5:   Low-status occupations.
   a)   Low-status workers employed in organizations (e.g., assembly-line
        workers).
   b)   Free low-status workers (e.g., taxi drivers).
Chapter 6:   Deviant occupations.
   a)   Deviant workers in organizations (e.g., Mafia leaders).
   b)   Free deviant workers (e.g., poolroom hustlers).

Obviously, all occupations are not covered by this categorization system, but
almost all of the major ones are included.

CONFLICT

In each of the occupational levels studied here the focus is on conflict and
change. In effect, this book constitutes an effort to examine and compare[10]
occupational levels on these two basic variables, and empirical generalizations
are made on the nature of conflict and change at each level. Although many
of these generalizations are not propositions, in Chapter 7 an effort is made
to distill some testable propositions from them. With the focus on comparative analysis and the development of propositions, an effort is also made to
respond to a traditional criticism of occupational sociology, "that the ethno-
graphic-organization studies of occupations have habitually looked at only
one or two occupations at a time, and have developed few propositions that
apply across a wide range of employments."[11]

---

[10] The comparative analysis of occupations is also of central concern to those from
the Chicago School. Hughes and his students "became convinced that if a certain problem turned up in one occupation, it was nearly certain to turn up in all. There is no absolute virtue in studying one kind of work rather than another, if the inward frame of
one's mind is comparative. The essence of the comparative frame is that one seeks differences in terms of dimensions common to all cases. . . . If he seeks common dimensions,
the differences become clearer, and more impressive." See Everett C. Hughes, "The
Humble and the Proud: The Comparative Study of Occupations," *Sociological Quarterly* 2 (1970), 149–150.
[11] Peterson, *Review of Occupational Sociology*, 777.

Individuals in all types of occupations are persistently confronted by various types of conflicts, of which a wide variety are discussed throughout this book. However, one of the main contentions here is that one or two types of conflict characterize each occupational level. In outlining all of the forms of occupational conflict, an attempt is made to state the occupational level or levels that are particularly prone to each form of conflict.

Conflict between subgroups. Within a given occupation there are various subgroups, and these quite frequently find themselves in conflict. This condition is most typical of the professions. A number of theorists have pointed to the existence of "segments" within each profession which are in a state of almost continual competition and conflict.[12] In medicine, for example, there are general practitioners, surgeons, and psychiatrists. The conflict among such segments offers a great deal of insight into the nature of the professions in particular, and occupations in general.

Conflict between occupations. A related form of conflict in occupational life is the struggle between different occupations. All occupations conflict with other occupations, but this form of conflict is most important to the so-called staff occupations. Staff occupations are found in most types of organizations and their defining characteristic is that they are supposed to serve as advisors to the line occupations, or those which are involved in producing the organization's goods or services. In seeking to give advice, those in staff occupations frequently meet with resistance from those in the line. This conflict is crucial to those in staff occupations, and many staff people spend a large portion of their workday living with and attempting to resolve it. Some examples of those in staff occupations are personnel specialists, accountants, and purchasing agents.

Conflict between occupational and organizational norms. There is often a conflict between the norms of an occupation and the norms of the organization in which those in an occupation are employed. This problem is most frequently found in the case of professionals who are employed in non-professional organizations. One of the defining characteristics of the professions is the norm of autonomy: professionals seek to make their own decisions and to allow only other professionals to assess the validity of those decisions. On the other hand, one of the cardinal principles of organizations is that control should come from the top. These two norms come into direct conflict when the professional is employed in an organization. The organization feels it cannot allow the professional free rein; the professional feels he cannot allow the organization to determine his decisions. Skilled craftsmen such as carpenters, electricians, and plumbers are confronted with the same type of

[12] Rue Bucher and Anselm Strauss, "Professions in Process," *American Journal of Sociology* 66 (1961), 325–334; or Harvey Smith, "Contingencies of Professional Differentiation," *American Journal of Sociology* 63 (1958), 410–414.

normative conflict when they are employed in a formal organization. Like professionals, skilled craftsmen traditionally worked on their own or in small groups of peers. Because of their lengthy training, skill, and past history, skilled craftsmen have developed a norm of autonomy similar to that of professionals. When craftsmen are employed in organizations they must cope with the conflict between their norms and the norms of the employing organization. Another instance in which occupational norms conflict with organizational norms is in the case of informal occupational groups within organizations. Blue- and white-collar workers frequently form informal groups, the norms of which often conflict with the norms of the organization. A good example is the fact that informal groups frequently develop norms concerning the productivity of individuals in the groups. These norms are generally aimed at producing less than the organization expects as a normal day's work. This phenomenon is known as "restriction of output" or "goldbricking," and is the cause of much strife between occupational groups and the organization.[13]

Role conflict. Other occupations in organizations, in particular managers, officials, and lower-level supervisors, are prone to role conflict.[14] Individuals in these occupations are most prone to role conflict because of their nature and their position in the organization. They are "men in the middle," faced with expectations from those above them, at their level, and below them in the organization. They are also often faced with conflicting expectations from two or more significant others; conflicting expectations from one significant other; conflicting expectations because of their occupancy of more than one role; expectations which conflict with their personal norms; and more expectations than it is possible to satisfy.[15] Again these types of conflict plague all those in occupations, but are particularly acute in the case of managers, officials, and lower-level supervisors.

Alienation. Those in low-status occupations in organizations, in particular, are characterized by the problem of alienation.[16] Because of their lowly status, persons in such occupations are faced with alienation, which results in a greal deal of psychological conflict. They work in an environment in which they are virtually *powerless* to affect the decisions which determine their worklives. In many cases they are also powerless to determine what they do, at what pace they do it, and how they do it. Their work is *meaningless* in the sense that it is so minutely specialized that they are unable to see its relevance to the finished product. Because of the structure of their work en-

[13] See, for example, Donald F. Roy, "Quota Restriction and Goldbricking in a Machine Shop," *American Journal of Sociology* 57 (1952), 427–442.
[14] Robert L. Kahn et al., *Organizational Stress: Studies in Role Conflict and Ambiguity* (New York, John Wiley, 1964), pp. 18–21.
[15] Ibid.
[16] Robert Blauner, *Alienation and Freedom: The Factory Worker and His Industry* (Chicago: University of Chicago Press, 1964).

vironment they are frequently *isolated,* unable to interact even with their peers. Finally, they are *self-estranged* in the sense that they are unable to utilize their skills and knowledge in their work. Their worklife is characterized by a struggle to "flesh out" some meaning in an alienating occupation. Another group which is faced with alienation is what is called in this book the nonemployed, in particular those who are unemployed, underemployed, retired, and in such nonoccupations as skid-row bum.

Conflict with customer clients. Persons in a number of occupations which either exist within organizations or are free of organizational control are confronted with conflict with customers or clients. These are generally known as the service occupations and include the automobile salesman, the taxi driver, the prostitute, and the physician in private practice. Professionals such as the physician deal with clients, while those in all other occupational groups deal with customers. The difference is that the client often surrenders judgment to the professional while the customer retains the right to judge those in all other occupations which serve him. In either case, the customer/ client is a source of difficulty to an individual in a service occupation. Of all occupations, professionals have the least trouble with clients, since clients have surrendered the right, in most cases, to evaluate the performance of the professional. Nevertheless, there is still friction in the professional-client relationship. This friction is exacerbated in the relationship between those in all other service occupations and their customers. There is conflict in the relationship between the taxi driver and his fare, the prostitute and the "john," and the car salesman and the buyer. Conflict with customers is ubiquitous in the service occupations.

Occupational-status insecurity. For those in a number of other occupations occupational conflict stems from the inherent insecurity. With his strong sense of status insecurity, the white-collar worker exemplifies this best.[17] Although white-collar workers have not been well paid, they have gained status by comparing themselves to blue-collar workers. In the past, their claims to greater status have been based on their cleaner work, white shirts, greater freedom, and the fact that they were physically and psychologically closer to management. However, recent changes in white-collar work have robbed them of many of these symbols. On the other hand, many blue-collar occupations have changed so that they more closely resemble white-collar work. The result has been more difficulty on the part of white-collar workers in differentiating themselves from blue-collar employees. Hence, the strong feeling of status insecurity among such white-collar workers as bookkeepers, clerks, and secretaries. Another occupational group characterized by status insecurity is the female semiprofessions, which include teachers, nurses, and

[17] C. Wright Mills, *White Collar: The American Middle Class* (New York: Oxford University Press, 1956), pp. 239–258.

social workers. Individuals in these occupations would like to be considered professionals, but are faced with serious barriers: most significant others have refused to grant them this recognition. Wanting to be something which they cannot be, at least at present, the female semiprofessionals must also deal with the resulting status insecurity.

Barriers to mobility. Individuals in a wide variety of occupations are faced with barriers to upward mobility, which in an achievement-oriented society such as ours are a very important source of occupational conflict. Such barriers are discussed throughout the book. Although these blocks occur in many occupations, they are more serious in some. Due to the revolution in education in this country, industry can now insist that its managers have at least a college education. The result, of course, has been a drastic reduction in the chances for upward mobility open to blue-collar workers, who simply lack the education which is fast becoming a prerequisite for a managerial position. Those who aspire to official positions within labor unions are also confronted with barriers to advancement, such as the relatively few official positions open. More important, union leaders, following Michel's Iron Law of Oligarchy,[18] generally resist all efforts to replace themselves.

Problems with the law. While those in deviant occupations must cope with conflict with their clients (the prostitute and her "john," the con man and his mark), they are also confronted with conflict with the police if their deviant activity is illegal. (Not all deviant occupations are illegal, however.) On the other hand, individuals in legal occupations often engage in illegal behavior and for them too dealings with the police are a source of occupational stress. Examples include the physician who performs abortions, the lawyer who bribes a court official, and the business manager who engages in price-fixing.

Economic and professional marginality. Finally, economic marginality, although it affects individuals in all occupations, is most characteristic of the contemporary small entrepreneur. Although small entrepreneurs have historically been economically marginal, their position has deteriorated in recent years. The major cause has been the proliferation of huge organizations in virtually every area of economic life. The neighborhood grocery stands little chance in its competition with chains of supermarkets such as the A&P. Those that have survived generally find great difficulty in eking out a living. Some small entrepreneurs are faced with another form of marginality, professional marginality. This faces those who seek to fuse the roles of entrepreneur and professional. The major example is the pharmacist who, although professionally trained, also attempts to run a business; other examples would in-

---

[18] The "Iron Law of Oligarchy" was first formulated by Robert Michels, *Political Parties: A Sociological Study of the Oligarchial Tendencies of Modern Democracy* (New York: Free Press, 1962).

clude the optometrist and the chiropractor. Quite simply, it is very difficult
to conform to professional norms when one is also trying to run a business.
As a professional the pharmacist may be opposed to advertising, but as a
businessman he finds it absolutely necessary for economic survival.

Here then is the list of major occupational problems which are dealt
with in this book under the occupation or occupations which are most plagued
by them:

1. Conflict between subgroups within an occupation.
2. Conflict between occupations.
3. Conflict between occupational and organizational norms.
4. Role conflict.
5. Alienation.
6. Conflict with customer/clients.
7. Occupational status insecurity.
8. Barriers to upward mobility.
9. Problems with the law.
10. Economic and professional marginality.

It must be reiterated that all of these problems occur in virtually every type
of occupation, but each type of occupation seems to be more prone to one or
at most two of these conflicts. I have, for example, contended that professionals employed in nonprofessional organizations are most prone to conflict between professional and organizational norms, but they are also at one time or
another subjected to all of the types of conflict listed above. Thus, George Miller has found that professionals in organizations are alienated.[19] Similarly, they
are faced with conflict with clients, role conflict, status insecurity, and all the
rest. Again, I have tried to locate the most characteristic type of stress in each
type of occupation, but the reader should keep in mind that all of the types
of conflict occur at each occupational level.

Conflict resolution

Along with focusing on conflict in occupational life, occupational sociologists
have been very interested in the ways in which these conflicts are dealt with.
Although there is a central concern with conflict resolution in this book, this
should not imply that conflict is regarded as necessarily dysfunctional. Indeed, as a number of recent theorists have pointed out, conflict can be highly
functional.[20] For example, it can spur social change in occupational life and
rouse individuals in some occupations to higher-quality productivity. How-

[19] George Miller, "Professionals in Bureaucracy: Alienation Among Industrial Scientists and Engineers," *American Sociological Review* 32 (1967), pp. 755–767.
[20] Lewis Coser, *The Functions of Social Conflict* (New York: Free Press, 1956).

ever, the fact remains that much of occupational life is taken up with efforts to reduce or eliminate conflict.

In some cases employing organizations can reduce the level of conflict. An organization may lessen the conflict caused by the employment of professionals by adapting itself structurally and normatively to them. Or organizations may strive to mitigate the conflict between informal occupational groups and the organization by supporting or even helping to create informal groups. In other instances, the occupation may act to reduce conflict. For example, some professions are now requiring courses on organizational life for trainees so that they can better adapt to life in an organization.

Normative conflict. Most efforts to reduce or eliminate conflict are, however, on an individual level. Let us return to some of the occupational problems listed above and outline some of the actions individuals may take to ameliorate the resulting conflict. A professional employed in a nonprofessional organization has four basic options open to him in terms of resolving the conflict between occupational and organizational norms.[21] He can orient himself toward the expectations of his employing organization and ignore his professional role ("job bureaucrat"). Choosing this option, he may satisfy the expectations of his employer, but at the cost of the approbation of his professional colleagues. Second, the organizationally employed professional can orient himself toward his profession and turn his back on his employer ("functionalist bureaucrat"). Although this will undoubtedly earn him the applause of his colleagues, he may not have his job for long. Third, he can attempt to satisfy the expectations of both his employer and his profession ("specialist bureaucrat"). Although this is undoubtedly the most satisfactory resolution for all parties concerned, it is very difficult to achieve. For example, a scientist employed in industry, if he were to choose this option, must contribute to both science and his employer. Yet what it takes to be a good scientist is often at odds with what it takes to be a good employee. Finally, the professional employed in a nonprofessional organization may become a "service bureaucrat," one who does not identify with profession or employer. Neither the profession or the employer is likely to be satisfied with such a resolution, but the individual may have coped with the normative conflict by withdrawing from it. A blue-collar worker faced with a conflict between the norms of his employing organization and his informal occupational group has the same possibilities open to him. He can satisfy the expectations of his informal group, his employer, both, or neither.[22] The same is obviously true of an individual in any occupation which is confronted with normative conflict. However, while the four resolutions are open to all, individuals in some occupations are more likely to choose a particular resolution than those in other occupations.

[21] Leonard Reissman, "A Study of Role Conceptions in Bureaucracy," *Social Forces* 27 (1949), 305–310.

[22] Fritz Roethlisberger and William J. Dickson, *Management and the Worker* (New York: John Wiley, 1964), pp. 409–447.

For example, professionals are probably more likely to identify with their occupation, blue-collar workers with their organization.

Role conflict. Basically there are five ways in which a manager, official, or first-line supervisor can resolve the role conflict inherent in his position.[23] He can choose to satisfy one of the conflicting expectations or he can choose to satisfy the other. In either case, of course, he has only solved part of his problem. Third, he can seek to compromise, which generally means attempting to satisfy all expectations to some degree. This in most cases is extremely difficult and very trying for the individual. Further, while he has partially satisfied everyone, he has also left them all partially dissatisfied. A fourth option in a role conflict situation is withdrawal, ranging from quitting the job to stating that one cannot satisfy the conflicting expectations. Last, there is the possibility of independent action, or taking action which the individual himself believes to be best in the particular situation. While this choice may be very satisfying to the individual, it is likely to cause virtually all significant others to be dissatisfied.

Alienation. Individuals in alienating occupations handle the problem in a variety of ways. Most typically such individuals seek to "flesh out" their occupational lives through a variety of informal practices. One such practice is known as "working the system,"[24] and involves escaping the more odious aspects of the job as well as attempting to illegitimately use or take property which belongs to the organization. Another informal practice involves efforts to make the job easier.[25] When the job is being set up or timed the worker works at a slower pace, going through every conceivable motion. Once the rate of work has been set by management, he can work faster by cutting out steps, thereby giving himself a considerable amount of free time on the job. A third informal practice is the setting up of unofficial production norms which are lower than the productivity expectations of management.[26] The work is made more meaningful by "beating" management and keeping workers who stray from the unofficial group norm in line. In addition to these and other actions, employees in alienating occupations seek to reduce their feelings of alienation. They may rationalize their position by focusing exclusively on the income they receive, or they may turn their attention to their children and concentrate on how their work will help to build them a better future.[27] Other workers in alienating occupations may seek to make

[23] George Ritzer and Harrison M. Trice, *An Occupation in Conflict: A Study of the Personnel Manager* (Ithaca, N.Y.: Cornell University, 1969), pp. 46–57.
[24] Donald F. Roy, "Efficiency and the 'Fix': Informal Intergroup Relations in a Piece-work Machine Shop," *American Journal of Sociology* 60 (1964), 255–266.
[25] Dean Harper and Frederick Emmert, "Work Behavior in a Service Industry," *Social Forces* 28 (1963), 216–225.
[26] Roethlisberger and Dickson, *Management and Worker,* pp. 409–447.
[27] Ely Chinoy, *Automobile Workers and the American Dream* (Boston: Beacon Press, 1955).

their worklife more comfortable by overemphasizing the status or importance of their work.[28] Still others may seize upon some highly valued aspect of their work and focus on it.[29] Thus, for example, the psychiatric attendant spends most of his time doing menial housekeeping chores, but says that the most important part of his job is caring for patients.[30] Or there is the night watchman who, despite the fact that no one ever comes into the plant at night, claims that one of his most important tasks is as a company representative.[31] Finally, those who exist in alienating occupations may seek to compensate by activity within unions. All in all, however, these numerous activities seem to be rather unsuccessful in reducing alienation in low status occupations.

Conflict with customer/clients. Many of those in the very diverse service occupations have difficulties with their customer/clients. In almost every case the solution attempted may be termed the "dramaturgical approach";[32] that is, the individual in a service occupation relies on his abilities as a performer to manipulate the situation in his favor. Dramaturgical manipulation is necessary because usually the power lies with the customer/client. The exception is the client-professional relationship, but even here the professional must frequently use dramaturgical devices to maintain his power. In the case of the general practitioner, clients in the first few visits frequently test the physician. In order to retain them as patients he may have to dramaturgically manipulate the situation. For example, if he senses that the patient wants to be treated as if he were sick, even though the doctor knows he is well he may prescribe a placebo to keep him satisfied.[33] Further, all physicians tend to follow a series of rules governing interaction with patients: the physician is supposed to appear interested in what the patient says and he is never to argue with a patient's prejudices.[34] These dramaturgical rules are designed to keep the patient satisfied and interested in continuing to give the doctor his business.

There are numerous other examples of dramaturgical manipulation by those in service occupations. A large part of the taxi driver's income is dependent on the size of his tip, and he has developed a number of dramaturgical devices to increase it. He may fumble with change so that the exasperated

[28] Joel Seidman, "Telephone Workers," in Sigmund Nosow and William Form, eds., *Man, Work and Society* (New York: Basic Books, 1962), pp. 493–504.

[29] Richard Simpson and Ida Harper Simpson, "The Psychiatric Attendant: Development of an Occupational Image in a Low Status Occupation," *American Sociological Review* 24 (1959), 389–393.

[30] Ibid.

[31] Harrison M. Trice, "Night Watchman: A Study of an Isolated Occupation," *ILR Research* 10 (1964), 3–8.

[32] Erving Goffman, *The Presentation of Self in Everyday Life* (Garden City, N.Y.: Doubleday Anchor Books, 1959).

[33] Eliot Freidson, "Client Control and Medical Practice," *American Journal of Sociology* 65 (1960), 374–382.

[34] L. J. Henderson, "Medicine," in Howard M. Vollmer and Donald L. Mills, eds., *Professionalization* (Englewood Cliffs, N.J.: Prentice-Hall, 1966), pp. 199–202.

passenger will finally tell him to keep it, or he may make change in such denominations that the passenger is forced to give a larger tip than he intended. The driver may also tell hard luck stories, exhibit fancy driving, or address customers as "sir" or "madam."[35]

Dramaturgical manipulation is probably most common in the sales occupations. Some salesmen use the "hard sell" and others the "soft sell" in order to increase the likelihood of a sale. In general, the salesman adapts his act to the nature of the customer.[36]

Dramaturgical manipulation is also of central importance to those in many deviant occupations. Individuals in these occupations are perpetually faced with the possibility of being caught in their deviant acts by customer/ clients or the police. The poolroom hustler makes his living by acting as if he is not a very good pool player.[37] Should he slip in his act and perform as well as he can, he will never be able to hustle again at the location where he has made his dramaturgical slip. The shoplifter must always act as if he is a legitimate shopper, or he will be spotted by salespeople or store detectives.[38] The jazz musician despises and fears his audience, since they insist on "square" music, while he generally prefers to play pure, noncommercial jazz.[39] In order to restrict the influence of the audience, he goes through some elaborate staging techniques.

Status insecurity. Individuals in those occupations which are faced with status insecurity also employ a variety of means to reduce their insecurity. Members of the female semiprofessions may try to reduce their insecurity by becoming more like the established professionals. Although occupations such as teaching, social work, and nursing may never be regarded in the same way as medicine, they can try to approximate this goal far more closely than they have in the past. Another resolution for those with status insecurity is to eschew the goal of becoming like the established professions and instead define a new type of professional status for themselves. In this way the female semiprofessions can cease seeking an unattainable goal, which is the basic source of their insecurity. The white-collar worker reacts to his status insecurity in several different ways. He may retreat into the psychological safety of informal white-collar groups and find solace with his peers, or he may become what has been called the "bureaucratic personality," an expert

---

[35] Fred Davis, "The Cabdriver and His Fare: Facets of a Fleeting Relationship," *American Journal of Sociology* 65 (1959), 158–165.

[36] Stephen Miller, "The Social Base of Sales Behavior," *Social Problems* 12 (1964), 15–24.

[37] Ned Polsky, *Hustlers, Beats, and Others* (Garden City, N.Y.: Anchor Books, 1969), pp. 31–108.

[38] Edwin H. Sutherland, *The Professional Thief* (Chicago: University of Chicago Press, 1967), pp. 48–51.

[39] Howard Becker, "The Professional Dance Musician and his Audience," *American Journal of Sociology* 57 (1951), 136–144.

on the rules and a strict adherent to them.[40] His expertise on the rules serves to differentiate him from the rising blue-collar workers.

Other types of conflict resolution. The other types of conflict constitute lesser problems in occupational life. Individuals who have superiors who refuse to be replaced have developed a variety of ploys. If none succeed, they may simply withdraw in search of an environment in which they can move upward. The problems those in illegal deviant occupations have with the law have been mentioned briefly above. One resolution was also mentioned, the employment of dramaturgical manipulation so that the police are unable to witness the illegal act, or apprehend the individual even if they have observed it. Another more direct resolution is to bribe public officials so that they will ignore illegal behavior.[41] Economic marginality is a problem which faces storekeepers in particular. The most typical resolution is to offer personalized service so that a loyal group of regular customers can be developed. Another is the attempt to enlarge the number of customers so that the economic position of the business may be improved.

Problems of minority groups

While the above conflicts and resolutions apply to all workers, additional difficulties beset workers who are members of minority groups. As will be remembered from the Smigel et al. study, the problem of minority groups in occupational life has been one of the focal concerns of occupational sociologists. Out of the large number of minority groups, this book concentrates on two major ones: blacks and women. (Sociologists define minority groups in terms of lack of power not numbers; therefore the inclusion of numerically dominant women as a minority group.) Both these groups face particularly acute problems in virtually all occupational levels. Table 1-3 offers some statistics on the question.

It is quite clear from Table 1-3 that blacks and females are discriminated against occupationally. They are found in smaller percentages in higher-status occupations and in greater numbers in lower-status occupations. However, at all occupational levels they face peculiar problems because of their minority-group status.

Blacks. That American society is prejudiced against blacks has been confirmed, once again, by the recent Kerner Commission Report, which labelled white America as racist.[42] Since work is one of society's most important

[40] Robert K. Merton, "Bureaucratic Structure and Personality," in Robert K. Merton et al., eds., *Reader in Bureaucracy* (New York: Free Press, 1967), pp. 361–371.

[41] William F. Whyte, *Street Corner Society* (Chicago: University of Chicago Press, 1969), pp. 111–146.

[42] Kerner Commission, *Report of the National Advisory Commission on Civil Disorders* (New York: Bantam Books, 1968).

TABLE 1-3

Projected Occupational Distribution for 1970 for White Males,
Nonwhite Males, and Females Between 35 and 44 Years of Age

	% of Females (35–44)	% of Nonwhite Males (35–44)	% of White Males (35–44)
Professional and managerial	8.0	8.5	25.0
Clerical and sales	19.0	8.0	13.0
Craftsman and operators	7.0	35.0	42.5
Private household workers	1.0	.4	—
Other service workers	5.0	10.6	3.5
Laborers, except farm	0.1	15.0	3.5
Farmers and farm managers	0.2	1.5	2.5
Farm laborers	—	5.0	0.8
Not in the experienced labor force (including occupations not reported)	59.7	16.0	9.2
	100.0	100.0	100.0

Adapted from Daniel O. Price, "Occupational Changes Among Whites and Non-whites with Projections for 1970," *Social Science Quarterly* 49 (1968), 571.

institutions, it is not surprising that racism extends deep into the workworld. Blacks have a more difficult time gaining employment of any sort as represented by the higher rates of black unemployment and underemployment. At every occupational level, they are faced with a host of problems which do not confront their white counterparts. This is true across the occupational spectrum; black professionals, managers, blue-collar workers, and those in deviant occupations share many of the same problems as well as some peculiar to their occupational level.

Females.   Females, like blacks, are faced with difficulties at each occupational level. In American society both blacks and females are supposed to be passive and subordinate, even when they are in the workworld. Females are accepted as long as their occupations are congruent with their sex roles. The same is true of blacks, but there are fewer black occupations of this type than there are female occupations. In almost all cases those occupations which are viewed as black are at the bottom of the occupational hierarchy. Thus we find it easy to accept blacks in the workworld as long as they are shoe shine boys, janitors, porters, farm hands, and the like. Female occupations, on the other hand, are spread more evenly throughout the occupational hierarchy. Females are acceptable in such low-status occupations as waitress and maid; such middle-level occupations as secretary, social worker, and teacher; and such high-status occupations as gynecologist and pediatrician. Even in these occupations, they must generally deal with hostility from peers and, at times, from customer/clients.

SOCIAL CHANGE AND ITS IMPACT ON OCCUPATIONAL LIFE

The preceding is an outline of the first basic concern of this book: occupational conflict and its resolution. The second theme is social change and its impact on occupational life. Under the general heading of social change two subtopics are dealt with: broad social changes and their effect on occupational life in general as well as on the structure of specific occupations, and change in the individual worker (a topic which is dealt with under the heading of career patterns). Each occupation has a hierarchy of positions through which an individual moves in the course of his career. By understanding the career pattern typical of a given occupation, we learn much about the structure of the occupation as well as the individuals in it. The following pages summarize the major social changes in American society and their effect on occupational structure.

Division of labor

The starting point for any discussion of changes in the division of labor must be Emile Durkheim's seminal work, *The Division of Labor in Society*.[43] Durkheim saw primitive society characterized by what he called *mechanical solidarity*. In this type of society solidarity stems from the fact that everyone does essentially the same kinds of things. There is little or no division of labor; everyone raises his own food, educates his children, polices, and so forth. Primarily because of population growth and increased interaction among people, mechanical solidarity is gradually replaced by *organic solidarity*. Because of the increasing size of society, a greater and greater division of labor is necessitated. A society characterized by organic solidarity is held together not by the similarity of individuals, but by their differences. That is, an individual in this more modern type of society must depend upon farmers, teachers, policemen, etc., in order to survive. Although it is clear that Durkheim saw the development from mechanical to organic solidarity as a universal evolutionary trend, he had many reservations about a society characterized by organic solidarity, and seems to have yearned for the continuation of some aspects of mechanical solidarity. In fact, Durkheim noted that while organic solidarity becomes dominant with the increasing division of labor, mechanical solidarity continues to exist. He noted three dysfunctional aspects of organic solidarity, and as is pointed out throughout this book, these

[43] Emile Durkheim, *The Division of Labor in Society*, trans. George Simpson (Glencoe, Ill.: Free Press, 1947).

three problems continue to plague those in occupational life. First he observed that anomie, or a sense of normlessness or isolation, may increase with the division of labor. Second, there is the problem of the forced division of labor, when an individual is forced to perform tasks which are not in line with his individual characteristics. Finally, the division of labor may be so minute that a task does not seem meaningful. Although these problems seem to be most characteristic of those occupations which are called low status in this book, they are also found in all types of occupations.

Contemporary American society may be viewed as an example of a society characterized by organic solidarity. This is true not only because of the high degree of the division of labor, but also because of the problems Durkheim saw as concomitants of a high degree of specialization.

Highly specialized labor. According to Wilensky there are roughly 30,000 occupations in the United States, with over 22,000 of these listed in the *Dictionary of Occupational Titles.*[44] Among these 30,000 there are some remarkable examples of the high degree of occupational specialization in the United States:

In the baking industry one can make a living as a cracker breaker, meringue spreader, a pie stripper, or pan dumper. In the slaughter and meat-packing industry one can specialize as: a large stock scalper, belly shaver, crotch buster, gut snatcher, gut sorter, snout puller, ear cutter, eyelid remover, stomach washer (sometimes called belly pumper), hindleg toenail puller, frontleg toenail puller and oxtail washer.[45]

Of course, the statistics and the list of exotic titles tell only a small part of the story of the increasing division of labor.

It is quite clear that we have witnessed an enormous proliferation of occupations. More important, however, is the effect of this division of labor on the worker. Many theorists and empiricists have noted the impact of a high degree of specialization on the worker. As work is subdivided and subdivided again, it becomes increasingly difficult for a worker to find satisfaction in the intrinsic aspects of his job. One need only ponder how much satisfaction the worker gets from pulling hindleg toenails hour after hour five days each week. Work on the automobile assembly line is generally regarded as the ultimate form of the extreme division of labor. A typical worker may fasten a bolt on an automobile every twenty seconds with only a rare respite. But assembly-line work is not the ultimate expression of the increasing division of labor merely because of its minute specialization and

[44] *Dictionary of Occupational Titles,* 3rd ed. (Washington, D.C.: U.S. Department of Labor, 1965).

[45] Harold Wilensky, "The Early Impact of Industrialization on Society," in William A. Faunce, ed., *Readings in Industrial Sociology* (New York: Appleton, 1967), pp. 78–79.

its repetitiveness; after all, many American occupations are minutely specialized. In addition to, and partly because of, its minute specialization and its repetitiveness, assembly-line work is one of the most alienating occupations in contemporary America. As is discussed at length in the chapter on low-status occupations, assembly-line workers are faced with a high degree of meaninglessness, isolation, powerlessness, and self-estrangement, which are the four components of alienation.

It must be noted, however, that the contention concerning assembly-line work may reveal an intellectual bias. Perhaps this work would not be significant to the intellectual, but is it not possible that the job is meaningful to the average high-school graduate employed at it? This argument appears to have merit, but a large number of studies of assembly-line workers all reveal strong negative feelings toward the job.[46]

Although specialization is clearest among low-status workers (in particular, assembly-line workers), it has occurred throughout the occupational hierarchy. In medicine we have witnessed the decline of the general practitioner and the increasing number of doctors in such specialties as pediatrics, surgery, psychiatry, and gynecology. In sociology few of us are generalists. Instead, sociologists are specialists in criminology, marriage and the family, social stratification, and even occupations. In the early days of personnel administration almost everyone was a personnel manager, but today we find specialists in labor relations, employment, benefits, and counseling. The secretary of the past who performed a variety of functions is being replaced with clerk-typists, typists, stenographers, and receptionists. The examples are legion, but the basic point is that virtually every occupation has become highly specialized.

Changes in the labor force

Related to the increasing division of labor are the changes which have taken place within the workforce. There have been enormous shifts in the occupational structure of the United States, as shown in Table 1-4.

The changes which have taken place become clearer when we collapse some of the categories given in Table 1-4. In Table 1-5, white-collar occupations include the first four categories of Table 1-4, service occupations include categories 5–6, manual occupations include 7–9, and farm occupations include categories 10–11.

Clearly the really startling changes have taken place in the white-collar and farm occupations. A marked increase in white-collar occupations has been paralleled by an even greater decline in farm occupations. One of the causal variables here is industrialization, which led to a need for many workers in industry and those organizations which service industry, and for fewer on the

---

[46] See, for example, Chinoy, *Automobile Workers*.

TABLE 1-4

Changes in Labor Force by Occupational Level—1900, 1930, 1960

	% in 1900	% in 1930	% in 1960
Professional, technical, and kindred workers	4.3	6.8	11.4
Managers, officials, proprietors, except farm	5.9	7.4	8.5
Clerical and kindred workers	3.0	8.9	14.9
Sales workers	4.5	6.3	7.4
Private household workers	5.4	4.1	2.8
Other service workers	3.6	5.7	8.9
Craftsmen, foremen, and kindred workers	10.6	12.8	14.3
Operators and kindred workers	12.8	15.8	19.9
Laborers, except farm and mine	12.5	11.0	5.5
Farmers and farm managers	19.9	12.4	3.9
Farm laborers and foremen	17.7	8.8	2.4
	100.2	100.0	99.9

Adapted from Philip M. Hauser, "Labor Force," in Robert E. L. Faris, ed., *Handbook of Modern Sociology* (Chicago: Rand, McNally, 1964), p. 183. Totals reflect rounding errors.

TABLE 1-5

Changes in Labor Force by Occupational Group—1900, 1930, 1960

	% in 1900	% in 1930	% in 1960
White collar	17.6	29.4	42.2
Service	9.1	9.8	11.8
Manual	35.8	39.6	39.7
Farm	37.5	21.2	6.3
	100.0	100.0	100.0

Adapted from Philip M. Hauser, "Labor Force," in Robert E. L. Faris, ed., *Handbook of Modern Sociology* (Chicago: Rand, McNally, 1964), p. 183.

farm. This trend is also reflected in changes which have taken place in the labor force by type of activity, as shown in Table 1-6.

Again, the changes clearly represent a decline in rural activities and an increase in industrial and related activities. As of 1968 over 72 million people were employed in nonagricultural industries while less than 4 million remained on the farm.[47] Also increasing greatly are governmental employment and a variety of other service occupations. Industrialization is one cause of growth in these areas, but certainly not the only one. The increasing number of Americans would necessitate increases in government and service

[47] *The American Almanac: The U.S. Book of Facts, Statistics, and Information for 1970* (New York: Grosset and Dunlap, 1970), p. 223.

TABLE 1-6

Change in Labor Force by Activity—1860, 1900, 1950

| | % of Labor Force | | |
	1860	1900	1950
Agriculture, fishing, and forestry	59	38	12
Industry, construction, and mining	20	30	33
Services (professional, administrative, transport, and commerce)	20	31	53
Other	1	1	2
	100	100	100

Joseph A. Kahl, "Some Social Concomitants of Industrialization and Urbanization," in William A. Faunce, ed., *Readings in Industrial Sociology* (New York: Appleton-Century-Crofts, 1967), p. 39.

jobs. Another factor in the growth of government positions is the changing American philosophy concerning the role of the government in the lives of its people. A major factor in the growth of service occupations has been the increased affluence of American society and the ability of the society to afford the "luxuries" offered by service occupations.

Professional, technical, and kindred occupations. Some of the trends outlined in the Tables 1-4, 1-5, and 1-6 need to be underscored. The percentage of workers in professional, technical, and related occupations almost trebled between 1900 and 1960. One source has projected that by 1975 over 14 percent of the workforce will be employed at this occupational level.[48] Two different dynamics account for the increase in occupations at this level. Technical occupations are growing because of an increasing need for technical skills in industry: as machines become more complex, more and more technicians are needed to design and service them. Part of the reason for the growth in the professions may be attributed to the increasing need for expertise as well as the increase in the population which requires and can afford their services. There is another causal factor here—the growing number of occupations which are striving for, and in many cases achieving, recognition as professions. Professional recognition is a desirable goal for many occupations because it carries enormous economic gains and prestige value. Thus personnel managers, morticians, and librarians are among the occupations currently striving for professional status. Others who have "made it" (at least in their own evaluation) include social workers, teachers, and nurses. However, there is a lively debate in the literature as to whether these occupations should be considered professional in the traditional sense. Historically, the title of

[48] *Manpower Report of the President, 1963* (Washington, D.C.: U.S. Government Printing Office, 1963), p. 100.

professional has been granted to free occupations such as medicine and law; newer occupations seeking professional recognition are generally not free, since they most often find themselves within formal organizations. Hence, this book contends that those occupations which are striving for or claiming professionalization are not in fact professions in the traditional sense. Further, I suggest that it is unrealistic for them to continue to strive for a goal which they are highly unlikely ever to achieve. (A new, more realistic goal is suggested for these occupations in the chapter on the professions.) The claim to professional status by such occupations as teaching, social work, and nursing is not accepted in this book; these occupations are discussed in the chapter on middle-level occupations rather than the chapter on the professions. In fact the major problem for this group of occupations is their strong desire for professionalization and their inability to achieve this goal.

Clerks and kindred workers. The biggest increase in the other types of white-collar work has been among clerks and kindred workers. By 1975 it is projected that over 16 percent of the labor force will be employed at this occupational level.[49] The major explanation for this large increase lies in the growing bureaucratization of American society, a topic discussed later in this chapter. Large-scale organizations require numerous clerks to handle the massive amount of paper work which has been generated, and this enormous increase in numbers has been one of the basic causes of the problems in clerical occupations. Formerly, clerks were rather high-status people who, despite their low wages, found satisfaction in their closeness to management and the superiority of their working environment in comparison to that of blue-collar workers. Now these sources of satisfaction have all but been eliminated—the clerk is no longer close to his superior and his workworld has become increasingly like that of the blue-collar worker. In fact, modern offices look very much like white-collar factories.

Manual workers. There have been significant changes among the three groups of occupations included under the heading of manual occupations, but the total percentage of manual workers has not greatly increased. There has been a marked increase in semiskilled manual occupations (operators and kindred workers) and a large decrease in the number of unskilled manual occupations (laborers). The explanation for this shift lies primarily in technological advances, for new machines have eliminated the need for many unskilled occupations. This trend is likely to continue—it is forecast that by 1975 only 4.3 percent of the workforce will be in unskilled occupations.[50] Most of those who were laborers have been elevated to the status of semiskilled machine operators and tenders. As has been discussed before, their basic occupational problem stems from the control machines exert over their lives.

[49] Ibid.
[50] Ibid.

Farm workers. Perhaps the most striking change of all has been the precipitous decline in farm workers of all types. Farming has been affected most by the impact of improved technology and the growth of huge farms, and far fewer workers are needed to produce the much greater quantity of farm produce. Taking up the slack has been the growth of organizations of all types which have come to employ many of the ex-farm workers and their children. Because of the decline in the numbers needed in rural areas, and the fact that large-scale organizations are usually found in cities, urbanization has been one of concomitants of industrialization and bureaucratization. Kahl notes:

The traditional world is a rural world . . . but the modern world is an urban world. Less than ten percent of the population (given good farmland and scientific techniques of production) can feed ninety percent living in towns and cities. . . . During the period of rapid development, there is an enormous flow of young people from farm to city.[51]

Technological advances

The professions. It is clear that one of the basic causes of the increasing division of labor and changes in the distribution of the workforce is the large number of technological advances which have affected every level of occupational life. Starting at the top of the occupational ladder, professionals have been affected significantly by technological advances. The days of the old general practitioner who practiced medicine almost exclusively out of his "little black bag" are swiftly passing. Specialties within medicine have proliferated rapidly and many of the newer specialties have been spawned by the new technologies. Further, a set of technical occupations which service the medical profession has developed. Medicine now consists of giving a series of tests, many of which depend on complicated machinery and require technical experts to administer and interpret. Relationships between general practitioners, medical specialists, and technicians have added a whole new dimension to the practice of medicine, and a whole new series of conflicts.

Scientific occupations. The biggest impact of technological change in the United States has been on the scientific occupations in general. Engineering, for example, was virtually unknown in the early 1800s.[52] Some growth occurred because of the construction of such public works as canals and railroads, and by 1850 there were about 2,000 civil engineers in the United States. The massive industrialization of the United States in the late 1800s and early 1900s led to a large increase in the number of engineers. For ex-

---

[51] Joseph A. Kahl, "Some Social Concomitants of Industrialization and Urbanization," in Faunce, *Readings in Industrial Sociology*, p. 32.

[52] Edwin Layton, "Science, Business, and the American Engineer," in Robert Perrucci and Joel E. Gerstl, eds., *The Engineers and the Social System* (New York: John Wiley, Inc., 1969), pp. 51–72.

ample, Layton, in discussing the period between 1880 and 1920 notes: "In these forty years the engineering profession increased by almost 2000%, from 7000 to 136,000 members."[53] Not only was there a vast increase in numbers, but also in specialties. "The civil engineer was overshadowed by the new technical specialists who emerged to meet the needs of industry, by the mining, metallurgical, mechanical, electrical, and chemical.[54] Paralleling the growth in engineering has been the proliferation of many other scientific occupations which have come to be linked either as employees of or consultants to industry.

In addition to the growth of scientific specialties and occupations, there has been considerable growth in technical occupations. Individuals in these occupations serve primarily as adjuncts to scientists or as operators of complex machinery. Examples include the computer programmer and medical, dental, and engineering technicians. That such occupations are proliferating is exemplified by the growth of engineering technicians in the 1950s from 112,000 to about 275,000.[55] The technician generally combines some professional expertise with manual skills. Thus the engineering technician knows some things about engineering theory, but his primary tasks are "the testing and development, the application, and the operation of engineering or scientific equipment or processes."[56] Technicians are generally highly skilled "supporting personnel" for the scientific and professional occupations. They owe the existence of their jobs to technological advances. For example, the occupation of computer programmer was not even listed in the 1949 *Dictionary of Occupational Titles*;[57] it owes its existence to the recent development and wide-scale use of the computer.

Other white-collar occupations. The other white-collar occupations have also been affected by technological advances. New types of managerial occupations have been spawned by these changes, such as the manager of computer services, an important new position in industry, government, and hospitals. Similarly, older managers have been forced to radically alter the nature of their jobs. A good example is the manager of the accounting department, who in many organizations is now also in charge of computer services. Many accounting managers have been forced to school themselves in the theory and functioning of electronic computers. Even clerical occupations have been faced with the problem of adjusting to technological change. The old highly skilled bookkeeper has been replaced by the young high-school graduate who is able to operate adding machines, billing machines, and the like. The dictaphone has eliminated the need for many private secretaries and has led to the

---

[53] Ibid., p. 53.
[54] Ibid.
[55] William M. Evan, "On the Margin—The Engineering Technician," in Peter Berger, ed., *The Human Shape of Work* (New York: Macmillan, 1964) p. 84.
[56] Ibid., p. 88.
[57] Ibid., p. 84.

formation of large stenographic pools. In fact, the coming of automation to the office has created a basic problem for the clerk. Many jobs are threatened with elimination, while others, such as the bookkeeper, are being greatly altered and reduced in importance and prestige. The continuing automation of the office has reduced the disparity between clerks and blue-collar workers. Since clerks have gained much satisfaction from this disparity, automation is highly threatening to them. In fact many automated offices cannot be differentiated from new automated factories. The machine operator in his white shirt in an automated chemical plant is little different from the billing-machine operator in the automated office. Sales occupations have been virtually untouched by technological change, except that many salesmen are now selling new machinery such as the computer.

Domestic occupations. The decline in the service occupations such as household workers is attributable to technological changes within the home. The maid is less important because of the development of the washing machines, automatic dishwashers, ovens which start, finish, and clean themselves, vacuum cleaners, and other similar household devices.

Foremen and craftsmen. The foreman has seen his job diminished in part by technological changes which have given increasing power to such staff departments as engineering and efficiency experts. Skilled workers have resisted the impact of technological changes most successfully, although not totally, since many (e.g., blacksmiths) were almost totally eliminated or reduced to semiskilled workers. In general however, the skills of the craftsman are not easily replaced by machines, and where they are, the powerful unions of the skilled trades have resisted their introduction into the workplace. Laborers have seen many of their jobs eliminated by machines and they have been fired or moved into the operative category to work with the machines.

Operatives. It is in the operative category that technological changes have been felt most. In the early days of industrialization much production was still done in the home, but with the advent of steam power and new, large machines, the early factories developed. Operatives were moved out of their homes and their ability to control their own work behavior was greatly reduced. The early machines required tending by the operatives, but these machines did not have the total control over the workers that were characteristic of some later machinery. Nevertheless, the shift from home to factory was a difficult adjustment for most operatives, and with each technological change and advance new adjustments were required. Thus there was constant tension caused by continual change as well as the ever-present possibility that one might be replaced or have his skill made obsolete by new machinery. Unemployment and technological obsolescence were feared by all early industrial workers, and realities for many. The next great technological change which had a profound effect on the operative was the development of the assembly

almost certainly affiliated with a hospital. The small independent proprietor is also fast becoming a thing of the past as he is forced out of business by larger retail organizations such as the A&P and Woolworths. In contrast, managers and officials were created by the spread of organizations, and it is only within organizations that they are needed to supervise the work of subordinates. The same is true of white-collar workers: they came into existence to handle the enormous amount of paper work generated by large-scale organizations. Blue-collar workers existed prior to the growth of organizations, but they generally worked alone or in small groups as skilled craftsmen. Technological advances and the resulting large and expensive machinery created the need for large organizations and these organizations lured workers into their employ. Even organized crime, in some cases, has found it more efficient to set up fairly large-scale organizations.

It is contended here that most formal organizations have the characteristics of Weber's ideal type of bureaucracy. However, as much of the recent literature on formal organizations has indicated, Weber's ideal type is a reasonable starting point, but an inaccurate description of almost all formal organizations. For one thing, there is considerable diversity in the forms of formal organizations, and for another, there are many processes which occur in organizational life which have been omitted in Weber's ideal type.

Types of organizations. Although there are many organizations in America, most can be categorized as one of the three types developed by Etzioni: coercive, utilitarian, and normative.[61] These types are all formal organizations possessing the characteristics of a bureaucracy outlined by Weber, but there are important differences. The following are Etzioni's definitions of each type of organization and the major examples of each:

1. "Coercive organizations are organizations in which coercion is the major means of control over lower participants and high alienation characterizes the orientation of most lower participants to the organization."[62] The major examples of coercive organizations are prisons and custodial mental hospitals.
2. "Utilitarian organizations are organizations in which remuneration is the major means of control over lower participants and calculative involvement (i.e. mild alienation to mild commitment) characterizes the orientation of the large majority of lower participants."[63] Industrial and commercial organizations of all types are the major examples of utilitarian organizations.
3. "Normative organizations are organizations in which normative power is the major source of control over most lower participants, whose orienta-

[61] Amitai Etzioni, *Comparative Analysis of Complex Organizations* (New York: Free Press, 1961).
[62] Ibid., p. 27.
[63] Ibid., p. 31.

tion to the organization is characterized by high commitment."[64] Examples include religious and political organizations, schools and universities, general hospitals, therapeutic mental hospitals, voluntary associations, and professional organizations. In addition to the three "pure" types, there are also a number of mixed types of organizations such as combat units and labor unions.

In developing his typology, Etzioni clearly focused on the compliance of lower participants in an organization and the means employed by the organization to ensure their compliance. This variable is a useful center around which to develop a typology, but it is certainly not the only possibility. One could also develop typologies based on the compliance of higher participants or on the basis of the locus of decision making. Another well known typological scheme was developed by Blau and Scott on the basis of the prime beneficiary of the organization's operation:[65]

1. " 'Mutual-benefit associations,' where the prime beneficiary is the membership."[66] Examples include political parties, labor unions, and professional organizations.
2. " 'Business concerns,' where the owners are prime beneficiary."[67] Examples are industry, banks, stores, and insurance companies.
3. " 'Service organizations,' where the client group is the prime beneficiary."[68] Major examples are schools, hospitals, and social work agencies.
4. " 'Commonweal organizations,' where the prime beneficiary is the public-at-large."[69] Examples include the government, the police, and the military.

Whatever typology one uses, it is quite clear that one loses a great deal of information about organizations if they are all lumped together under the general heading of bureaucracy.

Informal structure. The concept of a bureaucracy is inadequate because it includes under it a wide array of different types of organizations. It is also inadequate because it focuses on the formal structure and ignores the rather complex informal structure which develops within it. Early work on the concept of bureaucracy, including Weber's ideal type, tended to ignore the informal structure of formal organizations. This was particularly true of what was called the "Classical Administration School,"[70] which studied such formal organizational variables as the need for unity of command, specializa-

---

[64] Ibid., p. 40.
[65] Peter Blau and W. Richard Scott, *Formal Organizations: A Comparative Approach* (San Francisco: Chandler, 1962).
[66] Ibid., p. 43.
[67] Ibid.
[68] Ibid.
[69] Ibid.
[70] Names such as Gulick and Urwick are usually associated with this school.

tion, and the number of workers a supervisor could be expected to adequately supervise. The well-known Hawthorne studies led to the development of the Human Relations School and its emphasis on the informal structure which exists within formal organizations.[71] It was in the Hawthorne studies that the existence of informal groups and their ability to control the behavior of their members through group norms first came to light. Since the Hawthorne studies of the late 1920s and early 1930s, much of the sociological study of organizations has focused on the informal structure.

Peter Blau has called the informal organization "bureaucracy's other face" or "the unofficial activities and interactions that are so prominent in the daily operations of formal organization."[72] The informal organization may be highly functional or highly dysfunctional to the entire organization, but in either case it is an important reality of life in every formal organization. Participation in the informal group constitutes an important means for those in many occupations of resolving the conflicts they are faced with in formal organizations. For one thing, if the job is intrinsically meaningless, workers may turn to involvement in informal groups in the workplace as a source of worklife satisfaction. Participation in informal group activities designed to "beat the system" also constitutes a source of satisfaction both in terms of rewards gained and as a way of striking back at the formal organization. The informal group may even engage in illegal activities which serve the same kinds of functions: striking back at the organization and gaining unofficial rewards.

The literature is rich with examples of informal group activities within formal organizations. The manager or foreman who because of regulations cannot be granted formal rewards engages in informal activities which are designed to reward him despite official restrictions. Thus, in Dalton's study, *Men Who Manage*, foremen were allowed on company time to construct objects which were designed to unofficially reward themselves or those above them in the organizational hierarchy.[73] White- and blue-collar workers frequently engage in "goldbricking" in order to offset what they consider to be the unduly high expectations of management.[74] Mailmen structure their worklife so that they can finish their day's work early and they sanction anyone who deviates from this norm. Union stewards are supposed to push all the grievances of their constituents, but in many cases they arrange a "deal" with the foremen. They agree not to push many grievances and the foreman agrees to grant enough of the grievances to keep the steward's constituents content. Throughout this book there is considerable discussion of these kinds of informal practices. In the main, they serve to resolve some of the conflicts in

---

[71] Elton Mayo is most closely associated with this approach.

[72] Peter M. Blau, *Bureaucracy in Modern Society* (New York: Random House, 1956), p. 46.

[73] Melville Dalton, *Men Who Manage* (New York: John Wiley, 1959).

[74] Roy, "Quota Restriction and Goldbricking," 427–442.

occupational life within organizations and as a means of fleshing out the worklife in some of the more meaningless occupations.

Unionization

An important change in occupational life has been the growth of labor unions. In 1900 only 3 percent of the labor force in the United States belonged to labor unions, but spurred on by the competition between the AFL and the CIO, the percentage had grown to 23 percent by the end of the Second World War. However, since then this figure has remained stable, at slightly less than a quarter of the labor force.[75] Although the percentages have not changed much, there are today about 3 million more unionized workers than there were in 1950.[76] This increase is accounted for by the absolute growth in the labor force. Thus unions have been working hard just to maintain their position in terms of the percentage of the workforce that is unionized.

There are many reasons for the decline in union success in recent years. By the early 1950s unions had already organized a large proportion of the group most prone to unionization, blue-collar factory workers, and thus had to look elsewhere for members. Other occupations proved far more resistant to their membership drives. The scandals which rocked the union movement certainly did not help; names such as Dave Beck and James Hoffa became household words and symbols of union corruption. The merger of the AFL and the CIO in the early 1950s removed much of the competitiveness and dynamism from the union movement. In addition, to prevent the spread of unionism many nonunionized companies made the conditions of employment (wages, hours, and working conditions) equal to or better than those in unionized firms. Faced with these obstacles, the union movement tried to recruit members outside of its traditional domain. Needless to say, unions have not met with a great deal of success.

Unions have been strongest in the industrial states, so it was natural that they turn their attention to the less industrialized ones. However, while in states such as Michigan, New York, Pennsylvania, and West Virginia, between 35 and 45 percent of nonagricultural workers were in unions in 1966, in many southern and midwestern states at that time the percentage was less than 20. Nor does union strength in these states seem to be growing. Between 1964 and 1966 the percentage dropped from 7.4 to 6.7 in South Carolina, 13.5 to 12.3 in Mississippi, and 18.6 to 17.5 in Kansas.[77]

Unions have not made inroads in nonindustrial states, and have also lacked success in organizing white-collar workers. In 1956 12.9 percent of all white-collar workers were in unions, but by 1966 that figure had dropped to

[75] Joseph G. Rayback, *A History of American Labor* (New York: Free Press, 1966).
[76] *American Almanac* (1970), p. 236.
[77] Ibid.

10.7 percent.[78] A variety of factors account for this: white-collar workers tend to associate unions with blue-collar workers and hence consider it beneath their dignity to join; many white-collar workers are women whose involvement in the workforce is more transitory and they are less likely to be attracted to unions; and many white-collar workers cling to the dream that they will sometime rise to management positions and regard union membership as a hindrance to the attainment of that goal. Among professionals in particular, there are a large number of associations which perform functions similar to those performed by unions. Examples of such associations include the American Medical Association, The American Nursing Association, the National Education Association, and the American Sociological Association.

If unions have ceased to grow (at least for the time being), why are they included in this section on social change? For one thing, historically they have had an important effect on occupational life. More important, they continue to have an impact, albeit more indirectly. Management must continue to be on its toes if it wants to prevent the unionization of employees. Therefore, managers of nonunionized firms must be alert to the terms of collective bargaining agreements in unionized locations and seek to meet or exceed them. Thus, unionized firms often serve as a model for nonunionized ones. Further, unions often serve to put pressure on associations and push them into a more union-like posture. A good example is the more militant position that the National Education Association has had to take as a result of pressure from the American Federation of Teachers, an AFL-CIO affiliate. Finally, although the percentage of unionized workers has not increased, new groups of workers are being drawn into unions. Within the last few years, for example, the taxi drivers in New York City have been organized.

Revolution in education

Another important trend in contemporary America is the increasing educational level of the populace. In 1870 there were only 80,000 people enrolled in secondary schools in the United States, by 1960 there were over 10 million children, and it is projected that by 1980 over 15 million children will be enrolled in secondary schools. Also striking has been the growth in university and college enrollments. In 1870, there were only 52,000 young adults in colleges and universities in the United States, but by 1960 this figure had jumped to about 3.5 million students. Even more startling is the projection for 1980—that over 11 million persons will be enrolled in colleges and universities.[79] The revolution in education has affected virtually every occupational level.

First, it means that a vastly increasing number of people will have the

[78] Ibid.
[79] *Current Population Reports*, Series P-25, Np. 365 (May 5, 1967).

training needed to qualify for professional and semiprofessional positions. This seems to predict a huge growth in these occupational levels. An increasingly complex society will demand more and more services from these occupations. An increasingly affluent society will be able to afford the private kinds of services some of these occupations can offer. A large number of these college and university graduates will continue to flow into high-level managerial and official positions. For example, one of the areas of biggest growth has been and promises to continue to be in business schools. The old type of manager who rose from the bottom to the pinnacle of the organization will be even more uncommon in the future. Even today the vast majority of managers and officials are highly trained individuals with professional degrees. This increase in educational level also foretells that these high-level occupations, with their more and more trained personnel, will be involved in the drive of many occupations for professional recognition.

The personnel occupations.   A perfect example of this trend is what has happened in the personnel occupations. Personnel administration is a comparatively new occupation, first appearing in the early 1900s. Early personnel managers were usually female "do-gooders" who sought to bring welfarism into industry. With the growth of industry came a huge expansion of the functions handled by the personnel department. At first, these were what has been called "trash-can" functions, that is, tasks which no one else in the organization wanted. Examples included running the company cafeteria, parking lots, and similar kinds of relatively "unimportant" services. But changes within industry brought an increasing number of "important" functions into the personnel department. The development of industrial psychology, with its psychological and manual tests, was a big spur, and the testing of applicants and regular employees soon found its way into the personnel department. Unionism led to the need for an agency to handle collective bargaining and union relations for management, and these, too became an accepted part of the personnel function. Government legislation in the 1930s and 1940s forced companies, and consequently personnel departments, to become increasingly concerned with the question of benefits such as health insurance and pensions. Finally, the Human Relations School, with its emphasis on group problems at work, forced companies to abandon their focal concern with monetary factors. Personnel was delegated the job of studying and handling problems of communication, motivation, leadership, job satisfaction, and intergroup relations.

It is clear that the skills needed to be a modern personnel manager far exceeded those needed by early personnel officers. Labor relations representatives need to be lawyers or at least well versed in law to handle union contract negotiations and grievance settlements. The complexity of benefit programs requires highly trained personnel. The human problems of the workworld, as well as testing and training, require the personnel man to be well schooled in the behavioral sciences. The old personnel man was promoted up through the ranks or granted a personnel position as a sinecure. The new personnel man must be highly and specifically trained for his position. This need is reflected in the huge growth of personnel as a field of study at most colleges and universities. Most business schools offer a variety of graduate and undergraduate courses in personnel administration, and there are even a number of American schools which are exclusively concerned with the study of personnel administration. This trend is shown in a recent study by the author and Harrison Trice of personnel officers.[80] Ninety-six percent of the personnel managers and vice presidents of personnel had at least some college education, while 100 percent of the employment managers (who are in charge of hiring) had attained this educational level. Further, 49 percent of the personnel managers, 53 percent of the employment managers, and 64 percent of the vice presidents of personnel had some graduate work or an advanced degree.[81] In future years, it will be extremely difficult for anyone to find work in personnel administration without a Bachelor's degree. Further, few will be able to rise to high-level positions within this field without an advanced degree.

Thus personnel administration represents what has taken place in almost all managerial positions: a great rise in the educational level of the position's occupants. Personnel is also representative of these occupations in that, spurred on by increasing responsibility and rising educational levels, it is seeking to be recognized as a profession. There are a number of reasons why occupations such as personnel are seeking professional standing, including greater status, pay, and autonomy, and the ability to train and select new personnel officers and to weed out those without the necessary professional qualifications. The drive toward professionalization among this group of occupations is achieving some success, but those in managerial positions face a number of crucial barriers which are likely to prevent their full recognition as professionals. Some of these barriers are discussed in Chapter 2.

The blue-collar worker.   The other occupational group which has been most profoundly affected by the revolution in education is the blue-collar worker. In the early days of industrialization it was possible for a talented blue-collar worker to attract the attention of top management. If he displayed managerial ability he could become a foreman and still later move on to higher-level managerial positions. Such "rags to riches" stories abound in the popular literature of the late 1800s and early 1900s. However, the revolution in education has all but eliminated this possibility. Managerial positions now usually require at least an undergraduate degree and in many cases advanced degrees. Even the position of foreman is increasingly filled with new college graduates who are given this job to gain experience before moving on to

[80] George Ritzer and Harrison M. Trice, *An Occupation in Conflict: A Study of the Personnel Manager* (Ithaca: Cornell University, 1969).
[81] Ibid., p. 16.

higher-level positions. Management can now afford to fill its ranks with college graduates because so many people graduate from college. This leaves the blue-collar worker (usually with no more than a high-school diploma) stuck, with little hope of achieving a managerial position. The same situation, to a lesser extent, exists in nonmanagerial white-collar occupations. Increasingly white-collar workers either have some college training or have received some specialized training in business schools or high schools. Since the blue-collar worker does not have this kind of background, he has little chance of moving into these positions.

Other occupations. Although the professionals, managers, and blue-collar workers have been most affected by the increasing educational attainments of the population, all other occupational levels have also been affected to some degree. White-collar workers must have more training to fill the same level jobs they filled before, without any real pre-occupational training. Their chances, like those of the blue-collar workers, of moving into managerial positions have also been reduced because of the greater education required to fill managerial positions. A salesman now sometimes needs advanced training or a college degree to handle his job. The computer salesman of today bears little resemblance to the Willy Lomans of yesterday. Many storekeepers even find that the complexity of modern business requires at least some college-level training. Finally, even those in illegal deviant occupations have come to recognize the need for education if they are to make it to the top. Note, for example, the case of the Mafia: "Cosa Nostra members occupying the higher echelons of organized crime are orienting their sons to the value of education. . . . They are sending their sons to college to learn business skills, on the assumption that these sons will soon be eligible for 'family' membership."[82] In short, in virtually every occupation education has become a prerequisite to success.

An offshoot of this revolution in education has been the birth of a new problem in occupational life. We are in danger of becoming an overeducated society. Positions which formerly required only a high-school education now require bachelor's or even master's degrees. The problem is that many of the positions have not been altered to fit the new occupants; jobs which required a high-school degree often remain unchanged although they are now filled by college graduates. Thus the college graduate frequently finds himself in a position which he considers unworthy of his ability and training. In part, the fault lies with the colleges and universities; they lead the student to believe that he will immediately be placed in a responsible position. This is particularly true of business schools, most of whose students leave school believing they will assume responsible positions, and instead find themselves in menial positions or in training programs which are much like school. Thus there is much disillusionment and turnover in the first few years on the job. The

[82] Donald R. Cressey, *Theft of the Nation* (New York: Harper & Row, 1969), p. 241.

major fault however lies with organizations which have not revised the jobs to suit the training and abilities of the new type of occupant.

Increasing leisure time

A problem of particular importance to our affluent society is the great increase in leisure time. Leisure, as Nels Anderson puts it, was an "unintended creature of technological efficiency," and a "child not planned for."[83] Historically, only the elites had leisure, while the bulk of the population worked from dawn to dusk, with neither the time nor the energy for leisure activities. Now the industrial revolution has given the masses both the energy and the time. This book dwells on the problems created by our industrializing and bureaucratizing society, but it should be pointed out that despite these problems work is physically easier than at any time in the history of the world. The assembly-line worker may be alienated, but this work is not nearly as physically gruelling as that of the man who tilled the soil or shepherded the flock. Physically less taxed, the worker of today has the energy left at the end of the workday to enjoy his leisure, as well as more free hours to engage in such activities. Despite outcries that shortening the workday would lead to a moral degeneration in the population, there has been a steady decline in hours on the job. According to Faunce, the last century has seen a decline in the average workweek from about 65 hours to about 40.[84] This decline is likely to continue, and Faunce predicts "the four-day week may be feasible throughout the non-farm sector of our economy in the next twenty years."[85] Some skilled occupations already have an average workweek of 4 days and 25 hours. We have more time and more energy for leisure-time activity because of the machines we have created. Our automated factories tend increasingly to make each worker more productive as well as making the work easier. Thus the future promises to greatly increase the problem of leisure.

There are other factors involved in the boom in leisure time. One is the increase in vacation periods; it is not uncommon in some organizations for a worker to have a month's vacation every year. Retirement is another source of increasing leisure time, for the age at which one may retire has declined and at the same time life expectancy has increased. Thus the man who retires at 60 or 62 has a considerable number of leisure years to cope with. Then there is the problem of the unemployed and the underemployed. In recent years unemployment rates in the United States, have ranged from 3 to 6 percent,[86] and they are far higher for the young, women, blacks, and the old. The unem-

[83] Nels Anderson, *Dimensions of Work: The Sociology of a Work Culture* (New York: David McKay, 1964), p. 90.

[84] Faunce, *Problems of Industrial Society*, p. 73.

[85] Ibid.

[86] Alphonso Pinkney, *Black Americans* (Englewood Cliffs, N.J.: Prentice-Hall, 1969), p. 82.

ployment rate for blacks in the United States has generally been double that for whites.[87] Many others are underemployed—they do not hold full-time jobs. Underemployment rates are also far higher for the groups listed above than they are for white males. Finally, there are the dropouts from society who have nothing but leisure time. These include the hippie and the skid-row bum who reject society and are rejected by it.

Leisure is a problem in America because those who have an increasing amount of it do not seem to know what to do with it; they tend to be ignorant of how not to work and instead spend their time doing other types of work. Moonlighting, or taking a second job, is the prime example of this tendency. This is clearly not in line with Dumazedier's definition of leisure as an "activity to which the individual may freely devote himself outside the needs and obligations of his occupation, his family and society, for his relaxation, diversion and personal development."[88] While moonlighting is an extreme example, many other leisure-time activities also do not fit the definition. Is the "do-it-yourselfer" who builds an addition on his house exhibiting leisure-time behavior? Is the vacationer who drives two thousand miles to and from his destination at leisure? How do these differ from the carpenter or the truck driver?

Although leisure has created problems, it has also been a boon to occupational life, creating many new organizations and occupations. The automobile and related industries owe much of their existence to the growth of leisure, while some examples of the numerous occupations which exist primarily because of it include the work of the baseball player, actor, television repairman, movie projectionist, and stewardess. A large part of the American economy is based on supplying those who need things for their leisure-time activities.

The growth of leisure time has different implications for different occupational levels. Many managers formally work nine to five, but fill their leisure with work-related activities. It is not uncommon for them to get to work before nine and leave late in the evening. When they are at home they spend a great deal of time catching up on work which they could not complete at the office, and they even spend much of the morning and evening train ride at work. Weekends may be used for trips to outlying organizational locations to check on developments there. This behavior is not idiosyncratic; rather, it is expected in many organizations. Most organizations do not even pay their managers overtime, because the extra work is viewed as a normal part of their job. This is true of union and governmental leaders as well as of business executives.

On the other end of the occupational spectrum, many of those in middle- and low-status occupations literally flee from work at the five o'clock whistle.

[87] Ibid.
[88] Anderson, p. 93.

Overtime is not an expected part of their work, as is indicated by the fact that they must be paid for any hours in excess of the normal workday. Blue-collar occupations tend to be so meaningless that it is little wonder that individuals in them cannot wait for the workday to end. Much of the day is spent in day-dreaming and clockwatching. Machine breakdowns which give a moment's respite are welcome occurrences. Much of life's meaning comes from those activities which begin when the workday ends—drinking with buddies, playing with children, hobbies, and television. Thus, the meaningfulness of the occupation determines, in large part, the meaning of leisure time. Work is meaningful for most of those in high-status occupations; leisure time therefore is merely an extension of work. For most of those in low-status occupations, work is meaningless and leisure time is spent on other activities which, it is hoped, will make life more meaningful.

The changing status of females

The role of females in occupational life has changed enormously in recent years. Increasingly, women have moved out of the home and into occupational life. This trend has created enormous strains between sex and occupational roles. A mother who works has the very difficult task of balancing the expectations of those at home with those she finds at work. Further, at work the female has had to cope with conflicts with male peers, subordinates, and superiors. Thus, while males at each occupational level have problems, the female is in double or triple jeopardy. In addition to the general problems in the occupation she must deal with problems at home as well as additional problems in the workworld. Because of these additional problems, each chapter in this book devotes a brief section to the distinctive problems of females at each occupational level.

In 1890 about 18 percent of women above 14 were in the labor force, while by 1968 this percentage had more than doubled to 40.7 percent.[89] There are a number of explanations for this huge increase. For one thing, ideologies concerning the role of women in society have changed. Many women are no longer willing merely to accept roles as housekeeper, mother, and wife. They are more inclined to strive for success in the occupational world. Males have relented, at least in some occupations, in their willingness to accept female coworkers as long as they are in subordinate positions. Another factor has been the booming economy with its demand for workers, including females. Still another factor has been the increasing number of women going to college. They were originally supposed to get a humanistic or home economics degree, but many have found their way into the same educational programs as men. Buoyed by their success in competing with males at school, they have generalized this to a desire to compete in the work-

[89] *American Almanac* (1970), p. 220.

TABLE 1-7

Changes in the Occupational Distribution of Females 1900–1960

	% in 1900	% in 1960
Professional, technical, and kindred	8.2	13.3
Managers, officials, proprietors, except farm	1.4	3.8
Clerical and kindred workers	4.0	30.9
Sales	4.3	8.3
Private household workers	28.7	8.4
Other service workers	6.8	14.4
Craftsmen, foremen, and kindred workers	1.4	1.3
Operators and kindred workers	23.8	17.2
Laborers except farm and mine	2.6	0.6
Farmers and farm managers	5.9	0.6
Farm laborers and foremen	13.1	1.3
	100.2	100.1

Adapted from Philip M. Hauser, "Labor Force," in Robert E. L. Faris, ed., *Handbook of Modern Sociology* (Chicago: Rand, McNally, 1964), p. 183. Totals reflect rounding errors.

place. Another force in this change has been the proliferation of labor-saving devices in the home, which have given women the free time needed to work.

In venturing into the workplace women have historically sought positions in "female" occupations, such as teacher, librarian, nurse, maid, secretary, waitress, and telephone operator. However, because of the changes outlined above, women have recently tended to move beyond these into the world of male occupations. This trend is reflected in Table 1-7, which compares females in the labor force in 1900 and 1960 by occupational level.

Many of the changes shown in Table 1-7 reflect general trends already discussed. For example, the precipitous decline in females working on the farm reflects the general decline of farm work. Others, however, represent declines in traditional female occupations, the rise of new female occupations, *and* the movement of females into occupations in traditional male areas. Of particular importance to the focus here is the decline in household workers (a typically "female" occupation), and the increase of females working as professionals, managers, and clerks, occupations in which they are more likely to work with or deal with males.

The changing status of blacks

The position of the black occupationally in the United States has been very similar to that of females, as can be seen by comparing Tables 1-7 and 1-8. Note also the occupational status in 1960 of white and black males over 14 years, as shown in Table 1-8.

TABLE 1-8

Comparison of Occupational Distribution for Black Males
in 1910 and 1960 with White Males in 1960

	% of Black Males (10 yrs. of age and older) 1910	% of Black Males (14 yrs. of age and older) 1960	% of White Males (14 yrs. of age and older) 1960
Professional, technical, and kindred	1.1	3.9	11.0
Managers, officials, and proprietors	1.1	2.3	11.5
Clerks and sales workers	1.0	6.5	14.5
Foremen and craftsmen	3.6	10.2	20.5
Semiskilled operators	4.7	23.5	19.5
Unskilled	25.5	19.4	5.6
Service, incl. domestic	6.9	14.4	5.3
Farm workers	56.1	11.5	7.9
Not reported	—	8.4	4.3
	100.0	100.1	100.1

Adapted from Alphonso Pinkney, *Black Americans* (Englewood Cliffs, N.J.: Prentice-Hall, 1969), p. 79. Totals reflect rounding errors.

It is quite clear from Table 1-8 that although the occupational status of the black man has improved, he still is far from approximating the status of white males. Blacks continue to be grossly underrepresented in high- and middle-status occupations and overrepresented in low-status occupations. In addition, blacks are much more likely to be unemployed or underemployed.

Blacks have problems in the workworld precisely because there have been changes in race relations in the United States. In the slave era there were few black occupational problems because blacks "knew their place" and were mired in it. The end of slavery, decline of the farm, and industrialization, led many blacks into the workworld, but primarily in black, low-status occupations. In recent years however they have, albeit slowly, moved into every occupational sphere. Their entrance into these occupations has created a whole new series of work-related problems which are discussed throughout this book. Without these social changes these problems would never have existed. We are now in an era in which even greater social change is affecting race relations in the United States. Supreme Court decisions, government legislation, black pride, and black power, all indicate that blacks will move in greater numbers into every area of occupational life. As they do some problems will be resolved, while others will be exacerbated. The future holds turmoil for blacks in the workworld as it does in every other area of American life.

This concludes the rather extended discussion of the major social changes which have had an impact on occupational life. In the next section we turn to individual change in occupational life. "Career pattern" is the term used by occupational sociologists when they discuss individual change in occupational life.

Career patterns

According to Hughes the study of career patterns yields insights into the occupation, the individual, and society.[90] On the individual level Hughes sees the career pattern as "the moving perspective in which the person sees his life as a whole and interprets the meaning of his various attributes, actions, and the things which happen to him."[91] Hughes also contends that the study of career patterns tells us much about the structure of society. In an extremely rigid society career patterns consist "of a series of status and clearly defined offices."[92] In contrast, in less rigid societies career patterns are more highly variable. By studying careers one is able to "throw light on the nature of our institutions" and "reveal the nature and 'working constitution' of a society."[93] Although studying career patterns for insight into society is desirable, career patterns are not discussed here with that intention in mind, but because of what they tell us about the structure of occupations and individuals in them. This is consistent with our interest in occupations per se.

Steps in the career patterns. Every individual in every occupation follows a career pattern, and if he looks back over his career he can chart the sequence of upward, lateral, and downward moves. Although there is considerable individual variation, each occupational level has rather distinctive career patterns caused by the structure of the occupation. Beyond this there are very general steps all career patterns follow; Miller and Form have outlined five of these:[94]

1. Preparatory period (prior to the beginning of occupational life; important variables are family background and education).
2. Initial period (individual enters active worklife in his first job, usually while he is still in school).
3. Trial period (between the individual's first full-time job and his movement into a permanent position).
4. Stable period (some degree of occupational permanency).
5. Retirement.

The preceding five-step approach fits males in our society, while females go through an eight-stage career pattern:

[90] Everett Hughes, *Men and Their Work* (Glencoe, Ill.: Free Press, 1958), pp. 11–22.
[91] Ibid., p. 63.
[92] Ibid., p. 63.
[93] Ibid., p. 67.
[94] Miller and Form, *Industrial Sociology*, p. 541.

1. Preparatory.
2. Transitional (working and dating).
3. Marriage (generally entails withdrawal from the workforce).
4. Marital adjustment.
5. Settled domesticity.
6. Period of divided interest (may re-enter workforce).
7. Period of biological risk (husband may die) and preparation for leaving the workforce.
8. Retirement and widowhood.[95]

Both of these career patterns are ideal types with much individual variation in the "real world." Although true, they tell us very little about actual career patterns. In this book there is an effort to examine each occupational level in terms of the general types of career patterns found, and obviously many of the generalizations made will have a large number of individual exceptions. Nevertheless, it is important to look at the general career patterns common at each occupational level because of the insight they give into the relationship between occupational structure and the mobility of individuals.

Professionals. Professionals, because they are at the top of the occupational hierarchy, go through the most rigorous preparatory period of individuals at any occupational level. Frequently it begins in the home because a relatively large percentage of professionals come from homes in which either or both parents were professionals. College years are generally devoted to professional preparatory programs such as premed and prelaw. Training begins in earnest, however, in graduate or professional schools, where on a formal level there are a wide variety of courses and experiences designed to give the neophyte the needed information and skills. On a more informal level, graduate training is concerned with passing on to students the norms and values of the professions. For example, medical students learn informally that they are not omnipotent and that there are great gaps in what medicine knows, as well as how to view themselves as doctors rather than merely medical students. Once they have acquired enough of the needed skills, knowledge, values, and norms they are ready to begin the initial stage, in which the first professional positions are held. Internship, law firm jobs during the summer, and graduate research and teaching assistantships are examples of such positions. On the completion of training, they are generally actively recruited by organizations into their first position in the stable period. Hospitals actively recruit residents and other staff members, law firms seek new lawyers, and universities seek out teachers. The recruiting of professionals is a very complex affair, with a great deal of money often expended in the search for talent. Following recruitment the professions are characterized by

[95] Ibid., p. 545.

extremely diverse career patterns. Some professionals, like the Wall Street lawyer, are confronted with a series of well-defined steps leading to the top of the organization. Others, like the college professor, are faced with very few formal steps to the pinnacle of the occupation. Still others, like the general practitioner, have virtually no formal steps remaining once in the initial position. However, they can look forward to informal steps, such as, in the case of the medical specialist, acceptance in the inner fraternity of medicine. On retirement the professional has a large number of employment opportunities open to him because of his scarce and desirable skills and knowledge.

Managers and officials. Managers and officials have a less involved preparatory period. Generally they have no more than a bachelor's degree or, in some cases, a master's degree in business administration. Nevertheless, they are recruited at least as actively and with as much complexity as professionals. Like professionals they will fill strategic positions, and organizations seek through their recruiting processes to ensure good choices in hiring. Once in the stable period, managers and officials are generally confronted with the most possibilities for mobility of any occupational level. They generally start at the bottom and are faced with a veritable maze of moves which may be up, lateral, or down. In the course of their careers they may move up for a while, laterally, down for training purposes, and then up again. Some rise straight to the top, others ascend in a zig-zag fashion, still others may get stuck at lower level positions, and some may never move at all. The organizations in which the manager or official finds himself have a plethora of positions, and they may be used in an infinite number of combinations in each career pattern.

Middle-level occupations. In most cases middle-level occupations offer highly constricted career patterns. The foreman who is a recent college graduate and who is in the position for training purposes is an exception; he is usually a future manager who is to gain some experience in production. After a short time he will move on to low-level managerial positions and have the same potential career patterns as the managers discussed above. Other foremen are promoted from the blue-collar ranks and they have little possibility of further upward mobility because they lack the education to be considered for higher-level positions. Union stewards are in the same position as foremen—they have little possibility of upward mobility. The stewards' lack of mobility is caused by the few positions at the top of the union and the longevity of those already in these positions. Skilled craftsmen are also in a terminal position in terms of career mobility. They are very committed to their craft and most do not desire to move out of the occupation and up in the organization, but even if they did, they too lack the education and managerial skills needed for advancement. Although the semiprofessions offer slightly more career mobility than the skilled crafts or union stewardships, there is still little opportunity to rise, although there are occasional chances to move up by moving out of the occupation. For example, teachers can move up if they want to cease being teachers and become school principals or even higher-level administrators. The semiprofessions do, however, offer a good deal of lateral mobility. Teachers, social workers, and nurses can, because they have scarce and valued skills, move from organization to organization in search of what they consider to be the best work environment.

Clerical and low-status occupations. Most of the clerical and low-status occupations have almost no possibilities for career mobility because they lack the skills and education needed for advancement in modern American organizations. They are also the most insecure in their positions because they are easily replaced. In the case of some blue collar workers, this insecurity is ameliorated through the existence of a labor union at their location. Similarly, most of these in low-status deviant occupations are loners who have no organization in which to rise. They have some informal mobility—they can become the best poolroom hustler or the bookie with the biggest business in town. Some low-status occupations are attached to organized crime, but although there is a potential for upward mobility there is little actual opportunity to move up. The Mafia, according to Cressey, has not let in new members in the last ten years.[96] Even if there were openings in the Mafia, only a very small percentage of those in deviant occupations would be admitted. But there are very few positions, many jobs are granted on the basis of nepotism, and only Italians are allowed into official positions. Finally, there is some indication that even the Mafia is now requiring advanced education for admittance.

Career-pattern disorder. From the preceding discussion it might appear as though career patterns are very orderly in virtually all occupational levels. While it is true that each level is characterized by a general type of pattern, we must not conclude that all of the individuals in a given occupation conform to the general type. In fact there is much variation within each occupational level, a fact which is underscored in each of the succeeding chapters. More important, a considerable amount of disorder is characteristic of a number of careers. Wilensky defines a career pattern as "a succession of related jobs, arranged in a hierarchy of prestige, through which persons move in an ordered, predictable sequence,"[97] but goes on to conclude that no more than one-third of the labor force has had such a career. Most American workers have careers which are better viewed as disorderly than orderly. How can we reconcile Wilensky's view of disorder with our more orderly view of career patterns? Basically, Wilensky is talking about the career patterns of individuals, while we are focusing on the career patterns typical of a particular occupation or occupational level. Thus *occupations* are characterized by typical

[96] Cressey, *Theft of the Nation,* pp. 221–247.
[97] Harold Wilensky, "Work, Careers, and Social Integration," *International Social Science Journal* 12 (1960), 554.

and orderly career patterns, while the *individuals* in them have careers which vary greatly and in most cases are disorderly. Let us take the case of the college professor, who usually has four career steps open to him: instructor, assistant professor, associate professor, and full professor. While many individuals proceed in an orderly manner through these steps, many others have more disorderly careers in academia. An individual may be an instructor, move to industry for a few years, return to academia as an assistant professor, work for the government, return to academia as an associate professor, and so forth. Such individual variation and disorder does not negate the fact than an orderly pattern is associated with the occupation.

Wilensky relates the disorder of individual careers to the disorder in the labor market. Labor market disorder is due to a variety of factors:

Rapid technological change dilutes old skills, renders others obsolete and creates demand for new ones; a related decentralization of industry displaces millions, creating the paradox of depressed areas in prosperous economies; metropolitan deconcentration shifts the clientele of service establishments, sometimes smashing or re-structuring careers; and recurrent crises such as wars, depressions, recessions, coupled with the acceleration of fad and fashion in consumption add to the general unpredictability.[98]

Perhaps hardest hit by these chaotic conditions are individuals in low-status occupations, and Wilensky finds that their careers are marked by considerable disorder. In interviews with 108 blue-collar workers and 38 lower white-collar workers, he found that the median number of jobs held since graduation from high school was six and the median number of occupations was three. Wilensky presents the following case to illustrate career disorder among blue collar workers:

Helped on father's farm until 1932; 1932–34, part-time clerk in grocery store; 1934–37, plating work in a factory; 1937–39, father's farm; 1939–1959, machine work, 2 years; bricklayer's helper, 2 years; window repair, 2 years; assembler, 5 years; tool attendant, 8 years; truck driver, 1 year; drill machine operator, 8 months; all jobs in the same factory.[99]

Again, however, Wilensky is describing the career of one man, not the career pattern of a particular occupation.

Wilensky has a number of other insights into career patterns which deserve our attention. Although most people do not have orderly careers, the existence of orderly career patterns is a source of stability for society as a whole. Those who are in orderly careers provide a model for those who are not. Further, since orderly careers are most characteristic of those in high-status occupations, these skilled people are more likely to be careerists and less likely to use their skills against the system. Wilensky also sees the continuing indus-

[98] Ibid.
[99] Ibid.

trialization of society as leading to a number of changes in careers. He contends that careers will become even more disorderly because they will be more discrete with an increasing number of stages. The revolution in education will lead to even longer training periods required for occupations and the increasing bureaucratization in society will result in more and more careers taking place in organizations.

Along with Hughes, Wilensky sees an intimate relationship between one's career and his life style. The career of the much maligned "organization man" is characterized by considerable stability as he moves to the pinnacle of the employing organization. To ascend this hierarchy the organization man plays it safe and tries to avoid making decisions, especially those which might entail some risk. Further, he seeks to gain security and to develop his human-relations skills so that he can manipulate people in his drive to the top. A career with these characteristics clearly affects the off-the-job behavior of the organization man. Wilensky summarizes his view of this life style: "This is a life style which is active, group-centered, conforming and fluid—a pseudo-community pattern, unguided by stable values. Behavior both at work and off work is characterized by expedient conformity . . . and by other-direction, or conformity as a way of life whatever the content of values and norms conformed to. . . ."[100] In short, the nature of a man's career can tell us a great deal about the nature of the man.

PLAN FOR THE BOOK

This chapter has been devoted to a discussion of the themes which are discussed in the ensuing chapters. Each chapter, then, focuses on the particular acute form (or forms) of conflict at each occupational level and the means employed to resolve these conflicts. Each chapter also contains a discussion of the additional conflicts faced by two minority groups, blacks and females, at each occupational level. An explicit focus on career patterns and an implicit focus on broad social changes constitute the second major concern in each chapter. In Chapter 6, in addition to a discussion of deviant occupations in terms of conflict and change, there is a discussion of the problem of deviant behavior in all occupational levels. In the final chapter there is a summary of the book in propositional form as well as a discussion of the relevance of sociological theory in the study of occupations.

[100] Ibid., p. 556.

2

The Professions

Studying professional occupations has been the pre-eminent concern of sociologists interested in the workworld. For the period from 1946 to 1952, Smigel reports that 58 percent of all studies of occupations dealt with the professions;[1] later (1953–1959) Smigel et al. report a decline in interest, with only 48 percent of occupational studies concerned with the professions.[2] Despite this decrease in interest, from 1953 to 1959 studies of the professions continued to dominate studies of occupations, with their nearest rival being studies of proprietors, managers, and officials (22 percent of all studies from 1953–1959). The occupational sociologist must explain this intensive interest in the professions, and one explanation is clearly their accessibility. No occupational group is as likely to cooperate with the sociological researcher as fellow professionals. Second, a number of occupational sociologists view the process of professionalization as an excellent index into social structure and social change. The industrialization of Western society was paralleled by a proliferation of professional occupations and occupations which strove for professional recognition. It has been contended that the more advanced a society is industrially, the more dependent it is on professionals and their expertise.[3] There is a third reason for the dominance of the study of the professions, which relates to the history of the sociological study of occupations. The sociological study of lower-status occupations had its origin at the University of Chicago in the 1920s and 1930s. It was Robert Park's call for the study of low-status occupations as a means of gaining insight into urban structure and process which led Everett Hughes into his lifelong concern with occupational life. Most studies of low-status occupations were done by Hughes' students while they were at Chicago or after they moved to other

[1] Erwin Smigel, "Trends in Occupational Sociology in the United States: A Survey of Postwar Research," *American Sociological Review* 19 (1954), 398–404.
[2] Erwin Smigel et al., "Occupational Sociology: A Re-examination," *Sociology and Social Research* 47 (1963), 472–477.
[3] Everett Hughes, "Professions," in Kenneth S. Lynn, ed., *The Professions in America* (Boston: Beacon Press, 1967), pp. 1–14.

universities. Unlike the study of lower-status occupations, studies of the professions had two sources: Chicago and the Ivy League universities.[4] Following its early interest in low-status occupations, the Chicago School expanded its focus to include higher-status occupations and professions. On the other hand, Ivy League interest in occupations began at the professional level with Parsons' 1939 essay, "The Professions and Social Structure."[5] While the Chicago School was interested in *process* and *change* within the professions, the Ivy League School, dominated by functionalists, was much more interested in the structure of the professions. They were following Parsons' belief that before sociologists could study social change they must first be able to adequately describe social structure.[6] Thus the study of professions had a dual geographic and intellectual source which helped make it the focal concern of occupational sociologists. With this brief background of the history of interest in the professions, we can turn to empirical generalizations dealing with this occupational level.

PROFESSIONAL CONTINUA

1. All occupations can be placed on a continuum ranging from the nonprofessions on one end to the established professions on the other.

Most occupational sociologists subscribe to the notion that there are degrees of professionalization rather than a simple dichotomy between professions and nonprofessions. This notion of a continuum is more a product of the processualists from Chicago than the functionalists of the Ivy League. The continuum idea grows out of the processualists' focus on social change rather than on static structure. By viewing professionalization as a continuum they are able to study how and why an occupation moves up or down the scale. On the other hand, the functionalists are more concerned with describing the characteristics which differentiate the profession from the nonprofession. The two approaches, however, are not incompatible. One can view occupations as lying on a professional continuum *and* be concerned with delineating the characteristics which determine their position there. Position on the professional continuum depends not only on the number of professional characteristics an occupation possesses, but also on the degree to which it has each characteristic. For example, the position of social work is closer to the professional end. It is neither an established nor a new profession, because it lacks some professional characteristics and others, that it does possess, are not well developed.

4 James McCorkel, "Chicago and Ivy League Sociologies of Occupations: A Comparative Analysis of Assumptions, Theories, and Methods" (Paper presented at meeting of the Southern Sociological Society, New Orleans, La., April 11, 1969).

5 Talcott Parsons, "The Professions and Social Structure," *Social Forces* 17 (1939), 457–467.

6 Talcott Parsons, *The Social System* (New York: Free Press, 1964).

It is interesting to note that the reconciliation of the processual and functional perspectives in occupational sociology follows a similar attempt at reconciliation in general sociological theory. Dahrendorf, for example, outlines what he considers to be the major tenets of conflict (or process) and functional (or structural-functional) theory and concludes that neither approach, in itself, is complete.[7] For Dahrendorf they constitute complementary rather than alternate perspectives on total societies as well as various subsystems within society. Van den Berghe also sees the possibility of wedding the two perspectives.[8] He cites a number of commonalities in the two approaches, including a holistic view of social systems; concern with equilibrium models of these systems; and agreement that conflict can contribute to integration and, conversely, that integration can lead to conflict and change. The occupational sociologist can focus on the structure of an occupation *as well as* the inherent strains, conflicts, process, and change. Indeed sociologists such as Bernard Barber have been able to utilize both perspectives in discussing the professions.[9]

Once the notion of a professional continuum is accepted, its parameters must be ascertained. Hughes, in 1928, made one of the earliest attempts at developing such a continuum.[10] Hughes based his "classification of the types of places in the division of labor"[11] on how people enter an occupation, the individual's attitude toward his occupation, and the standing of the occupation "in the eyes of the community."[12] These three factors are used today by occupational sociologists in assessing the degree of professionalization of an occupation. Entry into the occupation relates to the existence of professional training schools and sponsorship patterns; attitude relates to commitment to the occupation; and standing in the eyes of the public refers to a label an occupation tries to acquire in order to win power and prestige. These factors continue to be relevant and we discuss them in greater detail later in this chapter. Based on these elements Hughes developed the following continuum:

1. Missions—the clergy is an example of an occupation Hughes would classify as a mission.
2. Professions and near-professions—medicine would be classified as a profession, while social work would fit into the near-profession category.
3. Enterprise or entrepreneur—for example, the business leader.

---

[7] Ralf Dahrendorf, *Class and Class Conflict in Industrial Society* (Stanford: Stanford University Press, 1965).

[8] Pierre Van den Berghe, "Dialectic and Functionalism: Toward a Theoretical Synthesis," *American Sociological Review* 28 (1963), 695–705.

[9] Bernard Barber, "Some Problems in the Sociology of the Professions," in Lynn, *Professions in America*, pp. 15–34.

[10] Everett Hughes, "Personality Types and the Division of Labor," in Hughes, ed., *Men and Their Work* (Glencoe, Ill.: Free Press, 1958), pp. 23–41.

[11] Ibid., p. 32.

[12] Ibid.

4. Arts—for example, authors, composers, and painters.
5. Trades—by this Hughes seems to mean the skilled trades, which he admits are very close to the arts.
6. Jobs—this appears to be a catch-all category which includes all of the less skilled or unskilled occupations.[13]

There are a number of difficulties with the Hughes continuum. Most occupational sociologists would classify the missions as professions. The clergy is often discussed as one of the original professions. Also, one could quarrel with the order in which Hughes has listed these occupational groups (e.g., why is arts placed below entrepreneurs and above trades?). Finally, the jobs category covers a wide range of occupations and might profitably be subdivided. Despite these shortcomings the Hughes spectrum is important historically and it comes strikingly close to later efforts at developing a professional continuum.

Reiss utilizes a classification system which focuses on the professional end of the professional continuum:[14]

1. Old established professions—occupations in this category include doctors, lawyers, and the clergy.
2. New professions—occupations here include the natural and social scientists.
3. Semiprofessions—Etzioni has described semiprofessions as a group of occupations which, in comparison to the professions, have less training, less legitimization, less well-established right to privileged communication, less specialized body of knowledge, and less autonomy.[15] Examples include social workers, teachers, and nurses.
4. Would-be professions—occupations currently aspiring for professional status include personnel managers and funeral directors.
5. Marginal professions—included here are occupations which are associated with professional occupations (e.g., laboratory and engineering technicians).

By differentiating the professional end of the continuum, the Reiss approach is a significant advance over the Hughes approach. However, it totally ignores the nonprofessional end. The NORC (National Opinion Research Center) list of occupational situses rectifies this omission, but with a loss of detail at the professional end of the continuum:

1. Free professions—doctors, clergymen, undertakers, public schoolteachers, etc.

[13] Ibid., pp. 33–34.
[14] Albert Reiss, Jr., "Occupational Mobility of Professional Workers," *American Sociological Review* 20 (1955), 693–700.
[15] Amitai Etzioni, ed., *The Semi-Professions and Their Organization* (New York: Free Press, 1969), pp. xiii–xiv.

2. Cultural/Communication-oriented professionals—artists, musicians, reporters, nightclub singers, etc.
3. Scientific professions—natural and social scientists.
4. Political/Government occupations—Supreme Court Justices, governors, policemen, etc.
5. Big businessmen—bankers, building contractors, etc.
6. Customer-oriented occupations—taxi drivers, bartenders, etc.
7. Artisans—skilled trades.
8. Outdoor-oriented occupations—airline pilots, mailmen, truck drivers.
9. Dead-end occupations—night watchmen, janitors, etc.
10. All-farm occupations—farm owners, farm hands, etc.
11. Other—Captains in the army, union officials, machine operators.[16]

Although this continuum is complete, it has enormous weaknesses. For example, a public schoolteacher is classified as a free professional when most occupational sociologists would consider him neither free (since he inevitably exists in an organization) nor professional. The NORC system also lumps a number of diverse occupations into each category. One might ask why Supreme Court Justices and policemen are both included in the relatively high-status Political/Government category. The status of the Justice is clearly far higher than that of the policeman. Finally, there are a number of occupations which cannot be placed in a specific category and are lumped together under "other" occupations.

In reviewing these efforts at developing a continuum of professionalization it is quite clear that as yet there is not an adequate one. The major inadequacy lies at the relatively nonprofessional end of the range. There clearly is a range, but one does not know where the less professional occupations and/or occupational groups lie. For example, is the industrial foreman more or less professional than the skilled craftsman? Theorists are more confident at the extremes since most would agree that the doctor is an old established profession and the janitor is a nonprofession. Past efforts to work with the entire spectrum of occupations have focused on the single variable of prestige. As will be pointed out later, this is only one dimension of professionalization. Occupational sociologists must use all of the professional variables in order to develop the entire professional continuum. The factors discussed later in Generalization 3 can be used to develop such a continuum.

2. Just as all occupations vary in their degree of professionalization, individuals in any occupation vary in their degree of professionalism.

[16] Robert Hodge, Paul Siegel, and Peter Rossi, "Occupational Prestige in the United States: 1925–1963," in Reinhard Bendix and Seymour Lipset, eds., *Class, Status, and Power: Social Stratification in Comparative Perspective*, 2nd ed. (New York, Free Press, 1966), pp. 322–333.

Occupational sociologists have focused on the question of what factors determine the position of an occupation on the professional continuum. Virtually ignored has been the important question of professionalism at the individual level. In every occupation there are some individuals who are more professional than others. Thus, while medicine is a profession there are some doctors who are more professional than others. By the same token, in a nonprofession such as janitorial work there are some professional individuals. It seems logical to assume that the more professional occupations have the greater number of professional individuals. However, this does not negate the contention that within each occupation there is individual variation. That there is such a level in the study of professionalism is stated in several places. In many of Hughes' essays on occupations there is a dual emphasis on structural *and* social psychological factors in the workworld. Specifically, in discussing professions Hughes contends that the

culture and technique, the etiquette and skill of the profession, appear in the individual as personal traits. . . . In general, we may say that the longer and more rigorous the period of initiation into an occupation, the more culture and technique are associated with it, and the more deeply impressed are its attitudes upon the person.[17]

This statement clearly implies that there is an occupational level of concern composed of etiquette, culture, and skill, *and* an individual level to which these are transmitted in the initiation period. There is the additional implication that the degree of inculcation at the individual level is highly variable. Hughes points out that it varies with the length and rigor of the training period, but the degree of individual professionalism might also be affected by a number of other factors. In discussing the process of becoming professionalized, Hughes in another essay says of the term "professionalized" that it is "here used to mean what happens to an occupation, but lately used to refer to what happens to an individual in the course of training for his occupation."[18]

The differentiation between structural and attitudinal levels of professionalism has recently been made by Richard Hall, who contends that the professional model consists of *both* structural and attitudinal variables.[19] I believe that combining both of these levels into one professional model confuses the issue. The two levels are conceptually and analytically distinct, as Hall himself discovers:

Among the major findings of this research is the fact that the structural and the attitudinal aspects of professionalism do not necessarily vary together. Some "es-

---

[17] Hughes, "Personality Types," p. 36.
[18] Hughes, "Professions," in Lynn, *Professions in America*, p. 4.
[19] Richard Hall, "Professionalization and Bureaucratization," *American Sociological Review* 33 (1968), 92–104.

tablished" professions have rather weakly developed professional attitudes, while some of the less professionalized groups have very strong attitudes in this regard.[20]

There is not one professional model; rather, there are two, and occupational sociologists must keep them distinct. In Generalization 4 variables which might be useful in differentiating individuals on their degree of professionalism are discussed.

    3. Where an occupation lies on the professional continuum depends on how many of the following structural characteristics it possesses and to what degree it possesses each:

a) General, systematic knowledge.
b) Authority over clients.
c) Community rather than self-interest, which is related to an emphasis on symbolic rather than monetary rewards.
d) Self-control through professional associations, training schools, and sponsorship patterns rather than outside control.
e) Recognition by the public and law that the occupation is a profession.
f) A distinctive culture.

According to Haug and Sussman, there are two major viewpoints on professionalization at the occupational level. One is that "professions do not constitute an identifiable sub-category of the range of occupational variation and that professionalism is merely a label used by occupations to win power and prestige."[21] The alternative view is that "professions are conceptualized as occupations with . . . core characteristics."[22] However, there is no real conflict in these points of view. Most occupational sociologists accept the idea that there are certain core characteristics which determine where on the professional continuum an occupation stands. The acceptance of this view does not, however, constitute a rejection of the first position outlined by Haug and Sussman. The use of the label of professional to win power and prestige is one of the core characteristics of a profession.

It must be pointed out that there is considerable disagreement in the literature on what are the core characteristics of a profession. The processualists see these characteristics embodied in steps each occupation must go through if it is to receive professional recognition. Caplow, for example, sees four steps in the process of professionalization:

1. A professional association must be established.
2. There must be a change of name which dissociates the occupation from its previous nonprofessional status and provides it with a title which is its exclusive domain.

    [20] Ibid., p. 103.
    [21] Marie Haug and Marvin Sussman, "Professionalism and the Public," *Sociological Inquiry* 39 (1968), p. 57.
    [22] Ibid.

3. There is the development and adoption of a code of ethics.
4. There is political agitation to gain popular and legal support and the setting up of a mechanism controlled by the profession to train new members.[23, 24]

Wilensky, another processualist, outlines a five-step sequence which is very close to the Caplow approach:

1. Creation of a full-time occupation.
2. Establishment of a training school.
3. Establishment of a national association.
4. Efforts to win legal support.
5. Establishment of a code of ethics.[25]

Combining the two approaches results in the following characteristics:

1. Full-time occupation.
2. Change of name, which becomes the occupation's exclusive domain.
3. National association.
4. Training school.
5. Code of ethics.
6. Political agitation to win popular and legal support.

The above steps need not be in order since some steps may take place concurrently or some later steps may precede earlier ones. The structural characteristics developed by the functionalists are outlined next, followed by an attempt to reconcile them with the characteristics developed by the processualists.

Huntington points out the general orientation of functionalists in their analysis of the professions:

Professions have attained a strategic position in modern industrial society as the occupational groups whose task it is to develop and apply abstract and technical knowledge to important problems of everyday life. The task, which is essential to the smooth running of the industrialized business economy and which must be carried on by highly trained personnel, is institutionalized in the various professional roles. Because of the functional significance of professions for the social structure, sociologists are interested in analyzing the social context in which professional activity is carried on.[26]

In studying the social context of professional activity the functionalists have developed a "constellation of characteristics" which differentiate professional

[23] Theodore Caplow, The Sociology of Work (Minneapolis: University of Minnesota Press, 1954), pp. 139–140.
[24] The goal here is to win the label Haug and Sussman discuss.
[25] Harold Wilensky, "The Professionalization of Everyone?" American Journal of Sociology 70 (1964), 137–158.
[26] Mary Jean Huntington, "Sociology of Professions," Sociology in the United States of America (Paris: UNESCO, 1956), p. 87.

activity from other occupations.[27] The major characteristics of this professional constellation are the six structural factors listed under Generalization 3. This approach of selecting characteristics which differentiate occupations by their degree of professionalization has been severely criticized by Habenstein.[28] Habenstein feels that the major problem with such an approach is the variation from one theorist to another in terms of which characteristics they select for their constellation. The six characteristics used in this proposition are inclusive and this is demonstrated later when it is shown how the characteristics developed by the processualists are subsumed under the six structural variables.

Characteristics of professions

The six professional characteristics used here constitute the most frequently mentioned variables which may be used in determining how professional a given occupation is. Established and new professions have all of these characteristics, would-be professions have some, and nonprofessions have none. One may select any occupation, ascertain how many of these characteristics it possesses, and thereby determine in a general way where it lies on the professional continuum. More specific placement depends on how much of each characteristic the occupation possesses. For example, some occupations have more general, systematic knowledge than others. With this background, a detailed discussion of each of the six professional characteristics follows.

General, systematic knowledge. Intellectually, the professions are differentiated from other occupations by general, systematic knowledge which is acquired through a long period of training in a professional school and informally in relationships with established professionals. Professionals have knowledge about their specialty which no one outside of the occupation could acquire. According to Greenwood:

The crucial distinction between professions and non-professions is this: the skills that characterize a profession flow from and are supported by a fund of knowledge that has been organized into an internally consistent system, called a body of theory. A profession's underlying body of theory is a system of abstract propositions that describe in general terms the classes of phenomena comprising the profession's focus of interest.[29]

The doctor's years of medical school, internship, and residency invest him with expertise no layman could possibly acquire. Similarly, law school, divinity school, and graduate school transmit knowledge, both formally and

[27] Robert Habenstein, "Critique of Profession as a Sociological Category," *Sociological Quarterly* 4 (1963), 296.
[28] Ibid., p. 292.
[29] Ernest Greenwood, "Attributes of a Profession," *Social Work* 2 (1957), 46.

informally, which could not be acquired in any other way. Occupations which are categorized as semi- or would-be professions frequently lack a systematic body of knowledge because their knowledge is a potpourri of expertise drawn from a number of disciplines. Social work, for example, is a field which is composed primarily of insights drawn from the social sciences. As yet it does not possess a systematic body of general knowledge, although it may be moving in that direction. Similarly, business management as a body of knowledge is also composed, in the main, of insights drawn from the social sciences as well as a number of self-generated practical ideas about industrial management. Business management lacks a general theory and seems further from achieving that goal than social work. As one descends down the professional continuum less and less general knowledge is found. Technicians have some general systematic knowledge, but much more of their expertise comes from practical know-how. Finally, taxi drivers have no discernible general systematic knowledge, although they may have acquired considerable expertise on the job.

Authority over clients. Authority over clients is a second factor which differentiates occupations in terms of their degree of professionalization. This characteristic actually has two aspects: existence of a clearly defined client and authority over him. Professionals have clients, while all individuals in nonprofessional occupations have customers. The difference between a customer and a client is that a customer can, and does, judge his own needs and evaluate the ability of the service or commodity to satisfy those needs. In contrast, the client is characterized by an inability to judge what he needs or the ability of the specific professional to satisfy the need. Because he has uncontested authority within this area of expertise, the professional has clients, not customers. In contrast, authority in the customer-occupation relationship lies with the customer. Theoretically, at least, the shopper knows what kind of automobile he wants and shops around in order to find the best car at the best price. A sick individual, in contrast, frequently does not know specifically what is wrong with him, nor can he assess the ability of the doctor to help him. The client, in general, has surrendered his ability to judge the quality of the service he receives to the professional authority. Whether an occupation receives recognition is dependent on its possession of a systematic body of knowledge which no one else possesses. Some occupations which are striving for professional authority will find it difficult to achieve their goal because they lack such knowledge. For example, personnel managers are striving for professional authority, but significant others refuse to grant this because they feel they are as expert in "people problems" as the personnel manager. The question of authority over clients is therefore related to the possession of general, systematic knowledge.

It is necessary to discuss the notion that the professional has complete authority over his client. Authority, like every other variable discussed in this section, is not a matter of "all or nothing," but is rather a matter of degree. Those in occupations on the professional end of the continuum have more authority over clients than those in other occupations, but they rarely have complete authority. Freidson points out that doctors do not have the ability to define a patient, at least initially, as ill.[30] The doctor must wait for the patient to define himself as ill before he will seek out a physician. The physician, especially the general practitioner, also has his authority limited since he must be responsive to the lay culture. It is by pleasing this culture that the general practitioner gets and keeps patients. "Whether their motives be to heal the patient or to survive, professionally, they will feel pressure to accept or manipulate lay expectations, whether by administering harmless placebos or by giving no unpopular drugs."[31] Many patients visit a physician for the first time on a "tryout" basis. The patient assesses the doctor's performance and may even compare his assessment with that of others who have used the same doctor. Only if his assessment is favorable will the patient return to the doctor. Although the physician, as a professional, is often viewed as free of client control, the above discussion demonstrates that this is not always the case. The doctor's authority is clear once he has been accepted by the patient—he then is free to dispense advice and medication and the patient is not in a position to assess the quality of these recommendations. In contrast to the general practitioner, the doctor who deals only with patients referred by other doctors has much more authority and has therefore much greater freedom from lay control. Instead, he must be more responsive to fellow doctors and this places a limitation on *his* authority. In sum, the more professional the occupation, the greater the authority, but this authority is rarely absolute.

Community rather than self-interest. It is generally conceded that those occupations on the professional end of the continuum are dominated by a community interest, while those occupations which stand near the nonprofessional end are more self-interested. In other words, professionals ideally emphasize helping others, while nonprofessionals are primarily interested in helping themselves. These contrasting emphases are related to the differences in reward structures. Professionals emphasize symbolic rewards, which reflect their success in helping others, while nonprofessionals seek primarily economic rewards, which exemplify successful self-interest. The doctor is concerned with healing the sick, while the assembly-line worker is generally interested in little more than his paycheck. Although most occupational sociologists accept this differentiation, Talcott Parsons disagrees. Parsons contends that both professionals and businessmen are interested in the same

[30] Eliot Freidson, "Client Control and Medical Practice," *American Journal of Sociology* 65 (1960), 374–382.
[31] Ibid., p. 378.

goal—success.[32] The difference between the two lies not in the goals, but in the means to the goals. Thus Parsons contends "doctors are not altruists, and the famous 'acquisitiveness' of a business economy is not the product of 'enlightened self-interest'."[33] However, the differences between Parsons' approach and the more traditional approach are not irreconcilable. The disagreement boils down to whether professionals and nonprofessionals differ on means or ends, but this disagreement is not central to the point made here. Means and ends are not relevant; what matters is action. Professionals are more likely to *act* with the community in mind and nonprofessionals are more likely to *act* in a self-interested manner. This is not to deny that much of what is considered altruistic behavior may, from another perspective, be seen as selfish behavior. A researcher who is seeking a cure for cancer is acting in the community interest, but he is also concerned with the impact of such research on his professional reputation. By the same token, the philanthropist who gives money to charity may also be viewed as seeking to enhance his reputation or to reduce his taxes. This argument, however, is a blind alley. All so-called altruistic behavior has elements of selfishness, while even some selfish behavior has elements of altruism. Thus the businessman who slavishly seeks profits is also helping the economy of the country and even contributing to the betterment of the poor. Parsons is right, therefore, when he contends that

the typical motivation of professional men is not in the usual sense "altruistic," nor is that of businessmen typically "egoistic." Indeed there is little basis for maintaining that there is any important broad difference of motivation in the two cases, or at least any of sufficient importance to account for the broad differences of socially expected behavior.[34]

However the focus should not be on motivation or on expectations, but rather on actual behavior, for although the motivation of the two groups might be the same, their actual behavior is quite different. Behaviorally, professionals are more altruistic (as defined by our society), while businessmen are more self-interested.

Parsons raises an important point which relates to all of the professional characteristics discussed in this section. He observes that the differentiation between altruism and self-motivation is not sufficient to account for the broad differences between occupations on the poles of the professional spectrum. None of the factors discussed here is in itself sufficient to account for the differences between occupational groups. It is only when these factors are used in combination that it is possible to place occupations on the continuum and account for differences between them.

[32] Parsons, "Professions and Social Structure," pp. 457–467.
[33] Ibid., p. 465.
[34] Ibid.

Self-control rather than outside control. Another distinctive character-istic of the professions is that only one professional can train or judge an-other. Thus the community surrenders to the profession the right to control the behavior of individuals in the group. In Hughes' terms this is the "li-cense" the community yields, and he believes the profession may then seek to expand its sphere of control by enlarging what he calls its "mandate."[35] Even without expansion of the professional mandate, there is a broad area in which the professional can only be evaluated by his peers. Thus the profes-sion is allowed to select its own recruits, train them formally in professional schools and informally in the professional culture and sponsorship system, develop a code of ethics, and judge individual professionals through the pro-fessional association. In sum, what the profession seeks is "a monopoly granted by the community to the professional group." In some cases the community may resist and the profession must then, through a public-relations cam-paign, convince the public that the profession has a right to its monopoly.

Recognition by the community and law that the occupation is a pro-fession. In reality, the preceding four professional factors are dependent on community recognition of the occupation as a profession. It is interesting to ponder which comes first: community recognition or one of the other four professional factors already discussed. When the sequential models of Cap-low and Wilensky are examined, it seems clear that the first goal of an oc-cupation seeking professional standing is to create for itself an exclusive body of general knowledge. It can then seek community recognition, after which it can proceed to institutionalize the other facets of professionalization. It can gain authority over clients, stress community rather than self-interest, and develop self-control through its professional association, training school, and sponsorship pattern. The recognition which a profession seeks is suc-cinctly summarized by Greenwood:

Every profession strives to persuade the community to sanction its authority within certain spheres by conferring upon the profession a series of powers and privileges. Community approval of these powers and privileges may be either informal or for-mal; formal approval is that reinforced by the community's police power.[36]

In the main the powers and privileges a profession seeks are the right to self-control, authority over clients, and the security of income which allows it to be interested in the good of the community. Others include the right to obtain confidential information from clients and to keep such information from inquiring government officials. Some of these powers and privileges are legalized while others are on an informal basis. For example, some professions have been able to have the government license individuals who seek to prac-tice it. Sometimes an individual desiring work in a profession must be exam-

[35] Hughes, "License and Mandate," in Hughes, *Men and Their Work*, p. 79.
[36] Greenwood, "Attributes of a Profession," p. 48.

ined on his qualifications by a board which is generally composed of individuals in the occupation. In contrast to this legalized community recognition, there are the more informal rights such as the right to obtain confidential information. It is this goal of formal and informal community recognition which is the primary concern of occupations nearing professional standing. Once they have achieved this recognition, monopoly within their area of expertise is secure. This accounts for the active public-relations campaigns waged by occupations striving for professionalization. It should be pointed out, however, that all occupations will not be able to achieve professional recognition merely by waging a public relations-campaign. At a minimum an occupation must have general systematic knowledge for the public to view its public-relations efforts as legitimate. With a strong knowledge base, an occupation can reasonably expect its public-relations efforts to win community recognition. Once this recognition has been achieved all of the facets of the "professional model" are likely to follow.

Freidson has extended this dimension of professionalization and views the successful political efforts of an occupation to win recognition as a profession as the sole defining characteristic of a profession.[37] Not even the professional label is important to him—all that an occupation need do is convince the public and state of its right to autonomy (or self-control) over work-related matters. In effect, Freidson contends that the characteristics of an occupation are irrelevant; all that matters is its political power. Although there is much to recommend this position, it is obviously not the one taken here. I feel that it is highly unlikely, if not impossible, that an occupation could wage a successful political campaign if it did not have at least some of the core characteristics discussed here (especially general systematic knowledge), and to a significant degree. Those in occupations such as social work, teaching, nursing, and personnel management have made a significant investment of both energy and money to gain professional recognition, but as of this date their efforts must be viewed as failures, although *not* for a lack of political power. Rather, they have failed because they woefully lack some of the dimensions of professionalization discussed in this section.

The preceding discussion raises an interesting question: should all occupations which desire professional recognition seek such status? The answer implied here is obviously "No." For one thing, an occupation without general, systematic knowledge is doomed to failure, but even if it could develop such a base of knowledge, it should not, in many cases, seek professional recognition. Many of the occupations now seeking professional recognition are creatures of formal organizations (e.g., social work, personnel management). Since they owe their livelihood to the organization, it would be difficult for them to gain some of the characteristics of a profession already discussed. The personnel manager, for example, is in a staff position

[37] Eliot Freidson, *Profession of Medicine* (New York: Dodd, Mead, 1970).

and hence has no authority over those who might be considered his clients. He cannot stress community interest in organizations which define success in terms of self-interest. Even if personnel could define a body of knowledge as its exclusive domain (which as yet it has been unable to do), it would find it difficult to fulfill the other aspects of the professional model. Thus, professional status, as we know it, does not constitute a realistic goal for occupations like personnel. This point was clearly shown by the author and Harrison Trice in a study of the American Society for Personnel Administration in which we found personnel administration to lack a number of professional variables.[38] These findings led the then president of ASPA to make the following statement:

> Inevitably, we have to come to grips with the matter of professionalism in personnel. As we learn more, a new concept is beginning to emerge . . . a new set of criteria for the professionalization of functions which operate within the framework of an established organization.
>
> Those of us who believe strongly that the practicing personnel man must be completely involved and immersed in the day-to-day operations of the enterprise if he is to properly focus "manpower management" as a key element in the success of the organization, would be reluctant to espouse a concept of professionalism which would tend to isolate the function from business reality.
>
> Thus while we may borrow from the criteria utilized by such established groups as medicine, law and teaching to determine what constitutes professionalism, we may also modify and add. Perhaps we will produce a model which will better serve those functions which, like personnel, demand and are willing to earn a better defined role in our rapidly changing society.[39]

Such occupations face insurmountable barriers in their efforts to professionalize. What is needed is a new concept of the professional-bureaucrat to cover the goal which these occupations are trying to achieve. In conclusion, all occupations that wish professional recognition should examine their own inherent liabilities in terms of the traditional professional model. Instead of striving to be like doctors they might be better served by defining a more realistic goal for themselves.

A distinctive culture. A profession which has the preceding professional characteristics will inevitably develop a distinctive occupational culture. These characteristics make its subculture different from that of any other occupational group. Greenwood points out that this culture develops around formal as well as informal groups within the profession. The formal organizations which help to create a distinctive culture are the professional associations, the training schools, and the organizations in which professionals work; supplementing these formal structures are a series of informal

---

[38] George Ritzer and Harrison Trice, *An Occupation in Conflict: A Study of the Personnel Manager* (Ithaca: Cornell University, 1969).
   [39] Ibid., p. 80.

groupings within the profession. The culture which develops is composed of a number of distinctive values, norms, and symbols.[40] Some typical professional values include importance of their service to the community, authority over clients, self-control, and theoretical objectivity. In addition, there are numerous norms within a profession which serve as specific guides for behavior. Some examples from the medical profession concern how to get into medical school, how to attract a sponsor, and how to find patients. Such norms are so pervasive that Greenwood contends that "there is a behavior norm covering every standard interpersonal situation likely to recur in professional life."[41] Finally, there are the symbols of the profession, which reflect the culture and are in addition part of it: included are "its insignias, emblems, and distinctive dress; its history, folklore, and argot; its heroes and its villains; and its stereotypes of the professional, the client, and the layman."[42] Training in a profession is focally concerned with transmitting this culture to the neophyte through formal training schools or informal devices such as sponsorship.

The idea of a professional culture has been expanded by Goode. He views a profession as a community[43] because the members are bound by a common identity: it is terminal in the sense that once in a profession few leave; it has common values, role definitions, and language; power over members; clear boundaries; and powers of reproduction via transmission of culture to succeeding generations. As with all of the other professional characteristics discussed in this section, there are degrees of community within professional occupations—some professions are more community-like than others. No matter how strong a community the profession has, it enjoys certain rights and privileges. However these are not obtained merely because a profession is a community; rather, they are obtained when the public grants them, recognizing the distinctive aspects of the professional community. Thus, as was pointed out in the preceding discussion, a professional community is dependent on public acceptance.

Reconciling structural and processual theories

The problem is now to reconcile these structural characteristics with those delineated by the processualists. It seems clear that in this area at least, the structuralists have made a greater contribution to the study of the professions than the processualists. The idea that an occupation must be full-time in order for it to be a profession seems to be obvious, as is the idea that the occupation have a name which is its exclusive possession. While these char-

[40] Greenwood, "Attributes of a Profession," p. 51.
[41] Ibid., p. 52.
[42] Ibid.
[43] William J. Goode, "Community Within a Community: The Professions," *American Sociological Review* 22 (1957), 194–200.

acteristics are obvious, other characteristics listed by the processualists are subsumed under some of the structural characteristics. For example, general systematic knowledge assumes a training school which is a storehouse of this theory and passes it on to recruits. The structural characteristic of self-control includes the notion of a professional association and code of ethics to institutionalize self-control, and a training school which passes on norms and values which help the professional to control himself. Finally, the proc-essualists and the structuralists agree on the need for public and legal sup-port. While all of the processualist steps may be included under the struc-tural approach, the reverse is not true. The structuralists have contributed important new characteristics to the professional model including control over clients, community interest, and a distinctive professional culture. Gen-erally, then, the structuralists have contributed more important variables to the ability of the sociologist to differentiate occupations in terms of their degree of professionalization.

Although the structuralists have a superior variable scheme, one need not accept their static approach to the study of the professions. Indeed, the structural characteristics can fit neatly into a dynamic view of professional-ization. The structuralists' contention that there is merely a dichotomy between professionals and nonprofessionals is inadequate. There is a profes-sional continuum, and occupations are not either professions or nonprofes-sions, but rather vary in their degree of professionalization. It is the six structural characteristics discussed under this proposition which determine where on the continuum an occupation stands. An occupation's position on the continuum is determined by the number of these characteristics it pos-sesses. However, the issue is not as simple as it first appears: each of the six characteristics is in itself a continuum. An occupation on the professional end of the spectrum has much systematic knowledge, a great deal of authority over clients, much more community interest than self-interest, considerable self-control, a substantial public and legal recognition, and a highly distinc-tive culture. Occupations in the middle of the professional continuum have some of each of these characteristics, while occupations at the lower end have very little of each. In ascertaining the position of an occupation of the professional continuum two questions must be answered: a) How many of the six characteristics listed above does it possess? b) To what degree does it possess each of them?

In a recent book on the professions Wilbert Moore has taken a position very similar to the one described above.[44] Moore sees professionalization as a scale which is composed of subscales. His scale of professionalization is the equivalent of the professional continuum described here and his subscales are the theoretical equivalents of the six subdimensions outlined in this sec-tion. Although there is disagreement between Moore's subscales and the six

44 Wilbert Moore, *The Professions: Roles and Rules* (New York: Russell Sage Foundation: 1970).

subdimensions used here (one of his subscales is the degree to which an occupation is full time), our basic approaches to professionalization are almost identical. Moore raises a question which has also been alluded to in the preceding discussion: What are the relative weights of each of the subscales or subdimensions? Clearly, all of the six subdimensions of professionalization discussed in this section are not of equal importance in terms of the degree of professionalization of an occupation. I have suggested that general systematic knowledge is the most important variable, while others are likely to have their own favorites. Although I cannot answer the question of relative weights here, it is important to point out that it must ultimately be answered if sociologists are to ever develop an accurate way of assessing the degree of professionalization of a given occupation.

4. Where an individual lies on the professional continuum depends on how many of the following attitudinal and experiential characteristics he possesses and to what degree he possesses each:

a) General, systematic knowledge.
b) Authority over clients.
c) Community rather than self-interest, which is related to an emphasis on symbolic rather than monetary rewards.
d) Membership in professional (or occupational) associations, training in professional (or occupational) schools, and existence of a sponsor.
e) Recognition by the public that he is a professional.
f) Involvement in the professional (or occupational) culture.

a) Individuals in any occupation vary in the amount of general systematic knowledge they possess. It is clear, however, that the amount of such knowledge an individual possesses is related to the amount possessed by the occupation. Thus any given doctor is likely to have more systematic knowledge than a particular plumber. However, there is a good deal of variation in knowledge *within* the medical profession; some doctors are more expert in general medicine, or in their specialty, than other doctors. Similarly, not all plumbers are completely lacking in general systematic knowledge concerning the theoretical aspects of plumbing. By ascertaining the amount of general systematic knowledge of individuals in an occupation one gains some insight into the range of individual professionalism. By utilizing all of the variables discussed in this section one can pinpoint where an individual stands in terms of *his* degree of professionalism.

b) Individuals in any occupation also vary in the amount of authority they have over clients. Some doctors have more authority over their patients than others. The Freidson study cited above indicates that in general specialists have more authority over their clients than do general practitioners. This finding can be extended so that it might be hypothesized that even within specialties of medicine there is individual variation in terms of authority over clients. By the same token, individuals in relatively low-status occupations also vary in their amount of authority over customers. For example, we allow some barbers to determine how our hair should be cut while with others we insist that they follow our directions.

c) Individuals in any occupation vary in their emphasis on community and symbolic rewards over self- and monetary rewards. While this variable and all others discussed in this section are highly related to occupational variation, there is much individual differentiation within an occupation. Most doctors emphasize community and symbolic rewards, but it is not rare to find a self-interested doctor who is focally concerned with money. Similarly, most taxi drivers are interested in self- and monetary rewards, but some do have a community interest and are concerned with symbolic rewards.

d) Self-control, at the occupational level, is exerted through professional associations, training schools, and sponsorship patterns. Although self-control is an occupational variable, individuals vary in experience in the means through which it is exerted. One might ask the following questions about individual involvement in the occupational means of self-control:

i. Is the individual a member of the professional (or occupational) associations? How active is he in these associations? Is he an officer?

ii. How much professional (or occupational) training has he had? How good was the professional (or occupational school) he attended?

iii. Did he have a sponsor? How active was the sponsor in his behalf? How did the sponsor help him?

e) Individuals in any occupation vary in the amount of recognition they receive from the public as professionals. Some doctors are viewed as more professional than others. Similarly, we may consider some taxi drivers more professional than others.

f) Individuals in any occupation vary in their degree of involvement in their occupational culture. All occupations are likely to have a culture of some sort and involvement in that culture is an index into individual professionalism. Involvement in an occupational culture has two aspects: activity and attitude. One can ask how active an individual is in the formal and informal culture of the occupation, and can ascertain how committed he is to his occupation. The individual who is active and committed is highly professional on this variable.

In discussing the individual level of professionalism we can appraise a debate which has raged in the literature on professionalism. The debate began with an article by Foote entitled "The Professionalization of Labor in Detroit."[45] Foote's major conclusion is that "labor itself is becoming profes-

---

[45] Nelson N. Foote, "The Professionalization of Labor in Detroit," *American Journal of Sociology* 58 (1953), 371–380.

sionalized." Wilensky, in a response to the Foote article, concludes that "this notion of the professionalization of everyone is a bit of sociological romance."[46] Interestingly, both of these seemingly antagonistic conclusions are correct, because the arguments are on different levels. Foote is really discussing individual professionalism and Wilensky is discussing occupational professionalization. Foote says that "the professionalization of labor in Detroit is . . . what is happening to the laboring men themselves."[47] Thus as individuals, *laborers* are becoming more professional. He notes that they are using an increasing amount of general theory. Wilensky, on the other hand, details the barriers to professionalization at the occupational level. Both writers are right: as individuals, laborers are becoming more professional, but as an occupation, laborers face insurmountable barriers to professional status. By differentiating the individual and occupational levels of professionalism this controversy, and other debates in the literature on professionals, can be clarified.

5. A profession is not monolithic, but rather is composed of a series of segments which frequently are in conflict.

While the structural functionalists have tended to view professions as monoliths, the processualists have presented evidence that professions are composed of a number of segments. I believe that the processualists have sufficient evidence to hypothesize that professions are "loose amalgamations of segments pursuing different objectives in different manners and . . . delicately held together."[48] By viewing professions in this way the sociologist is better able to account for the internal conflict and change endemic to all professions.

The notion of segments within professional occupations was raised by Bucher and Strauss in response to Goode's description of a profession as a community.[49] They present the community view of a profession which focuses on "the mechanics of cohesiveness" and "detailing the social structure." Analysis of cohesion and social structure are tasks "structural-functional sociology is prepared to do, and do relatively well."[50] After this brief acknowledgement of the structural-functional position, Bucher and Strauss proceed to the attack:

But this kind of focus and theory tend to lead one to overlook many significant aspects of professions and professional life. Particularly does it bias the observer against appreciating the conflict—or at least difference—of interests within the profession; this leads him to overlook certain of the more subtle features of the profes-

[46] Wilensky, "Professionalization of Everyone?", p. 156.
[47] Foote, "Professionalization of Labor in Detroit," p. 372.
[48] Rue Bucher and Anselm Strauss, "Professions in Process," *American Journal of Sociology* 66 (1961), 326.
[49] Ibid., pp. 325–334.
[50] Ibid., p. 325.

sion's "organization" as well as to fail to appreciate how consequential for changes in the profession and its practitioners differential interests may be.[51]

Bucher and Strauss go on to say that "the assumption of relative homogeneity is not entirely useful," and see their process approach as either a supplement or alternative to the functional model.[52] The segmental approach is best viewed as a supplement to the functional model rather than an alternate approach.

There are a number of commonalities throughout any profession including shared norms, values, interests, and role definitions. However there is also diversity within each profession, and the major indicator of these differences is the existence of frequently conflicting segments.

Pathologists.   Bucher uses the conception of segments in an examination of the pathology profession.[53] Like many other professions, pathology has been subjected to much social change; this has resulted in the growth of segments within the profession. These segments have developed their own identity, history, goals, and suborganization. Their growth was spurred by the development of new techniques, increased laboratory services, and a greater demand for the pathologist's services. Pathology has become less of a science and more of a clinical specialty serving physicians, and because of these changes has split into two segments. The practitioner segment views pathology as a medical specialty which must focus on clinical diagnostic activities and efforts to build closer ties with the medical profession. In contrast, the scientific segment is primarily concerned with scientific investigation and communication of results to fellow professionals. Further, it is devoted to the idea of "maintaining the scientific position of the specialty." These two segments were found to be so distinct that members of one segment were generally not interested in, or informed about, the activities of the other.

The practitioners constitute the newer segment and are seeking to carve out a niche for themselves despite the resistance of the entrenched old-liners. The practitioners have stretched the boundaries of the profession to include their activities. Pathology to them is not just the study of disease, and they have declared new missions for the science including servant and consultant to, and educator of, the physician. In addition, they have developed a new self-image which dissociates them from the old image of pathologist as a laboratory worker. They have sought to solidify their position by developing their own professional associations, which press for the establishment of practitioner-pathologist positions in hospitals. They have also sought to

[51] Ibid.
[52] Ibid., pp. 325-326.
[53] Rue Bucher, "Pathology: A Study of Social Movements Within a Profession," *Social Problems* 10 (1962), 40-51.

recruit new pathologists who accept their ideology and who will ultimately fill the positions they are developing.

The scientific segment, in contrast, has been long established and seeks to maintain its position in the face of the threat from the practitioners. The primary interest of the scientific pathologist is research; this is threatened if the service ideal of the practitioners is accepted. Because of their effort to defend their occupational position and ideology, the scientists find themselves in direct conflict with the practitioners. This conflict is not only ideological, but has extended to a battle between the two segments to attract recruits. In the face of this threat the scientific pathologists have taken a number of steps "to rejuvenate pathology as a science." They are trying to move away from the old techniques and emphasize the exciting new methods being utilized by the modern scientific pathologist. However, they continue to defend the old techniques because they constitute their exclusive domain. The scientists also are redefining their research mission to include traditional techniques as well as new scientific developments.

The conflict between the two segments has resulted in large-scale social change within the entire profession. By moving away from a monolithic view of professions, we are able to account for conflict and change within the group. The example of the pathologist may be extended to every professional occupation. Conflict within a profession may revolve around its mission, work activities, methodology and techniques, clients, colleagues, interests and associations, recruits, and public recognition.[54] Segments form around these issues and newer ones do battle with the established ones, which are seeking to maintain tradition. However, just as it is erroneous to view professions as monoliths, it is equally erroneous to view segments as monolithic. Segments have internal differentiation and are constantly in flux. A profession may witness the rise of a segment, its later decline and replacement by a new segment, or the resurgence of an older segment.

Viewing professions in this way has enormous implications for the overall study of these occupations. The places in which they work are the arenas for the battle between members of the rival segments. This conflict is affected by, and affects, the organization in which the profession operates. Careers within professions are not a well-defined series of steps, but vary between segments. Further, career ladders may disappear or come to the fore when a segment declines or a new segment arises. Socialization is not a simple process of indoctrination into the profession: instead, it involves a conflict between segments for recruits and a selection by the recruit of the segment by which he chooses to be socialized. In training schools the recruit is treated to the spectacle of competing segments vying for his commitment. Segments disagree on the image they wish to convey to the public and may seek to project differing public images. Finally, segments may relate differently to

[54] Bucher and Strauss, "Professions in Process," pp. 325–334.

other professions and may each possess their own leaders. In sum, viewing professions as segmental affects virtually all areas in the study of professions.

PROFESSIONAL TRAINING, RECRUITMENT, AND CAREER PATTERNS

6. Formally, professional schools are primarily concerned with teaching skills and communicating knowledge.

On the formal level virtually every type of professional school has courses designed to communicate knowledge and offer opportunities for recruits to learn the skills they need. Medical schools, for example, are designed to offer both formal courses and practical experience. In most graduate schools the focus is on formal coursework which is designed to enable the student to pass his preliminary examinations. In addition, graduate schools also offer their students opportunities to gain some practical experience. Thus, most schools require their students to assist a professor in a course or in a research project in order to gain experience in research design, methodology, and analysis, and dissertation research is also designed to give the student experience in designing, carrying out, and analyzing his own project. Some professional schools, however, do not accomplish both of these goals. In Lortie's view, law schools are almost totally involved in communicating knowledge.[55] This focus has its weaknesses because it leaves little time for the law student to learn the actual practice of law, how to handle clients and opposing lawyers, and how to handle the value conflicts inherent in the legal profession. No matter how well they perform their formal tasks, professional schools leave many of the important aspects of professional training to an informal system. In medical school, while the focus is formally on communicating knowledge and teaching skills, professional norms and values are acquired informally through contact with instructors and peers, patients, and members of the health team.

7. Informally, professional schools are primarily concerned with communicating professional norms and values.

Students entering professional schools generally have an unrealistic picture of the nature of the profession. The informal system in the professional school serves to communicate the norms and values of the profession and, in the process, generally changes initial idealism into a more realistic view. Lortie, supporting a position put forth by Hughes, feels that professional schools seek to replace an initial lay view of the profession with "more subtle, complex and even ambiguous perceptions."[56] There is a "gradual replace-

[55] Dan C. Lortie, "Layman to Lawman: Law School, Careers, and Professional Socialization," *Harvard Educational Review* 29 (Fall, 1959), 352–369.
[56] Ibid.

ment of the exotic and dramatized image by one which takes account of routine and pedestrian elements."[57] Although all professional schools try to achieve this goal, they are rarely completely successful, and because of their focus on formal training, law schools are probably least successful. Newly graduated law students are dissatisfied with their social preparation because "they left law school with a hazy and incomplete conception of what lawyers' work consists of."[58] Most of the value and normative socialization of the law student is left for his first job. Although other professional schools perform this task better than do law schools, there is inevitably a "reality shock" in the transition from school to practice. The remainder of this section outlines some of the ways in which professional schools informally socialize their students.

Medical students. Among the occupational sociologists who have studied the more informal aspects of socialization, focusing on medical schools, are Becker and Geer, who examined the change in idealism which takes place there.[59] A freshman enters medical school imbued with the wonders of medicine and the desire to save mankind, but the first year proves to be a rude shock. He is disillusioned because his courses seem irrelevant and, furthermore, they are not even taught by doctors. He realizes that there is far more knowledge in medicine than he could ever hope to learn, and learns to "play the game" by concentrating on passing examinations, pleasing the faculty, and utilizing shortcuts to learn the mass of facts. He views the first year as unimportant and becomes cynical about his activities. However, he retains the hope that subsequent years will prove better and that the knowledge learned will be more applicable to his lingering idealistic desire to help mankind. However, the second year proves to be little different, although there is some contact with "real" medical problems such as autopsies. In the third and fourth years he does have contact with the patients, and his performance is assessed by doctors, but instead of helping these patients, his primary concern is to understand them as a specific form of a general medical problem. "The student becomes preoccupied with the technical aspects of the case . . . because the faculty requires him to do so."[60] In addition, the medical student is plagued by his low status in the hospital system and is not in reality a central participant in the actual care of patients. As a result a sense of cynicism pervades the student culture and he tends to look at patients in terms of the problems they create for him. In the end, however, the medical school provides the student with an out. Although he has become more cynical, his cynicism is directed at the school; he is able to retain his idealistic belief that once he graduates he will be able to help society. As his

[57] Ibid.
[58] Ibid., p. 353.
[59] Howard Becker and Blanche Geer, "The Fate of Idealism in Medical School," *American Sociological Review* 23 (1958), 50–56.
[60] Ibid., p. 53.

student years come to an end his cynicism about medical school recedes and idealism about the profession regains center stage. However, this is quite different from the idealism he had when he entered medical school: he has acquired a more realistic picture of the profession which will enable him to handle the blows to idealism he will face in private practice or hospital work.

Many other changes take place informally throughout the student years. For example, a change in identity takes place. Huntington was concerned with the process by which first-year students, who think of themselves as students, come by the fourth year to think of themselves as doctors.[61] In a survey of three medical schools she found that only 31 percent of the first-year students but 83 percent of the fourth-year students thought of themselves as doctors. Further, throughout the four years there are times when the student sees himself as a doctor, while at other times he does not. Whether a medical student thinks of himself as a doctor depends on whom he interacts with and what he perceives their role expectations to be. The first-year student rarely views himself as a doctor when interacting with the faculty or fellow students. However, with patients or nurses he is much more likely to be viewed, and to view himself, as a doctor. As the years of medical school pass more of his significant others are likely to view him as a doctor, and hence by the last year of school the vast majority of medical students do view themselves as physicians.

Another change which takes place informally in medical school is the development of interest in a specialty. In their study of students entering Cornell Medical College, Kendall and Selvin found that most did not intend to specialize and that this intention slowly changed during their student years.[62] In this study 60 percent of the first-year students expected to devote most of their working time to general practice, while only 16 percent of the fourth-year medical students said they planned to go into general practice. Conversely, 35 percent of the first-year students and 74 percent of the fourth-year students said they would devote themselves to a specialty. Students generally begin with a broad interest in medicine, but it soon becomes clear that the field is so complex that it is possible only to master a small portion of the subject matter. Thus a majority of the students, by their fourth year, have decided to seek a specialized internship. However, not all who apply for specialized internships are accepted. These positions often go to the top-ranking students while lesser students are persuaded by faculty and staff to seek general internship appointments.

[61] Mary Jean Huntington, "The Development of a Professional Self-Image," in Robert K. Merton, George Reader, and Patricia Kendall, eds., *The Student Physician: Introductory Studies in the Sociology of Medical Education* (Cambridge: Harvard University Press, 1957), pp. 179–188.

[62] Patricia L. Kendall and Hanan C. Selvin, "The Tendencies Toward Specialization in Medical Training," in Merton, Reader, and Kendall, *Student Physician*, pp. 153–176.

One of the latent functions of medical education is to train the student to handle the uncertainty inherent in the occupation. Medical skill and knowledge is far from complete and along with the successes there will be a number of failures. Furthermore, no single doctor can ever master all the skills, or acquire all the knowledge, no matter how inadequate skills and knowledge are. In addition, the medical student must learn to differentiate "between his own ignorance and/or ineptitude and the failings of current medical knowledge." Renee Fox, in her discussion of training for uncertainty in medicine, has outlined a number of ways in which medical school formally and informally prepares the student to deal with that uncertainty.[63] Courses are not presented with clear expectations of what should and should not be learned. The student must decide for himself the boundaries of the subject matter. The student does not receive grades, and thus gets no clear picture of where he stands. Each course covers an enormous amount of material and the student learns that he cannot master all there is to know. Further, each course demonstrates the great gaps in medical knowledge. In contact with instructors the student learns that he knows far less than they do. When he gets to actual practice he makes errors (e.g., an improper autopsy), because of inadequacies in the field as well as his own failings. He also learns, in working on autopsies, of the unpredictability of death, the inability to prevent it, and the incorrect diagnoses which may have hastened it. Thus as the student learns more he also learns of the gaps in knowledge and the uncertainty in the field. In learning more he also learns to differentiate between personal inadequacy and inadequacies in the discipline, and in his relationships with peers he soon learns that he is not alone in his sensitivity of these dual sources of uncertainty. In addition to learning of uncertainty, the medical student has also been taught, informally, to cope with it.

Sociology students. Graduate training in sociology is in many ways similar to the experience of doctors. A graduate student in sociology enters with a number of vague and unrealistic ideas about graduate education. He frequently enters with the same kind of idealism that is found among medical and nursing students:

He may see sociology in a rather vague way as being an avenue for the betterment of mankind, a discipline sensitive to the sore spots in civilization and dedicated to alleviating them. This appeals to his idealism, since he is likely to be a person who would want his life in some way to serve the cause of human welfare and progress.[64]

During his years in graduate school the student quickly learns the realities

---

[63] Renee Fox, "Training for Uncertainty," in Merton, Reader, and Kendall, *Student Physician*, pp. 207–244.

[64] Alan P. Bates, *The Sociological Enterprise* (Boston: Houghton Mifflin, 1967), p. 116.

of life in sociology. He is not given answers to society's ills; instead, the subject matter tends to be ambiguous, with the professor more concerned with getting the graduate student to "show initiative, imagination, and a self-starting capacity"[65] than he is with teaching him facts. Like the medical student he learns that there is much more to sociology than he could possibly master. More frightening is the realization that "truth in sociology is provisional and problematic,"[66] and he begins to realize that because of limitations in himself and the field he may never find the answers he originally sought. If he survives the process, the graduating sociologist is in many ways a changed man. He is concerned with more realistic goals, such as passing his dissertation defense, getting a good job, and above all, accepting the basic goal of professional sociologists: "the search for reliable scientific knowledge about human social behavior."[67]

> 8. The nature of the socialization process in professional school depends on the nature of the entering student's commitment to the profession.

Most students who enter the training schools of the established professions already have a deep commitment. The schools therefore can concentrate on transmitting knowledge, values, norms, and a more realistic picture of the profession. However, among students entering the training schools of newer professions this is not always the case: students may be committed on entrance, but in many cases they have entered the training schools for a number of nonprofessional reasons. Hence, some professional schools must be concerned with engendering a sense of professional commitment. Much light is cast on this question by the comparative study of graduate students in physiology, philosophy, and engineering conducted by Becker and Carper.[68] Because of differing initial commitment the socialization processes for the three groups have some basic differences. Most physiology students enter graduate school with a commitment to another field. Graduate school must therefore be concerned with transforming this to a commitment to physiology. Philosophy students enter graduate school with a broad intellectual commitment and engineering students enter with a strong commitment to engineering. In both these cases, graduate school serves to maintain these attitudes.

Physiology students. A majority of the physiology students in the Becker and Carper study had originally planned a medical career and decided on graduate work in physiology only after they were rejected by medical schools. In general, they entered graduate work in physiology as a stop-

---

[65] Ibid., p. 117.
[66] Ibid.
[67] Ibid., p. 120.
[68] Howard S. Becker and James W. Carper, "The Development of Identification with an Occupation," *American Journal of Sociology* 61 (1956), 289-298.

gap, planning to enter medical school after the end of the first year of grad-uate school. Even those students who planned to study physiology entered without a strong commitment to the field. The first year of coursework makes it clear to the student that the field lacks many answers and is a fertile area for original work. This discovery, as well as developing skill in physiological techniques, makes for some degree of commitment by the end of the first year. Some may then reapply to medical school, but as medicine becomes more of an unattainable goal, physiology grows as a meaningful alternative. This meaningfulness is enhanced in the second year as the student begins laboratory work in which he finds himself in intimate contact with com-mitted students and faculty, and their formal and informal socialization helps to increase his commitment. By the end of the second year he is fairly well committed to physiology and "can even envision turning down a place in medical school if one materializes."[69] His developing dedication is the result of two factors: a growing identity with the field and a reluctance to give up the "investments" he has already made in physiology.

Engineering students. The engineering student is in a much differ-ent situation: he has developed a commitment to engineering long before he entered graduate school. Thus in the first year little attention is paid to developing commitment, since it already exists. Instead, the first year of graduate school is seen as a way of enhancing the salary offers the student will ultimately receive; attention is primarily on course work and gaining additional expertise. The student does not even greatly desire to ever get a degree since job offers are generally not contingent on his receiving a di-ploma. Having achieved their primary goal of enhancing their market posi-tion, most students leave at the end of the first year. Those who stay do so because they have been appointed to relatively high-paying research jobs in the university. They continue in these positions as long as they feel they are gaining more from the research job than they would in industry. Gradu-ate school in engineering is not marked by the close student-faculty relation-ship found in most other graduate programs. This may be because the stu-dents "feel themselves to be in school only temporarily and always have an eye on the outside world."[70]

Philosophy students. Philosophy students enter graduate school with a view, acquired as undergraduates, of themselves as wide-ranging intellec-tuals. Many chose graduate training in philosophy not because of an intrinsic interest in the field, but because it offered them the widest range of intellec-tual interests. The graduate department offers them a wide range of courses which serve to maintain the student's original inclination. Contacts with the faculty are limited by both parties and this allows the student to main-

[69] Ibid., p. 292.
[70] Ibid., p. 294.

tain broad-scale interest without facing the question of his ultimate occupational goal. Instead the commitment to philosophy gradually grows as he learns that it is only philosophy which offers him the opportunity to remain a wide-ranging intellectual. Furthermore, by now he too has made a number of investments in philosophy which make it costly for him to switch fields. Even after this commitment is made, his basic interest remains in broad intellectualism. Thus how a graduate school socializes its students depends on the nature of their commitment to the field.

9. Potential employers utilize elaborate recruiting procedures in their efforts to hire professionals to work in organizations.

As defined by Glaser, recruitment "is a process of screening, wooing, and eliminating before the career actually starts."[71] The elaborateness of the recruiting procedure depends upon the status of the occupations. Organizations seeking high-status occupations (e.g., lawyers, college professors) employ far more complex procedures than those used to recruit individuals in lower-status occupations (e.g., assembly-line workers, janitors). In part this is due to the high demand and low supply of professionals. In addition, an organization can live with poor choices at its lower levels because mistakes there are unlikely to upset the organization. An error in the hiring of high-status people, however, is likely to have enormous repercussions throughout the organization. Finally, it costs the organization so much to train a professional that it is likely to be very careful who it recruits, and it is much more difficult to fire a professional than it is to fire a low-status employee. This is due to the investment in training costs and the difficulty in finding a qualified replacement. In the next few pages the recruiting of professionals is discussed.

College professors. Caplow and McGee, in their insightful study of recruiting in academia, point out that the most striking thing about academic recruiting is its elaborateness. This complexity is a little difficult to understand since professorial salaries are low and professors are not generally expected to stay long at any given university. In part this may be explained by the importance of the position, and the fact that such recruiting has become an accepted part of the academic subculture. This is demonstrated by a professor's wariness of any job he is offered without the necessity of going through this recruiting procedure. Despite its elaborateness, academic recruiting is not an open process; usually no effort is made to seek out and hire the best-qualified individual. Instead, an acceptable candidate, with contacts in the department which is recruiting, is frequently offered the position.

The recruit may personally seek the position he would like. This is generally not done however, especially if he is from a major university and

---

[71] Barney G. Glaser, ed., *Organizational Careers: A Sourcebook for Theory* (Chicago: Aldine, 1968), p. 56.

is seeking a job at another major institution. A major university which is seeking to add personnel will tend to doubt the credentials of a recruit who actively seeks the position. There is a norm in academia that such contacts are generally to be made by the candidate's sponsor. At lesser universities it is much more common to find him making job contacts on his own. Although the above practices apply to individuals who have just completed graduate training, it is even more unlikely to find established professors formally and openly seeking new positions. Rather, as is pointed out later, individuals looking for jobs in academia are more likely to utilize informal contact networks.

It is also possible that a university with an opening will actively seek out the candidate it prefers. This procedure is used primarily when a university is interested in hiring a particular individual who is well known in the field; it is rarely used for recruiting unknown individuals or new entrants into academia.

The most common form of recruiting occurs when an individual in the recruiting university suggests someone he knows at another university, and by so doing vouches for his acceptability. This process is very attractive to the recruiting department because it eases the work of searching and they can be fairly sure that the recruit will prove acceptable.

Sometimes the department which is in the market may receive unsolicited letters recommending a particular person. Such a recommendation generally comes from the recruit's doctoral chairman. A recruiting department is particularly influenced by letters from a prestigious member of the discipline or from a less well-known sponsor who has recommended good people in the past.

Finally, some universities use professional placement services, including outside agencies or services which are run at the local and national meetings of most disciplines. However, such services are generally utilized only by lesser universities. As Caplow and McGee point out: "prestige is attached to the non-use of their services."[72]

No matter how he is selected the applicant chosen is generally asked to come for a visit. This is a fairly expensive process, especially when the university decides to examine several candidates. Prior to the visit letters of recommendation are solicited from professors who are familiar with the recruit. Such references are considered one piece of evidence and are rarely in themselves sufficient to cause acceptance or rejection. Once on the scene the applicant will generally meet individually with every member of the department. In these interviews the main topic of conversation is his past and present research as well as his future research plans. Although these inter-

[72] Theodore Caplow and Reece J. McGee, *The Academic Marketplace* (New York: Anchor Books, 1965), p. 103. Some of their findings have been recently supported by Diana Crane, "The Academic Marketplace Revisited: A Study of Faculty Mobility Using the Cartter Ratings," *American Journal of Sociology* 75 (1970), 953–964.

views are primarily for the members of the recruiting department, they also serve to pass on information about the members of the department which can help the recruit make his decision if he is offered a job. A seminar may be required in which the recruit is asked to make a presentation to the faculty and graduate students; this presentation yields some insight into his teaching ability. A party is also part of the typical recruiting visit, with the faculty and applicant given a chance to evaluate each other socially. Finally, the recruit will frequently meet with the Dean, who often has veto power over the recruiting department's choice. Most often the visit with the Dean is a formality which is devoted primarily to discussing the fringe benefits offered by the university. At the completion of this process the recruiting department theoretically has all the information it needs to make a decision. This procedure is repeated for each individual brought in for an interview. Once all applicants have been seen, a departmental meeting is held in which the final choice is made. In general, those faculty members at or above the rank of the opening will vote. The applicant receiving the most votes will be offered the position. After the offer has been made the recruit is given a stated period of time to make his decision. If he refuses the position, the offer may be made to the second choice, or a new group of applicants may be brought in for interviews. Clearly the most striking thing about this process of academic recruitment is its elaborateness. On this point Caplow and McGee also seem to be surprised:

When we examine the specific procedures of hiring in the American university, they turn out to be almost unbelievably elaborate. The average salary of an assistant professor is approximately that of a bakery truck driver, and his occupancy of a job is likely to be less permanent. Yet it may require a large part of the time of twenty highly-skilled men for a full year to hire him.[73]

Despite the time and energy expended, academic recruiting is not totally rational. On the surface such factors as publications, teaching ability, and letters of recommendation would seem to be of utmost importance. However, letters of recommendation are rarely crucial, and little attention is paid to teaching ability. Publications are considered to be of central importance, especially at major universities. Paradoxically, however, publications of a recruit are rarely read by the members of the recruiting department, because "men are hired for their repute, and not for what the repute is based upon."[74] The quality of the publications is not important; rather, of central importance is where the publications appeared. If they appeared in the major journals they are automatically considered to be of high quality. What the department is really concerned about is how good the publications look to others in the discipline. In effect, the department hires the man who they feel will most enhance their reputation in the eyes of the discipline.

[73] Ibid., p. 97.
[74] Ibid., p. 110.

Wall Street lawyers. In many ways the recruiting of Wall Street lawyers resembles academic recruitment.[75] For example, professional placement services play a negligible role in placing lawyers in Wall Street firms. The major similarity lies in the elaborateness of the process. Wall Street firms strive, before beginning active recruitment, to create a favorable image among law students. They utilize alumni in their employ and brochures to set the stage for their visit to the campus. The active stage of the process begins when representatives of the firm visit the law school. In the Wall Street firms, the high-status partners frequently perform this function. University placement officials arrange for interviews with interested students.

In Smigel's study about 13 percent of those interviewed at the university were ultimately hired, of which about half were direct hirings as a result of that interview. The other half were hired after visits to the New York offices. The firm pays the travel expenses of the law student and sometimes entertainment expenses. During his visit, the law student is interviewed by many of the important figures in the firm. Those who ultimately receive offers often have influence or contacts within the firm. If one looks solely at economic factors the complexity of the process is striking. Until very recently the newly hired lawyer earned little more than the new assistant professor. The explanation for this elaborateness, as was pointed out in the beginning of this section, lies not in the income, but in such factors as supply and demand, sensitivity of position, expense in training, and difficulty in firing.

Industrial scientists. Marcson's study of industrial scientists also points out the involved recruiting patterns used by organizations to attract professionals.[76] In the electronics firm he examined there is a specialist within the personnel department who concentrates on the recruitment of PhDs. His function is to maintain contacts with universities and possible recruits. Visits for interviews at a university are generally handled by teams of two scientists who have contacts there. At the university, the recruiting team seeks to contact department chairmen or professors in a given field who might have students searching for jobs. Initial interviews with students are not designed to screen them carefully, but to sell the electronics firm. Interested and eligible students are invited to the firm for a visit, and they are interviewed by a number of scientists in their area of interest who seek to determine their potential as researchers as well as to pass on information about the firm. Each interviewing scientist evaluates the candidate and the evaluations are compiled by the PhD recruiter. Assuming an offer is to be made, the evaluations are sent to a salary committee made up of technical staff, personnel

[75] Erwin Smigel, *The Wall Street Lawyer* (Bloomington: Indiana University Press, 1969).

[76] Simon Marcson, *The Scientist in American Industry* (New York: Harper and Row, 1960).

people, and research managers. This committee decides on the size of the salary offer.

Industrial laboratories have a difficult time attracting first-rate university graduates. Such graduates generally go to universities where they have freedom in terms of their research interests. To combat this the industrial laboratory attempts to show the recruit that it too is involved in basic research and places great importance on it. To foster this image industrial laboratories encourage their scientists to write papers and present them at scientific meetings. Despite these efforts, industrial laboratories must be satisfied with attracting second-level recruits, for the very best continue to go to the universities. Although it must settle for second-rank graduates, the industrial laboratory must compete for them with other laboratories and it must therefore employ a highly sophisticated recruiting system.

It should be noted that elaborate recruiting is not solely within the province of the professions. Most notable in the nonprofessions is the recruiting of top business executives, but complex recruiting procedures are typical of professional occupations.

10. Professions are characterized by highly variable career patterns.

Once hired, the professional is faced with the question of what form his career is likely to take. Unlike many lower-status occupations, there is much variability in professional career patterns. Once on the job individuals in such low-status occupations as janitor and taxi driver have virtually no mobility within the occupation. Most middle-level bureaucratic occupations have considerable mobility, but their potential career patterns are rather clearly defined. Within the professions a wide variety of career patterns are found.

Wall Street lawyers. Some professionals find themselves similar, in terms of career pattern, to the manager. That is, they are confronted with a clearly defined timetable for career advancement. The Wall Street lawyer is one such professional. Upon entering the firm he is made a beginning associate. In this position he is socialized into the life of the firm, since he works closely with established lawyers. Law school has probably best prepared him to do research, but as a beginning associate he learns how to "write memoranda and briefs, give advice, learn the 'ins and out' of the courts . . . also confer with partners, learn to dictate, gain familiarity with the filing system, and compete with older women stenographers for small power symbols."[77] Such a position is very important to the new lawyer since, as was pointed out earlier, law schools tend to do a poor job of communicating many of the realities of legal life. This first job serves to change idealism into realism in much the same way as this function was performed in medical professional and graduate schools. After four to eight years the lawyer may expect a

[77] Smigel, *Wall Street Lawyer,* p. 143.

promotion to middle-range associate. At this level he becomes more specialized and takes on greater responsibility: for example, he may personally negotiate a contract for the sale of a house. In his eighth year in the firm the Wall Street lawyer may expect to be promoted to senior associate. Here he has more wide-ranging responsibilities although he has less status and responsibility than the partners. The next step, permanent associate, is critical because in this position he may be asked either to be a partner or to leave the organization. There are three steps once a lawyer has become a partner: junior, middle, and senior partner. Junior- and middle-partner positions are viewed as *testing points* for those who aspire to senior partnership. The summit, of course, is the senior partnership. "When he arrives at that position he becomes the final interpreter of the law for the firm, its overall manager, and advisor to colleagues, clients and government, as well as in civic organization."[78] The career of the Wall Street lawyer thus follows a well-defined pattern. Early in his career he is a generalist, then a specialist, and and ultimately he becomes again a generalist, although at a much higher level in the organizational hierarchy. In many ways the career of the Wall Street lawyer is indistinguishable from the career of the business executive.

College professors. Within the university the professor's career is somewhat similar to that of the Wall Street lawyer or the business executive, and generally contains four well-defined steps. In most cases the first step is the position of instructor. In minor-league universities instructors are usually those who have not yet received their PhD. In major-league universities the instructor position is generally filled by new PhDs. Instructors in lesser universities are virtually assured of promotion once they get their degrees. In contrast, instructors in top universities will only be promoted when they have demonstrated professional competence by their publication record. An assistant professorship is the next step, although the position means different things in major- and minor-league universities. In the latter some publications will ensure progress to the next step, but in the best schools this position is often terminal, with few assistant professors having any hope of promotion. Those who are promoted must have demonstrated exceptional publication ability. The third step, associate professor, is therefore more difficult to achieve in a high-status university. The final step, a full professorship, is the most difficult to achieve in both types of universities, although the requirements are much greater at the major ones. In most universities one or more books and a number of articles are required in order to be considered for full professorship.

The above pattern of career progression applies mainly to universities which emphasize research. Smaller teaching colleges place less emphasis on research and promote more on the basis of teaching ability.

Unlike Wall Street lawyers or business executives, academicians are

[78] Ibid., p. 160.

usually confronted with a rather constricted career pattern. There are only a few steps, and once a man is a full professor there are very few alternatives open to him. A full professor at a minor university may seek a similar position at a major university or an endowed chair at his present school, or perhaps leave academia for industry or government. However, only a small number of full professors take any of these options.

A central variable in analyzing the career patterns of academicians is the status of the university. One general rule is that a new PhD cannot obtain a job at a university with greater prestige than the one from which he has gotten his degree. Thus, a PhD from Ohio State is unlikely to get his first job at an Ivy League university: he is more likely to receive offers from state universities or private colleges at or below the level of Ohio State. This first step down in the prestige hierarchy is perfectly acceptable in academia. More important for the graduate of a major university is his second position, which should be a step back toward the major league or directly into that level. A PhD from Harvard may take his first job at the University of Missouri, but his second job should represent a step up (e.g., to the Big Ten or right into the Ivy League). The Harvard PhD who moves from Missouri to the University of Alabama has taken a sharp step down; it will be difficult for him to make up for this retrogression and ultimately return to the Ivy League. A parallel move for the second job represents less of a liability. A change from Missouri to the University of Colorado is not an irremedial move, but it does make it more difficult to return to the major league. The individual who has moved up the prestige hierarchy after his first job will find it easier to move into the major leagues when he is looking for a senior academic position.

The PhD from a minor university has a different career pattern. His first job, following the rule discussed above, is likely to be at a university of lower status. He thus begins in one of the colleges or universities with lesser prestige, and is virtually impossible for him to ever make the major leagues. He has not received the proper socialization and lacks the contacts or prestigious label needed to ever be considered by a major university. At best, he can only hope to return to the level of the university from which he received his degree. There are some exceptions to this rule: the prolific publisher from a minor university might ultimately be considered for a position at a major university. However, there are few PhDs from the University of Alabama at Harvard.

Physicians. Other professions offer virtually no mobility in career-pattern terms. Once an individual has become a full-fledged doctor (that is, completed his residency), he has in most cases reached the pinnacle of his career. Although this is formally correct there is a great deal of informal mobility in the professions, and a professional at the formal top may still have a number of informal career steps open to him. Hall, for example, believes that there are four basic steps in the physician's career pattern.[79] However, three of these steps occur before he is firmly established as a doctor. It is in the fourth stage that some mobility is available, but this mobility is primarily informal.

a) In the first stage the focus is on generating ambition in potential doctors. Because it takes so long to receive rewards in the medical profession, a good deal of ambition is necessary. The family is central in this process and families headed by professionals seem best equipped to generate the needed ambition, as well as provide financial aid. Families headed by nonprofessionals may instill the ambition, but they frequently will be unable to supply the necessary material assets. Such a family may not have the money to pay for the necessary initial equipment or it may not have the informal contacts needed to guarantee success. b) In the second stage the new doctor must be able to place himself in a prestigious hospital. He faces much the same problem as the academician. If he isn't placed in a top hospital he will find it difficult to be successful in private practice. c) In the third stage the doctor seeks to acquire a clientele, and success in this venture is dependent on contacts with colleagues. Once he has successfully completed these three steps his career, in a formal sense, is over. However, informally, the fourth stage of the doctor's career involves several additional substeps. d) Once established he stands on the outskirts of the informal organization of the medical profession. Closer to the top are the general practitioners who refer patients to specialists. Just below the top are a group of doctors who are aspiring for acceptance in the inner fraternity. At the top of the medical profession is the inner fraternity, a group of high-status specialists who control access to the important hospital posts. Once established, the doctor turns to the informal career pattern in an effort to gain acceptance in the inner fraternity. The best way to gain such acceptance is to be sponsored by someone who belongs. This inner fraternity is open only to specialists, so that general practitioners find it almost impossible to reach the top of the informal organization of the medical profession.

Career contingencies. Professions are characterized by career patterns which are continually disrupted by career contingencies. These contingencies, which are chance events which occur at critical points in a career, occur throughout the occupational structure. It is interesting to note that they occur as well in the professions, the occupational group which theoretically should have career patterns which are more resistant to change. The success of a new doctor depends on whether he can attract the sponsorship of an established physician. A college professor may decide to change jobs after a chance meeting with a friend at another university. Professionals in the military probably exemplify best the duality in the professions of order and

[79] Oswald Hall, "The Stages of a Medical Career," *American Journal of Sociology* 53 (1948), 327–336.

contingency in the career pattern. After graduation from a military academy the formal steps in the career of an officer are clear: second lieutenant, first lieutenant, captain, major, lieutenant colonel, colonel, general. For the graduate of the naval academy the career steps are different although similar in their rigor: ensign, lieutenant (j.g.), lieutenant, lieutenant commander, commander, captain, admiral. Movement up either of these hierarchies is dependent on a series of factors, many of which may be considered career contingencies. One such contingency is the time when the cadet graduates from the academy: if it is just prior to wartime, his chances of rapid promotion are greatly enhanced. There is a greater need for officers and there is more opportunity to display one's abilities. Another contingency is visibility of action. The new officer who acts bravely will not be promoted unless his actions are seen or heard about by those in a position to promote. On a formal level there are continuous appraisals of officers to determine whether they are worthy of promotion, but beyond these formal rankings the opportunity for informal contacts with highly placed officers is an important contingency determining when, and if, an individual will be promoted.[80]

Retirement. As in all other occupations, the career of the professional ultimately ends in either death or retirement. It is at the point of retirement that the career of the professional perhaps differs most from the careers in any other occupational group. Individuals in most other occupations must retire at a certain age, but professionals, especially those who do not work in organizations, may retire when they wish. The private physician or lawyer may work as long as he feels he can perform adequately. Even professionals

TABLE 2-1

Organization Affiliations of Re-employed Generals

Type of Organization	% of Sample Employed in Each Organization
Manufacturing	15.8
Government	15.2
Education	10.5
Associations	10.2
Communication and transportation	8.7
Finance and banking	7.7
Medical services	6.5
Other	25.4
	100.0

Adapted from Leonard Reissman, "Life Careers, Power and the Professions: The Retired Army General," *American Sociological Review* 21 (1956), 220.

[80] Morris Janowitz, *The Professional Soldier: A Social and Political Portrait* (New York: Free Press, 1960).

TABLE 2-2

Organization Positions Held by Re-employed Generals

Type of Occupation	% of Sample Employed in Each Occupation
President or Manager	16.7
Vice president or Assistant	15.5
Chairman of the Board	5.0
Member of the Board	19.8
Divisional Manager	13.0
Technical Consultant	7.4
Educational position	5.6
Other	17.0
	100.0

Adapted from Leonard Reissman, "Life Careers, Power and the Professions: The Retired Army General," *American Sociological Review* 21 (1956), 220.

in organizations such as judges or clergymen may work far beyond the age at which individuals in lesser occupations are compelled to retire. Even when they do retire, professionals have far more work opportunities open to them. It is not atypical for retired doctors or lawyers to work after retirement on a part-time basis, or to serve as consultants. The army general has even more post-retirement opportunities than most other professionals, partly because he may retire at a relatively early age. In addition, upon retirement he has training, skills, and prestige which make him desirable to private industry. Further, he retires with contacts in government and the military which make him highly useful to industry. With these desirable characteristics, and a large pension, the retired general can afford to wait for the ideal offer from private industry. In his study of retired generals Reissman found that they were most likely to be re-employed in the certain types of organizations (see Table 2-1).

In some of these cases the primary motivation for hiring retired generals was the utilization of their skills, while in others it was for their contacts and public relations potential. Retired generals are likely to be hired at fairly high levels in organizations, as shown in Table 2-2. Although the general is not typical of other professionals, he does represent their greater employment possibilities after retirement.[81]

PROFESSIONALIZATION AND BUREAUCRATIZATION

11.   The professional who is employed in a formal nonprofessional organization is confronted with a number of inherent conflicts.

[81] Leonard Reissman, "Life Careers, Power and the Professions: The Retired Army General," *American Sociological Review* 21 (1956), 220.

Before proceeding with this discussion it must be noted that Etzioni differentiates three types of organizations in which professionals are employed:

1. Professional organizations are those in which at least 50 percent of the employees are professionals and the goals of the organization generally coincide with the goals of the professionals.
2. Service organizations are those in which professionals are provided with facilities, but are neither employed by the organization nor under its control.
3. Nonprofessional organizations are those in which professionals are in a small, subordinate subunit within the organization.[82]

In the ensuing discussion the focus is almost exclusively on the professional in nonprofessional organizations.

One of the major current trends in occupational life is the increasing employment of professionals in formal organizations. The professional model discussed in Generalization 3 is based on professions which were free of bureaucratic control. Free professionals such as the doctor and lawyer in private practice provided the basis for the model professional. With the bureaucratization of the professions this model has been retained, but because many of the tenets of organizational life are at odds with the professional model, the professional employed in an organization is confronted with a good deal of conflict.

A formal organization, according to Weber's ideal type, is characterized by a series of specialized positions which are arranged in a hierarchy with authority resting at the higher levels. In opposition to this is the professional's belief that he should be responsible only to himself, fellow professionals, and his professional association. Organizations believe that superiors should assess performance, while professionals believe that only a peer is capable of assessing their performance. A plant manager, hospital administrator, corporate executive, or government bureaucrat do not, in the eyes of the professional, have the right or ability to assess his performance. College professors have always faced this problem and have resolved it by carving out for themselves an exclusive domain within the university. Utilizing the notion of academic freedom, professors prevent the university administration from interfering with their classroom performance. Decisions on raises, promotions, and tenure are made by peers, although university administrators have some measure of control over these decisions. Other professions have not been as successful in solving this problem of assessment of performance.

Although conflict occurs whenever a professional is employed in a nonprofessional organization, there is not a perfect relationship between bureaucratization and professionalization. That it, it is not necessarily true that the

---

[82] Etzioni, *Semi-Professions*, pp. xii–xiii.

greater the degree of bureaucratization, the greater the conflict for the professional. Hall, for example, has examined the degree of bureaucratization of the three major work settings of professionals: autonomous professional organizations (medical clinic, law firm), heteronomous professional organizations (public schools, social-work agencies), and the professional department which is part of a larger organization.[83] The general assumption is that conflict for the professional is greatest in the professional department, since it is assumed to be as bureaucratic as the rest of the organization. Hall finds that while autonomous professional organizations are the least bureaucratic, the differences between heteronomous professional organizations and professional departments are not great. In fact, professional departments are actually less bureaucratic than heteronomous professional organizations on some dimensions of bureaucratization. On the basis of these findings Hall cautions us that we must not merely assume that since a professional is employed in a professional department or heteronomous professional organization he will inevitably face conflict.

Gloria Engel has selected one dimension of professionalism, professional autonomy, and related it to the degree of bureaucratization.[84] She seeks "to demonstrate empirically that it is not bureaucracy per se but the degree of bureaucracy that can limit professional autonomy."[85] Specifically, Engel is concerned with the autonomy of the physician in his relationship with patients and in research. In reviewing the contradictory literature she concludes that the highly bureaucratic organization does indeed act to limit the professional autonomy of the physician. Somewhat surprisingly, Engel also concludes that solo practice limits professional autonomy. "The solo practitioner may thus be limited in, or suffer a loss of, autonomy, not as the result of any administrative restrictions, as might be experienced by those employed within the bureaucracy, but from not having ready access to the various physical facilities typically available in the complex organization."[86] Thus she hypothesizes that it is the moderately bureaucratic organization which affords the physician more autonomy than either the nonbureaucratic or highly bureaucratic work setting. To this end she compared doctors in solo or small group practice, "a privately owned, closed panel medical organization," and a government medical organization. The findings of this study tend to support the hypothesis that there is a curvilinear relationship between bureaucratization and professional autonomy. However, there are differences for autonomy in clinical practice and autonomy in clinical research. In terms of their clinical practice physicians in moderately bureaucratic set-

---

[83] Richard Hall, "Some Organizational Considerations in the Professional-Organizational Relationship," *Administrative Science Quarterly* 12 (1967), 461–478.

[84] Gloria Engel, "The Effect of Bureaucracy on the Professional Authority of Physicians," *Journal of Health and Social Behavior*, 10 (1969), 30–41.

[85] Ibid., p. 31.

[86] Ibid., p. 34.

tings are more likely to have a high degree of autonomy than those in the other two settings. However, in terms of clinical research those in highly bureaucratic settings are most likely to have a high degree of professional autonomy. In explaining this second finding Engel noted that the highly bureaucratic organization was in fact less bureaucratic with respect to clinical research than the organization which was moderately bureaucratic. "In the highly bureaucratic setting, administrative procedures are less formal, and fewer rules and regulations are imposed upon physicians who are interested in pursuing research activities."[87] This latter finding further muddies the relationship between professionalization and bureaucratization. It points to the fact that perhaps we cannot even discuss organizations as a whole in terms of their degree of bureaucratization. An organization may be highly bureaucratic on one factor (e.g., clinical practice), moderately bureaucratic on a second (e.g., clinical research), and have a low degree of bureaucratization in terms of still a third factor.

A number of other studies have pointed to the fact that professionalization and bureaucratization are not necessarily irreconcilable. In fact, some see them as interdependent rather than antagonistic. Litwak points to the existence of a professional bureaucracy, which is an organization which synthesizes the professional and bureaucratic models.[88] Similarly, Smigel terms what he finds in the Wall Street law firm a professional bureaucracy.[89] This phenomenon was also uncovered in Montagna's study of the Big Eight public accounting firms.[90] In these firms accountants spend relatively little of their time on nonprofessional administrative duties, because most are involved in a small amount of administrative detail, thereby spreading it evenly among them. Broader decision making is centralized, removing this burden from most of the accountants. In addition, external rules formulated by professional associations were far more important than internal rules of the organization. Because of rotation through administrative positions, there are no full-time administrators who have vested interest in retaining and expanding the bureaucratic structure. The codification of formerly "mystical" procedures is seen as a threat to the accountant since: "the power of the expert disappears as soon as the area of uncertainty (professional judgment) can be translated into rules and programs."[91] Yet accountants have responded to even this threat by expanding into new areas of uncertainty. In these and other ways they have created for themselves a new type of organization, one which combines the professional and bureaucratic models.

Bucher and Stellings take virtually every other theorist and researcher

---

[87] Ibid., p. 37.

[88] Eugene Litwak, "Models of Bureaucracy which Permit Conflict," *American Journal of Sociology* 67 (1961), 182.

[89] Smigel, *Wall Street Lawyer*.

[90] Paul Montagna, "Professionalization and Bureaucratization in Large Professional Organizations," *American Journal of Sociology* 74 (1968), 138–145.

[91] Ibid., p. 143.

to task for assuming that organizations in which professionals are employed are bureaucratic.[92] By starting with this assumption most researchers are led to the inevitable conflict between professional and bureaucratic norms. Yet when professionals control an organization (such as in a hospital), Bucher and Stellings contend that they create an organization which is neither bureaucratic nor professional. They believe a professional organization has the following characteristics:

1. Professionals negotiate with significant others in their organization to create their own role and do not fit neatly into the established roles in the organization.
2. Professionals tend to cluster within an organization; this leads to spontaneous internal differentiation rather than differentiation legislated from the top of the organization.
3. The various professionals in an organization have different interests, goals, etc.; this leads to internal competition and conflict.
4. Through political means the different professionals seek to affect the policies and goals of the organization.
5. Power is constantly shifting rather than located in a particular office.

In a sense then, there is no irreconcilability between professionalization and bureaucratization, since professionals in organizations create an entirely different kind of organization which conforms to neither of these models.

The findings of all of these studies seem to cast doubt on the proposition that a professional employed in a formal, nonprofessional organization is confronted with a number of inherent conflicts. Or do they? In fact, most of these studies have focused on professional rather than nonprofessional organizations. It is clear that in professional organizations there is much less conflict, although it is not safe to conclude that the professional in a professional organization is free of these forms of conflict. Nevertheless, it is plain that in a nonprofessional organization the professional is inevitably confronted with normative conflict. Although, as Hall and Engel point out, we cannot say that the more bureaucratic the nonprofessional organization, the greater the conflict for the professional, we can say no matter how bureaucratic the nonprofessional organization, some conflict does exist. In the next few pages we discuss the conflict which faces the professional in a nonprofessional organization.

Israeli physicians. Ben David's study of the Israeli doctor illustrates how the organization can encroach on at least some of its professional employees.[93] Traditionally, final responsibility for the patient lies exclusively

---

[92] Rue Bucher and Joan Stellings, "Characteristics of Professional Organizations," *Journal of Health and Social Behavior* 10 (1969), 3–15.
[93] Joseph Ben-David, "The Professional Role of the Physician in Bureaucratized Medicine: A Study in Role Conflict," *Human Relations* 40 (1958), 255–274.

with the doctor, but in the Israeli Sick Fund "final responsibility for the pa-tient rests not with the doctor but with the organization."[94] A number of doctors surrendered their responsibility to the organization, and Ben-David found them to be dissatisfied with their work. On the other hand, those doctors who were satisfied with their work were those who were able to retain their autonomy when dealing with patients. There were two ways in which doctors in the Sick Fund could keep their autonomy. One group, which Ben-David calls "service oriented," were those who "in spite of the bureaucratic context . . . felt that they owed their first loyalty to a deter-mined circle of patients." The second group, the "science oriented," were those who focused exclusively on "the scientific quality of their work."[95]

Military psychiatrists.   The psychiatrist in the military is supposed to be concerned with the health of his patient while the military focuses on man-power needs.[96] In this conflict it is the manpower requirements of the military which overwhelm the concern of the psychiatrist for the health of his pa-tient. It is the military which decides which patients a psychiatrist will see and the reasons he may see them. Therapy is a secondary function for the military psychiatrist—he is engaged primarily in providing a service to the military, not the patient. Thus he is merely an advisor on such matters as discharges, special duty for soldiers, and military legal matters. Furthermore, he is not even free to make diagnoses on the basis of his professional judg-ment. For one thing, he is constrained by a variety of military rules which have an important impact on the kind of diagnosis he makes. Also, he is often asked to justify the decisions of a commanding officer or a military court and the need for such justifications affects the kinds of diagnoses he makes. In effect, these constraints transform him from a counselor to one of the control agents within the military. In addition to these constant constraints upon him, there are a variety of shifting or variable contingencies which af-fect his action. One is the "climate of opinion" at any given time. If, for ex-ample, there is a manpower crisis in the military there will be a great deal of pressure on him to be highly cautious in classifying soldiers as unfit. Logis-tics is a second contingency, with the psychiatrist generally being prevented from making a recommendation which would involve transfers to distant places. Finally, the nature of a commanding officer at any given time has a great effect on the practice of military psychiatry. Some types of commanding officers place greater restraints on the activity of psychiatrists than do others, depending on how they interpret military regulations. In short, the psychia-trist who works in the military is a "captive professional."

    [94] Ibid., p. 259.
    [95] Ibid., pp. 261–262.
    [96] Arlene K. Daniels, "The Captive Professional: Bureaucratic Limitations in the Practice of Military Psychiatry," *Journal of Health and Social Behavior* 10 (1969), 255–265.

Specific conflicts. The conflict between professional authority and bureaucratic control extends to a variety of levels. In addition to the general conflict discussed above, Kornhauser points out four specific levels of disagreement between the professional and the organization.[97] First, there is the issue of recruitment. "In most government establishments (especially military) and in commercial enterprises . . . personnel matters tend to be controlled by an administration that represents the organization rather than the profession."[98] This stands in opposition to the professional notion that only a peer can evaluate whether an individual has the necessary professional competence. Further, many organizations seek to hire lesser professionals, who might ultimately become administrators. Professionals, on the other hand, would prefer to hire the best qualified professional without regard to his managerial potential. Second, there is the problem of how the professional's work is to be organized. Organizations tend to prefer "task forces" made up of professionals from various disciplines to work on a specific problem; professionals are likely to prefer groups of individuals from the same discipline. Third, there is the question of who should lead a professional subgroup within an organization. Professionals would like their manager to be the most professionally qualified individual, while organizations tend to seek administrators who exhibit managerial rather than professional qualities. Professional managers selected by the organization are likely to be more oriented to managerial than professional norms of behavior. Finally, there is the conflict between the professional notion of free and total communication and the organization's desire for secrecy. If a professional in an organization makes a discovery he would like it published so that all those in the profession may see and utilize his contribution. The organization, however, would prefer that these discoveries be kept secret so that the benefits would belong exclusively to the organization.

From the organization's point of view professionals have narrow expertise, and ultimate decisions must therefore be left to managers, who have a much broader perspective. The professional who has high status outside the organization finds himself to be little more than an adviser when he works within it. In private practice a doctor has almost unrestricted authority over a patient, but when he is employed in industry he is more of an advisor than a decision maker. He may find an individual unfit for a certain job, but the decision on whether the man can, or should be, removed rests with a bureaucrat. Only a management official knows how important such an individual is to his department, or whether there are alternate positions open to him in the organization. This control from the top conflicts with the professional norm of authority over clients.

An organization utilizes monetary rewards and is generally incapable

[97] William Kornhauser, *Scientists in Industry: Conflict and Accommodation* (Los Angeles: University of California Press, 1962).

[98] Ibid., p. 45.

of rewarding the professionals with the symbols they desire. The professional can rarely find bureaucratic life totally rewarding, for he can enjoy the economic rewards but not the symbolic compensation. He must operate on two levels, simultaneously, trying to satisfy the demands of the organization and seeking symbolic recognition from his professional colleagues. The organization, however, acts in a number of ways to prevent the achievement of professional recognition. One example is the openness versus secrecy conflict discussed above. For another, if the professional finds a question which he feels needs research, he must reconcile this with the more insistent demands of the organization, which is paying him to solve problems of immediate importance to it and not some esoteric question which will bring no recognizable payoff. In such a situation the organization will frequently discourage or forbid such research, and if he chooses to stay in the organization, the professional must then work on such a question on his own time. This strain is what Kornhauser has called the conflict between pure and applied research. The American Association for the Advancement of Science has noted that "what is essential to the proper growth of science is often in conflict with the conditions of its service to military and political and, it may be added, industrial affairs."[99] The conflict between organizations and professionals is not irreconcilable, as the next two generalizations will attempt to demonstrate.

12.   There are a number of ways in which a nonprofessional formal organization can adapt itself to its professional employees.

It is clear that the conflict between the professional and the organization can never be eliminated. In fact, it may well be that this conflict, like many others, has a variety of functions for both professionals and organizations. There are, however, a number of things an organization can do to reduce the dysfunctional aspects of the conflict; Barber suggests some in his discussion of ways an organization can accommodate its professionals.[100] For example, it can place them into separate substructures where they can perform their specialized activities relatively free of organizational constraints, or set up a separate authority structure for them with the head of the professional group being a qualified professional. Barber also suggests a separate reward structure which would enable them to achieve professional recognition while continuing to serve the organization. Included in this separate reward structure would be the opportunity to attend professional meetings, salary increases based strictly on professional accomplishments, and time off with pay to further professional education. Although the institution of these recommendations would help alleviate the conflict, it would not eliminate the

[99] Ibid., p. 18.
[100] Bernard Barber, "Some Problems in the Sociology of the Professions," in Lynn, *Professions in America*, pp. 15–34.

inherent problems. Even if professionals had separate substructures they still would not possess the authority or organizational knowledge to have control over their clients. Such a separation, furthermore, would enhance the segregation of professionals within the organization and would do little to increase their authority. The suborganization, even with a professional head, would ultimately be responsible to higher-level bureaucrats. The professional head would find himself in an extremely difficult position: inevitably he would have to decide whether he was primarily a professional or a bureaucrat, and whatever choice he made would alienate some segment of the organization and reduce his effectiveness. If he chose to be a professional first he would lose favor with top management; if he chose to be a bureaucrat first he might alienate many of his professional colleagues. Given the role conflict inherent in the position it may be that it is impossible for it ever to function in the way it was designed.

The dual ladder.   The dual ladder is perhaps the technique most frequently utilized by employing organizations to resolve the conflict. In all organizations there is a hierarchy of statuses leading to greater and greater positions of authority. Professionals, because of the nature of their occupation, are ordinarily barred from this ladder, a condition which has led some organizations to set up a second ladder. This ladder also has a hierarchy of positions, but they do not carry with them successively greater authority. Instead, they carry greater salaries, status, autonomy, or responsibility. Organizations realize that if professionals were to move up the traditional ladder they would be moving out of the area of their expertise: the second ladder allows them to be rewarded and experience some mobility within their professional area. Although there has been widespread adoption of the dual ladder, Goldner and Ritti contend that, at least as far as engineers are concerned,[101] this is based on the false assumption that professionals are interested in professional rewards rather than power. Goldner and Ritti find that engineers do want power, and identify with their employing organization rather than the profession. Further, the professional ladder at best can only resolve the conflict (if one exists) between an individual professional and his employing organization; it cannot resolve the basic conflict between the profession as an institution and the employing organization.

If the professional ladder does not function the way it is supposed to, what then is its function? Goldner and Ritti note that for one thing it performs the function of "cooling out" professionals in organizations—it keeps them in the organization and productive even though they cannot aspire to the normal definition of success in organizations, power. But cooling out generally occurs after the fact, as when an individual has been fleeced by a confidence man. In organizations the construction of a dual ladder allows the

101 Fred Goldner and R. R. Ritti, "Professionalization as Career Immobility," *American Journal of Sociology* 73 (1967), 489–502.

professional to be cooled out even before he has actually failed in his quest for power (as most will). The organization has redefined success for the professional from power to moving up the professional ladder. The professional ladder might even be viewed as a face-saving device for professionals. Goldner and Ritti contend that organizations may even find it functional to define nonprofessions as professions, and in so doing continue to get efficiency from employees, even though they have failed in their quest for power. For example, if older salesmen have failed to achieve power, the organization can keep them productive by defining them as professionals. By the same token individuals in certain occupations would find it functional to define themselves as professionals since this "explains" why they have not succeeded in terms of their search for power. In the case of engineers, the professional ladder does not operate the way management set it up to operate. Nevertheless it still performs a number of functions. Whether these findings for engineers apply to other professions awaits further study. However, whether one examines its manifest or latent functions, the dual ladder continues to be one of the ways in which organizations seek to resolve the conflict between professionals and their employing organization.

Segregation of professionals. Hammond and Mitchell's study of the campus ministry suggests a radical solution to the professional-bureaucratic conflict.[102] The church handles radical ministers by sending them to college campuses where their ideology is accepted and where it does not affect the church-going public. Organizations can reduce the conflict between themselves and professionals by housing them in a physically separate structure. The only contact between the organization and its professionals would then be through the leaders of the professional suborganization. Although this will ease the conflict for most of the professionals, it will not eliminate the basic conflict between the two groups.

The problem of the professional in the nonprofessional organization is how "to gain access to the organization without becoming available for manipulation by the organization."[103] The professional never becomes fully absorbed in the organization "nor do professionals wholly absorb the organization."[104] Ultimately there must be a balance between those "conditions conducive to creativity and those conducive to control."[105] Although it can never solve the problem, the organization must seek to maximize the creativity of its professionals while minimizing its control over them, for if it imposes too much control, it will stifle the creativity it seeks. Nevertheless, organizations have goals and must be sure that their professionals are contributing to

[102] Phillip G. Hammond and Robert E. Mitchell, "Segmentation of Radicalism: The Case of the Protestant Campus Minister," *American Journal of Sociology* 71 (1965), 133–143.
[103] Kornhauser, *Scientists in Industry*, p. 196.
[104] Ibid., p. 197.
[105] Ibid.

the achievement of those goals: they cannot allow professionals to operate totally independently. The organization must set broad limits for professionals and then allow them to operate autonomously within these limits. Most organizations find it difficult to grant professionals such autonomy, but it is clear that they must if they are to progress as much as they would like.

13. There are a number of ways in which professionals can adapt to nonprofessional formal organizations.

Just as the organization can take steps to reduce the conflict, professionals can also act to resolve the dilemma. Vollmer and Mills suggest that one means for the professional is to "sell out" to the organization by becoming primarily a bureaucrat.[106] This would certainly eliminate the conflict, but few professionals are willing to take this step and few organizations would like to see it happen.

Resolutions open to the professions. Professional schools can offer courses in complex organizations in an effort to prepare the new professional for life in an organization. He will then know what to expect and, perhaps, how to handle some of the dilemmas which will confront him. Professional schools continue to socialize as if their products were going to be free professionals, but most new professionals will work in organizations and they need to be prepared for the inevitable conflict.

The profession can restructure itself so that there are symbolic rewards for those who work in organizations. For example, it could recognize the importance of applied research by accepting more of such papers for presentation at national meetings and publication in professional journals. Those professionals who achieve high status in their employing organization might also receive some recognition from their professional association. Kornhauser finds that the kinds of changes discussed here are occurring within some professions, particularly in science and engineering, where the professional-administrator is beginning to be viewed as a "valued activity" by some professional associations and to achieve high status in professional societies. Further,

in the scientific society, journals and conferences in applied science have been organized; permanent sections of the society have been established in applied areas; employment clearing houses have been created to facilitate contacts of industrial and governmental employers with scientists; and large grants have been solicited from industry to finance society activities.[107]

Resolutions open to the professionals. While there are a number of things the profession as a whole can do to reduce the level of conflict, there are also mechanisms available to the individual professional. It has generally

---

[106] Vollmer and Mills, *Professionalization*, p. 276.
[107] Kornhauser, *Scientists in Industry*, p. 198.

been assumed that a professional in an organization must either identify with the organization or the profession. Gouldner calls those who identify with the profession "cosmopolitans" and those who identify with the employing organization "locals."[108] Yet there is no reason to assume that these are the only possibilities. Reissman, for example, identifies four types of orientation: the functional bureaucrat who identifies with profession and not organization; the job bureaucrat who identifies with employing organization and not profession; the specialist bureaucrat who identifies with both; and the service bureaucrat who identifies with neither.[109] Thus Reissman adds two types to the cosmopolitan and local types developed by Gouldner. The most important type, for our purpose, is the specialist bureaucrat who identifies with both profession and employing organization, for this shows it is possible for the professional in an organization to fuse his dual orientations. This is the type Glaser has called the "local-cosmopolitan."[110] Much of the conflict is resolved by those who can identify with both occupation and organization. Again, however, it is unlikely that such a fusion can lead to the elimination of the inherent conflict, for it seems unlikely that these two diverse roles can ever be perfectly combined by all professionals.

It may well be that the conflict between professional and organization is not undesirable and hence should not be eliminated. Kornhauser notes that "the tension between the autonomy and integration of professional groups, production groups, and other participants tends to summon a more effective structure than is attained where they are isolated from one another or where one absorbs the other."[111] There is little evidence on this point and comparative studies of organizations in which there has, and has not, been accommodation are needed. Although there is little empirical support this notion is in line with the views of such theorists as Coser, Simmel, and Dahrendorf, who emphasize the functions of social conflict. From these theorists one might hypothesize that the conflict makes for unity in the professional subgroup. One might also hypothesize that the conflict leads to greater feedback between pure and applied research. In any event it must not be concluded without evidence that the conflict between the professional and his employing nonprofessional organization is necessarily dysfunctional.

14. The occupational problems of the free professional revolve primarily around the client.

The free professional is not employed in a formal organization on a full-time basis. The major examples have been doctors and lawyers in private

---

[108] Alvin Gouldner, "Cosmopolitans and Locals: Toward an Analysis of Latent Social Roles," *Administrative Science Quarterly* 2 (1957), 281–306.

[109] Leonard Reissman, "A Study of Role Conceptions in Bureaucracy," *Social Forces* 27 (1949), 305–310.

[110] Barney Glaser, "The Local-Cosmopolitan Scientist," *American Journal of Sociology* 69 (1962), 249–259.

[111] Kornhauser, *Scientists in Industry*, p. 198.

practice. Even these archetypes of the free profession are increasingly employed in formal organizations: many doctors, for example, who are in private practice are also on a hospital staff. Also, there is a trend among doctors to engage in joint practice, for by joining with several others the private practitioner eases many of the burdens of his occupational life. Lawyers, too, are increasingly found in small law firms. Although the trend is toward organizational involvement there remains a significant proportion in some professions who still may be classified as free professionals. Because they are free of organizational constraints they are also free of most of the problems faced by professionals in organizations. They are not faced with threats to their autonomy to the degree that such threats are common in organizational life, and they are free to retain their commitment to their occupation without pressure to also commit themselves to an organization. Although they avoid these and other problems, they are faced with a series of rather distinctive problems. For the free professional these problems primarily revolve around his relationship with his clients.

Conflicts of the free and organizationally employed professionals. Although conflict with clients is characteristic of free professionals and normative conflict is typical of professionals employed in nonprofessional organizations, the distinction is not as clear as we have tried to make it. While employment in nonprofessional organizations threatens the autonomy of the professional, the free professional is also confronted with threats to his autonomy. The professional who is hired by an organization implicitly agrees to sell some of his autonomy in exchange for the resources that the organization can provide. The free professional makes no such bargain, but while he retains his freedom he is unable to avail himself of the resources an organization can provide. This lack of resources constitutes a threat to his autonomy. He may, for example, lack the equipment he needs, or may have to handle so much detail work that he is left with less time to work on professional matters. In these and a variety of other ways freedom from organizational control may constitute a threat to the autonomy of the free professional. A second limitation on the distinction between the characteristic conflicts of free and organizationally employed professionals is that many professionals fall into both categories. The physician who is in private practice may also spend a good deal of his time in hospitals, or he may even work on a part-time basis for a university or industry. The third limitation is that professionals employed in nonprofessional organizations also have clients, although exactly who the clients are is often less clear for them. For example, the physician who works in industry clearly has patients, but are they his clients or is the organization he serves his client? If we view patients as his clients, it is plain that conflict exists between the clients and the professional although the clear guidelines laid down by the organization serve to mitigate the conflict. On the other hand, if we view the employing organization as the client, there is also conflict between the professional and his client, the organization. Yet, when we view the employing organization as the client, we are really saying that the source of the conflict lies in the conflicting norms of the professional and his organization. In fact, the conflict between the free professional and his client is also normative conflict in that it is a conflict between the norms of the professional and the layman. In a sense then professionals, whether they are free or employed in organizations, must deal with normative conflict. But by placing both types of normative conflict under one heading, much information is lost. Thus professionals in nonprofessional organizations are characteristically confronted with normative conflict, while the distinguishing conflict for free professionals is with their clients. This differentiation is adhered to here despite the fact that in the real world it is much less clear-cut.

The doctor and his patient.   Once out of school the problem for the free professional is how to attract and keep a clientele. Henderson's old, but seminal study, "Physicians and Patients as a Social System," is a lengthy list of "dos and don'ts" for a doctor when he interacts with his patient. The doctor should be interested in what the patient says and should not argue with the patient's prejudices; he should listen carefully, ask few questions about the psychological aspects of the problem, and "beware of bare statements, or bare truth, or bare logic."[112] In short, there are many pitfalls in the patient-doctor relationship. The physician and other free professionals must be careful not to alienate their clients. Most professionals find this difficult because their training emphasizes the scientific aspect of work and ignores the human problem.

The lawyer and his clientele.   The lawyer who works on his own is generally a marginal member of the legal profession. Much of his professional life is spent in seeking out clients who are deemed undesirable by the large law firms. Some must even engage in the unethical behavior of "ambulance chasing" in order to make a living.[113] Ambulance chasers are those lawyers who seek out customers who are involved in accidents and offer them their services, whereas those in the large law firms can generally sit back and wait for the clients to come to them. Carlin's study of lawyers on their own catalogs a long list of devices employed to build up a clientele.[114] The young solo lawyer may at first rely on friends and relatives of his family, but he soon finds that he cannot build a practice on this alone. Thus he joins organizations, caters to members of his ethno-religious group, becomes

[112] L. J. Henderson, "Physician and Patient as a Social System," *The New England Journal of Medicine* 212 (1935), 821–823.

[113] Kenneth Reichstein, "Ambulance Chasing: A Study of Deviation and Control within the Legal Profession," *Social Problems* 13 (1965), 3–17.

[114] Jerome Carlin, *Lawyers on Their Own* (New Brunswick, N.J.: Rutgers University Press, 1962).

involved in politics, and relies on brokers (e.g., another lawyer, policeman, a minister) in order to find clients. Life for him is a constant struggle to get and keep an adequate clientele, and he must engage in a number of activities which he may consider nonprofessional and/or distasteful because he does not have the prestige and administrative apparatus of a law firm. This is in line with the findings previously cited by Engel which point out that solo practice is a threat to the professional status of, in this case, the lawyer.

Nature of the client. Although strain is ubiquitous in the professional-client relationship, the nature of the strain is dependent on the nature of the participants. Hanley and Grunberg outline three types of patients (the hostile, the passive-dependent, and the manipulative-seductive) and three types of doctors, (the omnipotent, the anxious, and the detached), and discuss the nature of the strain in each of the nine possible relationships.[115] In only two of the nine possible relationships is there no real strain. The perfect relationship for the doctor exists when he is detached and is dealing with a passive-dependent patient: there is no strain of personalities and the detached doctor is given virtual carte blanche by the patient. The perfect relationship for the patient exists when he is manipulative and is dealing with an anxious doctor: in this situation the patient can completely dominate the relationship. In all of the other relationships there is considerable strain. When a hostile patient meets an "omnipotent" doctor the doctor is thwarted by the patient and there is a rapid termination of the relationship. In a relationship between a passive-dependent patient and an anxious doctor both try to please, but insecurities and guilt in both lead to strain and eventual termination. The Freidson article, discussed earlier, is also relevant here in its discussion of the strains between the general practitioner and the patient and the need for the doctor to satisfy the lay culture.[116]

A more knowledgeable clientele. All of these studies clearly indicate that the free professional does not have unrestricted authority over his clients. Even though the professional model was developed in terms of the free professional, even he no longer fits that model, at least in terms of the dimension of authority over clients. We are faced with the question of why clients are more likely to question, and conflict with, free professionals. Perhaps the major factor has been the increased familiarity of the public with medical and legal knowledge. The greater educational level of the public has played a crucial role. In addition, the mass media have widely distributed much information about medicine and law. Included here would be newspaper and magazine articles about health and legal problems as well as popular television programs and movies, which in the process of being entertaining also pass on some, albeit simplified, medical and legal knowledge. The result

[115] F. W. Hanley and F. Grunberg, "Reflections on the Doctor-Patient Relationship," *Canadian Medical Association Journal* 86 (June, 1962).
[116] Freidson, "Client Control and Medical Practice."

has been that an increasing number of clients consider themselves knowledge-able about medical and legal matters. At least one study indicates that the popular information they receive is fairly accurate. Kisch and Reeder found that patients' evaluations of physicians correlated rather well with professional characteristics of the physicians.[117] Thus clients are more likely to evaluate and question free professionals and they seem to be doing a pretty good job of it.

Although the professional man, in some cases, is free of organizational involvement, he is certainly not free of occupational strains. A different work environment does not eliminate his problems; it merely changes the nature of the strains.

15. Despite the rationality which characterizes the professions, minority groups face difficulties in professional life.

As in other occupational groups, there is discrimination in the profes-sions. Although the discrimination is less, it has by no means been totally eliminated. The scope of the problem is clear in data projected by Price for 1970 as shown in Table 2-3.

TABLE 2-3

Percentage of Whites and Nonwhites in All
Professional and Managerial Positions

White males (35–44 years of age)	25.0
Nonwhite males (35–44 years of age)	8.5
White females (35–44 years of age)	8.0
Nonwhite females (35–44 years of age)	6.5

Adapted from Daniel Price, "Occupational Changes Among Whites and Non-whites with Projections for 1970," *Social Science Quarterly* 49 (1968), 571.

Thus black males and black and white females are grossly underrepresented in the high-status professional and managerial occupational levels. Price's projections, however, combine professionals and managers while our focus here is on blacks and females in the professions. In 1969 there were about 692,000 nonwhites employed in professional and technical occupations while over ten million whites were employed in these two categories.[118] A little over 8 percent of employed nonwhites in 1969 were in professional or tech-nical occupations, while about 15 percent of the employed whites were in these two categories. Even in these figures we probably have an underestima-tion of the scope of the black problem in the professions. For one thing the

[117] Arnold Kisch and Leo G. Reeder, "Client Evaluation and Physician Perform-ance," *Journal of Health and Social Behavior* 10 (1969), 51–59.
[118] U.S. Department of Labor, *The Social and Economic Status of Negroes in the United States* (Washington, D.C.: U.S. Government Printing Office, 1969), p. 41.

figures are for all nonwhites, not just blacks. For another, technical occupations are combined by the Bureau of Labor Statistics with professions and it is probably easier for blacks to gain employment in technical occupations than in the professions. The picture for female professionals is not much different and one even gets an overly optimistic view if he looks at the statistics on the question, because the Bureau of Labor Statistics considers such semiprofessionals as nurses, social workers, and librarians as professionals while it is contended here that they do not conform to the professional model. Yet it is precisely in the semiprofessions that we find a predominance of females. For example, in 1960 97 percent of the nurses, 85 percent of the librarians, and 57 percent of the social workers were females. In contrast, 7 percent of the doctors, 2 percent of the dentists, and 6 percent of the clergymen in 1960 were females.[119] Discounting the semiprofessions, the status of females in the professions is about as bleak as the status of blacks.

Females

Before discussing the problems of females in specific professions, a more general analysis of females in the professions is in order. On the one hand, women in the United States are supposed to have "personal warmth and empathy, sensitivity and emotionalism, grace, charm, compliance, dependence, and deference," while on the other they are felt to have a "lack of aggressiveness, lack of personal involvement and egotism, lack of persistence (unless it be for the benefit of a family member), and lack of ambitious drive."[120] The problem for the would-be female professional lies in the fact that the positive characteristics she is supposed to possess are antithetical to the characteristics of the ideal professional. Conversely, those characteristics that the American female is supposed to lack are precisely those which are imputed to professionals. The professional is supposed to possess "persistence and drive, personal dedication, aggressiveness, emotional detachment, and a kind of sexless matter-of-factness equated with intellectual performance.[121] Given this contradiction between the professional role and the female role, most American women feel they must choose one or the other and usually prefer their sex role. For those who seek to fuse the two roles the result is a great deal of stress. It is beyond the province of this book to go into a detailed discussion of the causes of female underrepresentation in the professions, but a few of the more important factors need to be mentioned.

Boys are reared much more permissively in American society. They are trained to be aggressive and allowed to act out their aggressiveness. In con-

---

[119] Cynthia Fuchs Epstein, *Woman's Place: Options and Limits in Professional Careers* (Berkeley: University of California Press, 1970).
[120] Ibid., pp. 20–21.
[121] Ibid., pp. 23.

trast, females are reared to be unaggressive and dependent. Clearly this philosophy of female socialization is an important factor in the lack of female professionals. A related factor here is the role models available to boys and girls. The boy's role model (his father or other male relatives) is more likely to be a professional while the girl's role model (mother or other female relatives) is more often than not a homemaker. Even if the girl is dissatisfied with the role models in her family and looks outside, she is still highly unlikely to find a female professional to model herself after. The dependency and lack of aggressiveness stretches into the classroom, but has its greatset effect as one moves up the educational ladder. Thus, in 1965 about 34,000 more girls than boys finished high school, but about 100,000 more boys than girls graduated from college. Or to put it another way, even though over 50 percent of the population of the United States is female, only 41 percent of those who graduated from college in 1960 were female. The figures are more striking for advanced degrees: in 1966, only 33.8 percent of the Master's degrees and 11.6 percent of the Doctor's degrees in the United States were granted to women. College dropout rates are also revealing. While the percentage of male and female dropouts is about the same (40 percent), the reasons are very different. Men drop out of college mainly because of academic and personal difficulties, while for women the single most important reason is marriage. Despite these statistics females are being increasingly encouraged to get a college education, but the traditional image of a "woman's place" lingers. This contradiction is a major source of stress to college women and another important reason why females are less likely to get an advanced education. One girl sums up this contradiction best: "First my parents encourage me to get grades, and then they worry I'm not meeting any boys or having any fun. When I do go out and have fun, they worry about my grades. I feel pulled two ways."[122] There are many other barriers to female entry into the professions, but it would be more useful to discuss them in the context of particular professions. In the next few pages we turn to a discussion of females in some selected professions and the barriers to entry as well as the problems which result even if these barriers are overcome.

Female physicians. Kosa and Coker hypothesize that whether a profession is predominantly male or female depends on whether there is congruency between sex and professional roles.[123] Nursing and teaching are semiprofessions in which the role obligations are congruent with female sex roles; consequently, one finds a preponderance of females in them. On the other hand, one finds few women in medicine and law because there is con-

---

[122] Ibid., p. 64.
[123] John Kosa and Robert E. Coker, Jr., "The Female Physician in Public Health: Conflict and Reconciliation of the Sex and Professional Roles," *Sociology and Social Research* 49 (1965), 294–305.

flict between sex and professional roles. Kosa and Coker examine the female doctor in order to ascertain the problems faced by a female in a male profession, and the means employed by the female doctor to cope with these problems.

As a doctor the female is confronted with a series of distinctive problems. For one thing, the public is reluctant to accept a female physician, and most Americans would prefer a male. Second, the female physician is not fully accepted by her male colleagues. This lack of professional acceptance may take many forms. Male doctors might refuse to send their patients to female physicians, they might prevent females from holding offices in local or national associations, or they might, as Kosa and Coker point out, "ask for stricter selection among women than men applicants to medical schools."[124] Third, merely being a female in American society causes the woman doctor problems. She frequently finds that she cannot fully fulfill either her sex or professional role. For example, pregnancy and child rearing limit her professional involvement in the crucial early years of her medical career. Later, when she is able to fulfill her professional role, she finds that this interferes with her role as wife and mother. Finally, the female doctor has peculiar problems in handling "professional duties which are more or less incompatible with female tasks."[125]

Given the intrinsic conflict between her sex and professional roles, the woman doctor seeks in a variety of ways to lessen the strain. She is likely to marry later in life than the average female, so that she can complete her training without the interference of familial obligations. Once married, she does not work continuously in her profession; rather, she takes long periods off to tend to family affairs. Even later in her career the female doctor is unlikely to hold a full-time position. She prefers part-time positions which give her some time to fulfill her sex role expectations. For the same reason she is less likely to be a self-employed medical "entrepreneur." Because she earns less than her male counterpart, she is less likely to value economic rewards. In conformity with her general sex role expectations, the female physician expresses "a dislike for competition with other people, a willingness to renounce independence in work for close patient relationships, and a preference for the aid of experienced persons."[126] The woman doctor tends to prefer pediatrics as a subfield because it conflicts less with her sex role. Other medical fields in which she is able to reduce her role conflict are psychiatry and public health. Through these and other actions she is able to reduce to manageable proportions the conflict between her sex and professional roles. Analogous mechanisms are likely to be employed by females in all predominantly male professions.

Female engineers. There is a lower proportion of females in engineer-

[124] Ibid., p. 295.
[125] Ibid.
[126] Ibid., pp. 299–300.

ing than in virtually any other profession.[127] According to Robin, in the United States in 1960 females comprised 7 percent of physicians and surgeons, 9 percent of natural scientists, 2 percent of earth scientists, 4 percent of physicists, 26 percent of mathematicians, and 27 percent of biologists, but only 1 percent of engineers were females. Robin's basic question is, How do we account for such a small proportion of women in an occupation which is hungry for manpower? Robin separates his answer into general reasons why females do not enter professions and specific reasons why females do not enter engineering. Among the general reasons females do not enter professions is their socialization for domestic roles, the masculine image of most professions, fear of discrimination by male professionals, familial responsibilities, and societal norms on what is the "proper" role of the female. More specifically, women find that the characteristics of engineers are more at variance with the values of an academically trained female than the characteristics of other professions. Robin concludes that engineers "are narrow of interest, stolid, relatively uninterested in 'cultural' things and not involved in general intellectual pursuits."[128] In opposition, academically trained females are characterized by: "intellectual sophistication, defined as broad interests, emotional sensitiveness, a 'liberal arts' approach to learning, responsiveness to art and literature, and relative tolerance of intellectual creativity and deviation."[129] It is this basic conflict of values which makes for fewer females in engineering than any other profession.

Female scientists. The socialization of the female in childhood, previously mentioned, is an important factor in the difficulties she faces in professional life. This is brought out clearly in Rossi's analysis of the female scientist.[130] A well-known scientist is marked by high intellectual ability, intense channeling of energy in one direction, extreme independence, preference for working alone, and social withdrawal. The female in childhood socialization is not given the independence granted to boys. She is taught to be dependent, to prefer to work with others, and various social skills. Because of the early learning of these norms and values, she finds it difficult in school to develop the same analytic abilities as boys. Rossi contends that if the female is encouraged to show initiative and to solve problems on her own, she will develop the same analytic abilities as men. Because of the emphasis on social skills, the female scientist tends to be interested in teaching rather than doing research, preferring the interaction in the classroom to the relative isolation of research. The female socialization process also militates against

[127] Stanley S. Robin, "The Female in Engineering," in Robert Perucci and Joel E. Gerstl, eds., *The Engineers and the Social System* (New York: John Wiley, 1969), pp. 203–218.

[128] Ibid., p. 210.

[129] Ibid.

[130] Alice S. Rossi, "Characteristics of the Scientist and Implications for Women's Career Choices," in Jacquelyn Mattfield and Carol G. Aken, *Women and the Scientific Professions* (Cambridge, Mass.: The MIT Press), pp. 112–127.

the persistence and intense channeling of energy needed for successful scientific research; thus, the female scientist finds it extremely difficult to succeed professionally. Despite their own inabilities to attain scientific achievement, most college-trained women admire the rare female who is a well-known scientist. College women also sublimate their professional goals by desiring to be the mother of highly successful children and the wife of a prominent husband.

Female professors. The female in academia faces many of the same problems as the female scientist or doctor. In her book, *Academic Women*, Jessie Bernard discusses a number of problems which confront the female academic.[131] Women find it difficult to get the requisite education, but even when they succeed they are faced with the discriminatory hiring policies of most universities. Male college professors, like men in every other occupational group, dislike working with females and discriminate in their hiring practices in order to keep women out. In addition to this barrier, the academic woman faces the usual sex-role barriers to the attainment of an academic position. The expectations attached to their sex role prevent many from attaining the needed education or even entering the workforce. Marriage and children are obstacles on the route to success for the academic woman, while these are not troublesome barriers to most males. Even when she is able to overcome these barriers and enter academia, the female college professor finds herself faced with a series of distinctive problems. Increasingly, success in academia is defined in terms of research productivity, but Bernard points out a number of reasons why female academics tend to be far less productive than their male counterparts:

Because women have so many more outs for failure, because they are less sex-driven, because they are less involved, because they have less at stake, and because of a number of other sex-linked factors, it is quite possible that they are less likely to be in the driven, high-producing category.[132]

Because of these and other sex-linked characteristics, Bernard also concludes that female academics are also less creative and innovative than their male colleagues.

On a number of variables females have less chance at upward mobility. They have more difficulty moving into administrative positions, their academic ranks are inferior to those of males with similar qualifications and productivity, and their salaries, on the average, are lower than the mean salary for males. There are a number of reasons for this relative lack of success, not the least of which is discrimination by males who stand higher in the academic hierarchy. Another factor is that the reference group for many female academics is nonacademic women rather than male colleagues. Per-

131 Jessie Bernard, *Academic Women* (University Park: Pennsylvania State University Press, 1964).
132 Ibid., p. 156.

haps the most important factor, however, is "women are by and large less status-driven occupationally than men and are less competitive."[133]

In summation, the problem of the female professional is rooted in three areas: the socialization process which instills her with values that stand in opposition to professional values; the inherent conflict between her sex role and her professional role; and the resistance of male professionals and clients. Because of these conflicts females continue to be a minority group within the professions and are faced with distinctive difficulties if they achieve professional status.

Easing the conflict. In concluding this section on females in the professions it would be useful to return to Epstein's study and present some of her suggestions for reducing the strain between sex and professional roles. Although the female who chooses to be a professional must occupy both of these roles, she can avoid contact with specific individuals who cause her stress. She can refuse to marry a man who is unlikely to accept her professional status or she can avoid contact with fellow professionals who are likely to cause her trouble because she is a female. The female professional can also reduce the possibility of role overload by reducing the number of expectations attached to each role. She can, for example, have fewer children or avoid unimportant professional responsibilities. She can redefine her occupational role so that it is consonant with her sex role. Thus if her husband is also a professional, she can focus on helping him rather than on furthering her own career. Although this may reduce strain, the unpleasant result for some female professionals will be an undermining of their own careers. She can also seek to segregate her sex and professional roles so that she can focus on each intermittently. For example, she can send her children to camp during the summer to allow her to focus on her professional work, or she can seek professions with short hours and long vacations so that she can concentrate exclusively on her family during those periods. She can also compartmentalize her work schedule so that she can separate her two roles—days for work and evenings for family, or weekdays for family and weekends for work, are two possible strategies which might serve to reduce the strain. The female professional can also hire highly skilled help to take over a number of her family (or professional) responsibilities. She can also use her professional status to her advantage by allowing it to excuse her from a number of family and community responsibilities, because those around her know how busy she is with her work. (Epstein cautions here that many females in professional life overburden themselves by fulfilling all of the obligations attached to their roles in order to prove that they can handle both.) Finally, the female professional can rely on professional rules to temporarily relieve her of responsibilities at home. For example, a publisher's deadline or class times may be used to reduce or eliminate sex-role responsibilities during specific periods.

[133] Ibid., p. 181.

While the preceding paragraph focuses on specific actions a female professional can take to reduce stress, there are also a number of structural arrangements which perform the same function. The female professional can seek to work in settings where she shares a number of characteristics with her colleagues. If she shares the same educational background, class, and place of residence with her male colleagues, the stress which results from her sex will be reduced. Sharing professional practice with her husband is a helpful structural arrangement too. It might also be useful if husband and wife are in the same or kindred professions, for they would be both more aware of their professional responsibilities and more likely to work out a mutually acceptable relationship. The female professional can also ease her strain if her friends come from the same profession, or if her two roles can be made complementary. The example of the female gynecologist shows how the conflict between the two roles is lessened because they are consonant with each other. Strain is also less where one of the roles is less demanding. Thus the expectations attached to the wife-mother role will be reduced when the husband's occupation does not require her to spend much time in social engagements, and where the husband and/or children are absent for long periods. If her marriage is unsatisfactory and she spends even less time working on it, then the role strain is still less. The presence of a role surrogate such as a grandmother to take over some of her familial responsibilities is also helpful. If the woman is from an upper social class she will be freer to pursue her professional career and, conversely, if she has attained a high professional status she will be able to follow a more flexible time schedule which will enable her to handle her family obligations better. It will also be easier to fulfill the two roles if office hours, class hours, and other expectations are clearly defined, enabling the female to budget her time accordingly. Employing organizations can also help by structuring the hours of female professionals around their familial responsibilities or by providing day nurseries. In conclusion, there are a wide variety of things which can be done to reduce the conflict between female sex roles and professional roles. Despite these palliatives, the strain is unlikely to be eliminated in the near future—the stereotypes of females and professionals are too deeply embedded in the American value structure. It is only when these stereotypes change that females will experience no more conflict in the professions than their male colleagues. Perhaps the burgeoning Women's Liberation Movement will lead to such a change, but it will not come tomorrow.

Blacks

The black in America faces almost insurmountable barriers if he decides he would like to be a professional. These barriers constitute an index into American racism. The black man is often born in poverty and this lack of economic resources prevents most from attending college, let alone graduate school. Most often he must quit school to support his family. Even if he has the money, he faces other barriers. The family structure in black society frequently does not possess a successful father who can act as a role model for the child. Further, the black mother often seeks to emasculate the black male child so that he will not constitute a threat to white society. This emasculation is an adaptive device which serves to protect the black male from the hostility of the white community. One form of emasculation is a de-emphasis of education and intellectuality for the male child. The black child gets a second-rate education, which intensifies his lack of motivation. Teachers define the black child as dumb, so he begins to think of himself that way. The black student must almost inevitably deal with hostility from white students. If he makes it to college, it is usually a black college, which tends to be grossly inferior. Should he go to a white college he generally finds himself virtually alone in a sea of white faces. This isolation and the hostility from white students frequently force him to leave before he can graduate. Thus it is not at all surprising that blacks are underrepresented in the professions. When one adds to these factors the discrimination in graduate schools and the hostility of white professionals, the difficulties faced by the black who seeks to become a professional are even clearer.

Black physicians. Richard's study of the black physician in New York City offers great insight into the barriers which confront blacks in becoming and succeeding as professionals.[134] There are only two black medical schools in the United States, and white medical schools have discriminated against blacks in terms of admission. Hence 27 percent of the doctors in Richard's study felt they had had difficulty in getting into the medical school of their choice. Yet even this is an underestimation since many others had not even applied to schools where they thought they might be rejected or where black friends had in fact been rejected. One black doctor recalled: "When I graduated from Harvard College, I applied for admission to the medical school. The Dean of the school told me that they did not admit Negroes so I went to the University of Chicago."[135] Another said: "The Dean of Columbia tried to dissuade me; he said, 'You can make a good living as a shoemaker.'"[136] Because of this type of discrimination, two-thirds of black doctors in the United States were trained at the two black medical schools. Once in medical school the opposition of the American Medical Association to scholarships hits black students hardest, since they generally come from families with much lower incomes than those of their white counterparts. Some parents went heavily into debt in order to support them, while in other cases the black had to delay matriculation until he had earned enough money, or drop out of school for a time in order to earn enough to continue. The most typical pattern was for black students to work full time during the summer and

[134] Michael Richard, "The Negro Physician: Babbitt or Revolutionary?", *Journal of Health and Social Behavior* 10 (1969), 265–275.
[135] Ibid., p. 266.
[136] Ibid.

part time during the school year. Females could frequently find white-collar jobs while the males were forced to work as laborers, elevator boys, shoeshine boys, and Pullman porters. These kinds of financial and occupational hardships naturally made it far more difficult for a black medical student to finish medical school than a white student. If the black student makes it through medical school, other problems caused by his color remain.

Seeking a hospital internship constitutes another humiliation for the black physician. Once again 27 percent of Richard's respondents had difficulties getting the internship of their choice, and many others avoided these difficulties by not applying to those places which they expected would reject them. Following their internship, 59 percent of the respondents said they had difficulty in establishing their practices. Some had to borrow money to get started while others had to take on nonmedical work: "One older man became an elevator starter at Macy's department store after receiving his MD degree; another became a dining car waiter . . ."[137] In general a specialist is considered more professional than a general practitioner, but while 86 per cent of the white doctors in a parallel study were specialists, only 58 percent of the black sample were. Even this 58 percent is an overestimation, since less than 30 percent of the sample was board-certified to practice a specialty. The reasons for the relative lack of black specialists are manifold: they could not afford the extra money needed to acquire a specialty; it is difficult for a specialist to succeed economically in Harlem; and black patients tend to prefer to go to white specialists, since they regard them as more competent. Even fellow black doctors are a cause of the lack of specialists. Many black doctors prefer to refer their patients to white specialists, who would be reluctant to see them on a continuing basis, for it was felt that black specialists would be more inclined to "steal" these patients. Partly because there are fewer specialists, black doctors earn much less than their white counterparts. No blacks in Richard's study earn over $40,000 a year while 16 percent of the white doctors in the parallel study earned more than that amount; 45 percent of the black doctors earned more than $15,000 per year, while the 80 percent of whites earned more.

Hospital appointments are of growing importance to physicians, yet 64 percent of the black doctors studied by Richard had difficulty getting one. Once again this figure is low since other doctors did not even try for hospitals which they knew would reject them. Thus many black doctors are deprived of the technology, experts, more challenging patients, and the ability to offer patients adequate care which a hospital affiliation affords. Even when a black doctor gets a hospital appointment it tends to be a low-status appointment. One black physician remembered:

"I tried Presbyterian, but the director advised me to go to Harlem [hospital]. He said there was no place there even for Jews. Nevertheless, I went for rounds and

137 Ibid., p. 268.

attended lectures at Presbyterian for seventeen years without an appointment. Why did I do it? To pick up technical information and to show those black patients that not all members of their race are broom-pushers."[138]

The black doctors tended to have "monochromatic" practices. Almost 75 percent of those who answered the question admitted that their patients were 90 percent or more black. Only 8 percent of the black doctors who responded had less than a 50 percent black clientele. Richard concludes: "The Negro doctor is therefore one who doctors Negroes."[139] While black doctors refer patients to white physicians, 77 percent of the respondents had rarely or never received referrals from whites. This of course is explicable because few are specialists and they do practice in the ghetto. Yet even those black doctors who do get referrals get "garbage referrals." One said, "Sure I get referrals from white doctors, when they want to get rid of their cooks and servants, or the cooks and servants of their Park Avenue patients."[140] Richard has some optimism since younger black doctors seem to be moving away from monochromatic practices and garbage referrals. Thirty-four percent of the younger black doctors had more than 25 percent white patients, while only 12 percent of the older black doctors had that many white patients. In addition, 41 percent of the young physicians occasionally or frequently got referrals from white doctors, while the same is true of only 15 percent of the older ones. Although this offers some hope, the picture presented by Richard is far from bright.

Some of the characteristics of a professional individual are antithetical to the way a black is expected to behave in American society. For example, it was pointed out in Generalization 4 that a professional individual is supposed to have authority over clients. However, the black man in America is supposed to be passive. This conflict becomes especially acute when the black professional deals with a white client, for the white client is unaccustomed to dealing with a black authority figure. The black professional who is accustomed to being passive in other areas of life finds it difficult to be authoritative in his worklife. The professional individual also receives public recognition, but, the public is less likely to grant professional status to a black.

Black professionals and the black community. The major dilemma for the black professional probably lies in the reaction of the black community. The black community, most of which is economically depressed, is likely to resent the comparative success of the black professional. Further, although he is not totally accepted, the black professional is more acceptable to the white world than the rest of black society. This causes more resentment in the black community. Because he is more accepted, the black professional is likely to view integration as a meaningful goal, but as elements within black society

138 Ibid., p. 270.
139 Ibid.
140 Ibid., pp. 270–271.

are rejecting integration as a meaningful goal, the gap between the professional and the black society is likely to widen still further. For these reasons the black professional is truly a marginal man, standing with one foot in white society and the other in black society. Although he has a foothold in both places, he is not totally accepted by either group.

Given this dilemma, Back and Simpson, in an article entitled "The Dilemma of the Negro Professional," postulate several resolutions open to the black professional.[141] First, he can concentrate on dealing with black problems. The psychologist Kenneth Clark and the sociologist E. Franklin Frazier are examples of professional blacks who have chosen this direction. A similar resolution is employed by the black professional who retreats into the safety of the black community. Black doctors and lawyers who live and work in the ghetto exemplify this resolution. Finally, the black can be a professional first "who happens to be a Negro."

Attitudes toward competition. Howard's study of the attitudes of black professionals toward competition with whites sheds much light on which of these resolutions blacks are likely to choose.[142] Howard studied 21 black physicians, 19 black dentists, 20 black lawyers, and 40 black school teachers. He found that while they do accept some degree of competition with whites, they are ambivalent about it. They are less than whole-hearted and enthusiastic about competing with white professionals. Howard concludes that "they have a vested interest in a relatively closed system of competition. . . . They have a rather high degree of monopoly on services to Negroes through the professions of medicine, dentistry and teaching."[143] This seems to imply that black professionals are more likely to choose the first two resolutions postulated by Back and Simpson—they are likely to retreat into studying black problems or working in the safety of the black community. Conversely, the implication is that they are less likely to be professionals first who just happen to be black. Richard's more recent study, discussed above, implies that this might be changing. He sees some evidence that black physicians are becoming more professional, at least in the sense that they are less likely to have monochromatic practices and more likely to specialize and have patients referred to them by white doctors. This may indicate, although it is too early to tell, that younger black professionals are more likely to venture into competition with whites.

Which resolution the black professional chooses has important implications for the black community. If he chooses to work on black problems, or in the black community, he can be of immediate value to the black society. However, these contributions may be offset if he is retreating because of fear of

---

[141] Kurt Back and Ida Harper Simpson, "The Dilemma of the Negro Professional," *Journal of Social Issues* 20 (1964), 60–70.

[142] David Howard, "An Exploratory Study of Attitudes of Negro Professionals Toward Competition with Whites," *Social Forces* 45 (1966), 20–27.

[143] Ibid., p. 26.

competing with white professionals, for if he retreats out of fear, he will not be the successful role model the black community sorely needs. This problem is solved if he chooses to be a professional first and competes with white professionals. The danger here is that he may totally remove himself from the black community; if he lives outside and deals with white clients and problems, his ability to contribute to the black society is greatly diminished. Perhaps the ideal solution is exemplified by the black professional who makes it in white society, but devotes most of his energy to helping blacks.

Black baseball players. It has been pointed out that the professions are characterized by less discrimination than other occupational groups. In his discussion of the black professional baseball player, Blalock points out some of the reasons for less discrimination in the professions although baseball cannot be considered truly a profession.[144] Following the entrance of Jackie Robinson into the major leagues in 1947, an avalanche of black players came into professional baseball. A large pool of capable players had been built up in the minor and Negro leagues, and once the barrier was broken blacks rapidly entered the majors. There are a number of reasons for the successful integration of blacks into major-league teams. For one, performance in professional baseball is measured in highly objective terms such as "batting averages, slugging averages, home runs, runs batted in, fielding averages, earned run averages, strike outs, won or lost records, etc."[145] It is difficult to discriminate against a black .300 hitter or a black twenty-game winner. These records are widely publicized by the news media and a team's fans are unlikely to stand for discrimination against a talented black player. A team's success depends on the performance of its members. Profits come from having individual stars, winning teams, and playing in the World Series, and therefore a team is likely to play its best performers, regardless of race. Major-league cities also have large black populations and in order to attract this audience the team must utilize black players.

Another factor in the successful integration of major-league baseball is the inherent insecurity of the players. Every starting player is constantly faced with competition from second-stringers on his team as well as from aspiring minor-league players. Working in such a competitive atmosphere is an accepted part of the life of a professional baseball player. Thus when blacks entered the major leagues they were accepted as another competitor in an already competitive situation. Further, professional baseball teams are characterized by an egalitarian atmosphere. Other than the coaches and managers who are supervisors, there is no authority structure on a team. "There is little or no threat of a Negro teammate becoming the white player's boss, and an additional source of resistance to his employment is thereby removed."[146]

[144] Hubert M. Blalock, Jr., *Toward a Theory of Minority-Group Relations* (New York: John Wiley, 1967).
[145] Ibid., p. 94.
[146] Ibid., p. 96.

If a team hires a black player there is little that a white player who objects can do. The baseball culture does not permit him to change to a more biased team. He cannot prevent the player from gaining the skills he needs to perform capably. As much as a white player may dislike blacks he must, if he is a pitcher, throw him the ball as well as he can and the talented black will get his share of hits.

In this analysis of the black baseball player there are a number of general principles which might apply to integration in other occupations. From this discussion it is clear that there will be less discrimination in an occupation when:

1. Individual performance is central to the productivity of the group.
2. Employers must compete for talented individuals.
3. It is easy to assess individual performance.
4. Individual performance is to the advantage of others in the group.
5. There is a large black population to be served.
6. Competition and equality are an accepted part of the group's life.
7. Whites cannot prevent blacks from gaining the needed skills.

Since the professions have many of these characteristics, it is there that the black has the greatest chance of acceptance and success.

Professions and the social structure

The goal in this chapter has been to present a number of generalizations about professions and professional life. In conclusion, some mention must be made of the relationship between the professions and the changing social structure in the United States. Professions are clearly not a new social invention. Doctors, lawyers, and clergymen existed long before the industrial revolution, but the proliferation of the professions was a concomitant of this revolution. The widespread technological changes it brought about created the need for a massive number of technical experts. In Durkheimian terms, the need for professions grows with the transition from mechanical to organic solidarity. The division of labor which is the resultant of this transition requires highly trained specialists rather than the generalists characteristic of mechanical solidarity. This view was originally put forth by Carr-Saunders and Wilson:

For an explanation [of the rise of the professions] we must look primarily to the mechanical revolution and the progress of science which gave rise to engineers, chemists and physicists, and to the consequential social revolution which brought a demand for intellectual specialists to handle the new and complicated machinery, both material and institutional: actuaries, surveyors, realtors, secretaries, patent attorneys, and accountants (virtually unknown in Anglo-Saxon countries before the middle of the nineteenth century).[147]

[147] A. M. Carr-Saunders and P. A. Wilson, "The Emergence of Professions," in Sigmund Nosow and William H. Form, eds., *Man, Work and Society* (New York: Basic Books, 1962), p. 202.

In his study of the rise of the professional classes in nineteenth-century England, Reader expresses a similar view, contending that professions, in the main, were created to serve the needs of an industrial society.[148] The old established professions of medicine, law, and the clergy grew rather slowly, while what Reader calls the "new," "lower," and "unprivileged" professions (e.g., accountants and engineers) grew far more rapidly.

The whole notion of what a profession is was changed substantially by the industrial revolution. Previously professionals were viewed as learned men with generalized expertise. With the transition to organic solidarity the professional came to be viewed as a narrow specialist. He continued to be consulted on his specialty, but tended to lose his status as an overall expert. The new professionals who arose were also regarded as specialists. In addition, the old established professions were affected as well and they suffered a decline in their overall status.

Professions in different nations have many characteristics in common, but there are also important differences. In fascist Germany and Italy the professions were quickly brought under state control. By utilizing semicompulsory associations, expulsion of professionals who refused to conform, co-optation into the government, and government "watchdogs," the fascist countries were able to change the structure of the professions. Similarly, communist countries have sought to control the educational process of professionals and have brought many professionals into the government. The communist countries have sought to reduce the power of the professional association in the following way:

All teachers, lawyers, medical men, journalists, etc., are organized into trade unions . . . the distribution of persons among unions depends not on the personal function but on the function of the institution, so that a counsel of a textile factory belongs to the union of textile workers and . . . the union of medical men includes the janitors of the hospitals.[149]

Changes such as these have greatly altered the structure of the professions as they are known in western societies. The comparative study of professions cross-nationally offers a fruitful area for future research in occupational sociology. As with other institutions, the professions reflect the broader social structure.

The professions represent, in their ultimate form, the rationality Max Weber saw as a distinctive trait of western society. As such they represent a fertile field for the study of social structure and social change.

---

[148] W. J. Reader, *Professional Men* (New York: Basic Books, 1966).
[149] N. S. Timasheff, "Business and the Professions in Liberal, Fascist, and Communist Society," *American Journal of Sociology* 45 (1940), 867.

3
Managers, Officials, and Proprietors

There have been more studies of managers, officials, and proprietors than of any other occupational group except professionals. In the period from 1946 to 1952, 18 percent of all studies of occupations were concerned with this group.[1] What is more significant, the study of these occupations seems to be increasing in importance, with 22 percent of the occupational studies from 1953 to 1959 devoted to this category.[2] As Hall points out, managers, officials, and proprietors are members of a heterogeneous group of occupations sharing only high socioeconomic status and the fact that they exist in organizations.[3] We will use the following definitions for the three groups:

The term "manager" refers to business executives, itself a very broad category. Proprietors are owners of businesses, and in the majority of cases, proprietors are also managers performing the same kinds of functions and occupying the same positions as top executives. They also perform a wide variety of other non-managerial roles. Officials are in many ways identical to managers, the major difference being the fact that officials are employed in non-profit organizations, such as governmental agencies, school systems, hospitals, business and professional associations, etc. They are administrators in non-business organizations.[4]

Because both managers and officials exist in organizations in similar kinds of positions, they are more alike than different. They are dealt with together, leaving the discussion of proprietors to a later section of this chapter.

MANAGERS AND OFFICIALS

1. The basic dilemma for all managers and officials is role conflict.

[1] Erwin Smigel, "Trends in Occupational Sociology in the United States: A Survey of Postwar Research," *American Sociological Review* 19 (1954), 398–404.

[2] Erwin Smigel et al., "Occupational Sociology: A Re-examination," *Sociology and Social Research* 47 (1963), 472–477.

[3] Richard Hall, *Occupations and the Social Structure* (Englewood Cliffs, N.J.: Prentice-Hall, 1969), p. 138.

[4] Ibid., pp. 138–139.

One of the foci in the preceding chapter was the types of conflict faced by the professional. It was pointed out that the professional in an organization faces different types of conflict than does the free professional. In discussing managers and officials this differentiation is unnecessary, because all managers are by definition found in organizations. Because they exist in organizations and almost always find themselves with other managers above, below, and beside them, managers are particularly prone to role conflict. In a later chapter the foreman and similar occupations are discussed in these terms. Since it will be such an important theme, some of the basic ideas of the theory of role conflict and its resolution are dealt with in detail in the next few pages.

Role theory

Much of occupational sociology has been dominated by role theory, although to many occupational sociologists this orientation was not explicit. It is important to note that in a recent article Solomon concludes that Everett Hughes was in many ways a role theorist interested in the study of occupations from this perspective.[5] Moreover, Solomon contends that much of occupational sociology may be subsumed under the heading of role theory:

Occupation is, after all, a label for a class or category of persons, which, to be of sociological interest, must be characterized in some other way as well. Once an occupational label identifies a category of persons it is implied that they behave or can legitimately be expected to behave in the same or similar ways in given situations, that they have similar roles to perform. The occupational label and the behavioral expectations are equivalent to the notions of occupational status and role. An occupation can thus be thought of as *a* role. . . . The primary sociological interest in an occupation is, after all, as a role. Whatever other interests we pursue, or whatever other concepts we introduce are incidental to, or arise from, the fact that the phenomenon we are concerned with in studying an occupation is in essence a role. Moreover, such roles can be clearly identified by a single criterion: They are roles people are paid to perform.[6]

Just as role theory has been implicit in many sociological studies of occupations, it has also been a growing explicit orientation. Smigel's first survey of occupational sociology indicated that from 1946 to 1952 7 percent of all studies of occupations were explicitly from a role theory perspective.[7] In their follow-up study, Smigel et al. found that in the period 1953 to 1959 the percentage of occupational studies done from a role theory perspective had grown to 21 percent.[8] Given comparable growth in the last ten years, it may well be that role theory is the dominant perspective in occupational sociology. The plethora of studies done from a role theory perspective in the last few years

    [5] David N. Solomon, "Sociological Perspectives on Occupations," in Howard S. Becker et al., *Institutions and the Person* (Chicago: Aldine, 1968), pp. 3–13.
    [6] Ibid., pp. 6–7.
    [7] Smigel et al., "Occupational Sociology," p. 476.
    [8] Ibid.

indicate that if the growth of research with this perspective has not been comparable, it certainly has been substantial.

It is not within the province of this book to summarize the mass of material that constitutes the body of role theory. Rather, some of its basic concepts that have proven useful in the sociological study of occupations are briefly discussed. Before discussing these concepts it should be made clear that role theory is in fact *not* a theory. "The role field exhibits much speculation, and there are certainly hypotheses and theories about particular aspects of the subject, but there is no one grand 'theory.' "[9] Despite the lack of a grand theory, role theory does offer a number of useful concepts to the occupational sociologist.

Role theory had its origins in the early 1900s in the work of such social psychologists as James, Baldwin, Dewey, Cooley, and later Mead. Prior to 1930 the term "role" was commonly employed in speech and even discussed on several occasions in sociology. However, it was not until the 1930s that the technical form of the term was used in sociology and social psychology. The posthumous publication of Mead's *Mind, Self and Society* in 1934, with its discussion of "role theory," "generalized other," and "self," was a landmark. Also in 1934, Jacob Moreno published *Who Shall Survive*, in which the concepts of "role" and "role playing" were used in his discussion of psychodrama and sociodrama. Linton's differentiation of status and role was also gaining prominence during this period. These pioneering studies were soon followed by the work of such important figures in current sociology as Parsons and Newcomb. Because of its diverse history in sociology, social psychology, and anthropology, the basic concepts of role theory were defined differently and this resulted in a good deal of confusion in the field. Thus there are many definitions of the basic concepts in role theory, such as position (status) and role. These terms are defined in the next paragraph, but it should be pointed out that much disagreement remains on their definition.

The definitions used are the ones employed in what many consider to be the major piece of role analysis, Gross, Mason, and McEachern's study of the role of the school superintendent.[10] They define a *position* as "the location of an actor or class of actors in a system of social relationships."[11] A *role* is a set of expectations applied to the incumbent of a particular position. ("An *expectation* is an evaluative standard applied to an incumbent of a position.")[12] "A *role behavior* is an actual performance of an incumbent of a position which can be referred to an expectation for an incumbent of that position."[13] Before moving on to some other important role concepts, we need an example which

[9] Edwin J. Thomas and Bruce J. Biddle, "The Nature and History of Role Theory," in Bruce J. Biddle and Edwin J. Thomas, eds., *Role Theory* (New York: John Wiley, 1966), p. 14.
[10] Neal Gross, Ward Mason, and Alexander McEachern, *Explorations in Role Analysis: Studies of the School Superintendency Role* (New York: John Wiley, 1958).
[11] Ibid., p. 48.
[12] Ibid., p. 58.
[13] Ibid., p. 64.

will clarify the above definitions. A position relevant to this chapter is plant manager. In this position an individual is expected to fill many roles, including ultimate decision maker in the plant, agent for community relations, and communication link with top management. These roles constitute the expectations of a number of people in the plant for the individual who holds the position of plant manager. When the plant manager makes decisions, is involved in community relations, or acts as a communication link, he is exhibiting role behavior. It should be clear that the same concepts can be applied to any and all occupations.

Before proceeding to the focus of this section (role conflict), several other concepts must be defined. "A *position-set* is a series of positions and position relationships in which a person becomes involved simply as a result of occupying a particular focal position."[14] Thus, structurally, the position-set of our plant manager would include such other positions as foreman, personnel manager, and union president. While position-set is a structural variable, *role-set* is a perceptual variable. One's role-set "consists of a series of role performers with which a person perceives himself related, because of his involvement in, and performance of, a focal role."[15] Thus there will be significant others in the organization who will be in the plant manager's position-set, but not necessarily in his role-set. In other words, there are figures in the organization with whom the plant manager is supposed to be involved, but with whom he may not perceive the need to be involved. Two other concepts are needed: one is the notion of *sent-role* or the communicated expectations of the members of the role-set. Members of the role-set may have expectations, but they must be communicated to the focal role in order for them to qualify as a sent-roles. Finally, there is the idea of *role-pressures*, the attempts at influence by role-senders to bring about conformity with their expectations. It is clear that role-senders will expect different things of the focal role, and this fact brings us to the notion of role conflict.

Role conflict

In their book, *Organizational Stress: Studies in Role Conflict and Ambiguity*, Kahn et al. have pointed out there are five types of role conflict: role overload, inter-sender, person-role, inter-role, and intra-sender.[16] In the next few paragraphs each of these types of role conflict is discussed in terms of our hypothetical plant manager.

One type of role conflict developed by Kahn et al. is *role overload*, which occurs when the focal role is confronted with a large number of expectations, and finds it difficult if not impossible to satisfy all of them in a given period. For the plant manager it is simply a case of too many role expectations. A schematic representation of role overload looks like this:

14 Joseph A. Alutto, "Role Theory in Propositional Form," PhD Dissertation, New York State School of Industrial and Labor Relations, Cornell University, 1967, p. 40.

15 Ibid., p. 41.

16 Robert L. Kahn et al., *Organizational Stress: Studies in Role Conflict and Ambiguity* (New York: John Wiley, 1964), pp. 18–21.

Inter-sender role conflict is a situation in which the focal role is confronted with conflicting expectations from two or more significant others. The situation is such that the fulfillment of one expectation makes it difficult or impossible to satisfy the other. In our example of the plant manager, such a situation would occur when the manager of the accounting department wants him to cut personnel costs, while the personnel manager wants him to approve the hiring of more blacks. The following is a schematic representation of this conflict:

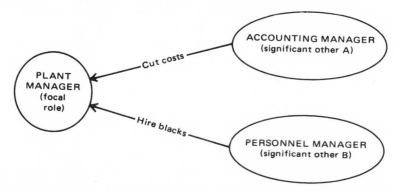

This is an overly simplistic illustration; very frequently there are a large number of significant others, each having conflicting expectations of the focal role.

Person-role conflict occurs when the expectations associated with a particular role violate the focal role's moral values, needs, or aspirations. In the case of the plant manager this may occur when he is expected to give preferential treatment to blacks in terms of hiring, but this conflicts with his egalitarianism. He may feel that all applicants should be given an equal chance to a job. Person-role conflict may be illustrated as follows:

A fourth type of role conflict outlined by Kahn et al. is *inter-role conflict*. This occurs when the expectations attached to one role conflict with the expectations of the same individual in another role. Let us take the plant manager in his roles as decision maker and in community relations. In the former he may be expected to give preferential treatment in the hiring of blacks, but in his role in community relations he may be expected to reassure the community that his plant is not giving preferential treatment to blacks. Schematically this conflict is:

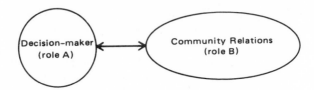

Intra-sender role conflict occurs when one significant other has conflicting expectations of the focal role. The expectations are such that to satisfy one expectation would make it virtually impossible to satisfy the other. As an example, one might examine a hypothetical relationship between the plant manager and his superior, the company president. The president might expect the plant manager to cut personnel costs, but also expect him, because of government pressure, to hire more blacks. The hiring of blacks is frequently costly, because they may require extra training as well as an allowance on the part of management for errors made in adjusting to work. Schematically, this example of intra-role conflict would look as follows:

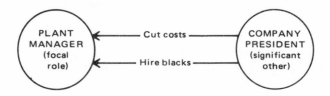

For illustrative purposes a situation in which there are only two conflicting expectations has been outlined. In the "real world" one would be more likely to find situations in which a significant other had many expectations of the focal role, and many of these may conflict with one another.

Another concept by Kahn et al. deserves mention although it is not directly related to role conflict. *Role ambiguity* occurs when the focal role receives an inadequate amount of role-related information. A focal role will find it difficult to satisfy the expectations of significant others when these expectations are ambiguous. The plant manager will be faced with role ambiguity when he is unsure what others expect of him.

Because they are in relatively high positions in an organization, managers and officials are particularly subject to conflicting expectations from significant others within the organization. Professionals are far less likely to suffer from role conflict, because by definition fellow professionals are their major significant others. Similarly, those in low-status occupations such as assembly-line work are also not as likely to face role conflict. One of the basic tenets of organizational structure is that those in low-status occupations have only one superior, and are not subject to the conflicting demands of several supervisors. Although low-status employees face little role conflict, this is not to say that they suffer none. For example, when their boss demands a certain level of productivity and peers set a norm of lower productivity, they are faced with inter-sender role conflict. However, the low-status employee in an organization suffers far more from alienation than he does from role conflict. Thus, role conflict is faced by everyone in organizational life, but it is particularly acute for managers and officials. As is pointed out later, it is also a difficult problem for those in lower-level managerial positions, such as the foreman.

Role overload

Business executives. Because of the nature of their position at the top of an achievement-oriented organization, business executives are subject to virtually every type of role conflict, and are particularly prone to role overload. William H. Whyte, Jr., the popular "sociologist," notes that the executives he studied worked an average of 45 to 48 hours per week.[17] (These are his hours in the office, but the executive's work does not stop there. Whyte's executives worked four nights a week.) Nights are taken up with business entertaining, catching up on office work, and conferences. During the day the executive's lunch hour is rarely passed idly—it is usually spent in conference. Add to this trips to outlying corporate locations and early morning and weekend work, and it is not unusual for the business executive to put in 70 or 80 hours per week on the job. William H. Whyte, Jr. asks, Why do executives work so hard? His respondents indicated that they do it because they can express themselves in their work, they feel they are making an important contribution to their organization, they have a great deal of responsibility and take this

[17] William H. Whyte, Jr., *The Organization Man* (Garden City, N.Y.: Anchor Books, 1957).

responsibility quite seriously, they enjoy the prestige their position offers them, and they feel that hard work gives them job security.

Union business agents.   It must be noted that managers and officials are not alone in being confronted with role overload: many individuals in lower-status occupations are also faced with it. However, the literature seems to indicate that as one ascends the organizational hierarchy, he is more likely to be faced with an overload of expectations. In the category of managers and officials, executives are not the only group faced with role overload. Rosen and Rosen found that role overload was one of the most striking characteristics of the role of the union business agent.[18] A business agent is a full-time, paid union official who is most likely to be found in craft industries. He represents a number of craft workers who work for a large number of employers, and he is the most important official within the craft local. In many craft unions it is the union, not the employer, who does the hiring. The union business agent is in charge of hiring as well as negotiations with the numerous employers. Another major element of his job is defending the jurisdiction of his local from the encroachment of other craft locals. The union business agent is particularly prone to role overload. Rosen and Rosen found that the business agent's day does not end with the passing of daylight. During his regular hours he deals with employers, writes reports, and attends and runs meetings.

At the end of the work "day," the second phase of the business agents' expected activities began: formal meetings with the membership in shop and local, joint board meetings, organizational drive meetings, and informal, but highly necessary social interaction with the membership. Duties relative to civic affairs, and legislative and political duties were also expected to be fitted into the already tight schedule.[19]

These job demands limited family and social life, both in the evenings and on weekends. Weekends were frequently spent catching up on work which could not be fitted into the busy regular schedule. All this work was not merely on the initiative of the business agent, but was expected by the membership, "and any reluctance to give unsparingly was viewed critically by others in the organization."[20] The result was considerable social and physical isolation from family and friends. Union business agents are primarily problem solvers, and the problems they must solve are not their own, but rather the very pressing problems of the local members. Because these problems are invariably important to the members, the business agent cannot put them out of his mind. He must be continually available to members who need his help, and the fact that he is always carrying around others' problems and the necessity for him to be constantly accessible contributes to role overload.

[18] Hjalmar Rosen and R. A. Hudson Rosen, "Personality Variables and Role in a Union Business Agent Group," *Journal of Applied Psychology* 41 (1957), 131–136.
[19] Ibid., pp. 131–132.
[20] Ibid., p. 132.

Elected public officials. Elected public officials also face role overload, as well as all the other forms of role conflict. Mitchell notes that at all levels the politician complains of the number of demands made upon him.[21] Rather than detail the demands which can possibly be made upon the elected politician, let us note the comments of two United States Senators on the role overload which confronts them.

Senator Downey of California:

Each day Senators have matters come before them which could, if they could spare the time, occupy their attentions for months . . . yet here we are compelled to dispose of weighty and complicated matters after being able to listen to arguments only for perhaps an hour or two. . . . Observe for a moment the volume of business that is done in my office alone. It is so great as almost to break me and my whole staff down. In mail alone we receive from 200 to 300 letters every 24 hours. And this in addition to telegrams and long-distance calls and personal visits. We do the best we can. We try to have every letter answered the day it is received. My staff is departmentalized. That is, each girl is an expert in some particular field. . . . If the office were not so organized, we could not possibly begin to carry the load. Yet, Mr. Chairman, I can say to you truthfully that even if I had four times the amount of time I have I could not possibly perform adequately and fully the duties imposed upon me as ambassador from my state. In the departments of government there are always delays or injustices or matters overlooked in which a Senator can be of very great assistance to his constituents. The flood of duties in my office has reached such proportions, and is so steadily increasing, that I am almost totally unable to enter into the study of any legislative matters. That means that frequently I have to inform myself concerning matters of importance by listening to arguments on the floor of the Senate. And yet even my presence on the floor is only intermittent, so great is the burden of my office duties if I am to efficiently carry out my responsibilities with respect to the state of California.

Senator Fulbright of Arkansas:

But the fact is that the multitude of requests for minor personal services comes close to destroying the effectiveness of a great many capable representatives. The legislator finds himself in a dilemma. If he refuses to see the constant stream of visitors or to give personal attention to their requests, they may become offended and withdraw their support. In addition, it is personally gratifying to be able to be of help to one's friends. On the other hand, if he does give his attentions to these matters, he literally has no time left for the intelligent study and reflection that sound legislation requires.[22]

One of the defining characteristics, then, of managers and officials is role overload. Business executives, union business agents, and politicians have been discussed in these terms. Virtually all managers and officials are particularly subject to role overload.

---

[21] William C. Mitchell, "Occupational Role Strains: The American Elective Public Official," *Administrative Science Quarterly* 3 (1958), 211–228.

[22] Ibid., pp. 222–223.

Inter-sender role conflict

Business executives. Let us turn now to studies of managers and officials which indicate the types of inter-sender role conflict faced by such individuals. The business executive is supposed to make decisions and because of this role he is subjected to a great deal of conflicting pressure. Top-level decisions affect many subgroups within the organization and each subgroup strives to affect the executive's decisions. Kahn et al. have composed the following list of groups or significant others which may make conflicting demands of any manager in an organization:

1. Management or company in general.
2. Person's direct supervisor(s).
3. Coworkers within organization.
4. Person's subordinates.
5. Union or its representatives.
6. Extraorganizational associates (e.g., clients, customers, suppliers).
7. Others (e.g., family, friends).[23]

When the expectations of one of these groups conflict with the expectations of another, inter-sender role conflict exists. Although everyone in an organization is faced with such role conflict, some types are more typical of the business executive. For example, one of the current vogues in business is the delegation of some of the executive's authority to subordinates. Delegation performs two functions: it gives subordinates who may someday occupy the executive's position experience in making decisions, and frees some of the executive's time for other types of work. Because it is fashionable, many subordinates have come to expect the executive to delegate some of his authority to them. Conflicting with this expectation is the accepted organizational reality that the executive's superiors will hold him responsible for decisions made by him or his subordinates. Thus the executive is expected by his superior to be responsible for decisions coming from his office, and is faced with a dilemma: should he delegate decision making and risk his status in the organization if the decision made by his subordinate is a poor one? Or should he deny his subordinates authority, and fail to fulfill their expectations?

Another typical inter-sender conflict for the business executive occurs in his relationship with customers. He finds that they expect him to give them the best possible deal, but against this is the expectation of his superiors that he get the best possible deal for the company. Quite clearly he can never satisfy both parties. All the significant others listed above have conflicting expectations of the business executive, and the fulfillment of one expectation frequently entails the inability to satisfy the other. That is the basic dilemma of

---

[23] Kahn et al., *Organizational Stress*, p. 56.

the business executive. Although inter-sender conflict occurs at all levels of organizational life, it is particularly acute at the top because that is where the major decisions are made.

School superintendents. Gross, Mason, and McEachern's study of the school superintendent focused on four situations where the school superintendent faced inter-sender role conflict.[24] The first situation involved a hiring situation and 71 percent of the respondents felt that this situation exposed them to role conflict. They felt that a local politician, school board member, or personal friend might ask them to recommend a friend or relative. "Big taxpayers" might expect the superintendent to give special consideration to their choices. Community groups such as the PTA or the teachers might feel he should not give special consideration to any interest group, but should base his decision solely on merit. A second area of conflict involved the allocation of the school superintendent's time. Fifty-three percent of the respondents felt that they were confronted with role conflict over how they spent their time. Professional associations expected them to attend meetings and participate on committees. Local groups such as the Chamber of Commerce and the Rotary Club expected the superintendent to be active in their programs. Further, the school board and staff members expected him to devote the bulk of his time to their needs.

The third conflict situation for the superintendent concerned salary recommendations. The PTA and local teachers associations undoubtedly expected the superintendent to fight for the maximum possible salary increases. Other groups, however, wanted him to hold the line on salary increases. These groups included property owners, those who lived on fixed incomes, local taxpayers associations, and others which were opposed to the tax increases which might follow a salary increase. Also, political figures were likely to resist salary increases because the resulting higher taxes would reduce their chances of reelection. Eighty-eight percent of the school superintendents perceived role conflict over this situation. The fourth and final conflict situation involved the school budget, which 91 percent of the responding superintendents viewed as a situation involving role conflict. Such groups as the taxpayers association, local politicians, and the city council, were likely to expect the superintendent to give priority to the community's financial resources when making budgetary decisions. On the other hand, groups such as the teachers and the PTA were perceived as expecting the superintendent to give priority to educational needs.

Thus the majority of school superintendents perceived each of these four situations to be fraught with role conflict, especially the inter-sender type. But not every superintendent perceived these situations as containing role conflict. The following is the percentage of respondents who instead perceived each situation to involve role congruency: a) personnel hiring—29 per-

[24] Gross et al., *Studies of the School Superintendency*, pp. 258–280.

cent; b) time allocation—47 percent; c) teacher salary recommendations—12 percent; d) budget recommendations—9 percent.

Therefore, even in those situations which appear to be laden with discord, there are those who do not perceive any. The implication is that a large part of the school superintendent's job contains no conflict. This is true of every occupation: there are always long periods of normality interrupted by periods of crisis and stress. Although I have chosen to emphasize the conflict aspect of occupational life here and in the rest of the book, it is not denied that much of occupational life is relatively routine. It is pointed out, however, that in looking at conflict in occupational life one can learn much about the nature of the workworld.

Local union presidents. The local union presidency is another occupation which is prone to role conflict, particularly the inter-sender role variety. Instead of a general discussion of this occupation, some of the author's research on one local president, which relates to this type of role conflict, is examined. Although the ensuing discussion relates to a particular local president, the literature indicates that these conflicts are general throughout the occupation. The local union studied is one of 11 organized under a System Council composed of the 11 local presidents, an elected Council president, and a recording secretary. There are approximately 2700 members in the 11 locals and all work for one company which supplies electrical power to a large area composed primarily of rural communities. All of the company's blue-collar workers belong to the union, as well as a majority of the white-collar workers. The local concerned has 330 members.

Most of the work is of an outdoor nature. Because there is some danger involved the union members do not work outside in inclement weather, and it has become a custom for them then to play cards on company property while waiting for the weather to clear. The workers enjoy this time off and object to any attempt by the company to limit their activities during these periods. Under pressure from the System Council and the company, the local president was asked to get his members to use the time off for training in new job techniques. Balancing this was pressure from the membership to prevent interference with their customary activities. Another example of inter-sender role conflict facing the local president arises over the issue of grievances. The rank and file of the local expect the union president to vigorously pursue all of their grievances—obviously, the problems which have caused a member to file a grievance are extremely important to him. However the importance of the grievance to the member involved often conflicts with the demands made upon the local president by the company and the System Council. On the issue of grievances the local president is truly a man in the middle. He must satisfy his constituents as well as the System Council, while being sure that he does not antagonize the company and adversely affect the good relations which have prevailed between the company and union. On the issue of grievances the System Council is an extremely conservative body which has committed itself to a policy of settling grievances as quickly as possible and thereby avoiding conflict with the company. This policy places them in direct opposition to the individual member who wants to see his grievance pushed as hard as possible no matter what its effect on overall union-management relations. The third group in this triangle of pressures on the local president is the company. The company dislikes grievances because they are expensive and time-consuming. Consequently, it expects the local president to bring as few as possible to its attention. It implicitly threatens a breakdown in the good company-union relations if the local president does not keep grievances to a minimum. There are many other types of inter-sender role conflict faced by the local union president and many other managerial and official occupations with this form of conflict.

Members of boards of directors. A wide variety of types of organizations are headed by boards of directors, including businesses, schools, hospitals, and government agencies. According to Zald boards of directors have two basic functions.[25] One is internal control and here the major responsibility of the board members is appointing, perpetuating, and overseeing the management of the organization. The second is an external function in which the board promotes and represents the organization to such outsiders as stockholders, suppliers, customers, and the government. It is because a board member must balance internal and external demands that he is particularly prone to inter-sender role conflict. Let us examine a few examples in order to illustrate the possibilities for this type of conflict. One of the major responsibilities of most boards is the appointment of chief executives. In choosing a new chief executive the board must frequently resolve conflicting expectations from internal and external sources. A major stockholder may favor one candidate while the management of the organization may be stumping for a different individual. Another example occurs when the organization contemplates a major change in its labor policy. Management may propose that the organization begin negotiations with a particular labor union, but there may well be several unions vying for the right to organize the organization's employees. Thus the board is caught between the demands of its management and pressure from several unions to gain bargaining rights. Boards of directors exist at the boundaries of an organization and because of this precarious position (and because of their great power) the members frequently find themselves subjected to rather severe cross pressures.

Person-role conflict

Navy disbursing officers. A third type of role conflict is person-role conflict, illustrated by Turner's study of the Navy disbursing officer.[26] The dis-

[25] Mayer N. Zald, "The Power and Functions of Boards of Directors: A Theoretical Synthesis," *American Journal of Sociology* 75 (1969), 97–111.
[26] Ralph H. Turner, "The Navy Disbursing Officer as a Bureaucrat," *American Sociological Review* 12 (1947), 342–348.

bursing officer's chief function is to serve as a paymaster at his location. There are certain rules of action for him, which he has internalized as norms of behavior. Conflict for him generally occurs when his superiors expect behavior which contradicts his normative orientation. This is person-role conflict because the stress centers on the contradiction between what the disbursing officer feels he should do and the expectations of superiors. The major source of conflict for the disbursing officer is commanding or executive officers. Turner points out that they "have little knowledge of and patience with disbursing regulations, and . . . are generally not accustomed to being asked by a subordinate to discuss the advisability of an order they have issued. . . ."[27] The conflict facing the disbursing officer is complicated by the fact that his own superior is likely to support the demands of the commanding or executive officer; if the officer does not accede to these demands he is threatened with notations on his permanent fitness report. Thus powerful forces within the Navy expect him to go against the regulations and his own view of how the job should be handled.

School superintendents.   There were elements of person-role conflict in two of the role conflict cases in the Gross et al. study of school superintendents. On the question of hiring new personnel most of the school superintendents studied felt that decisions should be made solely on the basis of merit. In effect, the superintendents took a very professional view of their role in hiring new teachers. However, as we have pointed out previously, a number of significant others had contradictory expectations of the school superintendent on the hiring question. They expected the superintendent to make choices which would satisfy their interests and this contradicted the superintendent's desire to base hiring decisions strictly on merit. There are also elements of person-role conflict in the area of teacher's salaries. The superintendents studied by Gross et al. favored higher salaries for teachers:

The interviews with the superintendents revealed that most of them are acutely aware of and concerned about the relative lag in teacher salary increases as compared to those of other occupational groups. They mentioned particularly that married male teachers frequently must take outside jobs to provide their families with minimum living standards. Most superintendents are former teachers and know from first hand experience that difficulties of maintaining a "middle class" standard of living on a "lower class" wage level.[28]

Despite their own predisposition to increase teacher salaries, there are powerful forces within the community which oppose such increases. Thus on these two issues the school superintendent is exposed to person-role conflict as well as inter-sender role conflict.

[27] Ibid., pp. 343–344.
[28] Gross et al., *Studies of the School Superintendency*, p. 268.

Business executives. White-collar crime constitutes a major source of person-role conflict for the business executive. He is supposed to be Machiavellian in that any form of behavior which is good for the company is desirable for the company. However, he is frequently placed in a position where an action which may be good for the company conflicts with his own morality. As Sutherland shows in his classic work on white-collar crime, these behaviors may include

misrepresentation in financial statements of corporations, manipulation in the stock exchange, commercial bribery of public officials directly or indirectly in order to secure favorable contracts and legislation, misrepresentation in advertising and salesmanship, embezzlement and misapplication of funds, short weights and measures and misgrading of commodities, tax frauds, misapplication of funds in receiverships and bankruptcies.[29]

It is not unusual for an organization to expect its executives to perform any actions which will improve the company's financial position. With these demands posed, the executive must face a conflict between his own morality and the morality of business life.

Local union presidents. Let us examine one more example of person-role conflict before moving on to inter-role conflict. In my study of the local union president, the electrical company had recently instituted a number of technological innovations which had complicated the work and made it much more dangerous. A number of workers, although recognizing the additional safety hazards, were seeking higher pay for the new work rather than safer working conditions. The local president took the opposite view, feeling that it was much more important for the union to seek safer working conditions. This brought him into direct opposition to the workers, who felt that he should be pressing management for higher wages. This is not an unusual situation for the union president, who frequently finds that what he believes conflicts with the expectations of the group of major significant others, the membership.

Inter-role conflict

Heads of professional organizations. The fourth type of role conflict is inter-role conflict, in which the expectations attached to one role conflict with those of another role. Etzioni points out that the institutional head of a professional organization is subject to this type of conflict.[30] Professional organizations are organizations whose major goal is to institutionalize knowledge and sustain its creation. Under this heading Etzioni includes such organiza-

---

[29] Edwin H. Sutherland, "White Collar Criminality" in Gilbert Geis, ed., *White Collar Criminal* (New York: Atherton Press, 1968), p. 42.

[30] Amitai Etzioni, *Modern Organizations* (Englewood Cliffs, N.J.: Prentice-Hall, 1964), p. 82.

tions as research centers, schools, universities, and hospitals. When an individual is at the head of such an organization he has two basic roles: expert and administrator. He must fill the role of expert so that the major goals of the organization will be kept in the forefront and so he can be responsive to the needs of the professionals in his organization. On the other hand, he must also be an administrator because "Organizations have to obtain funds to finance their activities, recruit personnel to staff the various functions, and allocate the funds and personnel which have been recruited."[31] If he underemphasizes his administrative role the institutional head "may endanger the integration of the professional organization by overemphasizing the major goal activity, neglecting secondary functions, and lacking skill in human relations."[32] If the institutional head overemphasizes his administrative role, he will alienate the professionals and tend to lose sight of the major goals of the organization.

Prison supervisors. The supervisor of a prison is also particularly subject to inter-role conflict. He is at the top of the hierarchy and has two major roles to fulfill; one is that of chief custodian, with the expectation that he focus on "maintaining discipline and control over inmates."[33] His other major role requires him to focus on treatment and rehabilitation of prisoners. Historically, the custodial goal came first, with the treatment role coming to the fore more recently. Built into these two roles is an inherent conflict. As Grusky, in his study of prison officials, comments:

If he stressed discipline by establishing new restrictive rules and hence curtailing the inmate's freedom, he would be seen as decreasing the probability of achieving the quasi-milieu treatment goal, since such a policy would serve to increase inmate resentment toward the officials. On the other hand, if he was overly permissive in his policies, discipline and control would break down and he would not be able to sustain the custodial goal.[34]

The supervisor's problems were exacerbated by division between his subordinates in their emphasis on the two goals. Some were oriented toward the custodial function and others were more concerned with treatment, while the supervisor was faced with the problem of maintaining a cohesive staff.

Elected public officials. The elected public official is also confronted with inter-role conflict. Mitchell uses Parson's pattern variables to illustrate the politician's inter-role conflict.[35] Two of the conflicting roles the politician is expected to fill are administrator and partisan. Mitchell contends that the

---

[31] Ibid., p. 82.
[32] Ibid.
[33] Oscar Grusky, "Role Conflict in Organizations: A Study of Prison Camp Officials," *Administrative Science Quarterly* 3 (1959), 456.
[34] Ibid.
[35] Mitchell, *"Occupational Role Strains,"* p. 214.

conflicts between these two roles "are contrary at every relevant choice point."[36] As an administrator the politician is expected to be affectively neutral, but as a partisan he is supposed to be affectively involved with his constituents. His role as an administrator is functionally specific, while his role as partisan is diffuse. In making decisions the administrator is supposed to utilize universalistic criteria, while the partisan is supposed to use particularistic orientations. As an administrator the elected politician is expected to be oriented toward achievement, while the partisan is expected to be oriented toward ascription. Finally, as an administrator the elected public official is expected to be oriented to the public, while as a partisan he is supposed to be more self-oriented.

The plight of the politician is complicated by the fact that he has two other roles attached to his position: executive and judicial. With the addition of these two roles we get a more complex picture of the inter-role conflicts endemic to the position of politician. Table 3-1 shows a cross-classification of the politician's four roles with Parsons' five pattern variables: Reading down the five columns we get a good idea of the number and variety of the politician's inter-role conflicts. For example, on specificity versus diffuseness, the administrative and judicial roles conflict with the executive and partisan roles. Mitchell contends that the offices with the greatest number of roles are likely to have the greatest inter-role conflict. Executive political positions such as Mayor, Governor, and President have more roles and, therefore, more inter-role conflict than legislative or judicial positions. Another important variable is the heterogeneity of the constituency. If the constituency is highly heterogeneous the politician is likely to have more roles to fill and therefore a greater likelihood of inter-role conflict.

TABLE 3-1

The Pattern Variables and Role Conflict of Elected Public Officials

Role	1	2	3	4	5
Administrative	Specific	Affective-Neutrality	Universalistic	Collectivity Orientation	Achievement
Executive	Diffuse	Affective-Neutrality	Universalistic	Collectivity	Achievement
Partisan	Diffuse	Affective	Particularistic	Self-oriented	Ascription
Judicial	Specific	Affective-Neutrality	Universalistic	Collectivity	Ascription

William C. Mitchell, "Occupational Role Strains: The American Elective Public Official," *Administrative Science Quarterly* 3 (1955), 216.

[36] Ibid., p. 215.

Inter-position conflict

Before discussing the final type of role conflict developed by Kahn et al., it is necessary to point out an area of conceptual confusion in their typology. Kahn and his colleagues define inter-role conflict as a situation in which the "role pressures associated with membership in one organization are in conflict with pressures stemming from membership in other groups."[37] However, what they are describing is a conflict between positions, not a conflict between roles. There is, therefore, another type of conflict to add to the five developed by Kahn and his colleagues—inter-position conflict. A typical inter-position conflict for those in high-status occupations is between their occupational and family positions. In fulfilling the demands of the occupation many individuals find that they cannot adequately handle their familial responsibilities. In their study of union business agents Rosen and Rosen found that the demands of the job resulted in "considerable psychological, as well as physical, isolation from family and friends. . . ."[38] Gross, Mason, and McEachern also discuss this inter-position conflict for the school superintendent:

Over 90 percent of the superintendents in discussing the impact of their jobs on their families reported that their wives were concerned about the infinitesimal amount of time they were able to spend with their families. Some of the wives, however, apparently recognized that the superintendency demands large family sacrifices and reluctantly accepted this unfortunate but "irremediable" state of affairs. Others were quite insistent that their husbands stay home most evenings. Many superintendents also said that their children expect them to be at home "like other fathers."[39]

Intra-sender conflict

The final form of role conflict is intra-sender, or conflicting expectations from one significant other. There are few examples of this type of conflict in the literature on occupational sociology, but it is not uncommon in occupational life. Let us use the example of personnel executives to illustrate this type of conflict. Within any unionized organization there is a personnel officer who is in charge of relations with the union. Although he is a manager, he is subordinate to the personnel manager who has broad responsibility for all the personnel functions. The personnel manager frequently has contradictory expectations of the labor relations manager. He expects him to maintain harmonious relations with the union, but also expects him not to "sell out" to it. That is, he expects him to be tough on the handling of grievances and in contract negotiations. These dual expectations are laden with conflict for the

[37] Kahn et al., *Organizational Stress*, p. 20.
[38] Rosen and Rosen, "Personality Variables and Role," p. 132.
[39] Gross et al., *Studies of the School Superintendency*, p. 263.

labor relations manager. If he is too soft with the union, the union will win too many grievances and get too good a contract. On the other hand, if he is too hard on the union, it will upset union-management harmony and possibly lead to lengthy and costly strikes or slowdowns. Thus the labor relations manager must attempt to balance these conflicting expectations. Although there is little empirical evidence, this type of conflict would seem to be endemic in all occupations at the managerial and official level.

Role ambiguity

Finally, although it is not actually role conflict, some mention must be made of role ambiguity. Mitchell discusses role ambiguity in his analysis of the elected politician: "Instead of being pulled in opposite directions by well known forces, the elected official is often in the position of a lost hunter seeking direction."[40] This ambiguity applies to both the politician's administrative and partisan roles. In his administrative role the ambiguity stems from inadequate knowledge of means he may utilize in the attainment of goals. The ambiguity surrounding the partisan role concerns a difficulty in discovering what are the goals of the community. These types of ambiguity would also seem to occur in all managerial and official positions. The job of business executive is another example of an occupation at this level which is plagued by role ambiguity. Much of the ambiguity the executive finds stems from inadequate communication from below. Many studies have shown that for a variety of reasons subordinates restrict information flow up through the organization's hierarchy. In his classic study of government agencies, Blau found that subordinates were unwilling to ask superiors questions,[41] for in asking the question the subordinate was confessing his ignorance to the man who evaluated him. To circumvent this, subordinates with problems would consult with more knowledgeable peers in other departments. The questioning subordinate thus became indebted, in exchange-theory terms, to his more knowledgeable peers, but deemed this indebtedness preferable to letting a superior know about his ignorance. This example is not unusual and presents a problem for managers and officials in virtually every organization. One of the thrusts of the Human Relations School was to attempt to ease this problem by emphasizing two-way communication in organizations. However, the Human Relations School overlooked the fact that the interests of subordinates were frequently not compatible with the interests of superiors. Because of this incompatibility, subordinates will almost always attempt to restrict communication to superiors, and therefore superiors must always make some decisions in the face of ambiguity. This is complicated by the fact that other groups in the organization also find it to

[40] Mitchell, "Occupational Role Strains," p. 218.
[41] Peter M. Blau, *The Dynamics of Bureaucracy*, 2nd ed. (Chicago: University of Chicago Press, 1963).

their benefit to restrict information flow. In Simon's view this is one of the reasons managers can never optimize, but must almost always be restricted to satisfactory types of decisions.[42]

2. Managers and officials employ a variety of means to resolve the role conflict endemic in their positions.

Literature on the theory of role conflict resolution

The literature on the resolution of role conflict comes from two sources. One is the theoretical literature on role-conflict resolution, which has focused on the theoretical question, rather than descriptive material on how individuals in particular occupations resolve role conflict. The other source is this mass of descriptive studies, which contain a great deal of information on role conflict resolution. The goal here is to summarize the theory of role conflict resolution and then show how the material from the descriptive studies can be fitted into the theoretical framework.

The theory of role conflict resolution developed by Gross, Mason, and McEachern offers a major conceptual base for the study of occupations. The Gross group hypothesized that there were four basic devices for resolving role conflict:

1. Conform to expectation A.
2. Conform to expectation B.
3. Perform some compromise behavior which represents an attempt to conform in part to both expectations.
4. Attempt to avoid conforming to either of the expectations.[43]

Based on these hypotheses, the authors went on to develop a "theory" of role conflict resolution. Their goal was to be able to predict which of the means an individual would adopt. With information on three factors, they believed that they would be able to predict modes of role conflict resolution. The first factor is legitimacy, or the right others have to expect the focal role to behave in conformity with their expectations. Using only the legitimacy dimension the following predictions are made: a) where expectations A and B are both perceived as legitimate, they predict some sort of compromise behavior; b) when expectation A is perceived as legitimate and expectation B is perceived as illegitimate, they predict conformity to A; c) when expectation A is perceived as illegitimate and expectation B as legitimate, they predict conformity to expectation B; d) where both expectations A and B are perceived as illegitimate, they predict some sort of avoidance behavior.

However, there is more than one factor involved, and this complicates

---

[42] Herbert Simon, *Administrative Behavior,* 2nd ed. (New York: Free Press, 1957).
[43] Gross et al., *Studies of the School Superintendency,* p. 284.

the authors' power to make predictions. The second factor is the ability of the significant others to sanction the focal role for nonconformity to their expectations. Considering sanctioning ability alone, the authors predict: a) compromise behavior where both A and B have strong negative sanctions; b) conformity to A when A has strong negative sanctions and B does not; c) conformity to B when A has weak negative sanctions and B has strong negative sanctions; d) Gross et al. are unable to make any prediction where both significant others have weak negative sanctions.[44]

When the Gross group tried to look at both factors together, they found that they were unable to make predictions in a number of situations, specifically when "the legitimacy and sanctions elements predisposed him [the focal role] to undertake different behaviors."[45] What was needed was some knowledge of what predisposes an individual to give primacy to one factor over the other. They posited three distinct orientations individuals have to role conflict situations. The first is a moral orientation, where the individual tends to emphasize legitimacy and minimize sanctioning ability. The second is the expedient orientation, in which the actor gives primacy to sanctioning ability over legitimacy. The third is the moral-expedient, where the individual sees a net balance between sanctioning ability and legitimacy. In order to ascertain which of the three types each respondent belonged to, the authors constructed a series of questions which they felt differentiated the three types.

On the basis of the ratings of the significant others on legitimacy and sanctioning ability, and knowledge of the individual's orientation, Gross et al were able to predict 264 of the 291 role conflict resolutions correctly (91 percent).

The impressive results of this study led to a series of follow-up studies. Miller and Shull (1962) modified the approach used by Gross et al.[46] Legitimacy, in this study, was defined as the right significant others have to expect the focal role to conform to their expectations. Sanctions were defined as penalties perceived as a consequence of following either of the conflicting role expectations. Miller and Shull decided to use just these two variables and not use the individual's orientation; they felt that they could do as good a job predicting with two variables as Gross and his associates had done with three. In addition, they felt that there was no stable personality trait which determined how a person would resolve role conflict. Rather they felt that one's orientation would shift with the situation.

Miller and Shull's basic research hypothesis was "the decisions of a position incumbent when confronted with role conflicts can be predicted with a high degree of accuracy if the incumbent's perceptions of legitimacy

44 Ibid., p. 287.
45 Ibid., p. 289.
46 Delbert Miller and Fremont Shull, "The Prediction of Administrative Role Conflict Resolutions," *Administrative Science Quarterly* 7 (1962), 143–160.

and sanctions are given."[47] Overall, the authors found that they were able to correctly predict role conflict resolution 71 percent of the time.

Ehrlich, Rinehart, and Howell (1962) compare the results of three of their studies of role conflict with the findings of Gross and associates and Miller and Shull.[48] In their interviews the authors probed for situations in which there were conflicting expectations. When such situations were located, they sought to determine the legitimacy and "obligatoriness" of the expectations, and how the respondent resolved the conflict.

After their discussion the authors present an alternative method of predicting role conflict resolution. They observe that, rather than knowing about such factors as legitimacy and "obligatoriness," it might be more helpful to know which audiences are more important to the focal role than others. They conclude: "it seems likely too that an actor will be more likely to conform to what he perceives to be the expectations of an audience of his 'significant others' than to the expectations of any other audience group."[49] They find, in testing this notion, that they can predict as well from knowing this information as they can from knowing about "legitimacy, sanctions, or even personal preference."[50] They conclude that use of these variables might not be the most parsimonious way of predicting role conflict resolution.

Despite the caveats of the Ehrlich research, Magid (1967) proceeded to use legitimacy and what he calls "obligation" in studying role conflict resolution of local officials in northern Nigeria.[51] Magid's procedure was similar to preceding approaches. On the basis of interviews, participant observation, and documents, five cases were developed. The subjects of the study were 71 district councilors and local officials in Idoma division, northern region of the Federal Republic of Nigeria. Each of the five cases was described to each of the focal roles. "It is hypothesized that the Idoma district councilor who perceives a role conflict situation will fulfill the role which he evaluates as more legitimate and/or more obligatory."[52] Magid found that by using this method he was able to predict whether an individual will go along with one expectation or the other. However, he cannot predict such actions as compromise, withdrawal, or an independent stand. He admits "a more comprehensive model is needed for predictions from equal legitimacy and/or obligation to such behavior as withdrawal or compromise."[53]

Finally, it is necessary to summarize the relevant findings of a study of

[47] Ibid., pp. 85–86.
[48] H. Ehrlich, J. Rinehart, and J. Howell, "The Study of Role Conflict: Explorations in Methodology," Sociometry 25 (1962), 85–97.
[49] Ibid., p. 95.
[50] Ibid., p. 96.
[51] Alvin Magid, "Dimensions of Administrative Role and Conflict Resolution Among Local Officials in Northern Nigeria," Administrative Science Quarterly 12 (1967), 321–338.
[52] Ibid., p. 331.
[53] Ibid., p. 335.

personnel managers conducted by the author with Harrison M. Trice, which designed to expand on the theory of role conflict resolution developed by Gross, Mason, and McEachern.[54] The major finding of this study was that independent action is a fifth alternative available in the resolution of role conflict. Independent action was operationally defined as listening to both significant others in an inter-sender role conflict, but then making one's own decision. Surprisingly, independent action proved to be not only a viable alternative, but the most frequently chosen of the five modes of resolving role conflict. As a matter of fact, in 11 of the 12 situations employed in the study independent action was chosen significantly more often than the next most frequently chosen alternative.

This brief review of the literature on the theory of role conflict resolution leaves us with two important tools for analyzing the resolution of role conflict by managers and officials. First, the theory has given us five types of actions one may employ in resolving role conflict. In analyzing particular actions by managers and officials we can ascertain whether they fit into one of the modes of resolving role conflict. Second, the literature has indicated a number of variables which can help us explain why an individual in an occupation chooses a particular resolution. Many of the variables discussed in the preceding pages really relate to the power of significant others. Using some general measure of the power of significant others we can hypothesize the following about role conflict resolution:

1. If significant other A has more power than significant other B, the focal role will resolve the conflict by conforming to expectation A.
2. If significant other B has more power than significant other A, the focal role will resolve the conflict by conforming to expectation B.
3. If both significant others have a great deal of power, the focal role will seek to compromise or withdraw.
4. If both significant others have little power, the focal role will take independent action.

These hypotheses have received some empirical support in the Ritzer and Trice study of personnel managers. The theory of role conflict resolution gives us the types of actions an individual may take in resolving role conflict, and provides an explanation of why a particular action is taken. One of the problems, for our purposes, with this explanation is that it focuses on the social-psychological level. It helps explain why an individual chooses a particular resolution, but fails to explain why a mode of resolution is chosen by the occupation as a whole. For example, later in this chapter there is a discussion of the way in which the Navy disbursing officer resolves the conflict between regulations and orders from the top. Most, if not all, such officers

---

[54] George Ritzer and Harrison M. Trice, *An Occupation in Conflict: A Study of the Personnel Manager* (Ithaca: Cornell University, 1969), pp. 46–57.

resolve the conflict between regulations and orders from the top in the direction of orders from above. In part this is due to the power of superiors, but it has also become a norm within the occupation. Thus at the occupational level the resolution of role conflict is determined by a combination of the power of the significant others and norms within the occupation. In all, the preceding discussion enables us to understand better the means employed in managerial and official occupations for resolving role conflict.

Studies in role conflict resolution

School superintendents. The school superintendents studied by Gross et al. employed each of these resolutions, although differentially across the four cases. The hiring situation was seen as a conflict between basing hiring decisions on merit or giving preferential treatment to some individuals. Eighty-five percent of the superintendents resolved this conflict in the direction of a decision based on merit rather than on the basis of personal preference, while 10 percent resolved it in the other direction, allowing the preferences of some significant others to determine their decisions. The remaining 5 percent chose to attempt to compromise between the merit and preferential expectations of significant others. The time-allocation situation was seen as an inter-role conflict. In terms of how they spent their time the superintendents were torn between their work role and their family role. Sixty-six percent of those superintendents who perceived a conflict on this issue resolved it in favor of their work role. One who did so explained his decision in this way: "The school board and the PTA," he said, "would get sore if I didn't, and I'd worry too. I don't think I'd be able to do a good job as superintendent of schools if I didn't."[55] Only 8 percent of the superintendents resolved this conflict by giving greater priority to the demands of their family; the remaining 26 percent compromised. "One superintendent used the device of showing up just frequently enough at important meetings in the community to avoid the charge of not being interested in school and community affairs."[56]

The question of teacher salary increases was the third situation discussed by Gross, Mason, and McEachern. Of those who perceived role conflict in this situation, 64 percent conformed to the expectation of giving the highest possible salary increase, while 9 percent conformed to the expectation that they give the lowest possible salary increase. This situation was seen, therefore, as involving inter-sender role conflict. Of the remaining superintendents, 21 percent sought to compromise by satisfying both demands to some degree, while 6 percent withdrew from the situation. One of those who withdrew placed the problem in the hands of the school committee stating that "it's a hot potato so I let the school committee handle it. The

---

[55] Gross et al., *Studies of the School Superintendency,* p. 266.
[56] Ibid., p. 267.

teachers feel I should represent them; I'd hang myself by getting involved. But I go along with the school committee recommendation 100 percent, whatever they decide."[57] Of the compromisers, some acted as intermediaries while others acted as salesmen. As has been pointed out before, Gross et al. ignore the possibility of independent action. However, 13 of those who were classified as compromisers were in reality independent actors. Three of these compromisers are described as follows: "when exposed to the salary dilemma [they] rejected both sets of expectations and substituted a new criterion in making their recommendations. . . . One of the superintendents recommended that the salary increases be contingent on a cost of living index."[58] The other 10 superintendents, whom we would classify as independent actors, "resolve[d] the salary dilemma by trying to modify the expectations of one group so that they more nearly approximate[d] the expectations of those with whom they had initially agreed."[59] The actions of these 13 superintendents are qualitatively different from the actions of those who compromised. They were being innovative in their approach, rather than merely seeking a middle-ground position.

The fourth situation which confronted the superintendents involved the budget. This too was a case of inter-sender role conflict, with 69 percent of the superintendents conforming to the expectations of those who emphasized educational needs and 3 percent going along with those who stressed the financial resources of the community. In addition, 27 percent sought to compromise, while only 1 percent withdrew in the face of this conflict.

Personnel managers. The Ritzer and Trice study of personnel managers was designed as a test of the theory of role conflict resolution developed by Gross and his associates. Two cases drawn from pretest interviews were designed to expose the respondents to inter-sender role conflict. The first case involved a storm which forced a number of employees to miss work and lose pay. The respondent was then given six situations based on this case in which he was asked to make a decision in the face of incompatible expectations from significant others in his organization. The six situations based on case one were:

1. The man immediately above you in the personnel department is in favor of paying for the time lost, but the top company official at your location is opposed.
2. The manager of the accounting department is in favor of paying for the time lost, but the man immediately above you in the personnel department is opposed.

[57] Ibid., p. 271.
[58] Ibid.
[59] Ibid., p. 272.

3. The top company official at your location is in favor of paying for the time lost, but the manager of the accounting department is opposed.
4. The manager of the accounting department is in favor of paying for the time lost, but your immediate subordinate whose knowledge would be relevant to the situation is opposed.
5. Your immediate subordinate is in favor of paying for the time lost, but the top company official at your location is opposed.
6. Your immediate subordinate is in favor of paying for the time lost, but the man immediately above you in the personnel department is opposed.

After each of these situations the respondents were given the following choices of action:

1. Recommend pay for the time lost (operationalization of conform to expectation A of Gross et al.).
2. Do not recommend pay for the time lost (conform to expectation B).
3. Talk to the two parties and attempt to resolve their differences (compromise).
4. Listen to both, but make your own recommendation (independent action).
5. Hold your recommendation in abeyance (withdraw).

A second case was also employed in which the personnel manager had to decide what to do about some changes recommended by an outside consultant, including changes in the personnel function. The same six situations were employed, although this time the significant others made recommendations concerning action on the consultant's suggestions. The only changes in the choices of action open to the personnel manager after each situation were that the conform to expectations A alternative read "Recommend the changes," and the conform to expectation B alternative read "Do not recommend the changes."

Table 3-2 summarizes the findings for the two cases:

TABLE 3-2

*Comparison of Resolutions of Two Role Conflict Cases
for Personnel Managers*

	% in Case I	% in Case II
Behavioral Alternatives		
Conform to Expectation A	15	11
Conform to Expectation B	10	9
Compromise	24	17
Independent action	50	62
Withdraw	1	1
	100	100

There are some rather striking findings here in terms of the theory of role conflict resolution and the way individuals in managerial and official occupations resolve the role conflict inherent in their occupations. The major finding, as pointed out previously, is that independent action is a viable means of resolving role conflict. As a matter of fact, for the personnel managers in the Ritzer and Trice study it was by far the dominant choice. If individuals in such a traditionally passive occupation choose independent action in resolving role conflict, then individuals in higher-status official and managerial positions are even more likely to be independent decision makers.

The findings on independent action in role conflict situations are also interesting because they reveal an entirely different means of resolving conflict in occupational life, adherence to a mythical occupational image. Publicly, personnel managers deny that they ever make decisions. A recent article on personnel managers describes them as "glorified clerks . . . they have no backbone and always find some way to accommodate the wishes of the strongest forces acting on them . . . the personnel officer is traditionally nonactivist, not a positive force . . . he isn't sufficiently assertive."[60] This theme of passivity is repeated over and over in the literature describing personnel managers and mentioned by practicing managers when asked about their role in the organization. Nevertheless, such observers as William Foote Whyte have noted that in reality personnel managers play a dynamic and assertive role within organizations. Whyte reports: "engineers in particular, but also personnel men and some other specialists, are expected to be innovators, to get operating people to adopt new products, machines, processes, and systems of doing work or organizing relations among men."[61] Whyte again:

The personnel man calls himself an advisor to line management on its human problems, but in most cases little time is spent upon such consultation. . . . Now he is beginning to be called on before the crises so that he has an opportunity to apply some preventive social medicine. This represents a sharp departure from past practice. It involves redefining of the personnel man's role in management, rising above the comfortable security of present strategies and procedures and learning new skills of social diagnosis, consultation, and action.[62]

The question is, Why do personnel men contend that they are merely passive advisors when they do make decisions? The answer is that they are preventing role conflict by adhering to a mythical occupational image. If

[60] O. Glenn Stahl, "Tomorrow's Generation of Personnel Managers" (Paper presented at the Public Personnel Association, International Conference, Victoria, B.C., October, 1967).
[61] William F. Whyte, Men at Work (Homewood, Ill.: Dorsey Press and Richard D. Irwin, 1961), p. 561.
[62] William F. Whyte, "The Impact of the Union on the Management Organization," in Conrad Arensburg et al., eds., Research in Industrial Human Relations: A Critical Appraisal (New York: Harper & Brothers, 1957), pp. 171–181.

they were to state they were decision makers, relations with line managers would be severely strained. Part of the ideology of line managers is that they make all the critical decisions in the organization, whereas in fact staff officers such as the personnel manager are making an increasing number of decisions for them. This reality is handled by both parties through adherence to mythical occupational images: the line manager believes he makes all the decisions and the staff manager believes he is merely an advisor. To support these myths interesting behavior patterns have emerged. Let us take, as an example, the hiring of blue-collar workers. The personnel man receives an order to hire so many blue-collar workers for the following week. He interviews some applicants and decides which to hire. He then brings those he has already chosen to the line manager for a decision. However, the decision has already been made by the personnel man. The line manager perfunctorily looks the applicants over and "decides" to hire the men the personnel man has already hired. By acting out this charade both parties can continue to believe in their mythical occupational images. If the personnel man did not continue this charade, the line manager could not accept the fact that personnel was making decisions for him. Should the personnel man make it clear to the line manager that he makes the decisions, the line manager would declare war on the personnel department. To forestall this conflict, personnel men are content to accept their passive image and are prepared to fight anything which threatens this image.

Controllers. The controller, like the personnel manager, is a staff officer, and as a staff officer is also supposed to be an advisor rather than a decision maker. However, because he controls monetary matters, the controller is generally a more powerful figure than the personnel manager. Nevertheless, his authority is supposed to be very limited. A recent study by Henning and Moseley indicates that this view of the controller, like the view of the personnel manager, is largely mythical.[63] They interviewed the controller, his superior, and a peer executive in 25 medium-sized firms. It was found that the controller had a great deal of authority on some matters and much less on others. He had much authority in making government reports and internal auditing and comparatively little in budgeting and making accounting reports. Thus like personnel managers, controllers do have a great deal of authority, at least in some areas. More important, there is a difference between controllers' perceptions of their own authority and the perceptions of superiors and peers. "These data suggest that controllers generally perceive themselves as having more authority than either their superiors or peers perceive them to have."[64] This, as was pointed out above, is also true of personnel managers. When dealing with others within their organization

[63] Dale A. Henning and Roger L. Moseley, "Authority Role of a Functional Manager: The Controller," *Administrative Science Quarterly* 15 (1970), 482–489.
[64] Ibid., p. 487.

staff officers downplay their authority, but that authority is clear to the staff officer although he prefers to keep the knowledge to himself.

Staff-line conflict. The preceding discussion has touched on one of the most typical conflicts in industry, staff-line conflict, which is basically a form of person-role conflict. Line managers tend to object to the expectations of staff officials. As Dalton points out, staff personnel are really specialists in change and reorganization. In contrast, line people are "sworn to stable technology" and "see changes as interfering with production."[65] The staff's orientation toward change is a direct threat to the line manager. By the same token, the conservatism of the line is threatening to the staff. Here is a case in which both parties are subjected to person-role conflict. Let us focus first on what the line manager can do to resolve this conflict. For one thing, he can reject staff proposals outright. In doing this he is rejecting the expectations of the staff in favor of his own view of the situation. When outright rejection is employed, it threatens the already precarious relations between line and staff. In order to maintain this delicate balance, line managers are more likely to compromise in the face of this conflict. The major form which compromise takes is formal acceptance of staff suggestions followed by informal rejection. Thus rules promulgated by the staff are accepted, but informal evasion of them is approved by line managers.

In Dalton's study, as well as in industry in general, staff officers quickly learn that power in the organization rests in the line. As Dalton points out, in a very real sense "the line *is* the firm."[66] The staff officer must learn to accommodate himself to this reality of organizational life. One means, discussed above, is to make decisions, but act as if the staff is merely an advisor. Another is to discover who the powerful figures in the informal organization of the line are, and attempt to learn what ideas they will welcome that will not offend his staff superiors. The staff officer learns what proposals both line managers and staff managers will accept. In Simon's terms, he no longer seeks to maximize, but instead seeks positions which will satisfy virtually everyone concerned. This effort at compromise is very difficult for many staff managers, and is one of the reasons for their high turnover rate (withdrawal). A related reason for this high turnover is that in always seeking to compromise, the staff officer finds it difficult to utilize his unique training and ability. Another withdrawal technique employed by the staff officer is transfer to line management. In doing this he recognizes the inherent conflicts in his position as well as the fact that the line organization is the only route to the top of the organization, for few staff officers ever make it to the top in American industry. A final resolution attempted by staff managers may be included under the general heading of independent action. Instead of withdrawing or accommodating himself to the line, the staff officer shifts his focus to his

[65] Melville Dalton, *Men Who Manage* (New York: John Wiley, 1959), p. 75.
[66] Ibid., p. 99.

own department. If he cannot gain status within the organization he will turn to gaining status within his own department, often by becoming expansionist and concentrating on gaining more departmental personnel and privileges. By getting some gratification in this way the staff officer compensates for some of his problems with the line.

Prison camp officials. The prison camp supervisor is confronted with a conflict between custodial and treatment orientations. Grusky contends that the prison camp supervisor's typical resolution is to take a position of administrative neutrality in terms of these conflicting goals. This is exemplified by the statement of one supervisor: "Another thing I found out is that you *can* be custodially-minded as well as treatment-minded. You don't have to be one or the other."[67] This neutrality tended to enhance the supervisor's position within the camp. Both the treatment-oriented and custodial-oriented factions were forced to work through him if they wanted to extend their influence throughout the organization. The prison camp official is, therefore, typically a compromise in the face of the role conflict inherent in his position.

Elected public officials. Mitchell[68] has noted that politicians tend to withdraw in the face of inter-role conflict. When in this situation the politician typically takes a "no comment" position, at least until the situation becomes clearer in terms of expectations and alternative actions.

Navy disbursing officers. In the person-role conflict faced by the Navy disbursing officer, he is generally not able to take a compromise position. When confronted with a clash between rules and the orders from above, the disbursing officer tends to resolve the conflict by obeying the order. He does so because of the sanctions superiors may impose on him if he fails to follow their orders. Further, in following orders from the top, he knows he cannot be held responsible for violating a rule. The Navy has recognized the inherent dilemma of the disbursing officer and provided him with two possibilities for withdrawing from the conflict. He can point out the discrepancy between orders and rules to his superiors and, if no understanding is reached, he can bring the problem to the attention of the Bureau of Supplies and Accounts for a decision. Or, he can bring the conflict to the attention of the commanding officer, "who may order the disbursing officer to make the expenditure 'under protest,' the commanding officer thereby assuming full financial liability."[69] However, these two withdrawal possibilities are infrequently utilized. Rather, the disbursing officer finds a variety of ways to get around the formal rules and fulfills orders in a variety of informal ways.

There are many other studies of occupations which describe specific modes of resolving role conflict. The basic point is that wherever there is a role conflict in occupational life, individuals seek in a variety of ways to re-

---

[67] Grusky, "Role Conflict in Organizations," p. 458.
[68] Mitchell, "Occupational Role Strains."
[69] Turner, "Navy Disbursing Officer," p. 345.

solve the problem of incompatible expectations. All of these idiosyncratic resolutions can be categorized as conformity to expectation A, conformity to expectation B, compromise, independent action, or withdrawal. Rather than a discussion of these studies, the focus in the remainder of this section will be on the author's study of a local union president. In resolving his conflicts the union president utilizes many of the elements of Goffman's dramaturgical approach to social interaction.[70] He is able, through dramaturgical manipulation, to take independent action.

Local union presidents. In general, the local union president manages to resolve the conflicts inherent in his position by managing the impressions he makes in various conflict-laden situations. Goffman contends that when what an individual ought to be (his virtual social identity) varies from what he actually is (his actual social identity), he is stigmatized. (Goffman feels that stigmatized individuals are not necessarily those with physical deformities. Normal individuals with a half-hidden failing have a gap between their virtual and actual social identity and are, therefore, stigmatized.) Much of the gap between the local president's virtual and actual social identity is caused by the demands made on him by conflicting groups. (Goffman differentiates two types of stigmatized individuals. The discredited individual is one who assumes his differentness is either known or immediately perceivable; the discreditable individual assumes that his differentness is neither known nor immediately perceivable.)[71] In some cases the local union president is discredited, while in others he is discreditable.

As discussed earlier, the workers of the local studied enjoy their card playing during inclement weather and did not wish to lose this time off. The local president, however, accepted the demands of the System Council and decided that these periods could be usefully employed to train the men in new job techniques. The workers were unaware of the union's attempt to interfere with their card games; if they had known there would have been a tremendous uproar. The local president's position on this issue would have stigmatized him in the members' eyes if they had known his stand. His virtual social identity was to represent the desires of the members while his actual social identity, in this case, was opposed to the desires of the members. He was discreditable, not discredited, since his differentness was unknown to the members. The major issue is, How did the local president maintain this position? For the discreditable individual the major problem is managing information. Here Goffman's concepts of front and back behavior are useful. Goffman defines the front as part of the performance which generally functions in a general and fixed fashion to define the situation for those who observe the performance. The back region is where suppressed facts make their

[70] Erving Goffman, *The Presentation of Self in Everyday Life* (Garden City, N.Y.: Anchor Books, 1959).
[71] Erving Goffman, *Stigma* (Englewood Cliffs, N.J.: Prentice-Hall, 1963).

appearance. Generally no member of the audience of the front region will intrude in the back. The local president exhibited his stigmatized behavior (his support of the effort to train the workers in inclement weather) only in the back region, which in this case was the System Council meetings. In the front region, the local meeting, he de-emphasized his goal—he kept it a "dark secret." To make sure his desire remained a secret he had to take several precautions: one was to make sure that his two audiences remained separate. He also took care that no members of the front region normally appeared in the back region. A tradition helped to accomplish this—no members of the local other than the local presidents, the chairman of the clerical unit, and the System Council officials could attend System Council meetings, except in emergencies. When a member of the back region entered the front (as he might have when an individual had a particular grievance he wanted to present to the System Council), Goffman tells us that there were two methods of handling the situation: a) The audience (the System Council in this case) colluded with the performer (the local president) to keep the information from the intruder. b) They welcomed the intruder as someone who should have been there all the time, thereby making him privy to the secret and a new member of the group. Thus by skillfully manipulating his front and back regions the local president was able to continue to push for training in inclement weather without the knowledge of the local members.

Another interesting conflict existed between the local president and the members. As previously mentioned, the company had introduced new techniques which had made the work much more dangerous. Although they realized the additional safety hazards, some workers sought higher pay rather than safer working conditions. The local president, however, stressed safer conditions rather than higher pay. In this situation he was discredited, not discreditable, since his differentness was known to his audience. Therefore, his problem here was not one of managing information. He had to devise means of controlling tension since this is the central problem for a discredited individual. The local president used two basic methods of handling this tension. One was through a series of in-group alliances: he allied himself with the other union officials who supported his view that safety is more important than monetary gain. In so doing they tended to reinforce their own position and were better able to handle the tension produced by the difference of opinion. The other method was a series of out-group alliances. Here the local president identified himself with management. The company was opposed to higher pay for this more dangerous work, and preferred more stringent safety rules, which were more important to them as well as being much less expensive. The company in general had a sincere interest in improving safety conditions. The president's identification with the management view further reduced his tension.

Let us now turn to a conflict between the local president and another officer of the local. The chairman of the Executive Board proved to be a difficult problem for the local president. Since this chairman is elected and the Executive Board is empowered to overrule the local president, the chairman has the power to cause great difficulty for the local president. The basic conflict was caused by the chairman's desire to move on to a management position—because of this he was reluctant to pursue any policy which jeopardized his chances. The local president was much more anxious to push local demands even if they conflicted with management's position. Thus the two came into direct conflict over this issue. Goffman's ideas about a team are helpful here in understanding the actions the local president took to try to solve this problem. Goffman defines a team as any set of individuals who cooperate in staging a single routine (the running of the local, in this case, by the president and chairman). The relationship between the team members is characterized by a) reliance of each upon the other since each is capable of disrupting the performance; b) familiarity of each with the fact that the other is putting on an act.

In any team someone is the director and controls the progress of the dramatic action. The director, in this case, was the local president. The director has two basic duties, to a) bring dissidents into line and b) allocate parts. By using these two procedures the local president attempted to bring the chairman of the Executive Board into line. One device was to isolate the chairman from the membership, underemphasizing his role and reducing his importance as well as the importance of the Executive Board. However, the chairman remained a thorn in the side of the local president as well as a bottleneck to local activity. To alleviate this situation, the local president tried to talk down the chairman's accomplishments and attempted to find a candidate to oppose him in the next election.

The local president was supposed to be deeply involved in the local's activities. One of his major duties was conducting the local meeting. Although these were poorly attended, those who did attend expected the president to be very concerned with the proceedings, well prepared, and to take charge of the meeting. However, because the meetings were dull and routine, the president was hard-pressed to be deeply involved. This is the type of situation which Goffman defines as "tight": that is, the local president could not act uninterested. Bored by the meetings, but yet required to appear involved, he resolved the problem by engaging in three types of behavior (described by Goffman). One is what Goffman calls subordinate involvement, which occurs when the individual is not in a dominant involvement. (The dominant involvement is one which the individual is required to recognize.) In this case the dominant involvement was the local meeting. Some subordinate involvements used by the local president to relieve the boredom were social meetings, honorary banquets, or pizza parties following the local meeting. Another method of relieving the discomfort is the use of side involvements, which Goffman defines as those the individual can carry out while carrying on the main involvement. By structuring the meeting the local president could become involved in issues which interested him, although they might have been extraneous to the business at hand. Besides side and subordinate involvements the president used a third device for easing his boredom, one which Goffman calls "role distance." (Role distance is defined as an expression of a separateness of the individual from his role.)[72] Goffman feels that role distance gives us a sociological understanding of the gap between role obligations and actual role performance. By displaying the fact that he was better than his role of local president, the president was able to ease the difficulty caused by acting out a role he disliked. The local president displayed role distance in a number of ways: one was the lackadaisical manner in which he performed his duties at the meeting, acting as if conducting the meeting was no challenge. Another was his continual allusions during the meetings to his desire to get "this petty business" over as quickly as possible.

The rank and file expected the president to vigorously pursue all of their grievances. However, the importance of these problems to the individual involved often clashed with the demands of the company and of the System Council. How did the president resolve these conflicting demands? The concept of "passing" is useful to us here. By passing Goffman means an attempt by an individual to pass himself off as something he is not. Thus the local president attempted to be different things to different groups. To the rank and file he tried to appear as the great protector of their rights, blaming the failure of their grievances on company resistance or lack of support by the System Council. To the Council he tried to pass himself off as a reasonable union leader who was more interested in the good of the union than in the good of particular individuals. To the company he tried to appear as a rational union leader who was more interested in maintaining harmonious union-management relations than he was in the good of the union or the good of individual members. In reality he was interested in all three, good relations with management, status in the System Council, and the respect of his constituents. In each situation the fact that he accentuated one aspect created a number of problems for him. Goffman summarizes the problems created by passing:

1. Need to lie.
2. Inability to avoid disclosing discrediting information.
3. Possibility of revealing other undesired behavior while attempting to avoid displaying undesired behavior.
4. High anxiety to the passer.
5. Possibility of exposure.
6. Passer is torn between possible roles.
7. Necessity to be more alert to events which might prove discrediting.

[72] Erving Goffman, *Encounters* (Indianapolis: Bobbs-Merrill, 1961).

8. Need for passer to stay close to the place where he can replenish his disguise.

Related to this difficulty was a problem encountered by the union president when he was discovered acting in concert with management. It was certainly to his benefit to be on good terms with the company officials, for through these good relations he was able to gain things for the union he would never have been able to obtain formally. (In labor-management relations there inevitably develops a trading relationship between union and management. In exchange for the union's dropping certain grievances the company will agree to grant others.) This presented a moral dilemma for the president—by trading he was bound to ignore the rights of certain individuals for equal representation. His rationale for trading was that it helped him make the best deal possible for the union. On a number of occasions local members saw him enter the personnel manager's office alone. This, along with personal dissatisfactions, led to accusations that he was selling out. Thus, in Goffman's terms, the local president was discredited when he was caught alone in the personnel manager's office. Once again his problem was to manage the tension created by this apparent difference between his virtual and actual social identity. Goffman tells us that there are a number of things the local president could have done to alleviate the tension, aside from the previously mentioned in-group and out-group alliances:

1. Physically corrected his stigma. The local president could have accomplished this by making sure that when he met with company officials he was accompanied by at least one other union official.
2. Mastered things he was supposedly not able to do. Since the local president was supposed to be selling out to management he could have contradicted this by actively pushing a number of grievances despite severe company opposition.
3. Used his stigma as a crutch to gain the upper hand. Here the president could have thrown himself on the mercy of the union by claiming that only through close contact could he gain the union's goals.
4. Believed that his stigma taught him about life. He could have accepted it, believing that only through close ties with management could he be an effective local president.
5. Reassessed the limitations of the normals. He could have rationalized his position by believing that the other union officers were less effective because they did not have as close ties with management.

The fact that the local president was also a full-time skilled employee in the company presented a number of problems for him. One such problem occurred when he was forced to press a grievance which involved his own supervisor. Unlimited grievance activity against this supervisor was unwise, because this man possessed a number of weapons he could have used to hurt the president on the job. He could assign him to the most distasteful jobs, give him poor or outdated equipment to work with, or assign him to poor work crews, which would complicate his own work. To prevent this the local president was again faced with a problem of information control. He used a variety of methods (which Goffman presents in *The Presentation of Self in Everyday Life*) to alleviate this difficulty. One was to foster the impression that the act he was putting on at the moment was the most important one. Thus he tried to impress upon the supervisor that while he was on the job he was primarily a worker and should have been judged on his work record, not his record as a union leader. Another useful method here was audience segregation. If management people were prevented from attending local meetings, they had no way of knowing who was the driving force behind the grievances. The local president was then able to blame the union hierarchy or adamant members for the grievance activity. Conversely, he did not allow union members to observe his relationship with his immediate supervisor. This allowed him to blame others for grievance activity without incurring the wrath of the union membership.

While I observed the local president conduct a meeting, the applicability of Goffman's ideas on what must be concealed in a performance became clear. I will list these discrepancies between appearance and reality and apply them to the president's behavior at the local meeting.

1. Inappropriate pleasures. It is quite clear that the local president enjoyed the power he held in the union. However, he had to hide his enjoyment of power in front of the rank and file since such pleasure was incompatible with their view of his role. They saw him as a servant to their needs instead of one who wielded power over them. Thus at the local meetings he had to present a self which did not reflect his feelings of superiority.

2. Activities incompatible with their view of him. Aside from his secret enjoyment of power the local president performed other duties which were incompatible with the membership's perceptions of what he should be doing. For instance, he took a number of precautions to prevent the members from observing the behind-the-scenes deals he negotiated with management. He made such deals in good faith, believing that it was for the good of the union. However, the rank and file would not have viewed it this way; they were more interested in their own individual welfare than in the abstract "good of the union." They generally felt that the local president should support all grievances equally and not sell out some in order to win others.

3. Errors, and the fact that they have been made. An interesting example of error concealment took place at one local meeting. The president proudly announced that he had negotiated an increase in the per diem allowance for those who were required to work out of town. However, when he read the company's letter of intent on this issue he discovered

that they had only agreed to raise the allowance in the present situation and that pay in future situations would revert to the old rate. He was extremely embarrassed that this error had come out before the membership, and managed to save face by explaining that it was the company, not he, who was in error. He promised to have the company rectify the mistake. To my knowledge the company has not changed its position. Ordinarily the local president would do a more careful job of screening before presenting such information at the meeting.

4. Showing only the end product and hiding the process. In order for the local president to gain some concessions from management he had to yield to them on other issues. As was discussed, an exchange relationship developed between them. The local president, however, attempted to hide this exchange by announcing only union victories and allowing defeats to pass unnoticed. Thus the process of trading off grievances was hidden from the members.

5. Dirty work involved in producing the end result. Once again the behind-the-scenes deals made with management are applicable here since they may have been considered "dirty work" by some members.

6. Hiding the fact that he let other standards slide in order to pursue public activity. The local president was required to attend a number of functions which took much of his time. Official and unofficial union meetings as well as meetings with the company prevented him from pursuing goals desired by the membership. For instance, many of the members were reluctant to write grievances themselves because they feared retaliation from their foreman. They wanted the union president to prepare the grievances himself and push them as if they emanated from him and not the individuals. This was time-consuming and secondary to his desire to maintain good relations with management. He was, therefore, more likely to let these slide rather than his contacts with management. In order to conceal this he was more likely to blame management's obstinacy than his own lack of time.

7. Hiding insults, humiliations, and deals made to get the role. The lack of power of the union in relation to management left the president open to humiliations from management. They could ignore many of his requests because they were aware of their superior position. The local president, of course, hid such humiliations from his constituents.

Dramaturgical manipulation, as employed by the local union president, may be categorized as a means by which one can take independent action in a role conflict situation. The focal role is manipulating the situation in order to do what he wants. Although there are few studies which deal directly with the dramaturgical handling of conflicting expectations, it is undoubtedly a major means of resolving role conflict, especially for those in managerial and official positions. Failure to keep the front and back stages separate can have dire consequences, as indicated by a study by Cicourel of a president of an informal group.[73] Cicourel studied a small organization of senior citizens in upstate New York. After about four years of existence, the group elected a president who had exhibited devotion to group goals. The fact that no one else was interested in the position also helped her to get elected. At the same time a Board of Directors was selected, appointments being based on influence within the community. Given these two groups (members and directors), the president ran into dramaturgical difficulties because she failed to keep her front and back regions separate. For example, she committed the major error of contradicting the organization's policy and the director's adherence to it before the director and members. As a result of these and other dramaturgical failures the president gradually lost the support of both members and directors. Although dramaturgical manipulation is an important means of resolving role conflict, it is not without risks to the focal role.

3. In recruiting managers and officials, industrial organizations utilize processes almost as complex as those they use in recruiting professionals.

For the same reasons that organizations use complex procedures in recruiting professionals, they also employ involved procedures in hiring managers and officials. The reasons include low supply and high demand, the importance of mistakes made by individuals at this level, the high training costs, and the difficulty of firing incompetent managers and officials. Before we proceed, a caveat is in order. There are some important exceptions to the above generalization. In voluntary organizations in particular, an official position frequently goes to the most interested individual, with little or no recruiting involved. For example, the position of local union president often goes to the person who is most active in the organization. Frequently, an individual interested in the presidency is unopposed because there is no one else in the union who wants the position. This seems to be true of official positions in many voluntary associations. For this reason our discussion will be restricted to industry, with the recognition that little or no recruiting takes place in voluntary organizations. Although the focus will be on industrial organizations, it is quite clear that other types of organizations, including hospitals and prisons, also utilize involved processes to recruit officials.

Campus recruiting. Industry recruits so actively on university campuses that it has had a profound effect on the structure of the university, the curriculum, and the student. Universities have adjusted a large part of their curriculum to mesh with industry by instituting a large number of courses which provide the student with skills and knowledge he will need when he enters the workworld. By the same token, industry has striven to adjust

[73] Aaron Cicourel, "The Front and Back of Organizational Leadership: A Case Study," *Pacific Sociological Review* I (1958), 54–58.

itself to the university by making the first few years of organizational life little more than an extension of academia. Although industry has pervaded much of academia, its most profound influence has been in the business schools. According to William H. Whyte, Jr., the number of students majoring in business doubled between 1940 and 1950. By 1955 business majors "had become the largest single undergraduate group—more than the majors in mathematics, all the natural sciences, all the physical sciences, all the biological sciences, and English put together."[74] Added to this has been the proliferation of graduate schools of business administration, many of which offer MBAs as well as PhDs. In recruiting future managers industry focuses its attention on the graduates of these programs. The result has been that the university placement officer has emerged as a central figure in most universities. It is his job to bring potential employer and recruit together. In most universities the recruiting season lasts for virtually the entire academic year. There is a constant procession of potential employers through the placement center. Preceding them is a barrage of advertisements on the center's walls and in the college newspaper. Some of these have such provocative leads as:

"The Horizons are Unlimited for College Graduates at Union Carbide."
"To the Young Man Bent on Conquering the Unknown."
"A Man can Grow and Keep on Growing with Owens-Illinois Glass Co."
"An Equitable Life Insurance Man is 'a Man on the Way Up.'"
"The Sky is our World."
"The Sky is the Limit."

With the stage set, the recruiters appear on campus and the real action begins. William H. Whyte, Jr.'s description of the clinical atmosphere at the Purdue placement center reflects the situation at most other major universities:

It is probably the largest and most effective placement operation in the country, yet, much as in a well-run group clinic, there seemed hardly any activity. In the main room some students were quietly studying company literature arranged on the tables for them; others were checking the interview timetables to find what recruiter they would see and to which cubicle he was assigned; at the central filing desk college employees were sorting the hundreds of names of men who had registered for placement. Except for the murmur from the row of cubicles there was little to indicate that scores of young men were, every hour on the half hour, making decisions that would determine their whole future life.[75]

The placement director performs an important function even before the recruit begins interviewing. He teaches students the proper way to look, act, and dress. Some universities even go so far as to design courses to prepare

[74] William H. Whyte, Jr., *Organization Man,* p. 93.
[75] Ibid., p. 70.

the student for his encounter with the recruiter. For his part the recruiter has checked with faculty and placement officers for suitable candidates for his organization. Frequently he is an alumnus of the university he visits, with contacts among the administration, the faculty, and the students. With both parties well schooled the actual recruiting interview takes place. It usually takes about a half an hour, with both parties feeling each other out. If the interviewer is impressed the recruit is invited for a visit to the company. The expenses for the trip are paid for by the company as well as any entertainment costs incurred. The crux of the visit is generally a series of interviews with officials in the department the recruit is being interviewed for. Many companies also insist on a battery of tests to be sure the recruit is the type of individual who will fit into the company and the specific department. After the recruit has left, a meeting is held in which the results of the interviews and tests are evaluated. Should the recruit be considered acceptable, he is notified of the job offer.

Training programs. The recruiting process does not end with the hiring of an individual. In many cases the first few years on the job are seen as an extension of the recruiting process. Many companies have formal training programs for recruits who are potential managers, and these programs perform a variety of functions. They allow the company to assess the potential of their new acquisition under circumstances which pose no threat to the organization if he should fail. Many recruits are in reality not hired until they have successfully negotiated the trials of the training program. These training programs are similar in many ways to university life and they therefore serve to ease the transition from university to industry. Some organizations, such as General Electric, have a separate "campus" on which the recruit receives his training before he is allowed in the "real" world of industrial life. Another function of the training period is to allow the recruit to get some exposure to various areas of industrial life. He is frequently given a series of different assignments and he rotates among these positions during his training period. Only after he has "graduated" from this training program (and some organizations even give diplomas) can we say that he has completed the recruiting process.

4. The career patterns of managers and officials offer more mobility than those of any other occupational group.

If one looks merely at the formal steps in the careers of managers and officials, he would get the impression that they follow a number of clearly defined steps to the top. Actually there are a number of informal factors which affect career patterns and there are also a number of dead ends, horizontal and downward steps built into the careers of the manager and official. Again we will focus on the industrial manager, although the same principles apply to managers and officials in other organizations. Perhaps the career of the business manager has greater opportunity for mobility than the others, but all managerial and official occupations exhibit a great deal of career mobility. Let us pick up the potential business manager as he leaves his management training program and enters the real world of industrial life.

Investments. In the course of his training program the potential manager has been developing a commitment to his employing organization. In Gouldner's terms, he begins his career with a local rather than a cosmopolitan orientation.[76] His education as well as his training period has instilled a strong loyalty to the employing organization. As his years in the organization pass, this initial loyalty is transformed into a strong commitment. The major factor in this transformation is the investments the manager makes in his employing organization. The more he has invested, the more committed he will be. What are some of the investments an individual makes in his organization? One is that he learns a number of things which are not readily transferable to other organizations. He may develop a series of skills which are useful in his organization, but which may well not be applicable to others. In addition to skills the manager learns the informal workings of his organization and the shortcuts which make his job easier. Were he to change organizations he would have to learn anew the informal organization and acceptable shortcuts. Another investment lies in the fringe benefits most organizations offer. A manager may have developed a great deal of equity in a retirement program and he would lose this if he left the organization. Or he may have acquired, through stock option plans, a considerable investment in the company and would lose this too if he left. The manager has friends within the community and the organization whom he may be reluctant to give up. His family has also made investments within the community: wives have friends and organizational involvements and children have schools and peers to which they are tied. Finally, the mere passing of time is an investment. The more years a manager spends in one company, the more difficult it will be for him to move. All of the investments discussed above increase with the passing of years. Further, the older the manager is the more difficult it will be for him to find alternative positions.

Side-bets. Becker has called the investments described above "side-bets."[77] He contends that the more side-bets, the greater the commitment. An empirical test of Becker's side-bet theory by Ritzer and Trice has indicated that his theory is overstated.[78] In the Ritzer and Trice study a number of investments were correlated with a score on commitment to the organization,

[76] Alvin Gouldner, "Cosmopolitans and Locals: Toward an Analysis of Latent Social Roles—I," *Administrative Science Quarterly* 2 (1957), 281–306.

[77] Howard S. Becker, "Notes on the Concept of Commitment," *American Journal of Sociology* 66 (1960), 32–42.

[78] George Ritzer and Harrison M. Trice, "An Empirical Study of Howard Becker's Side-Bet Theory," *Social Forces* 47 (1969), 475–478.

and very few of the correlations were statistically significant. Ritzer and Trice conclude that commitment to organization cannot be explained solely by structural side-bets; the additional component is the initial psychological commitment. As was pointed out previously, in the process of going through the transition from college to organizational life the new manager makes a psychological commitment to his organization. Once he has accepted a position he goes through a process of emphasizing the strong points of the organization he has chosen and downgrading organizations which rejected him, or which he rejected. This commitment is enhanced by the first few years on the job in the management training program, for one of the functions of this program is to sell the recruit on the company and allow the recruit to convince himself of the organization's worth. There is also a process of self-selection occurring here—those who are not sold, or who cannot sell themselves, leave the organization by the end of their training program. Those who remain are in all likelihood already highly committed to the company. It is at this point that the side-bets or investments play a role in enhancing this initial commitment. However, because the commitment is already strong, investments do not play the essential role given them by Becker.

Career patterns

Given a strong commitment to his organization, the new aspiring manager or official is confronted with what appears to be a series of well-defined steps leading to the pinnacle of the organization. It is popularly believed that anyone with ambition and skill will rapidly climb to the top; however, this is the formal picture of a manager or official's career pattern. Reality varies greatly, as the next few pages attempt to demonstrate.

Moving up in an organization. First of all, there are a great many lower-level managers, but far fewer within the top echelon. There is no room at the top for all of those who desire lofty status, and many management careers are therefore terminated at relatively low levels. Many individuals reach a low-level managerial position which they fill well, but they may remain there because the organization feels that they do not have the abilities to move up further. There are even potential managers who do not make it to this level—some fail so miserably on simple assignments that they never even attain a low-level position. Others, in looking at the prospects for moving up and what it takes to move up, decide that it is not worth the effort. Such individuals may remain as low-level bureaucrats, or leave the organization altogether.

There are those who do move steadily up in their organization. However, it is quite clear that it is not ability alone which determines whether an individual will reach the top. The dynamic, aggressive decision maker who fights his way to the top seems to be a thing of the past. Those who succeed are often those who are best able to understand the system and manipulate it for their own benefit. Brilliant decision making is not required; as a matter of fact, it frequently appears that the top positions go to those who never "stick their necks out" by making decisions. Another important quality is the ability to understand what the superior wants and give him exactly that, no more or no less. All of these points are neatly summarized by Mills in his discussion of success in the business world:

So speak in the rich, round voice and do not confuse your superiors with details. Know where to draw the line. Execute the ceremony of forming a judgment. Delay recognizing the choice you have already made, so as to make the truism sound like the deeply pondered notion. Speak like the quiet competent man of affairs and never personally say No. Hire the No-man as well as the Yes-man. Be the tolerant Maybe-man and they will cluster around you, filled with hopefulness. Practice softening the facts into the optimistic, practical, forward-looking, cordial, brisk view. Speaks to the well-blunted point. Have weight; be stable: caricature what you are supposed to be but never become aware of it much less amused by it. And never let your brains show.[79]

Mills is being ironic in the above statement, but the same theme has been repeated many times in both the sociological and popular literature on management.

There are also a number of informal factors which help a man to move up. What it really takes to get ahead in an organization is often at variance with what is formally stated. In his study, *Men Who Manage*, Dalton points out a number of informal conditions required if one was to move up in the organizations he examined.[80] For one thing it was informally recognized that one had to be a Mason in order to move ahead. Collins' study of a New England factory revealed the same processes:[81] virtually all of the top management positions at this New England factory went to Yankees. In contrast almost all of the foremen positions were manned by the Irish. In Dalton's study the vast majority of managers were either Anglo-Saxon or German. In addition, most managers were members of the yacht club and all had to be, at least officially, Republicans. These informal factors may vary from organization to organization, but it is clear that they are important for upward mobility in all organizations. It is clearly not what you know, but who you know that counts. Related to this is the informal importance of sponsorship in managerial life. One of the surest ways to move up in an organization is to be sponsored by someone who is already in a lofty position. As he rises, the sponsored individual also moves up.

Even if an individual has all of the informal attributes, he is not guar-

---

79 C. Wright Mills, *The Power Elite* (New York: Oxford University Press, 1959), pp. 142–143.

80 Melville Dalton, *Men Who Manage* (New York: John Wiley, 1959).

81 Orvis Collins, "Ethnic Behavior in Industry: Sponsorship and Rejection in a New England Factory," *American Journal of Sociology* 51 (1946), 293–298.

anteed a series of inalterable steps to the top. There is much zigzagging in the career of the typical manager or official.

Demotion. In addition to moving up in organizations it is also possible to move down. Dalton mentions demotion, but does little with it. Goldner has a much better analysis of demotion in industrial management.[82] He is concerned with the ways in which organizations make failure (demotion) "socially acceptable." Outstanding performance is not needed to move up, or even to stay at a given level. Adequate performance is generally sufficient to maintain one's position. Even when performance is inadequate, however, the organization is unlikely to fire an individual.[83] By rarely firing and gently demoting, the company removes most of the fear elements from its environment. However, anxiety is not totally eliminated from the manager's life. An occasional firing or outright demotion serves to keep him on his toes. Thus, demotion at a later point in the career is accepted as likely by most of Goldner's respondents.

The fascinating portion of Goldner's study is the ways in which organizations and individuals adapt to demotion. The following are some of the ways in which the organization adapts:

1. Demotions are often obscured. Organizations hide them in a mass of ambiguity and constant movement between positions, which makes it difficult to be certain a move has been a demotion. These ambiguities tend to soften the blow.
2. Another ambiguous demotion is movement to a less desirable geographical location, even though the position remains the same.
3. Another means of easing demotion is to give, along with the demotion, such side payments as a free trip or no reduction in pay.
4. Since many demotions may be followed by promotions, it is difficult to separate the manager demoted for further training so that he can fill a higher job from the manager demoted for inadequate performance.

The individual who has been demoted also has a variety of means of adaptation.

1. Redefining himself, both prior to and after demotion. For example, he may emphasize the high "price" one must pay to move up in the organization.

[82] Fred H. Goldner, "Demotion in Industrial Management," *American Sociological Review* 30 (1965), 714–725.

[83] On a more general level Goode has argued that the protection of the inept is ubiquitous. He notes that groups do not expose or expel members because of lack of achievement or talent. In fact, one of the major reasons for the effectiveness of industrial societies is their ability to use the inept and restrict the amount of destruction they can cause. William J. Goode, "The Protection of the Inept," *American Sociological Review* 32 (1967), 5–19.

2. Shifting attention to other activities such as leisure time and community involvement.
3. Managing embarrassment in facing others in the organization after demotion.

Dalton points out that the sinecure office, such as "assistant-to," is an effective place to which to demote people. Such offices rarely have any real function, but at least it appears as if the individual has been promoted, rather than demoted. Sinecures may also be used as holding positions for individuals who will be promoted when a position opens up.

Douglas More develops a more elaborate typology of demotion than does Goldner.[84] In addition to the types described by Goldner, More adds:

1. Lowered status with lower compensation.
2. Retention of the same job with a cut in salary.
3. Being bypassed for a promotion.
4. Being moved to a less desirable function.
5. Keeping the same job but having some of the subordinates moved.
6. Being bypassed in a general increase in salary.
7. Having steps added in the hierarchy above one's position.
8. Lateral movement from the high-status line to the lower-status staff.
9. Staying essentially where one is, but being moved out of the line of promotion.
10. Elimination of one's position and reassignment.

Some of More's types of demotion are much more subtle than those discussed by Goldner. They are in the main so subtle that one's fellow workers would be unlikely to be aware that one has been demoted. Others (for example, lowered status with lower compensation) are so blatant that they are likely to have important repercussions.

More observes that there are certain things about an organization which increase the likelihood of demotion. Demotion is more likely to be used and accepted in a utilitarian type of an organization. Where there is a strong benefits package it can be used more frequently, because a demoted individual would be wary of quitting and losing these side-bets. If the labor market is tight, companies can demote with less fear of losing employees. Where a company is losing money or suffers a cutback in orders it is more likely to demote. Mergers with other companies or intracompany reorganizations may result in excess managerial baggage. Finally, if the business in which the company is engaged is faced with contracting demand, it is more likely to demote.

More pursues his analysis by discussing individual reaction to demotion. The individual who has been demoted may show "increasing negativism, bit-

[84] Douglas More, "Demotion," *Social Problems* 9 (1962), 213–221.

terness, resistance to direction within the firm, and may go as far as to express a defeatist attitude with respect to his total life goals."[85] Demotion may also have positive functions for the individual, causing him "to work hard to recapture former status, resulting in increased effort and output. The man may become more realistically self-critical and may drive himself toward more thoroughness and perfectionism."[86] Others may be happy that they are no longer in positions they found too difficult to handle.

Demotion may have a number of impacts on middle-level managers in general. Because of a demotion, or a series of them, productivity, creativity, loyalty, and protective cliques may decrease, while turnover, illness and absenteeism, abuse of privileges, and moonlighting may increase. While demotion may have some positive functions for the middle management group in general, its negative effects are likely to be dominant. For this reason, most demotions are handled in the subtle way outlined by More.

Horizontal movement. In any career pattern there are also a number of horizontal moves. In such cases, an individual is transferred laterally from department to department to give him the experience he needs for top positions. In personnel administration, for example, it is generally believed that one must have experience in each area of the field before he can fill the personnel manager position. Such positions also act as "testing points" in which it is determined "whether he moves on along a line to intermediate or higher management, horizontally to other staff or line jobs, or terminates his career at the level involved."[87] In personnel, such a crucial testing point is an assignment in labor relations, which is usually the most difficult area in the field. If one can succeed there he is a good bet to be a capable personnel manager. In such critical positions top management can determine his ability to handle the kinds of difficult problems he will be faced with as he moves up the hierarchy. In every managerial and official occupational hierarchy there are a number of such testing points; success here generally means continued upward movement. Timing now becomes a problem. If the organization has an individual who has successfully completed his task at a given testing point, it must have a higher-level position open. Frequently, however, it finds the next higher position filled by a job incumbent who cannot be moved up, down, or laterally. Since organizations are unlikely to fire such an individual, the man below who is ready to move is likely to be stuck. The result may be that he will become unhappy over his prospects and seek a transfer, or seek to leave the company. In addition to being testing points, lateral moves may also constitute, as was pointed out previously, subtle demotions. Finally, one may move horizontally simply because there is nowhere else to go. If upward mobil-

[85] Ibid., p. 219.

[86] Ibid.

[87] Norman H. Martin and Anselm L. Strauss, "Patterns of Mobility within Industrial Organizations," *Journal of Business* 29 (1956), 101–110.

ity is blocked, the organization may move a manager around laterally to give him the illusion, at least, that he is moving.

Skidders. Although they are certainly atypical, there are even some circumstances in which managers are demoted as far down as blue-collar work. In their study of the "skidder," Wilensky and Edwards focus on the managers and officials in one company who have been demoted to blue-collar work.[88] The study is not totally applicable to this section, since people demoted from all types of white-collar work (professionals, sales workers, self-employed businessmen, etc.,) are lumped together with managers and officials. Nevertheless, the findings of Wilensky and Edwards are instructive for those interested in the career patterns of managers. They differentiate two types of skidders: the intergenerational skidder is an individual in a blue-collar occupation whose father was a white-collar worker; a worklife skidder is a blue-collar worker who had held a white-collar position prior to entering the factory. When Wilensky and Edwards compare skidders and nonskidders some interesting findings emerge. Those who have skidded are more likely to accept the social stratification system of the United States than those who have not. Apparently those who have been demoted have not changed their views about the system, and are more likely not to identify with the working class, to believe in the possibility of upward mobility based on ability, to continue to want themselves and their children to be middle class, and to expect to soon leave the factory. The authors explain their findings in this way: "Like a man falling from a skyscraper, our skidder reaches not in the direction of his fall, but back up the structure. The values and beliefs of the middle class family or the white collar workgroup retain their force despite later status loss."[89] Thus those who have skidded do not become opponents of the system that has hurt them, but continue to applaud it. The manager or official who is demoted copes with this crisis by maintaining his values and continuing to believe that somehow he will rise again to his "rightful" position.

Adjusting to a new position. Even if the manager is rapidly promoted up the line, he is not free of problems. Each time he moves into the next higher position he must make adjustments to his changed situation. Gouldner's study of a gypsum plant illustrates the kinds of problems a manager faces when he moves into a new position.[90] Prior to the arrival of the new plant manager, an elaborate informal system has developed. This Gouldner labelled the "indulgency pattern" because the workers were allowed to violate many of the organization's rules. The new manager came with a mandate

[88] Harold Wilensky and Hugh Edwards, "The Skidder: Ideological Adjustments of Downward Mobile Workers," *American Sociological Review* 24 (1959), 215–231.

[89] Ibid., p. 228.

[90] Alvin W. Gouldner, *Patterns of Industrial Bureaucracy* (New York: Free Press, 1964).

from top management to make the plant more efficient. To do this he had to strictly enforce the existing but previously unenforced rules. Such an action clearly left him with very few friends within the plant. Soon afterwards he strove to replace some of his strategic subordinates with his friends. Once his friends were in office he was able to operate more informally and less bureaucratically. All things considered the successor's entrance into the plant created serious strains and made it difficult for him to adjust to his new work environment. Virtually all new managers face similar kinds of informal arrangements when they assume their new positions, and adjusting to the new environment is a difficult problem for them.

The successful executive. Given the role conflict endemic in the positions and the circuitous route to the summit, one wonders what kind of person is able to make it to the top in an organization. Henry's old but important study of business executives sheds some light on this question.[91] In a study of over one hundred business executives, he isolated several personality characteristics which most had in common. Foremost, perhaps, is his finding that successful business executives have a high need for achievement. They possess the desire to work hard and to succeed. The business executive is action-oriented, rather than a dreamer. Another central characteristic of the successful executive is a strong drive for mobility. They seek movement up the career ladder, as well as greater competence, more responsibility, and the expeditious completion of tasks. Another similar desire is for greater prestige both in the organization and in the community. All of these serve as a spur to greater and greater productivity. Despite their drive, successful executives respect authority and the right of their superiors to issue them directives. They also have a superior "ability to organize unstructured situations and to see the implications of their organization."[92] Henry found that successful executives are able to make decisions when confronted with several alternatives, have a strong self-identity, are very active, and aggressively seek out what they want. It should be pointed out that his finding is, on the surface, contradictory to the views of such people as C. Wright Mills and William H. Whyte, Jr. They contend that the route to success entails being a yes-man and a non-decision-maker. It seems however that there is a difference between those who are striving for success and those who have made it. The route to success requires the aspiring executive to be a yes-man, but when he makes it he must reverse himself and be able to make decisions. Thus there is a discontinuity between the behaviors required on the route to success and in success itself. It is frequently difficult for the former yes-man to become a decision maker. Henry also makes passing note of some of the negative aspects of the successful executive's personality. For one thing,

[91] William E. Henry, "The Business Executive: The Psychodynamics of a Social Role," *American Journal of Sociology* 54 (1949), 286–291.
[92] Ibid., p. 288.

there is a constant anxiety and fear of failure. This is one of the costs of success in our high-powered industrial organizations. For another, the constant need to work often prevents him from enjoying his leisure time if, indeed, he has any.

5. Blacks and females face distinctive problems in managerial and official occupations.

Females

As at any occupational level, female managers and officials are confronted with a series of distinctive problems. When subordinates are also females the problems are lessened, but few such positions are available. Life is difficult for the female manager whose peers and subordinates are males. As Cussler points out, "if there is one thing women are not supposed to be it is the 'boss'."[93] This belief is a serious barrier to the woman who seeks to rise to the top of an organization. It is clear that a few women do overcome it, but the real question is how they do it. Cussler points out several factors which help a woman reach the top of an organization. For example, it seems to be easier in times of rapid social change, or when there are no qualified males available. The woman who makes it has frequently been sponsored by someone high in the organization and the sponsor is most often a man.

One hotel executive, younger than her fellow candidates, was selected and trained for the job by a sponsor. The head of an institution had been remembered by her professor at Columbia, and when the opportunity came, was recommended for the position. A hospital administrator said that a good friend, a hospital physician, got her to leave the South and come to New England for a better job. The head of a catalog department urged his protégé to go get a library school degree; he foresaw that specialized training would help toward her advancement on the library staff.[94]

The above indicates that in a wide variety of organizational settings female managers were sponsored by males.

Once she is in the executive position, the woman's problems really begin. Her sponsor is likely to have left the scene, but not before he had made the adjustment to executive life somewhat easier. The departure of the sponsor is likely to be a traumatic period for the female executive. But this is only one of the difficult problems with which she is confronted. Social contacts are important for executives, but the female executive finds it almost impossible to be accepted in these all-male gatherings. This inability to make contacts limits her effectiveness and may drive her into more social contacts with other females who are not likely to do her much good in her work. On the job, she must exhibit competency, but be extremely careful that she is

[93] Margaret Cussler, *The Woman Executive* (New York: Harcourt, Brace, 1958), p. 3.
[94] Ibid., p. 17.

not threatening to male peers and superiors. The line between nonthreat-
ening and threatening competency is thin, and this complicates her worklife.
Her male counterparts frequently treat her like the female stereotype, rather
than as an individual. The difficulty here is that there is no agreement on
what the stereotype is. Some males may believe that females have "a tendency
to think in broad terms," while others view the woman as "too fussy about
details." She may want to move still higher in the organization, but must be
careful that she does not appear too aggressive. Thus she must often wait
to be summoned to a higher position by male superiors. Perhaps her biggest
liability is the noncompetitiveness which is part of the female role in American society. She is at a decided disadvantage when she deals with male
executives who are supposed to act in a highly aggressive manner.

Being in an executive position affects every aspect of the female's life.
High-ranking females are less likely to be married. In the Cussler study only
one-third of the executive females were married, while in society as a whole
about two-thirds of all females are married. Given the nature of her position
she finds it more difficult to date. As an executive she is threatening to many
males. She makes a good salary, and this often precludes the possibility of
her marrying one of the large number of men who earns less than she does.
The longer she is an executive the more difficult it is for her to marry, because she becomes increasingly unwilling to give up her executive life. For
those female executives who are married, the problem is to combine the frequently incompatible expectations of home and office.

Despite the inherent strains, some females do manage to survive in executive life. It is instructive to inquire into the means they employ to handle
their stressful position. For one thing, they tend to choose positions in organizations which emphasize the feminine value of humanitarianism. Thus
Cussler found a number of female executives in such organizations as the
Red Cross, the Girl Scouts, hospitals, and government agencies with humanitarian goals. Even in nonhumanitarian organizations, female executives behave in a humanitarian way. Many are very concerned with the welfare of
subordinates. When confronted with problems on the job, the female executive is more likely to be patient than aggressive in her efforts to solve them.
Some, however, do behave in a male manner and attack problems aggressively. In relations with male executives, many of the older female executives
are content to take a back seat and allow the male to believe that he has
made all the decisions. New, younger female executives seem to be less willing
to take this position. But the aggressive female executive is still in the minority and most are content to display their competency quietly.

Blacks

Black union officials. Interestingly, the black executive is similar in many
ways to the female executive. He finds it harder to reach the top, and when

he does he is faced with the same kinds of problems as she finds. For example, black executives, like females, frequently need a sponsor to help them rise. Most often this sponsor is white. This position is stated quite clearly in Kornhauser's study of the Negro union official.[95] Virtually all unions are controlled by whites; thus, for a black to move into an official position requires the sponsorship of white leaders. White leaders do not sponsor blacks for humanitarian reasons, but rather when it is in their own best interest. There are a number of variables which enhance a black's chances of being sponsored for an official position by a white union leader. If the black membership in the union is large, whites are more likely to sponsor a black. Further, sponsorship is more likely when the black membership is centralized. The likelihood of sponsorship is also increased when harmonious race relations are important to the union leadership.

There are also a number of strategic reasons for the selection of a black union official. Negro officials enhance the ability of the local to organize black workers. In jurisdictional disputes with other unions it is important that a union have the support of all its members, and black union officials help to rally blacks in support of their union in the face of this external threat. When a white union leader is confronted with competition within the union, his chances of success are enhanced if he has sponsored a black official who can gather support for him among the black members. The black union official also serves a symbolic function; he is supposed to represent to the black membership the fair-mindedness of the white leadership. The black official also performs a liaison function between the white leadership and the black membership. The entire process puts the black union official in an extremely difficult position. He must satisfy the white leadership to retain his position, but at the same time he must be responsive to the needs of the black membership. Because of the realities of his position, the black leader frequently is more responsive to the needs of the white leaders than of his black constituents.

Black personnel managers. Hughes notes an important similarity between the black personnel man and the black union official. The Negro personnel man is one of the latest straw bosses; he acts as a liaison man between management and Negro help.[96] He has little hope of moving up in the organization and is retained only as long as there are significant numbers of black employees. The black personnel manager is also a man in the middle, and he is also likely to be more responsive to white superiors than black employees.

Black politicians. Wilson's study of Negro politics shows many of the

[95] William Kornhauser, "The Negro Union Official: A Study of Sponsorship and Control," *American Journal of Sociology* 57 (1952), 443–453.
[96] Everett C. Hughes, *Men and Their Work* (Glencoe, Ill.: Free Press, 1958), p. 114.

same kinds of processes as described above.[97] William Dawson was a prominent leader of the black political machine in Chicago who was sponsored early in his career by white political leaders. That black political machine was one of the most powerful in the United States, yet it had to be very careful not to alienate white political leaders. It was very conservative and intimately tied to the white Democratic organization. The black politician must not antagonize the white bosses, for the rewards of appreciation by the black constituency cannot make up for the possibility of sanctions from the white boss.[98] Silberman contends that Dawson was coopted by the white political machine and that this caused him to be inactive on important issues within the black community.[99] In fact, most black managers and officials have been coopted in one way or another. In acceding to the demands of the white leaders they have tended to lose their militancy, and end up working more for the white leaders than the black constituency. In many cases the white power structure has handled the problem of the black militancy by sponsoring a few blacks into important posts and then coopting them into the white organization. As a matter of fact, Silberman sees this as an inevitable process. He says,

for if Negroes are to be elected and appointed to high office—if they are, in fact, to enter the "power structure" and help shape the decisions that count—they will have to give up a good deal of their freedom to criticize and protest. No member of a city, state or federal administration can expect to keep any influence over that administration if he is always denouncing it; to be an effective advocate of Negro interests within the power structure, he must abandon his role as social actionist. He cannot have it both ways.[100]

This is the real dilemma of every black in a managerial or official position.

Wilson also analyzes black civic leaders in Chicago and finds that they fall into several types. One is the "prestige leader," who is generally successful in business or professional life. He too tends to avoid controversy, and is highly valued by the black community because of his contacts among white leaders. His major function is to give legitimacy to any black organization to which he lends his name. The token leader has been selected, most often by whites, to represent the black community. He is used by the white community to legitimize their policies within the black community. Because of the nature of his position, the token leader is rarely active in racial matters. He is also useful to whites as an advisor on the black community. The "organizer" is the activist, the one who raises and pursues issues through a variety of organizations within the black community. Organizers have not "made it" as have the other leaders discussed, and hence are able to be activists because they have far less to lose. Wilson was unable to find any "mass agitators" in

[97] James Q. Wilson, Negro Politics (New York: Free Press, 1960).
[98] Charles E. Silberman, Crisis in Black and White (New York: Vintage Books, 1964), pp. 204–211.
[99] Ibid.
[100] Ibid., p. 211.

Chicago such as Adam Clayton Powell in New York. There is hope in the black community that more militant leadership will come from the younger leaders of the black community.

In sum, the picture of the black manager and official is a bleak one from the perspective of the needs of the black community. Because of the nature of their position and how they got there, black leaders tend to be far more responsive to the white leadership than the needs of the black community.

PROPRIETORS

There is not a great deal of literature on proprietors in occupational sociology. There is virtually no material on some of the major foci of this book, including career patterns and the problems of black and female proprietors. Thus, due to paucity of studies, this section will be brief.

6. The major problems for proprietors are relations with customers and economic and professional marginality.

One clear source of strain for the proprietor revolves around relations with customers. The days of the huge, powerful entrepreneur are swiftly passing in the United States. Small shops and firms are increasingly swallowed up by huge organizations. Left, primarily, is a group of small businessmen-proprietors who have great difficulty in eking out a living. Many people who go into private business today are inadequately financed and this is one of the reasons for their high rate of failure. Because of their marginal status, proprietors must be highly responsive to the needs of the customers. Since the proprietor deals with customers rather than clients, the power in the relationship does not lie with him. In order to stay in business he must please his customers and build up ties with them. Thus, his success depends on his relationship with customers, as Kriesberg's study of furriers indicates.[101]

Furriers. Kriesberg found two basic types of furriers, each of whom handles his customers differently. The custom furrier emphasizes quality and personal relationships; he builds his patronage slowly and his main interest is in selling fine merchandise. If he is able to please a customer early in their relationship, the customer is likely to remain with him. The customer is more interested in quality than in price, and initial satisfaction with material and/or workmanship encourages him to allow himself to become dependent on the custom furrier. The custom furrier can better afford to be an artisan because he has a small group of devoted customers. He knows he can never earn a great deal and thus he can wait out slack times on his savings or on doing repair work.

[101] Louis Kriesberg, "The Retail Furrier: Concepts of Security and Success," *American Journal of Sociology* 57 (1952), 478–485.

The business furrier is more like the old-style entrepreneur. Unlike the custom furrier, he is the head of a small organization. Because he has an organization to support, he concentrates more on building a fairly large clientele than on quality, and he is far more dependent on this clientele. Since the business furrier deals with something more like a mass market, his customers do not have the close ties to him which characterize the customer relations of the custom furrier. The problems of the custom furrier are characteristic of many one-man businesses, while the problems of the business furrier are similar to those of all small entrepreneurs.

Pharmacists. Other proprietors, such as pharmacists and chiropractors, are faced with a professional dilemma. They are businessmen who would like to be considered professionals. The druggist, for example, finds it difficult to fulfill the often incompatible roles of businessman and professional. McCormack catches the essence of this conflict:

The role of the pharmacist is unstable to the degree that it is beset by the cross-pressures of the business and professional worlds. . . . The "collective" or service objectives of a profession are at odds with pecuniary goals of a business—continually. The pharmacist faces decisions which involve a choice of one or the other. How these decisions are made will depend to some degree on his value-system—whether he sees himself as a professional performing a social service or acting in the capacity of a seller.[102]

The most commonly employed resolution in this conflict is compromise. Most of the pharmacy students McCormack studied wished to own retail drugstores in medium-sized cities and carry out their business in residential rather than business districts. "There was a decided disinclination to run a small business in a large city or commercial district where conditions would be strongly competitive and the conflict between professional and commercial demands greatest."[103] They expect to combine and fuse the roles of independent professional and proprietor. However, they blunt the entrepreneurial aspect of pharmacy in two ways: they criticize big business and retreat from highly competitive situations. To lessen the professional aspect of their position they subordinate the professional service orientation "to individual achievement for its own sake." In effect, pharmacists attempt to resolve their inter-role conflict by blunting the conflicting roles and thereby reducing the discrepancy.

Other pharmacy students indicated other resolutions of the conflict. Some indicated that they would resolve the dilemma in the direction of professionalism, while others favored the direction of business.

Another of the conflicts inherent in the pharmacist's position is his relatively lowly status in relation to other professionals. This is a psychological

[102] Thelma H. McCormack, "The Druggists' Dilemma: Problems of a Marginal Occupation," *American Journal of Sociology* 61 (1956), 308.
[103] Ibid., p. 311.

conflict rather than a role conflict; hence the resolution employed is psychological rather than behavioral. On the Hatt-North scale the pharmacy students ranked only 4 of 89 occupations above the pharmacist. They viewed Supreme Court Justices, physicians, nuclear physicists, and scientists above them, and saw themselves on a par with dentists and chemists. Hence, they enhance their lowly status by adopting an idealized occupational image.[104]

One may also examine, as Denzin and Mettlin have, pharmacy as a would-be profession.[105] In their view, pharmacy has failed to achieve total professionalization; "they have taken on a number of the characteristics of a profession, but they failed to escape the marginality associated with professions which still contain within themselves elements of an occupation."[106] According to Denzin and Mettlin, pharmacists have failed to achieve professionalization for several reasons:

1. They continue to advertise, a singularly nonprofessional act.
2. They have not recruited truly committed and altruistic individuals to the occupation.
3. They have not been able to achieve "control over the social object around which their activities are organized, e.g., the drug."[107]
4. There is not a systematic body of scientific knowledge.
5. Because of many specialties, pharmacy has not been able to build up a strong organization to control the members.

Despite its failures, pharmacy has achieved some trappings of a profession, including a code of ethics, specialized skill, and "the common label of pharmacist." However, professionalization, as far as it has gone, has not been equal throughout the occupation. Hospital pharmacists are clearly much more professional than retail pharmacists. Retail pharmacists continue to advertise, emphasize personal rather than professional goals, and sell nonprofessional items. Thus there are clearly segmental elements within the pharmacy occupation which hold the potential for both internal conflict and change.

Chiropractors. Wardwell views the chiropractor as a marginal role in comparison to doctors.[108] In comparison to doctors the chiropractor has less technical competence, a lesser scope of practice, is illegal in some areas, has lower income, and lower prestige. He wants to be recognized as a doctor, but physicians are in opposition as is the public, although it is less so. Because of their established status, physicians are the major role definers of chiropractors. However, they refuse to recognize chiropractors as doctors and have even

[104] McCormack, "Druggists' Dilemma," 313–314.
[105] Norman K. Denzin and Curtis J. Mettlin, "Incomplete Professionalization: The Case of Pharmacy," *Social Forces* 46 (1968), 375–381.
[106] Ibid., p. 376.
[107] Ibid., p. 377.
[108] Walter Wardwell, "A Marginal Professional Role: The Chiropractor," *Social Forces* 31 (1952), 339–348.

gone so far as officially condemning them through the AMA. Wardwell outlines a number of devices employed by the chiropractor to reduce the conflict.

1. "Unit[ing] for mutual aid."
2. "Participat[ing] in civic and fraternal activities in order to gain community acceptance."
3. "Attempting to get favorable licensing law by engaging in campaigns to
   educate the public, organizing patients into layman's units for the purpose of exerting pressure on legislators, and forming friendships with
   politically important people."
4. "[Using] aggressive patterns—either toward the source of frustration, or
   a substitute."
5. "[Using] deviant means, such as secret remedies, fee-splitting, soliciting
   patients and advertising."
6. "Practicing under the guise of physiotherapists or masseurs."
7. "Restricting practice to 'safe' illnesses and trusted patients."[109]

In addition to these behaviors Wardwell discusses a number of things chiropractors do psychologically to reduce the conflict. One such rationalization is
embodied in the following quotation from his study:

Chiropractors have a new type of healing art which the medical monopoly wants to
keep from the public in order to prevent financial loss to themselves; until chiropractors obtain sufficient public support to get the laws changed, they are justified in
technically violating them; they are bringing relief and health to the suffering sick,
many of whom medicine has failed to help.[110]

Furthermore, some chiropractors never question the chiropractic "art," view
themselves as separate and distinct from medicine, and see themselves as an
oppressed minority.

In sum, trying to stay in business by satisfying customers and occupational or professional marginality constitute the two major problems for most
proprietors.

7. Proprietorship is a terminal occupation in career-pattern terms.

Once an individual becomes a proprietor there are few, if any, career
steps open to him in that occupation; he has formally reached its apex. Any
formal step up, such as to executive of a large company, is a move out of the
occupation. If the business fails he may be forced to move down, but such a
step is also out of the occupation. For example, the owner of a machine shop
which fails may go back to being a machinist, but in so doing he is no longer
a proprietor. While formal career steps are impossible, informal steps are a
possibility. If his firm grows or merges with another firm he is a more important proprietor than before. If, because of the success of his firm, he is elected

[109] Walter Wardwell, "The Reduction of Strain in a Marginal Social Role," American Journal of Sociology 61 (1955), 16–25.
[110] Ibid., p. 21.

president of the local Chamber of Commerce, he has also moved up in an informal sense. However such progression is not generally considered when one discusses career patterns. Having chosen to be a proprietor an individual is at the formal end of his career in that occupation.

8. Blacks and females have been notably unsuccessful in their efforts to become proprietors outside of a few areas which are defined as black or female.

As is true with any other position of authority in our society, blacks or females are not supposed to be proprietors. Proprietorship, like other high-status occupations, does not fit into the passive, subordinate stereotype of blacks and females. Further, proprietorship frequently means the supervision of subordinates, and whites or males intensely dislike working for a black or female. The only exceptions have been firms which cater to either blacks or females. In such cases it is possible, but not probable, that a black or a female can succeed as a proprietor.

In a Drexel Institute study of small businesses in Philadelphia, discussed by Foley, only about 10 of the 4,242 Negro businesses in 1964 were classified as "quite successful."[111] The types of businesses owned by blacks reflected nationwide patterns:

Nearly all were retail and service trades, and most were single proprietorships. Personal services were the most numerous, hairdressing and barbering comprising 24 percent and 11 percent respectively, of the total number of Negroes in business. Luncheonettes and restaurants comprised 11.5 percent of the total. Many of the businesses would be submarginal if free family labor were not available. For example, median sales for a sample of Negro-owned beauty shops were $2,500; for Negro-owned luncheonettes, $6,800; and for barber shops, $4,400.[112]

Virtually all black businesses were in predominantly black neighborhoods, while whites owned about half of the businesses in these areas. "While the white businessman is free to pass through the walls on either side, the Negro businessman cannot look beyond 'his neighborhood.' "[113] In one area of Philadelphia 12.1 percent of black businesses were rated as "neat and clean," 55.9 percent as "not eye-appealing," and 32 percent as "run down."[114] "The picture, then, of the Negro in business is that of a small businessman—a very small businessman—who is generally not a very good businessman and, frankly, not a very significant factor in the Negro community."[115] Blacks and females have not made major inroads as proprietors. There are some signs of change, but much remains to be done if these minority groups are to become significant forces in the world of small business.

[111] Eugene P. Foley, "The Negro Businessman: In Search of a Tradition," in Talcott Parsons and Kenneth B. Clark, eds., *The Negro American* (Boston: Beacon Press, 1966), pp. 555–592.
[112] Ibid., p. 561.
[113] Ibid.
[114] Ibid., p. 562.
[115] Ibid., p. 563.

4
Middle-Level Occupations

In the preceding two chapters we have dealt with the functional occupational categories of professionals, managers, officials, and proprietors. The occupations in each of these categories have marked similarities and it is therefore possible to make generalizations about the categories as a whole. In this chapter such generalizations are impossible because we are not dealing with a functional occupational category. Under the heading of middle-level occupation, four very different occupational groups are discussed: first-line supervisors (foremen and union stewards); white-collar clerical workers (including salesmen); skilled craftsmen; and the semiprofessions of teaching, social work, and nursing. No generalizations are made for all middle-level occupations; rather, they are derived for each of the four groups listed above.

The heading "middle-level occupations" has no functional significance and is merely used for convenience to denote a wide range of occupations which would be found in the middle of the professional continuum. Obviously, all such occupations are not discussed in this chapter; the four selected represent those which have received considerable attention from occupational sociologists. First-line supervisors have been the focus of considerable research because of their marginal status and the conflictive nature of their position. White-collar clerical workers have been extensively researched because of the growing numbers employed at this level and their endemic status insecurities. Much more has been done on skilled craftsmen because they represent a throwback to preindustrial times. Finally, the semiprofessions have received much attention because of the drive of individuals in them to become professionals and their overall failure to achieve this goal. Some might quarrel with a discussion of the semiprofessions in a chapter on middle-level occupations and prefer to cover them in a chapter on the professions. The placement of this group in this chapter represents my view that these occupations are not professions. Further, they frequently are not even viewed as high-status occupations. Thus it is most appropriate to discuss them in a chapter on middle-level occupations.

Just as this chapter is unlike the preceding two chapters, it is also unlike the ensuing two chapters. In Chapter 5 the focus is on low-status occupations and it is possible to make broad generalizations about occupations under this heading, although it is not a functional category. The same is true of Chapter 6, in which generalizations are made about deviant occupations. In both cases, despite the differences between particular occupations, it is possible to make broad generalizations because of the important similarities between them.

FIRST-LINE SUPERVISORS

Foremen

1. The foreman's basic dilemma is role conflict, and his resolutions are similar to those employed by managers and officials.

Social change. The industrial foreman has been subjected to substantial social change in the last fifty years. Changes within the occupation have been caused both by technological innovations and by changes in the structure of industrial organizations. In his analysis of this question, Miller has isolated five major changes to which the foreman has had to accommodate himself.[1]

a) The foreman of fifty years ago was supposed to be a rugged individual who issued directives and was obediently followed by his subordinates. Today, this ideology has changed and the foreman is warned by top management to be neither too authoritarian nor too close to his subordinates. Social science has played an enormous role in these changes. Its emphasis on the social factors in the workworld has forced the foreman away from either a too authoritarian or too lenient approach to supervision. The authoritarian supervisor is likely to incur the enmity of the workgroup, and increase both their propensity to restrict productivity and the likelihood of other retributive actions aimed at management in general. On the other hand, the foreman who is too close to his subordinates is unable to supervise their work adequately.

b) The growth of engineering departments was a second factor altering the role of the foreman. In the past the foreman made most of his own decisions on technical questions. Now he must rely on the engineering department for "instructions as to what machines he [is] to have, how they [are] to be placed, how he [is] to operate them, and how they [are] to be cared for."[2] Further, he must rely on blueprints drawn up by the engineers even when his own judgment tells him to do the job differently. c) Third, there is the growth of personnel departments, which have removed the job of hiring from the foreman and also taken over the functions of placement, training, transferring, making merit increases, and firing. d) A fourth factor has been the

---

[1] Delbert C. Miller, "Supervisor: Evolution of An Organizational Role," in Gerald D. Bell, ed., *Organizations and Human Behavior* (Englewood Cliffs, N.J.: Prentice-Hall, 1967), pp. 282–289.
[2] Ibid., p. 284.

proliferation of such departments as production control, quality control, accounting and finance, and overall organizational planning. Each of these has initiated changes which have further circumscribed the foreman's role. Each department has also required detailed reports from the foreman and he has been required to serve as a buffer between the staff and the production employees. e) Finally, the advent of labor unions with their local presidents, stewards, and other officers has placed still added pressure on the foreman. This pressure however is not from the top as was the case with the other new forces—now the foreman is also subjected to organized pressure from below, in the form of the union. Overall, the foreman has lost many of his original prerogatives. In their place have come a large number of new obligations; "He must know more about production, personnel, engineering, organizational procedures, and labor relations. His obligations have increased, his authority has diminished."[3]

Foreman: two views. These changes have resulted in an increase in role conflict with a corresponding decline in the ability to handle such conflict. Many occupational sociologists have examined the foreman from this perspective. Wray feels that there are two basic views of the foreman.[4] The first, which is in line with the preceding discussion, depicts him as "subject to two sets of demands, which are frequently in conflict; the foreman must satisfy both top management and his work force which is usually organized." In the other, more traditional, perspective, the foreman is viewed as "the most important link between management and the worker."[5] Wray was dissatisfied with both views and undertook an empirical study of foremen to test both positions. He analyzed foremen in two plants; one was a large plant which was part of a larger company, and the other a company which was made up of only one small plant. Wray found two similarities in the behavior of foremen at these locations. In neither plant did the foreman make any real decisions; he was merely the transmitter or interpreter of decisions made at the top. Second, Wray found foremen to be passive in union-management relations. The basic decisions on union matters were made by representatives of the union and higher-level managers. The foreman did little more than conform to the agreements made at this higher level. In sum, Wray concludes that the foreman, in reality, is neither a "key man" nor a "man in the middle." Instead he is in general a passive, noncrucial agent in the relations between top management, the workers, and the union.

That the foreman is not an important link between management and the worker can be easily accepted. This finding is in line with the changes which have greatly reduced the importance of his position. Wray's conclusion that the foreman is not a man in the middle is highly debatable. His finding that

[3] Ibid., p. 287.

[4] Donald Wray, "Marginal Men of Industry: The Foreman," *American Journal of Sociology* 54 (1949), 298–301.

[5] Ibid., p. 298.

the foreman is passive and unimportant does not deny the fact that he is caught in a crossfire of conflicting expectations. What Wray is describing is a characteristic way in which a foreman resolves the inherent problem—in the face of opposing demands from above and below, he typically withdraws by becoming merely a passive middleman in the conflict. Further, Wray is wrong in limiting the source of the foreman's problem to two parties. As the ensuing discussion points out, the foreman is confronted with a host of conflicting expectations from a variety of sources.

Inter-sender role conflict. Roethlisberger's analysis of the role of the foreman is much more comprehensive than Wray's study.[6] In role theory terms, the foreman in Roethlisberger's view is primarily subject to inter-sender role conflict. The conflict emanates from the clashing expectations of the following members of the foreman's role-set:

1. Immediate superior.
2. Staff specialists.
3. Heads of other departments.
4. Subordinates—e.g., subforemen, group leaders.
5. Workers.
6. Shop steward (where unionized).

The major inter-sender conflict is between the immediate superior and subordinates. The foreman's major orientation is toward his superior and he is preoccupied with making a good impression on the boss.

Thus the foreman, like each individual in the modern industrial structure, is in effect painfully tutored to focus his attention upward to his immediate superiors, and the logics of evaluation they represent, rather than downward to his subordinates and the feelings they have. So rigid does the conditioning of superiors and executives in the industrial structure become in this respect, it is almost impossible for them to pay attention to the concrete human situations below them, rich in sentiments and feelings.[7]

The superior has all the power in the situation, and consequently the foreman will ordinarily resolve the conflict by conforming to the expectations of the more powerful superior.

Another inter-sender conflict exists in the contradictory expectations of staff specialists and subordinates. Staff specialists (e.g., personnel, engineering) expect the foreman to get his subordinates to conform to the standards, policies, rules, and regulations developed by them, while subordinates expect more personalized treatment from the foreman. Instead they expect that he will elicit their spontaneous cooperation through personal contact.

Person-role conflict. Other aspects of the foreman's relationship to his

[6] Fritz Roethlisberger, "The Foreman: Master and Victim of Double Talk," *Harvard Business Review* 23 (1945), 285–294.
[7] Ibid., p. 288.

role-set entail person-role conflict. Superiors expect a free flow of information from the foreman concerning his own and his subordinates' performance. However, he is reluctant to pass on much information which concerns negative aspects of performance. According to Roethlisberger, the foreman uses a variety of devices to reduce or eliminate this conflict, including such withdrawal techniques as complete silence, avoidance of the boss, or communication of only positive aspects of his job performance. Independent action is represented by a variety of aggressive devices which he uses. Finally, he may "play it straight," giving the superior all information, good and bad. This conformity to the expectations of the superior at least indicates to him that the foreman is following the rules.

Another person-role conflict occurs in the foreman's relationship with staff specialists. Staff specialists are sources of change as well as sources of control over the performance of the foreman and his subordinates. Double-talk seems to be a foreman's most characteristic resolution in this situation. In order to appease staff specialists he tells them what he thinks they want to hear even if he does not believe it himself, and he tells his friends something different. Double-talk is a rather creative form of role conflict resolution which can be included under the category of independent action.

In sum, the foreman position is subjected to a good deal of inter-sender and person-role conflict. Given these types of conflict, the foreman employs a variety of resolutions which fit into the revised Gross et al. framework discussed in the preceding chapter.

Four modes of resolution. Miller and Form's discussion of the conflicts faced by the foreman and the ways in which he can resolve them fits very neatly into the Gross, Mason, and McEachern theory of role conflict resolution. Miller and Form take a rather limited view of the foreman's conflict, since they view it as one between the expectations of management and labor. As Roethlisberger has pointed out, the conflict is much more complex than this. Nevertheless, Miller and Form present a rather insightful discussion of the opposing expectations of these two groups and the resolutions the foreman may employ. They view the conflict and the resolutions in terms of ideologies. Management has an impersonal ideology of cost and efficiency which it seeks to have accepted by the foreman. Workers, however, do not see themselves in profit and loss terms, but rather as human beings. The foreman is caught between these two ideologies and recognizes that conformity to either one involves danger. Yet he must do something, and Miller and Form outline four modes of resolution which he may employ. a) The first is identification with his superior and therefore with management. In accepting management's ideology "he tends to be critical of his workers, find fault with their work, and presses them for ever greater output."[8] This position is most often taken by

[8] Delbert C. Miller and William H. Form, *Industrial Sociology* (New York: Harper & Row, 1964), p. 215.

those foremen who have been brought in from the outside with the expectation that they will soon move up in the organization. However, whatever type of foreman chooses this resolution, he moves toward increased social distance between himself and his subordinates. The almost inevitable result of this choice is the withholding of information, restriction of output, and increased union activity by subordinates. Despite these dysfunctions, some foremen, especially those who are upwardly mobile, are willing to put up with them in order to be acceptable to top management.

b) The second possible resolution involves identification with subordinates. "A foreman in this situation considers the sentiments of his men, is friendly toward them, and has social contacts with them on and off the job."[9] This reduces the social distance between superior and subordinate as well as the dysfunctions outlined above, but creates a different set of problems. Along with an increase in social distance between the foreman and management, free communication up is reduced, and the foreman "tries to cover up for his men, resist changes imposed from above, understand the union's demands, and modify his orders to fit the local situation."[10] This resolution is chosen most frequently by the foreman who has risen from the ranks and has little hope of any further upward mobility. Miller and Form hypothesize that since the chances of upward mobility for foremen are declining, there may be an increase in this type of resolution.

c) The third resolution available to the foreman is what Miller and Form call dual identification, that is, identifying with both labor and management. This is a difficult position, but most studies of foremen have found it to be a very common resolution (although it should be noted that this is not Miller and Form's view). They feel that this resolution is most commonly employed by newly appointed foremen who retain ties with the workers as well as some hope of moving up in the organization. Although undoubtedly true, it is likely that this ambivalence continues throughout the careers of most foremen. It is probably more costly to identify with labor or management than it is to straddle the fence.

d) The fourth resolution posited by Miller and Form is identification with other foremen. This is in effect an independent resolution in which the foreman chooses to attempt to be a third party in the struggle between labor and management. (An extreme form of this resolution is the institution of a union of foremen.) For legal reasons the formation of a foremen's union is difficult; thus, foremen may more typically band together informally to resist labor and management.

2. In terms of their career patterns, foremen have few chances of moving up the organizational hierarchy unless they are in the position for training purposes.

[9] Ibid., p. 216.
[10] Ibid.

There are really two types of foremen. The first has been promoted from below and the second is in the position for training and will soon move up in the organization. The career patterns for the two types are vastly different.

Many organizations use some of their foreman positions as training slots. They fill these openings with new college graduates in an effort to give them some practical experience in production. These training positions are generally in the less important production areas, for management is unwilling to entrust crucial positions to "green" college graduates. Individuals in this type of foreman position have a great deal of career mobility open to them. After a brief stint as foreman they are moved into other low-level managerial training positions. Ultimately, the best of this group will become the top managers of the organization.

The foreman who is recruited from among the workers faces a far different future. Few, if any, will ever be considered for or aspire to higher management positions. They may make excellent foremen, but they lack the education and background required of higher managers. Many soon return to their old blue-collar positions. There are a number of reasons for this downward mobility. The foreman's pay is typically not much greater than that which his blue-collar subordinate earns. As a matter of fact, with overtime pay many of his subordinates earn more. For this small increment in pay the foreman is expected to shoulder far more responsibility than he ever had as a blue-collar worker. Many newly promoted foremen find the added responsibility not worth the slight increase in pay. For this type of foreman there is the added problem of being in a position of authority vis-à-vis those who were formerly his peers, and many find it difficult to develop enough role distance between them. If he is able to establish this role distance, the foreman risks incurring the animosity of his former coworkers. Many new foremen feel that this dilemma makes the job not worth the small increase in salary. Still another problem for the newly promoted foreman is the lack of acceptance by management. Management generally has different educational and social backgrounds and is unlikely to accept into its inner circle a foreman who was formerly a blue-collar worker. For all of these reasons many newly promoted foremen soon return to their old blue-collar positions. Those who remain are locked in with little hope of moving any further. Thus for the trainee the foreman position offers much mobility, while for the man promoted from the blue-collar level it is a dead end occupationally.

That blue-collar workers promoted to foremen positions regard them as dead end is supported by a study by Coates and Pellegrin.[11] They contrasted the self-concepts and concepts of each other of executives and supervisors. Their findings on the self-concepts of executives are in line with Henry's

[11] Charles H. Coates and Roland J. Pellegrin, "Executives and Supervisors: Contrasting Self-Conceptions and Conceptions of Each Other," *American Sociological Review* 22 (1957), 217–220.

findings discussed in the preceding chapter. The supervisors recognized that executives were different.

Supervisors tended to be acutely aware of the handicaps of their socio-cultural backgrounds, education and training, and occupational opportunities. As derivatives of these self-conceived personal limitations, they tended to concede to executives: better social and educational backgrounds; more ambition and motivation; higher level attitudes, values and life goals; more energy, alertness, and initiative; better understanding of human nature; better rounded, more magnetic personalities; more ability to handle large numbers of people; more ability to solve problems and make long-range plans; more willingness to delegate authority, accept responsibility, and make decisions.[12]

In short, the supervisors recognized the discontinuity between their careers and the careers of those above them in the organization. Implicit here is a recognition by supervisors that they can never aspire to higher-level positions within the management hierarchy. Further, when Coates and Pellegrin asked their supervisors if they would like to become executives, the majority responded negatively. Typically, among their reasons was that they had too many worries, headaches, and responsibilities. Not only did the supervisors recognize the differences between themselves and executives, but they had rationalized their inability to move up by stressing the negative aspects of executive life.

3. Members of minority groups find it extremely difficult to handle the position of foreman, especially when their subordinates are not from the same minority group.

The basic problem of the minority-group foreman who supervises members of his own group revolves around lateral and upward relations. He has few problems stemming from his minority-group status with his subordinates, but he does have problems with peers and superiors. A black or female foreman in a sea of white or male foremen is faced with enormous interpersonal conflict. According to the American stereotype, blacks and females are not supposed to be foremen, and when they are they are likely to be confronted with ostracism and conflict from their white or male counterparts. Since top management is also dominated by white males the black or female foreman is confronted with opposition and ostracism from this source as well. For the black or female who supervises subordinates who are not from their minority group, the problems are exacerbated. Given their orientation, white male subordinates are unlikely to accept working under a black or a female. This is a problem that blacks and females have in all managerial positions, but it is greatly increased when the position is at the first-line level, where the almost continual interaction between the superior and subordinates on a face-to-face basis serves to enhance the likelihood of conflict. Because of this high likeli-

[12] Ibid., pp. 219–220.

hood of conflict we find few black foremen in white departments, or female foremen in male departments.

Union stewards

4. The basic dilemma of the union steward is role conflict, and his resolution is determined by the nature of his workgroup.

The counterpart of the foreman in a union is the steward. There are a number of similarities between stewards and foremen, but two are most important for our purposes. Like the foreman, the position of the steward has declined in importance in recent years. Also like the foreman, the union steward is a "man in the middle." The description of the steward position by Sayles and Strauss is strikingly close to the preceding description of the foreman: "Not only is his authority restricted, but he is also subject to almost irreconcilable pressures. For he is a member of three different social systems— the union, the company, and the departmental work group—each with its special claims for loyalty."[13] In the next few paragraphs some of the similarities between foremen and stewards will be outlined in terms of social change and social conflict.

The steward is the first-line officer within the local union. Typically, it is a part-time position, with the steward holding a regular blue-collar position. When a union member has a problem, the steward leaves his job and is usually the first union official on the scene. Historically his major function has been to deal with management, but over the years the position has declined significantly in importance. The steward rarely deals with management now and problems he formerly handled are now performed by high-level union officers. For example, when a member had a grievance he would contact his steward, who met with the foreman involved to settle the problem if possible. Now however, both steward and foreman are bypassed. An aggrieved member usually brings his problem to top union officials, who then meet with top management. Even when a member brings a problem to him, the steward is generally quick to turn it over to higher-level union officials. Sayles and Strauss point out a steward's manual which notes that "the shop steward is to the union what the foreman is to the company."[14] Formerly this meant that they were both essential; now it means that they both are almost inconsequential.

Resolution of conflict. The decline in importance of the steward has placed him in a position similar to that of the foreman; left with few weapons, he is faced with radically conflicting demands. Sayles and Strauss feel that

[13] Leonard R. Sayles and George Strauss, *The Local Union: Its Place in the Industrial Plant* (New York: Harper & Brothers, 1953), p. 83.
[14] Ibid., p. 37.

there are three types of stewards, who resolve the role conflict inherent in their position in different ways. The first type is the social leader, who resolves the conflict in the direction of the union membership. He has given up hope of rising either within the union or within management and gets his major satisfaction from helping his friends within the union. The second type is the active unionist, who aspires to higher positions within the union. This is probably the most effective type in terms of winning grievances for the members. Some are close to the members, but others, because they are so ambitious, are somewhat distant. The final type is the self-seeker, who becomes a steward to win his own grievances or to increase his chances of promotion into management. He is probably the least able in terms of member grievances and frequently looks on them "as a necessary evil to maintaining [himself] in office." It is interesting to note that the steward is likely to resolve his conflict in the direction of one of the three groups of significant others. Thus he is quite different in this respect from the foreman. One of the reasons for this lies in the sanctioning ability of the groups of significant others. If the foreman resolves in the direction of subordinates he will be sanctioned by superiors, while the reverse is true if he resolves in the direction of management. Both of these groups have powerful sanctions to apply to the foreman which frequently cause him to withdraw. The steward is in a much different position vis-à-vis his significant others, since their sanctioning power is much less important to him. If he chooses to be a social leader, there is little the union or management could or would do. If he chooses to be an active unionist, management is not involved and the membership will not care as long as its grievances are pursued. If he chooses to be a self-seeker, the union and its membership are unlikely to care as long as he adequately represents their interests. Because of these factors the steward can make a choice in his role conflict situation.

The choice that the steward makes is most frequently dependent on the nature of his workgroup. If the workgroup is strongly pro-union it is likely to be run by a social leader, while if it is apathetic no one will want to be the leader, and the door is open to the self-seeker. In the middle are such groups as the moderately pro-union, and in these groups either active unionists or social leaders will be the stewards. Thus the way a steward resolves the conflict inherent in his position is more a result of the nature of his workgroup than the power of the significant others involved. The resolutions adopted by the foreman cannot be chosen for this reason. He is not a member of a cohesive workgroup and is therefore far more affected by the relative power of significant others.

5. Union stewards have few chances for upward mobility in the union or in management.

Many workers accept positions as union stewards in the hope of moving into the higher echelons of union leadership. There are many stewards, however, and very few top-level positions. The union, like virtually every other organization, is shaped like a pyramid with many positions on the bottom, fewer in the middle, and only one on the top. Frequently, even the slim chance of reaching the top is eliminated, for once an individual has reached the pinnacle of the union structure he is extremely unwilling to give up his place. This unwillingness, when combined with the powers the union president has to keep himself on top, make it highly likely that he can stay in power as long as he wishes. The long tenure of union leaders reduces the chances of the aspiring steward to almost zero.

Not only is mobility within the union virtually unattainable, but the steward has little chance of moving on to managerial positions. In the past some stewards may have been able to move on to careers in management, but this avenue is now almost totally closed. As discussed before, new managers are, increasingly, university graduates. The aspiring steward finds it impossible to compete against the new graduate. Management has closed its eyes to the able blue-collar worker as a candidate for a managerial position. The type of steward Sayles and Strauss label the self-seeker is in for a rude shock, for there is no room at the top for such an individual in today's modern industrial organization.

6. Members of minority groups find it extremely difficult to handle the position of steward, especially when their constituents are not from the same minority group.

Little can be said here which has not been said in discussing the black or female foreman. Since the steward position, like the foreman position, requires face-to-face contact, the steward who is a member of a minority group is faced with particularly acute problems. Because of this the union is unlikely, to put it mildly, to appoint a black or female steward in a primarily white, male workgroup. Where stewards are elected, one would be hard-pressed to find a female steward elected by a male workgroup or a black steward elected by a white workgroup. When one does find black or female stewards, it is in workgroups which are predominantly black or female. Even these stewards must face conflicts from peers and union leaders. Since most union officials are white males, black and female stewards are likely to face hostility from them.

WHITE-COLLAR WORKERS

White-collar work is here defined as any occupation below the supervisory level and above the blue-collar level. Thus included is a wide array of occupations (e.g., clerks, typists, bookkeepers, salesmen), but there are a number of commonalities among them which are discussed in the next several pages.

7. The major problem for the white-collar worker is his status insecurity.

As is every other member of an occupational group discussed in this book, the white-collar worker is plagued by a variety of problems at work. Like managers, officials, and foremen, he is undoubtedly subjected to role conflict. He also faces problems with customer/clients just as do professionals and proprietors. He may also be troubled by alienation as are low-status employees. Although the white-collar worker must deal with all of these problems in his worklife, his pre-eminent problem is status insecurity.

Social change and status insecurity

One of the major causes of the insecurity of white-collar workers is the enormous social change which has affected their occupational level. For one thing, an increasing percentage of the workforce is employed at this level. The greatest growth has been among clerical and kindred workers; these composed 3 percent of the workforce in 1900, and by 1960 that percentage had multiplied five times to almost 15 percent. The percentage of sales workers has also grown, but not nearly as rapidly as clerical workers. In 1900 sales workers made up 4.5 percent of the workforce and by 1960 that percentage had grown to 7.4. Thus by 1960 clerical and sales workers made up almost one quarter of the workforce. When we add to this the over 11 percent in professional, technical, and kindred occupations and the 8.5 percent who were managers, officials, and proprietors, we see that over 42 percent of the workforce in 1960 went to work in white collars.[15] By 1970 48.6 percent of the workforce was employed in all of these white-collar occupations.[16] It is clear that we are in the midst of a white-collar revolution within the workforce, and the trends indicate that we will see an even greater percentage of white-collar workers in the future. The causes of these massive workforce shifts are manifold. Technological advances have reduced the need for many blue-collar workers and increased the need for white-collar workers to produce service, and man the new machines. The proliferation of bureaucracies has created the need for a mass of white-collar workers to handle the large number of new functions. Consumers have become increasingly interested in services.

The large increase in numbers was in itself a source of anxiety to white-collar workers: the older ones felt threatened by the newer ones. The newer bureaucrats were unsure of their status in the rapidly changing bureaucracies in which they were employed. More important, the influx led to other changes which further increased the status anxiety of white-collar workers. For ex-

15 Philip M. Hauser, "Labor Force," in Robert E. L. Faris, ed., *Handbook of Modern Sociology* (Chicago: Rand McNally, 1964), p. 183.
16 U.S. Bureau of the Census, *Statistical Abstract of the United States: 1970,* 91st ed. (Washington, D.C.: Government Printing Office, 1970).

ample, the growth of huge organizations led to the development of large groups of white-collar workers. Clerks or secretaries no longer had personal relationships with their superiors; instead, they were herded into giant secretarial pools or became one of many clerks doing essentially the same kind of work. With the growth in numbers came the need for specialization. Thus the position was subdivided and then subdivided again, until the clerk was performing a highly specialized task. Increasingly, the white-collar worker became the tender of files and business machines. All of these changes tended to minimize status differences between white-collar workers and bring them closer and closer to the blue-collar worker. The result of course was, at least on the surface, the same kind of alienation as the low-status worker faces on his job. The high degree of specialization has made it difficult for the bureaucrat to get any meaning or self-actualization from his work. The growing size and impersonality of the organizations in which he is employed have rendered him powerless to affect decisions made above him in the organization, and the increasing factory-like structure of the office has made him almost as isolated as his coworker on the assembly line. The essence of the "new" office is caught by C. Wright Mills:

The modern office with its tens of thousands of square feet and its factory-like flow of work is not an informal, friendly place. The drag and beat of work, the "production unit" tempo, require that time consumed by anything but business at hand be explained and apologized for. Dictation was once a private meeting of executive and secretary. Now the executive phones a pool of dictaphone transcribers whom he never sees and who know him merely as a voice. Many old types of personnel have become machine operators, many new types began as machine operators.[17]

Although Mills is undoubtedly overstating the case, it is clear that office work has moved in the direction he describes.

   Bookkeepers. These changes have greatly altered virtually all white-collar occupations. It is useful to outline Mills' description of the impact of these changes on two white-collar occupations, the bookkeeper and the secretary. Prior to these changes the bookkeeper was a central figure in any office. With the proliferation of white-collar occupations, there arose the need for an office manager whose major responsibility was the supervision of these bureaucrats. This manager has taken over many of the functions formerly performed by the bookkeeper. High-school girls with a few months training on machines are now able to do the same things he had tediously performed with pen and ink. Many bookkeepers have been eliminated altogether, while others remain with highly circumscribed functions. Those who remained, as well as the high-school girls with their machines, are now being threatened with almost total extinction by the big new computers. The result has been that when the

    [17] C. Wright Mills, *White Collar* (New York: Oxford University Press, 1956), pp. 204–205.

bookkeeper has not been eliminated, he has been demoted to the level of the clerical mass.

Secretaries. The secretary too has been subjected to an enormous reduction in function and status. In the past this position has been excellent for the ambitious young woman. The typewriter has been a status symbol and the typist "equipped with stenographer's pad, has managed to borrow prestige from her close and private contact with the executive."[18] An informal hierarchy had developed, with the private secretary on top, followed by the stenographer-typist, and then the typist. There was strong competition among the girls to move up in this hierarchy. However, in the new, impersonal, rationalized office this hierarchy has become increasingly less meaningful. Private secretaries seem to be a dying breed. The advent of dictaphones hastened the trend toward secretarial and stenographic pools. This has made many secretarial skills, such as stenography, unnecessary and obsolete. In addition to a loss of skill there has been the loss of the direct, personal contact between secretary and boss. The position has an increasing number of similarities to blue-collar, assembly-line occupations. Finally, the pooling of secretaries has reduced status differentials and robbed the aspiring secretary of her opportunity to move up the old hierarchy.

Intrinsic and extrinsic aspects. Despite the alienating tendencies of modern white-collar work, evidence seems to indicate that white-collar workers do not feel as alienated as those in lower-status occupations. Nancy Morse's study of white-collar workers indicated that the majority are satisfied with a wide array of things including the community in which they live, their employing organizations, hours, company publications, and fringe benefits.[19] In terms of the well-known differentiation made by Herzberg et al. between intrinsic and extrinsic job factors, white-collar workers are more satisfied with the extrinsic[20] than the intrinsic aspects of their jobs. Gurin, Veroff, and Feld compared a number of occupational groups on job satisfaction; Table 4-1 shows some of their findings.

It is clear in Table 4-1 that clerical workers are far less satisfied with their work than are professionals and technicians. As a matter of fact, they are closer to unskilled workers in terms of job satisfaction. Despite their comparative dissatisfaction, white-collar workers do not appear to be alienated. This point is made clear by Morse:

Most of the employees do not think in terms of autonomy and individuality or the lack of it in describing the work situation (sixty-four percent), nor do they talk

---

18 Ibid., p. 207.

19 Nancy G. Morse, *Satisfactions in the White Collar Job* (Ann Arbor Survey Research Center, University of Michigan, 1953).

20 Frederick Herzberg, Bernard Mausner, and Barbara Snyderman, *The Motivation to Work*, 2nd ed. (New York: John Wiley, 1959).

TABLE 4-1

Job Satisfaction Among Professional, Technical,
Clerical, and Unskilled Workers

Job Satisfaction	% of Professionals Technicians	% of Clerical Workers	% of Unskilled Workers
Very satisfied	42	22	13
Satisfied	41	39	52
Neutral	1	9	6
Ambivalent	10	13	13
Dissatisfied	3	17	16
Not ascertained	3	–	–
	100	100	100
Number of Cases	119	46	84

Adapted from G. Gurin, J. Veroff, and Sheila Feld, *Americans View Their Mental Health* (New York: Basic Books, 1960), p. 163.

about equality or inequality in describing the social situation in the office (eighty-seven percent).[21]

If white-collar workers are dissatisfied but not alienated, we are confronted with the problem of ascertaining what is the major source of their dissatisfaction.

Status panic. The greatest source of work satisfaction for white-collar workers is their greater prestige vis-à-vis blue-collar workers. However, this source of satisfaction is being threatened by changes in white- and blue-collar work which are greatly reducing the discrepancy between the two occupational levels and creating what Mills has called "status panic" among white-collar workers. It is this panic caused by threats to their prestige, which is their major problem.

Historically, those in white-collar occupations have claimed to have greater prestige than blue-collar workers for a variety of reasons: one of the major ones has been the difference in appearance. White-collar workers wore white shirts and suits or neat dresses, while blue-collar workers were attired in the proverbial blue collar. Related to this is the cleanliness of the work. Office work did not dirty hands or clothing, while blue-collar work was very likely to dirty both. White-collar workers felt that their work allowed more individuality and that they were "middle class," while blue-collar workers were of the "working class." They also believed that their work brought them closer to management and provided higher salaries. The brain work of the office was felt to be superior to the brawn work of the factory, to require more mental activity and therefore more training. White-collar skills could

[21] Morse, *Satisfactions in the White Collar Job,* p. 10.

only be learned in schools, while blue-collar skills, if indeed there were thought to be any, could be readily acquired on the job. There are undoubt-edly other reasons for the claim by white-collar workers to greater prestige, but the above will suffice as illustrations.

However, a number of social changes (alluded to earlier in this section) indicate that these claims to prestige are being increasingly threatened. The following is a partial list of some of these changes:

1. The great influx of people into white-collar clerical occupations has helped to downgrade the importance of this occupational level.
2. Organizations have downgraded the importance of white-collar clerical occupations, and this has resulted in a decline in the need for special edu-cation or training.
3. White-collar salaries have been levelled, while there has been a corre-sponding increase in blue-collar salaries.
4. The decline in immigration has narrowed the old differences in nativity between white- and blue-collar workers.
5. Both white- and blue-collar workers may now find themselves unem-ployed.
6. White-collar workers no longer have a significant say in the decision making of top executives.
7. Blue-collar workers have obtained increasing power, especially through their involvement in labor unions.
8. Some highly skilled blue-collar occupations require more skill and train-ing than many white-collar occupations.
9. Blue-collar work has become much cleaner, especially in automated fac-tories. In such factories it may now be impossible to see any differences between white- and blue-collar work.[22]

All of these factors have been important in reducing the status differen-tial between white- and blue-collar workers, but perhaps the most important factor has been the growth of "white-collar factories": "The new office is ra-tionalized: machines are used, employees become machine attendants; the work, as in the factory, is collective, not individualized; it is standardized for interchangeable, quickly replaceable clerks; it is specialized to the point of automatization."[23] It is difficult to see any difference between a white-collar worker employed in such a setting and the blue-collar assembly line worker. The fact that there are no apparent differences is part of the cause of Mills' "status panic" among white-collar employees. The white-collar worker seeks to flesh out his increasingly meaningless worklife through status symbols, but changes in his work situation have made it increasingly difficult for him to believe that he has any more prestige than his blue-collar coworkers.

[22] Mills, *White Collar,* p. 249.
[23] Ibid., p. 209.

Office automation.   Another important threat to the status of the white-collar work is the automation of the office. Automation threatens to eliminate many office jobs and radically alter those that remain. In the office automation takes the form of high-speed computers and their accessories. The computer can compute and prepare customer bills, inventories, cost statements, premium notices, payrolls, and a host of other simple and complicated tasks which have long provided the workbase for the white-collar worker. The specific impact of automation on the office is reflected in a study by Mann and Williams:

> Prior to the change, there were 140 jobs and approximately 450 positions in the central accounting area. It is estimated that 80 per cent of the jobs were either substantially changed or eliminated, and that this affected 90 per cent of the positions. Moreover, there was about 50 per cent reduction in the number of jobs.[24]

The positions that are eliminated tend to be those that are routine and menial. The coming of the computer creates new jobs, but they require different skills than were previously utilized. This means that many of the people who lost their old jobs may lack the skills or desire to fit into the newly created positions. Another byproduct of computerization of the office is the advent of shift work for white-collar employees. The company may very well find it profitable to run its computers on a two- or three-shift basis. This brings the white-collar work closer to blue-collar work, as well as demanding enormous readjustments on the part of white-collar workers who have never had to work on a shift basis. Still another offshoot of computerization is a decline in tolerance for error. An error made somewhere along the line can destroy an entire program. Along with this, because of greater specialization, it is far easier for management to locate the individual who is responsible for the mistake. "For the white collar worker, accustomed to the somewhat anonymous conditions of the typical office organization, this accountability is a new experience."[25] Because the positions are more highly specialized, each individual has a crucial role to play in the process. The result is that the organization is less likely to tolerate such things as lateness, absenteeism, and high turnover. Finally, the office worker now finds himself to be, like the assembly-line worker, paced by a machine.

The outcome of all of this is another important threat to the status of the white-collar employee. The mere possibility of automation, even if it never comes to a particular office, is threatening to him. When it does come the fears are generally realized, and the status of the white-collar worker is, in fact, threatened. The decline of white-collar occupations, the upgrading of blue-collar occupations, and automation have all posed threats to the white-collar worker.

[24] Floyd C. Mann and Lawrence K. Williams, "Organizational Impact of White Collar Automation," in Faunce, *Readings in Industrial Psychology*, p. 202.
[25] Ibid., p. 203.

Salesmen. The salesman is a rather peculiar white-collar occupation, although he is faced with many of the status insecurities discussed above. He is different because he most often works alone without interacting with peers. His workday is spent in interaction with his customers and his success on the job is directly related to his success in handling them. He must seek to control the customer, but much of the power in the relationship lies in the customer's hands. There are two basic types of salesmen: those who seek out customers and those who are sought out by them. The door-to-door salesman of encyclopedias, Fuller brushes, cosmetics, and insurance falls into the first type. He has two basic problems: getting into the house and selling the product. He must often ring a number of doorbells before he finds an amenable customer. Part of his sales pitch is spent in selling the customer on the idea that he should be allowed into the house. Fast-talking, subterfuges, or offers of free gifts are frequently employed. Once in the door the most important part remains, selling the product. The second type of salesman has only to sell the item. Car salesmen, salesgirls in department stores, etc., don't have to gain entrance since the customers most often come to them. Both types however, must sell their product, since their income is frequently determined in large part by commissions on sales. Many salesmen are paid a small salary, but this is generally not enough to live on. Thus the salesman's livelihood depends on his ability to sell to customers, who have the balance of power. They have the power to refuse to allow a salesman even to talk to them, or to walk out without buying anything after he has spent a good deal of time with them. It is not atypical when a customer takes up a good part of a used-car salesman's day and then decides not to buy a car. This time spent by the salesman is totally wasted since he has derived no income.

8. White-collar workers can respond to the threats to their status in a variety of ways.

Informal group structures. Most frequently white-collar workers respond to status threats by developing informal group structures which perform a variety of functions. Studies by Homans and Gross cast considerable light on some of these groups and functions. In the main both studies indicate that in order to compensate for external status threats, white-collar workers turn their attention inward and get satisfaction from informal relations with peers. Gross studied an office of one hundred white-collar workers in a manufacturing firm of 1600 employees.[26] He found this office to be characterized by small differentials between the office workers, a high division of labor, much passing back and forth of forms which must be worked on by a number of people, a great deal of physical mobility, and the traditional clean, white-collar atmosphere. Within this one-hundred person office, Gross

---

[26] Edward Gross, "Cliques in Office Organizations," in Neil J. Smelser, ed., *Readings on Economic Sociology* (Englewood Cliffs, N.J.: Prentice-Hall, 1965), pp. 96–100.

found eleven cliques made up of thirty-seven office workers. Within a clique no member was a competitor of another member—that is, no two clique members did the same work and had the same supervisor. In nine of the eleven cliques members came from different supervisor-subordinate groups, and all of the cliques were found to be very congenial. These cliques were not formed for protection as are cliques among blue-collar workers. Blue-collar cliques restrict production because of real or imagined threats from management and fellow workers who are rate busters. Gross found that there was restriction of output in the office, but that it was not controlled by the cliques. Since the members of an office clique were not competitors, it was not necessary to control competition between them and prevent rate busting. Threats from management were apparently handled by white-collar employees on an individual basis, rather than through their informal groups. The functions of the office cliques revolved around their ability to yield their members informal work gratification. Thus they served as media of communication, enabling members to find out what was happening in the rest of the organization. Second, they allowed the highly specialized clerk to understand the significance of his role in the organization. Finally, the clique's congeniality and noncompetitiveness gave its members a great deal of satisfaction. All in all the Gross study reveals a turning inward of white-collar workers in an effort to escape the external threats and gain a measure of informal satisfaction.

Cash posters and ledger posters.   Homans' study of clerical workers reveals other functions of informal office groups in the face of external threats.[27] Homans found two groups of workers, the cash posters and the ledger posters. We need not go into detail about the nature of these two occupations other than to point out that they are different but related clerical operations. Both the cash posters and the ledger posters were classified at the same pay grade, although it was generally agreed that the ledger posters had more status. Because of the differences in their work and their status, the two work groups formed separate informal groups. Homans concentrated on the ledger posters and found them to be generally satisfied with their work. Specifically, they liked such things as the friendliness on the job, the superiors, the pay, security, responsibility, variety, opportunity for outside contacts, and the chance to solve problems. Despite their satisfaction they, like most white-collar workers, were faced with a status problem. Although they were supposed to have more status than cash posters, they received no more pay. They frequently complained when they were taken off their jobs to do lower-status cash posting. The separation of the informal groups was very functional, especially for the ledger posters. By excluding lower-status cash posters they were able to maintain an elite informal group. Thus they were able in-

[27] George Homans, "Status Among Clerical Workers," *Human Organization* 12 (1953), pp. 5–10.

formally to gain the greater status they were unable to gain in a formal manner on the job.

Formality. While informality offers one way of alleviating status threats for white-collar workers, formality offers another. By becoming an expert on the formal rules, the white-collar worker is able to define for himself a specific area of proficiency which differentiates him from blue-collar workers and makes him safer from the encroachment of machines. This also serves to reduce the threat from another source, the client. With his expertise he gains status vis-à-vis the client and by rigidly following the rules he remains safe from criticism by superiors. This is the "bureaucratic personality" described by Merton, with its "unchallenged insistence upon punctilious adherence to formalized procedures."[28] Most studies of the bureaucratic personality, red tape, the civil service mentality, etc., have emphasized the factors within the structure of a bureaucracy as the main causes. This is not debated here; instead, the goal is to point out that devices such as the bureaucratic personality are in part created by the insecure bureaucrat in order to give himself a greater measure of security and status.

Unionization. In the face of their external threats one might think that white-collar workers would turn to unions for self-defense, especially for protection against automation. Many blue-collar unions have been able to prevent or delay automation; why could not white-collar unions do the same? Despite logical reasons for the formation of white-collar unions, there has not been much unionization at this occupational level, mainly because the concept of a union in itself constitutes a status threat to white-collar workers.

The overwhelming majority of salesmen, typists, file clerks, and professionals will not join because they consider it beneath their dignity, because they feel differently from blue-collar workers about their jobs and their status, because they are afraid it will hurt their advancement, and because the face of the labor movement seems to them crude and exploitative.[29]

White-collar workers ignore a major opportunity to reduce the threats to their status, because of what Bruner calls their "will-o'-the-wisp dignity."[30] Thus, as of 1968, only 11.2 percent of all white-collar workers belonged to unions. Astonishingly, this percentage represents a decline from 1956 when 12.8 percent of white-collar workers were unionized.[31]

Saleswomen. There are an almost infinite number of ways in which

[28] Robert Merton, *Social Theory and Social Structure* (New York: Free Press, 1957), pp. 195–206.
[29] Dick Bruner, "Why White Collar Workers Can't Be Organized," in Sigmund Nosow and William H. Form, eds., *Man, Work and Society* (New York: Basic Books, 1962), p. 188.
[30] Ibid., p. 190.
[31] Albert A. Blum, "The Office Employee," in Blum et al., eds., *White Collar Workers* (New York: Random House, 1971), p. 7.

the salesman may seek to wrest control of the situation from the customer. These approaches range from the "hard sell" to the "soft sell." Basically, the salesman attempts to dramaturgically manipulate his performance to suit the particular situation. With one type of customer he is likely to take a vigorous approach, while with others he is likely to operate in a relaxed manner. Mills discusses the almost infinite variety of approaches used by female salesgirls in large stores.[32] He notes that this variety is a function of the nature of the girl, the customer, and the store. The "wolf" is one of the most aggressive, prowling the store and pouncing on customers, rather than waiting for them to come to her. One wolf says, "Every well-dressed customer, cranky or not, looks like a five-dollar bill to me."[33] An even more aggressive wolf is an "elbower," who is determined to get every customer. "While attending to one, she answers the question of a second, urges a third to be patient, and beckons to a fourth from the distance. Sometimes she will literally elbow her sales colleagues out of the way."[34] The elbower is very expert in differentiating between those who are looking and those who intend to purchase, as well as distinguishing the small buyer from the big buyer. "Why waste good selling time with the folks who can't make up their mind, the ones who want to tell you their life-history, the bargain wolves, the advice-seekers, and the 'I'm just looking' boobs?"[35] The "charmer" is the salesgirl who relies on her looks and smile to make sales. The "ingenue" is new to the job and relies on her self-effacing manner and the help of more experienced salesgirls to make sales. The "collegiate" is a part-time college girl who relies on "her impulsive amateurishness" to make a living. The "drifter" is more concerned with gossiping with her colleagues than with making sales. The "social pretender" alienates her colleagues with her "airs," but she is attractive to wealthy customers in particular. The salesgirl who lasts to be an "old-timer" is either the "disgruntled rebel or a completely accommodated saleswoman. In either case, she is the backbone of the salesforce, the cornerstone around which it is built."[36]

Automobile Salesmen. A more detailed analysis of the sales process is outlined in Miller's study of the automobile salesman.[37] He analyzed the relationship between the automobile salesman and his customer, for it is this relationship which is the major defining characteristic of the automobile salesman's job. Miller breaks the sales relationship into these parts: the contact, the pitch, the close, and cooling out.

a) *The contact,* which may either be random or solicited by the salesman. Those who are unsolicited are not ideal customers. Many are not really

32 Mills, *White Collar,* pp. 161–188.
33 Ibid., p. 175.
34 Ibid.
35 Ibid.
36 Ibid., p. 177.
37 Stephen J. Miller, "The Social Base of Sales Behavior," *Social Problems* 12 (1964), pp. 15–24.

in the market for a car while others are, but salesmen are reluctant to deal with them because the customer controls the negotiation and the sale. Much more important are recruited customers who are clearly in the market and who the salesman is able to control. Thus, one of the defining characteristics of a good salesman is the ability to recruit customers.

b) *The pitch* is begun when the customer makes it clear he really seeks to buy a car. The pitch is analyzed by Miller in dramaturgical terms. There is a social drama taking place in which the salesman tries to understand his customer and to modify his pitch to fit the customer's character. In discussing a trade-in, taking a test drive, and seeking the customer's old car, the sales-man is able to discover things about him which help in selling the car. The salesman seeks to find out what the customer is thinking at all times. He ac-complishes this by "taking the role" of the customer as well as by keeping him talking. At all times "the salesman desires to keep control, in fact, achieve mastery of his relationship with the customer."[38] Control is much more im-portant than profit.

c) *The close* is marked by the salesman figuratively changing sides, tell-ing the customer, in effect, "that he has gotten the best of the deal."[39] In ad-dition, the salesman now says he will act in behalf of the customer in trying to get the sales manager to "OK" such a magnificent deal. The salesman feigns a battle with the sales manager and returns telling the customer how much trouble he had closing the deal. Throughout the entire drama it is em-phasized that the buyer is the shrewdist negotiator imaginable.

d) *Cooling.* After the purchase the salesman tries to disengage himself from the customer. He now has nothing to gain from him and seeks to pass him on to others in the organization so he can move on to other sales. "The buyer is ushered to the service department where he is literally promoted from the role of buyer to that of owner and presented with the purchased au-tomobile. The salesman foists the customer on the agency and the service manager now enters into a relationship with owner. . . . The 'cooling' of the buyer becomes a continuing feature of the service manager's role."[40]

9. White-collar workers have highly constricted career patterns.

Immobility. Once he is at his occupational level, there are few upward steps open to the white-collar worker. Most individuals who achieve white-collar status have already experienced some upward mobility. In their profile of the typical white-collar career, Miller and Form point out that the white-collar worker usually comes from a lower-middle-class background and fre-quently has only one or two years of college.[41] For one reason or another he leaves school and his first position is usually at the white-collar level. In

[38] Ibid., p. 19.
[39] Ibid., p. 20.
[40] Ibid., p. 21.
[41] Miller and Form, *Industrial Sociology*, pp. 590–591.

achieving this status he has probably far outdistanced his father in terms of occupational status. Nevertheless, in his first five years on the job he is likely to change positions twice in an attempt to find a higher-paying job. After this, however, he tends to stop looking and reconciles himself to the fact that, all things considered, he is in the best possible position. He must reconcile himself because there are very few better positions open to him. In this sense he is little different than the blue-collar worker. Increasingly, the managerial positions to which he might aspire are manned by college graduates. Top management is unlikely even to consider him for a management position, even if he performs his work in an outstanding manner. With no possibility of movement up he becomes proud of his white-collar status and finds satisfaction in the fact that he is better than blue-collar workers, believing this although many blue-collar workers earn more money.

The white-collar worker is also similar to the blue-collar worker employee in that both turn outside the workplace for satisfaction. Hobbies, sports, and numerous other leisure-time activities assume central importance. Realizing his own career limitations, the white-collar worker turns to his children. He attempts to give them the necessary prerequisites so that they can move into high-level organizational positions. He instills in them the importance of education and tries very hard to enable them to attend college. While the above applies mainly to male children, girls are also instilled with the importance of education, although the goal is a good marriage rather than a good job.

If one examines the nature of various white-collar occupations, other reasons for the immobility experienced in them become clear. In the case of the secretaries, one barrier is the fact that they are almost always female. In our society all females face added barriers to upward mobility, as has been made clear throughout this book. As a matter of fact many white-collar workers are female, and for that reason alone are immobile. The secretary's skills are hardly usable at the managerial level. If she excels at typing and shorthand she can expect job security, but little in the way of promotions. The same is true for all white-collar occupations; the skills needed to succeed are irrelevant to managerial success. The clerk may know how to handle the files, but this hardly prepares him to manage a clerical department. The bookkeeper may be very skilled at making ledger entries, but this hardly prepares him to be the manager of a highly complex accounting department.

Demotion. Although the white-collar worker finds it difficult to move up, he may find some solace in the fact that he is also unlikely to move down. As has been pointed out before, status differences within white-collar work have been levelled. Thus the white-collar workers in any office are at essentially the same level. Poor performance, within bounds, is unlikely to have any impact on their careers. Organizations hate to fire people, and the barely adequate clerk is fairly secure. Demotion to the ranks of blue-collar work is

extremely unlikely in most organizations. Although organizations dislike firing workers, white-collar workers are less secure on this issue than other occupational groups. For a number of reasons already pointed out, organizations
are very unlikely to fire professionals or managers. Even the lower-status blue-
collar worker is more secure about retaining his job, mainly because he has
the protection of the labor union. Although the white-collar worker is more
insecure about being fired, he is unlikely to be really concerned about the
possibility. It is quite clear that merely adequate performance is enough to
ensure him of his position for life. If he is in the civil service he is even more
secure, because the civil service rules make it very difficult to fire a white-
collar worker.

Salesmen.   The sales occupation, like other white-collar occupations, has
very constricted career patterns. Once one is a salesman there are few steps
left in formal career-pattern terms. If he moves on to be a salesmanager he
has moved out of the sales occupation and become a manager. As in most occupations there are informal career steps open. Bigger sales, a better territory,
or an award from the company for service may all be considered informal
steps up. Formal steps down are also unlikely since almost all of these would
lead out of the occupation.

10.   Blacks and females at the white-collar level face few problems
other than those which are common to them at all occupational
levels.

Since they generally do not deal with customers or supervise subordinates, these two causes of racial and sexual strife cause little problem for
blacks and females in white-collar clerical occupations. Females, in particular,
are at home at this occupational level because many white-collar occupations
are defined as female positions. Nevertheless, here as everywhere else in the
workworld, blacks and females face discriminatory hiring practices and the
prejudice and discrimination of peers and superiors.

Although many firms continue to discriminate against hiring blacks for
white-collar positions, others are discriminating in the other direction, and are
hiring blacks in preference to whites with similar qualifications. This "racism
in reverse" is in response to pressure from the government and civil rights
groups. White-collar occupations offer the firm an excellent showcase to indicate to these pressure sources that they do hire blacks, for the black receptionist,
secretary, or typist is often highly visible to outsiders. Quite frequently however, this type of hiring degenerates into tokenism. A few blacks are placed in
highly visible white-collar jobs, while the company continues to discriminate
against blacks in virtually every other area. Obviously the token black is in a
highly uncomfortable position: he must function among whites and with the
realization that he is merely a token and that the company continues to discriminate against blacks.

Black or female salesmen have the same problems as blacks or females in any service occupation. As long as they serve members of their own sex or race they have no more problems than other minority group white-collar workers. But when the customers are from the majority groups, the problems begin in earnest. Basically it is the same old problem of whites or males being unable to accept blacks or females in positions of authority. Thus members of the majority groups are less likely to come to minority-group sales people, and if they do they are more likely to give them a difficult time and less likely to buy.

SKILLED WORKERS

11. The major problem for skilled craftsmen is threats to their autonomy.

History of the craftsman. The craftsman, as we know him, dates back to fourteenth-century Europe.[42] It is at this time that we find the first craftsman who "owned not only the tools but also the raw materials and, in some cases, the workshop."[43] These early craftsmen were organized into guilds which served to further their interests as well as assume a responsibility to the community for quality goods at a fair price. They worked on an individual basis mainly because there were as yet no large industries, and since there were no industries the major work organization was the occupation and its guild. It is from involvement in the guilds and lack of involvement in industry that the craftsmen developed their sense of autonomy. However, the old guild system broke down in the wake of modernization:

The regulated economy of the guild town disintegrated with the growth of a centralized state organization, unification of large economic areas and radical changes in the technique of production and distribution which came in the seventeenth and eighteenth centuries. Commercialization and later mechanization of industry resulted in a regrouping of occupations and eventually in the creation of a new occupational order.[44]

That new occupational order forced the vast majority of skilled craftsmen into large industries in which their old notions of autonomy were opposed: the principles of formal organizations stood in direct contrast to the principle of autonomy. Some skilled craftsmen have avoided employment in formal organizations and continue to work on their own, but their problem is more one of survival than of autonomy. In effect, they have avoided the problem of maintaining their autonomy, but have substituted for it the problems involved in being a small proprietor.

[42] Arthur Salz, "Occupations in Their Historical Perspective," in Nosow and Form, *Man, Work and Society,* pp. 58–63.
[43] Ibid., p. 62.
[44] Ibid., pp. 62–63.

Autonomy. The skilled craftsman is in many ways similar to the professional. Like the professional he feels a sense of autonomy: after all, only he knows how to perform his particular task. Despite this ideology, his autonomy is continually threatened. One reason is that he lacks the general, systematic knowledge of the professional. Instead, he has a series of skills which are picked up in training for the job and are therefore not theoretically based. The lathe operator need know little physics to operate his machine effectively. Our society has far more respect for the theoretical knowledge of the professional than for the practical knowledge of the skilled craftsman; hence he is accorded far less status by the outside world. Because he has less status and little theoretical knowledge, laymen are much more likely to question the skilled worker than the professional. Further, the skilled craftsman does not have a powerful professional association for protection. The most important threat to his autonomy stems from the fact that, with the growth of huge industries, he is increasingly an employee of an organization, subject to control from above, frequently from superiors with little knowledge of his specialty. As we have seen in the case of the professional, it is difficult to sustain autonomy within an organization. In the case of the skilled worker it is even harder to maintain because of his lower status and lack of a powerful professional organization.

Construction workers. While we contend that skilled craftsmen are "like" professionals, Stinchcombe goes further in his discussion of "professional" construction workers,[45] in which he argues that construction workers go through a process of technical socialization and as a result are recognized as being competent in their area by the public. He sees the construction union as analogous to a professional association and an agency which ensures that those who are trained by it are hired preferentially. Stinchcombe proceeds to make the familiar distinction discussed in Chapter 2 between the professional and bureaucratic ways of organizing work. For a number of reasons which relate to the structure of the construction industry, it cannot be, and is not, run bureaucratically. For one, the amount and kind of work done are highly variable—there are periods when there is much work and periods when much of the workforce is laid off. The kind of work required also varies from one site to another. In addition, the work is widely dispersed geographically. For all of these reasons it would be inefficient to organize construction work bureaucratically, and thus, according to Stinchcombe, it is organized professionally. Decisions are made autonomously by the work crews rather than dictated from the top. The construction industry has an attenuated organizational structure with relatively few clerks and professionals employed. Communication is not from the top down, but built into the contracts. Further, the contracts specify only goals of the work and prices; how the

[45] Arthur Stinchcombe, "Bureaucratic and Craft Administration of Production: A Comparative Study," *Administrative Science Quarterly* 4 (1959), 168–187.

job is to be performed is left to the construction worker. Stinchcombe contends that these specifications do not have to be there because of the "professionalized culture" of the construction workers.

While Stinchcombe is correct in his analysis of the construction industry, he is using the term "professional" far too liberally. In effect he is making the same error made by Foote in his discussion of the professionalization of labor in Detroit. Just as the laborers in Detroit are not professional, the skilled crafts are not professions. Skilled craftsmen have many characteristics in common with professionals, but these crafts lack a number of aspects of the professional model (for example, as pointed out above, systematic knowledge in the sense that members of the professions possess it). Thus although the skilled crafts are certainly *not* professions, the similarity between them and professions leads us to conclude that the skilled craftsman faces the same types of problems on the job as the professional employed in an organization.

The threat of management.   Management, generally in the form of the immediate supervisor, poses the greatest threat to the skilled craftsman's autonomy. Most craftsmen take a great deal of pride in their work and feel that since only they have the skills, only they should judge their work. Yet management frequently has different goals, and this is the source of the conflict. Management may need a job done quickly, but the craftsman may feel that it must be done right, and to do it right takes time. Management feels that only it has the "big picture," and that therefore it must supervise the activities of all its workers, including skilled craftsmen. Knowing it must meet a deadline, management may request its skilled craftsmen to work harder or take shortcuts.

12.   Skilled workers employ a variety of formal and informal means to resolve the problem of threats to their autonomy.

Formal means

The major function of skilled trades unions is to prevent managerial encroachment on autonomy. The typographers and their union, the International Typographical Union, have been extremely successful in retaining their autonomy on the job. According to Perlman and Taft, the ITU has "the most complete control over job conditions of any union in the world."[46] It won a closed shop although the Taft-Hartley law made the closed shop illegal. Thus, all workers in the composing room, even foremen, must belong to the ITU before they can be considered for a job. The inclusion of foremen means that they are far more responsive to the union than they are to man-

---

[46] Seymour Martin Lipset, Martin Trow, and James Coleman, *Union Democracy* (Garden City, N.Y.: Anchor Books, 1962), p. 24.

agement. If the foreman violates union regulations he is subject to a fine. In this way, a major tool for managerial encroachment is brought under the union's control, and this fact alone has severely restricted the management's power to dictate terms to the skilled workers. The ITU has, however, gone far beyond this in its efforts to maintain the autonomy of its members.

The composing room. In the printing industry it is the workers, not management, who run their workplace, the composing room. Management has only the broad right to determine the way the work is supposed to be done. The job, however, belongs to the printer, not to the foreman or the shop. A good example of the printer's control over his job is the way in which replacements are selected should the worker decide to take a day off. In almost every other job it is the company which determines the substitute; in the printing industry the regular printer decides who shall temporarily replace him. An even clearer example of the printer's power is the fact that no non-union employee is allowed on the shop floor. This means that the union could prevent the owner of the company from setting foot in the composing room. Lipset et al. point out that this rule is rarely enforced: "Yet its existence is a reminder of a power relationship, and it may be invoked when the workers in a given shop have a grievance. In one New York newspaper some time ago the men stopped working when a well-known anti-labor columnist who had written articles attacking the ITU walked into the composing room to deliver his copy."[47]

Hiring. The ITU controls hiring in the printing industry. Union rules, which are accepted by management, state that workers must be hired (or fired) in accord with the union's seniority list. The union has a list of substitute workers and when a permanent opening occurs it must be given to the substitute with the most seniority "regardless of the employer's or foreman's opinion of the relative capabilities of available men."[48] When there is to be a reduction in force the company must lay off the employee with the least seniority.

Union law. The ITU has a series of laws which "determine conditions of employment, maximum length of work-week or work day, priority, closed shop, use of reproduced material, control over all composing-room work, and other work conditions."[49] These laws are defined by the union as nonnegotiable; that is, management must accept them if they wish to be in the printing business. If management objects to any portion of union law, or wishes to lay off a worker with seniority, it must make its appeal within the union structure. It can appeal to the local union, the national union, or to the conven-

---

[47] Ibid., p. 26.
[48] Ibid., p. 24.
[49] Ibid., p. 25.

tion, but the final decision rests with the union. There have been many disputes between publishers and the union on this issue, but in general the union has been able to maintain its control. "In large measure printers have demanded and won the right to be treated as independent craftsmen who control their own work and maintain and enforce their own standards of workmanship."[50]

Other devices.   Although the ITU has been more successful than other craft unions in protecting its members' autonomy, it is not atypical. Almost all craft unions have been able to employ a variety of techniques to protect member autonomy. Most are able to control job entry through the apprenticeship system. (Apprenticeship usually involves the lengthy training of the neophyte by an established journeyman.) This program performs a variety of functions for the skilled trades. Management may only hire as skilled craftsmen those who have successfully completed the program. The training of new skilled workers is determined by the union and its members, not the management: this keeps the number of skilled tradesmen low, giving them high job security and wages. Finally, the union sets the wages for the apprentice and prevents him from competing with the journeyman when he nears the end of his training program. Many skilled trades unions also utilize a closed shop despite the fact that it has been outlawed by Taft-Hartley. In order to circumvent the law they call their agreement a union-shop agreement, and this in fact gives them control of the selection of new employees. Under this system the employer may hire whom he wishes, but the new employee is required to join the union within a specified period of time. This is less effective than the closed shop, but it still gives the union a great deal of control. Skilled trades unions frequently have hiring halls in which unemployed members are referred to employers who have reported vacancies. After Taft-Hartley many of these hiring halls had to accept nonunion workers, but these nonmembers were referred only on a token basis.

There are a number of other devices employed by skilled trades unions in particular to increase the autonomy of their members. Some have rules that determine the number of workers which must be used on a given job. Such efforts to set work crews, which management generally feels forces them to use unneeded manpower, are common among railroad workers and musicians. A variant of this is union efforts to set up "make-work" requirements. For example, painters are frequently forbidden to use rollers although it is more efficient to do so. Other skilled unions attempt to set the workplace as well as the general union goals of wages, hours, and working conditions. Seniority rules are utilized in virtually all types of unions, skilled and nonskilled, to give the union control of hiring and firing. In sum, virtually all practices of the skilled trades unions may be viewed as attempts to prevent managerial encroachment on the autonomy of the skilled craftsman.

[50] Ibid., p. 31.

Informal means

In addition to the formal methods employed by the unions, skilled craftsmen employ a variety of informal means to protect their sense of autonomy. Note that the emphasis here is on the sense of autonomy rather than the autonomy itself. The union structure is a much more important contributor to actual autonomy than is the informal organization. Nevertheless, the informal organization does also, to some degree, contribute to actual autonomy. However, the preeminent function of the informal organization in the skilled trades is the preservation of a feeling or sense of autonomy.

The printers are the best example of the development of such an informal organization. Lipset et al. point out that printers have traditionally considered themselves an elite blue-collar occupation because of their great skill and the high degree of literacy they need. They were one of the first cohesive, informal work groups, and this informal structure, after first serving to preserve the autonomy of its members, was soon transformed into a formal union. Today an elaborate informal structure coexists with the formal union hierarchy. It fulfills a variety of social functions, some of which are related to the preservation of autonomy. For example, there are a series of informal norms, violations of which are punished by the group. As mentioned earlier, since foremen are members of the union, this is an important method of preventing encroachment on autonomy by first-line supervisors. Should the foreman try to interfere with the printers' traditional activities, he is likely to be sanctioned severely by the informal group. This is a weapon which is peculiar to the printing industry, since in few other industries are members of management also members of the union.

Social interaction. The fact that there is a high degree of informal, off-the-job interaction among printers also helps preserve their sense of autonomy. Social interaction does little to preserve actual autonomy, but it does give the printer a sense of his different and elite status among blue-collar workers. As Lipset et al. point out, the informal relations among printers are almost unbelievably elaborate:

Social clubs, organized leisure activities such as bowling leagues, and union newspapers are of course not unique to the printers, although we know of no other occupation which has as many and diverse forms of organized extravocational activities as the ITU. . . . In interviews many printers reported that their best friends are other printers, that they regularly visit the homes of other printers, that they often meet in bars, go fishing together, or see each other in various places before and after work. . . . In addition to the extensive social relations between printers away from the job, there is also more socializing among printers on the job than we find in most occupations.[51]

[51] Ibid., p. 78.

All of these informal relationships function to give the printer a sense of his differentness, his elitism, and his autonomy vis-à-vis other formal and informal groups.

The French bureaucracy. Crozier's study of French bureaucracy reveals another aspect of the informal autonomy of skilled craftsmen[52] (in a section on the relationship between the unskilled production workers and the skilled maintenance employees). The maintenance workers, because of the nature of their work, are free and independent from control by production workers. On the other hand the production workers are highly dependent on the maintenance employees. The autonomy of the maintenance workers and the dependency of the production worker center around machine stoppages. When a machine breaks down only the maintenance worker has the skill to fix it and he cannot, because of his skill, be directly supervised by anyone in the organization. Hence in this central event in the life of an industrial organization, the maintenance man is almost totally autonomous, while the production worker cannot fix the problem himself and therefore must rely on the maintenance person. Also, the breakdown of the machines is a highly important event for production workers: "Production workers are displeased by the consequences of a machine stoppage. It disrupts their work; it is likely to make it necessary for them to work harder to compensate for lost time; and if it lasts long enough, they will be displaced, losing friendship ties and even status."[53] Because he has power over both production workers and supervisors in this situation, the maintenance worker emerged as the most powerful figure on the shop floor. His power stemmed from his ability to control uncertainty, specifically the centrally important event of machine breakdown. Although he has power, it is not legitimate power. Thus he is insecure in his power position due to threats to that power from other actors on the shop floor. Nevertheless, his skilled status has given him a great deal of autonomy within the French bureaucracy studied by Crozier. This finding may also be generalizable to other industrial settings in the sense that many skilled tradesmen have the rather unique ability to control uncertainty and hence gain informal power in the organization.

Although the discussion in this section has focused on only two skilled crafts, there is evidence that many skilled trades utilize these devices to protect autonomy. If one looks at the formal and informal organization of carpenters, plumbers, electricians, etc., he will find many of the same protective mechanisms. They all have strong unions, apprenticeship programs, hiring-hall type arrangements, and strong informal organizations. One of the major goals of each of these devices is the protection of the skilled craftsman's autonomy.

[52] Michel Crozier, *The Bureaucratic Phenomenon* (Chicago: University of Chicago Press, 1967).
[53] Ibid., p. 109.

13. The career patterns in the skilled trades are rigid and highly restricted.

The skilled craftsman generally comes from a lower-middle-class background and is typically a high-school graduate. He may work for several years in semiskilled occupations until he is accepted in the apprenticeship program of a skilled occupation. Apprenticeship periods vary in length, but six years might be the average length of the program. He cannot be employed as a journeyman until he has completed the program, at which time he is almost immediately employed in a skilled position for which he has been trained.

Once in his selected trade, the skilled craftsman has virtually nowhere to go. It must be pointed out that most do not want to go anywhere else since they are very proud of their skill and very committed to their craft. However, even if he should want to move, he would find it extremely difficult. One type of mobility which he does have is geographic mobility. Seamen, carpenters, electricians, etc. can find similar work in many locations throughout the United States. However, he has little chance of occupational mobility. He could conceivably move down to semiskilled or unskilled occupations, but he is unlikely to because of the decline in status, security, and pay. His specialized training makes it almost equally impossible for him to move into other skilled occupations: a plumber cannot become an electrician, nor can a carpenter become a printer. There is some possibility of upward mobility into foreman-level positions, but few are likely to desire this move because of the greater responsibility without a corresponding increase in pay. More to the point, there are far more skilled trades positions than there are foreman positions for those who desire this kind of move. Higher-management positions are almost entirely out of reach, for his skilled training does not suit the craftsman for top-management positions. Further, he most frequently has no more than a high-school education, and management positions are increasingly restricted to college graduates. Thus once in his position, the skilled craftsman has little mobility. It should be reiterated that for most this is not a problem, since they are generally contented.

14. The skilled trades have been, and continue to be, highly discriminatory.

We need not discuss females in this section since there are relatively few, if any, who have been interested in entering the skilled trades. This reluctance is due to the nature of female socialization process as well as the resistance of the male dominated craft organizations. In discussing blacks in the skilled trades the focus must be on the discriminatory practices of the skilled unions since they are such a dominant force in the life of the skilled craftsman. As Marshall shows, craft unions have employed both formal and informal means of discriminating against blacks.[54]

[54] Ray Marshall, The Negro Worker (New York: Random House, 1967).

Formal barriers. Marshall discusses three craft unions in terms of their formal policies for excluding blacks. The Brotherhood of Railway and Steamship Clerks (BRSC) had a "white only" clause in its first constitution (1899). During World War I the union expanded to take in freight handlers, many of whom were black. To keep the blacks out of the union, they were put in separate locals linked directly to the AFL. This was unsatisfactory to both groups; the BRSC lost dues and the blacks were placed in a position of lower status. In the late 1930s the BRSC decided to allow blacks in, but in separate locals with white leaders. A 1946 New York State law outlawing black auxiliaries and color barriers impelled the union to drop its white-only clause and most of its separate black locals. The changes were approved by the union members only after the president assured them that these formal changes would really not alter very much. In fact, despite the formal changes, many union lodges continued to be virtually all black. Thus informal barriers had obviously replaced the formal barriers to equality for blacks within the union.

The International Brotherhood of Boilermakers, Iron Ship Builders, Blacksmiths, Forgers, and Helpers had a constitutional bar against black members until 1937. In that year separate auxiliary lodges for black members were begun. The reason, however, was far from humanitarian—the change was pushed by southern members because they feared competition from lower-paid blacks. During World War II the Boilermakers resisted attempts by government agencies to force the end of formal discrimination. The beginning of the end of black lodges came in 1944, with a California Supreme Court decision "that the union could not enforce the closed shop against the members of auxiliary locals."[55] This meant that black workers would be allowed to work without joining the union. "Faced with this possible loss of revenue and economic control, the Boilermakers' Executive Committee authorized the elimination of auxiliary locals."[56]

The Machinists (now the International Association of Machinists and Aerospace Workers) first formally barred blacks from membership in 1888, and this bar was not removed until 1948. Between 1888 and 1948 there were a variety of factors which led to the elimination of the barrier: The AFL dropped its formal barrier to blacks in 1895 (although it retained informal barriers); the union lost much of its southern character; the bar limited its growth, embarrassed its leaders, and it hurt its ability to compete for members with other unions; and the union would have lost its bargaining rights in the face of increasing government legislation. Even after the end of the formal barrier in 1948, the Machinists continued to have locals segregated on the basis of informal agreements.

Informal barriers. Unions which had formal bars have continued to have informal barriers, and some unions which never had formal barriers have

[55] Ibid., p. 62.
[56] Ibid.

always employed informal means. Marshall gives a good summary of the variety of these informal discriminatory practices:

These include agreements not to sponsor Negroes for membership; refusal to admit Negroes into apprenticeship programs or to accept their applications, or simply ignore their applications; general "understandings" to vote against Negroes if they are proposed (for example, as few as three members of some locals can bar applicants for membership); refusal of journeyman status to Negroes by means of examinations which either are not given to whites or are rigged so that Negroes cannot pass them; exertion of political pressure on governmental licensing agencies to ensure that Negroes fail the tests; and restriction of membership to sons, nephews, or other relatives of members.[57]

Marshall finds these informal barriers a nationwide practice and not merely a southern phenomenon. Although some industrial unions do informally discriminate, this process is practiced far more frequently by the craft unions. One reason lies in the fact that craft unions were the first unions and are therefore older and more traditional. They have not kept pace with, and have even resisted, the changes in race relations in the United States. Another factor is that many crafts require contact with white customers (e.g., plumbers). Finally, the skilled trades are the highest-status blue-collar jobs, and given white racial attitudes, it is understandable why whites should seek to exclude blacks from such positions. There is also a factor which relates to the general attitude of craftsmen to their jobs: they have, as has been discussed before, a strong sense of autonomy and a view that their job is their property. Hence any attempt at outside interference is likely to be resented and fought.

As witnessed by current attempts by blacks across the United States to gain equal treatment in skilled trade unions, there is the likelihood of change in the near future. The old-line skilled unions are likely to be one of the last bastions to fall in the face of black pressure for equality, but it is probable, given the change in the racial climate in the United States, that this bastion will ultimately fall. In the case of the crafts it is the union which is the focus of black protest. This sets the crafts apart from most other occupations in which the focus is on the discriminatory policies of the employer.

THE FEMALE SEMIPROFESSIONS

One of the most interesting occupational groups is the semiprofessions, which are dominated by females. The three major occupations included under this heading are teaching, nursing, and social work. These occupations are not professions, and the fact that they are dominated by females is a central barrier to their professional status.

[57] Ibid., p. 63.

15. The major problem for semiprofessionals is the barriers they face in their efforts to gain professional recognition.

As semiprofessionals, teachers, social workers, and nurses stand closer to the professional than the nonprofessional end of the continuum. However, most occupational sociologists would not include these occupations under the heading of professions. A useful way of determining the place of the semi-professions on the professional continuum is to examine them in terms of the six structural characteristics discussed in Chapter 2. As you remember, the six characteristics are:

1. General, systematic knowledge.
2. Authority over clients.
3. Community rather than self-interest, which is related to an emphasis on symbolic rather than monetary rewards.
4. Self-control through professional associations, training schools, and sponsorship patterns rather than outside control.
5. Recognition by the public and law that the occupation is a profession.
6. A distinctive culture.

In the next few pages the three semiprofessions are discussed in terms of each of these dimensions.

General, systematic knowledge. Teachers, social workers, and nurses probably lack most in this category. Teachers have little general systematic knowledge of teaching because in fact there is no such knowledge base in teaching. Rather there are a series of ideas about how to teach which are picked up either in school or on the job. There has been an influx of principles from social sciences such as psychology, social psychology, and sociology, but as yet these theoretical insights have not been developed into a theory of teaching. More important, these insights are not the exclusive domain of teaching. They "belong" to the sociologist, the social psychologist, and the psychologist. Teaching must use some of these insights to develop a theory of its own if it is to be regarded as a profession, at least on this characteristic. The same lack of general systematic knowledge also plagues nurses and social workers. Katz notes that nurses have no clearly formulated body of professional knowledge that is recognized and accepted by others.[58] Toren, in discussing social workers, makes essentially the same point: "This means that the knowledge base of social work is still, to a large extent, drawn from experience—i.e., generalizations inferred from many specific cases—and that a great deal of intuition is required in the application of this knowledge."[59] Thus all of the semiprofessions share this lack of a firm base of knowledge.

[58] Fred E. Katz, "Nurses," in Amitai Etzioni, ed., *The Semi-Professions and Their Organizations* (New York: Free Press, 1969), pp. 54–81.

[59] Nina Toren, "Semi-Professionalism and Social Work: A Theoretical Perspective," in Etzioni, *Semi-Professions*, p. 146.

Courses in school are generally atheoretical, much of the knowledge which does exist is practical and is drawn from other disciplines, and on-the-job behavior is determined by practical know-how rather than by general principles.

Authority over clients. The semiprofessionals also have far less authority over clients than do those in the established professions. One of the major reasons for this is the lack of general systematic knowledge and the resulting lower prestige. For these reasons clients are far more likely to question the authority of nurses, social workers, and teachers than they are to question the authority of the doctor or the lawyer. A patient will often give his doctor unlimited authority, but he is unlikely to grant the same to a nurse. For the same reasons students and their parents are more likely to question teachers and clients are more likely to question social workers. Another factor in the relative lack of authority of the semiprofessionals vis-à-vis clients is the fact that the semiprofessions are dominated by females and regarded as feminine occupations. As has frequently been pointed out in this book, women in our society are supposed to be followers, not leaders. Thus clients are far less likely to allow females, or those who work in female occupations even if they are males, unrestricted authority. Finally, there is the fact that the semiprofessions are almost entirely creatures of a formal organization. Authority over clients often has been granted to free professionals, but because the semiprofessionals are employees, clients are less likely to grant them such authority.

Community vs. self-interest. Semiprofessionals are as likely as established professionals to be imbued with community rather than self-interest, but because of certain structural factors they tend to lose sight of their community interests. This is not to say, by any means, that they lack community interest. Clearly, teachers, social workers, and nurses are concerned with helping mankind. There are two basic structural reasons why semiprofessionals have less community interest than established professionals. The first is that they are employees of formal organizations, and as such many develop what Merton has called a bureaucratic personality, which carries with it a displacement of goals. They become far more concerned with their position in the organization and their own security. By focusing on this they may lose sight of the goals of the occupation and the organization. The other factor here is their marginal status. Semiprofessionals are insecure about both their status as professionals and their status in their employing organization. One of the reasons established professionals can eschew many self-interested goals is their security: they do not have to worry about improving their status occupationally or organizationally. On the other hand, semiprofessionals frequently cannot afford to ignore their own interests, and must always be concerned with trying to maintain or improve their position in the occupation or the employing organization. This greater self-interest manifests itself in the semiprofessions in a greater concern for economic rewards. Again, this should not imply that semiprofessionals are not interested in symbolic rewards. The established professionals can afford to focus on symbolic rewards, because even with this focal concern they are guaranteed an adequate income. Semiprofessionals, however, are notoriously low paid, hence the almost constant concern with improving their economic position. Thus teachers join unions and strike for higher wages even though it hurts the community. Further, many are forced to moonlight in order to make a living wage, even though it may affect their ability to adequately perform their major function of serving the community.

Self-control. There is somewhat less self-control within the semiprofessions than in the professions. One reason is the weakness of the semiprofessional associations as compared to the professional associations. The national associations of teachers, nurses, and social workers are far less powerful than those of doctors and lawyers. Although they are intrinsically weaker, a more important source of their relative weakness is the power of the organizations which employ their members. Semiprofessionals are for the most part not free professionals—they are hired, paid, and owe their prime allegiance to the employing organization. It is this fact more than any other that restricts the power of their national associations. Since they are paid by their organizations, semiprofessionals are more likely, when there is a conflict, to conform to the norms of the organization than those of the national association. The reason, basically, is that the organization has far more power over the semiprofessional than does the national association. After all, being fired by one's employer is far more painful than the disapprobation of a national association. The free professional does not face this dilemma because he is not employed by a formal organization. As the old free professionals increasingly become employed in organizations, they are likely to face the same types of dilemmas and also more likely to resolve them in favor of the employing organization. However most of the established professionals retain private practices and this makes them better able to withstand pressure from an employing organization.

The semiprofessions also have training schools, but they are not nearly as important as the training schools of the established professions. For one thing, one can enter the semiprofessions with only undergraduate training. In a number of cases even this requirement has been waived—there are practicing teachers, nurses, and social workers who have had no specifically related training at the undergraduate level. For example, because of the shortage of teachers in some metropolitan areas, school boards have been forced to hire college graduates without any specific training in teaching. There are nurses, in particular practical nurses, who have no collegiate training in nursing. The semiprofessions are also less likely to employ sponsorship patterns. Once again, the primary reason is the power of the employing organization and the relative lack of power of the professional organization.

For all of the above reasons the semiprofessions are much more likely to be controlled by forces outside the occupation, in particular the employing organization. This point is made over and over again in the literature. In discussing all of the semiprofessions, Toren says: "They will also be less able to insist on complete freedom from control, whether by the public, special groups of laymen, or their administrative superiors."[60] Scott makes the important point that there is diversity within any occupation in terms of its attitudes toward autonomy.[61] In analyzing social workers he found four types of professional orientations:

1. Professionals—those with graduate training and responsiveness to the professional groups.
2. Reference group only—those without graduate training, but responsive to the professional groups.
3. Training only—those with graduate training, but responsive to the employing organization.
4. Bureaucrats—those who both lack professional training and are responsive to the employing organization.[62]

Scott found 56 of the 79 individuals he studied could be classified into Categories 3 and 4. This means that a vast majority of his respondents do not have autonomy and are not likely to be concerned about it. When he asked his respondents about routine supervision by superiors in the organization, half felt this to be "a good arrangement," while the other half found it to have both "advantages and disadvantages." None of his respondents felt that this was "not a good arrangement."[63] Thus social workers, in the main, are subjected to external control and are not displeased by this. (One could contrast this to the established professions, in which all efforts aimed at outside control by nonprofessionals are likely to be bitterly fought.) Nurses must face external control from two sources: one is the administrative hierarchy within the hospital and the other is the doctor. Since the doctor is of significantly higher status, the nurse frequently finds herself in a position of subordination in her relationship to the doctor. The teacher is in the same sort of position in that she must be responsive to the administrators of the school. The domination of females in the semiprofessions also reduces semiprofessional autonomy. Once again, females in our society are not supposed to be independent, but are supposed to be in a subordinate position.

Nurses. The semiprofessional's lack of autonomy on the job has been demonstrated in a variety of studies. In his study of psychiatric nurses Rush-

[60] Ibid., p. 154.
[61] W. Richard Scott, "Professional Employees in a Bureaucratic Structure: Social Work," in Etzioni, *Semi-Professions*, pp. 82–140.
[62] Ibid., p. 90.
[63] Ibid., p. 93.

ing found that deference characterized the nurse's relationship to the physician.[64] Relying on a number of other studies, Rushing did not even bother to test the relative authority of nurses and physicians. Rather, he "assumed that the nurse is the subordinate in the doctor-nurse relationship. . . . she carries out the doctor's 'orders.'"[65] This assumption was expressed well by one of the head nurses in Rushing's study:

As I see it, the function of the psychiatric nurse, the major function, is to carry out the doctor's care and treatment plan. The doctor is head of the team and it is the nurse's responsibility to carry out his treatment plan. . . . She is the go-between between the doctor and the patient. She relates to the patient so as to support him when he needs it and so on. [But] she relates to him in terms of the doctor's care plan.[66]

While the nurse accepts the authority of the physician, she also accepts the norm that she help the patient. The interesting research question raised by Rushing is, What do nurses do when these two norms conflict? That is, what does she do when the doctor does something which she feels is not in the patient's best interest? Fifteen of the sixteen nurses Rushing studied had experienced such a conflict. Four of those resolved the conflict by doing what the doctor ordered even though they believed it was not in the patient's best interests. These nurses have completely surrendered authority over the patient to the doctor because of his superior status, knowledge, and competence. The remaining eleven nurses tried to do something about the doctor's decision, but, interestingly, they never confronted him directly with their knowledge about the patient. Rather than challenge the authority of the doctor, they sought to influence his decision. Some went over the doctor's head and took the issue up with his superior. Others presented him with information about the patient which seemed to contradict his evaluation, but even these were careful not to contradict him: "I will tell him things about the patient that are contrary to the order given. I just let him know about these things in hopes that he will change the order."[67] Still others asked the physician questions in the hope that in answering he would see his error. These attempts at influence represent the subordination of the nurse to the doctor, and the deference she feels she owes him. She is supposed to be expert on the patient, yet she is unwilling to question the judgment of the physician even in her area of expertise. How can an occupation with these characteristics be considered a profession? One need only think of the reverse situation. A physician who is confronted by a nurse with judgments which he doubts would be quick to express his dissatisfaction. Because nursing is not a profession, nurses do not have very much autonomy on the job. A more important reason,

---

[64] William Rushing, "Social Influence and the Social Psychological Function of Deference," *Social Forces* 41 (1962), 142–148.

[65] Ibid., p. 143.

[66] Ibid., p. 144.

[67] Ibid.

though, for this lack of autonomy is the fact that nurses work hand-in-hand with physicians, members of the occupation which is at the pinnacle of the professional continuum.

In an essay about nurses, Katz makes essentially the same kind of points.[68] In hospitals, physicians are considered to be more important than nurses or any other occupation. This results, according to Katz, in a "caste-like system" which "puts an unscalable wall between the physician and the semi-professionals in the hospital."[69] The nurse must "know her place" by not passing information directly to the patient, but instead transmitting it to the physician whose job it is to pass that information on if he so desires. The nurse must always be aware of her place, even to the point of not daring to sit at a doctor's table during lunch. Further, physicians hold nurses in low esteem and frequently treat them as if they were "nonpersons." The nurse is clearly a second-class citizen in the hierarchy of the hospital system.

Teachers. The same lack of autonomy applies to the other semiprofes-sionals, although their position is not quite as lowly because they are not forced to work side-by-side with established professionals. Let us examine one more example here, the schoolteacher. Her autonomy is threatened by school principals. She is in a much weaker position vis-à-vis the principal than is the established professional in his relationship with his superiors. Goss, for ex-ample, found that physicians in a clinic are likely to comply with routine decisions made by the physician in charge.[70] However, when the physician in charge made judgments about patients, these judgments were taken by the doctors as *suggestions*, with the final decision left to the particular doctor. No such differentiation between routine and core duties is made by the school-teacher: she accepts the principal's authority totally. This is exemplified by the comments of one teacher interviewed by Becker: "After all, he's the principal, he is the boss, what he says should go, you know what I mean. . . . He's the principal and he's the authority, and you have to follow his orders. That's all there is to it."[71] It is inconceivable that a physician could ever make such a statement concerning another doctor in charge of a clinic.

Legal and public recognition. The semiprofessions are, by definition, not recognized as professions by the public. They are, in the main, licensed by governmental agencies. Hence on the variable of public and legal recog-nition, the semiprofessions are not fully professional.

Professional culture. Semiprofessionals seem to have a rather distinctive culture, but given their dual commitment to occupation and organization, it

---

[68] Katz, "Nurses."
[69] Ibid., p. 69.
[70] Mary Goss, "Influence and Authority Among Physicians in an Outpatient Clinic," *American Sociological Review* 26 (1961), 39–50.
[71] Howard S. Becker, "The Teacher in the Authority System of the Public School," *Journal of Educational Sociology* 27 (1953), 133.

is unlikely that they are as involved in their culture as are established professionals. This point is made quite clearly by Lortie in his discussion of the "incomplete subculture" in elementary teaching.[72] One of the major functions of the professional culture is the development of a "professional conscience" in neophytes. However, "elementary teaching represents, at best, a faint replica of such inculcation of technical and moral practices."[73] In the professions much of the early socialization is in the hands of the culture, but for teachers most of the socialization takes place on the first job. The major barrier to the development of a professional culture is the restricted possibilities for interaction and communication open to teachers. Their day is spent in almost constant contact with students, and this prevents interaction with peers. "Such conditions are neither likely to produce a culture marked by rich, specific, and detailed technical terms and procedures nor calculated to develop norms which operationalize values."[74] Once again it is the organization which is the villain. Because of the structure of schools, interaction is inhibited and, consequently, the development of a professional culture is inhibited.

In sum, then, these occupations are, not surprisingly, semiprofessional, but the crux of their problem is that their members want to become professional. In their efforts to attain professional recognition, however, they face two seemingly insurmountable barriers. The first is that they are employees of organizations, and as such can never attain the recognition attained by the old free professionals. Second they are female occupations and females face peculiar problems in terms of professionalism even when they are in the established professions. A female doctor has a far more difficult time gaining acceptance than her male counterpart. However, she is assured of a high degree of status and success merely because she occupies the prestigious position of doctor. In the semiprofessions the problems are greatly complicated. The problems of public acceptance for the female are exacerbated by the fact that there is not a prestigious occupational image for the semiprofessions. Thus the semiprofessions are characterized by a dominance of females in a series of occupations defined as feminine. In discussing social workers, Toren makes this point, which applies as well to the other semiprofessions: "Social work is thus identified in the mind of the public as a feminine occupation; the helping, nurturant functions of the social worker are associated with the traditional roles of women."[75]

16. There are a number of alternatives open to semiprofessionals in their efforts to resolve the problems caused by the barriers to professionalization.

[72] Dan C. Lortie, "The Balance of Control and Autonomy in Elementary School Teaching," in Etzioni, Semi-Professions, pp. 1–53.
[73] Ibid., p. 26.
[74] Ibid., p. 28.
[75] Toren, "Semi-Professionalism and Social Work," p. 156.

Although there is little they can do about the predominance of females, they can seek to alter their public image as members of feminine groups of occupations. However, such a change of image is unlikely because of the nature of their work and the predominance of females in these occupations. There is also little chance of moving out of the organization for the majority of semiprofessionals. There are some private nurses, private tutors, and independent social workers, but a mass exodus in the direction of independence is not a viable alternative for most semiprofessionals. Hospitals, schools, and social work agencies will continue to employ the great bulk of them. However, "freedom" will be open to some. For example, Cohen has written of the movement from organizations to private practice among social workers.[76] The occupations as a whole must work at a more general level to resolve the professional dilemma of their members. There are really two alternatives: to become more like the established professionals or to seek a redefinition of what a professional is.

Acceptance of the professional model. One thing those in the semiprofessionals can do, and really have done, is to accept the professional model and attempt to approximate it. Following the six structural characteristics used to determine the place of an occupation on the professional continuum, (see pp. 56–63), here are some of the things semiprofessionals can do to move toward the professional end of the continuum:

a) They must carve out for themselves a distinct general base of knowledge which is their exclusive domain. This means moving away from a dependence on the social sciences for theoretical insights. Each semiprofession needs to take theory drawn from other disciplines, theory developed internally, and practical insights and combine these into a new body of general systematic knowledge which is its own. This may indeed not be possible, but if it is not the semiprofessions are highly unlikely to ever attain full professional stature.

b) Whether semiprofessionals can gain greater authority over clients depends on various factors, the foremost of which is their ability to develop their own knowledge base. Once this is achieved, acceptance by clients will undoubtedly increase greatly. Although the development of knowledge is necessary, it is not sufficient in itself. Something must be done to combat the feminine image of the semiprofessions as well as to reduce the control by the employing organization.

c) The development of a stronger community interest is also contingent on changes in the factors discussed above. Although semiprofessionals will continue to exist in formal organizations, their autonomy within these organizations must be broadened. One means would be a significant increase in semiprofessional salaries so that they can afford greater community interest.

[76] Michael Cohen, "The Emergence of Private Practice in Social Work," *Social Problems* 14 (1966), 84–93.

Their ability to insist on higher pay depends on the other factors already discussed: more power within the organization and a change in their feminine image.

d) An increase in self-control is contingent, in part, on reducing the influence of the employing organization, but semiprofessionals can also strengthen training programs, professional associations, and sponsorship patterns. For example, they might insist, as they have in some areas, that only those with advanced degrees in the particular area may practice. Further, the training programs themselves might focus much more on socializing the neophyte, rather than leaving much of that socialization for the first job.

e) Public recognition that the occupation is indeed a profession is really contingent on the above factors. If semiprofessionals gain general systematic knowledge, autonomy, authority over clients, and stronger community interest, public recognition will follow, although there is likely to be a lag between achievement of the above goals and such recognition. Thus semiprofessionals might wage an active public relations campaign to inform the public of the changes which have taken place. They might also campaign for more stringent licensing.

f) Like public recognition, the development of a distinctive culture also depends in large part on the development of the first four factors listed in this section. If the other goals were to be obtained, a distinctive professional culture would soon follow.

Becoming more like established professionals constitutes one resolution for semiprofessionals, but they have been trying to do this for years, without a great deal of success. Many occupational sociologists have had and continue to have optimism about semiprofessionals' chances of success, while others recently have become more pessimistic. In a recent article, Goode takes a middle ground, contending that teaching and nursing will not become professions, while social work will.[77] He believes that teaching and nursing "will never reach the levels of knowledge and dedication to service the society considers necessary for a profession."[78] Although Goode is optimistic about the chances of social work, its lack of systematic knowledge continues to stand in the way of full professionalization.

Bureaucratic professionalization. A second solution open to semiprofessionals is for them to eschew interest in becoming like doctors and lawyers. After all, the professional model is built on these occupations which were, historically, free of organizational involvement. Because the semiprofessions are creatures of formal organizations, it is unrealistic to evaluate them in the same terms as the free professions. As was discussed in Chapter 2, perhaps a new concept of professions must be defined for the semiprofessions, as well

[77] William J. Goode, "The Theoretical Limits of Professionalization," in Etzioni, *Semi-Professions,* pp. 266–313.
[78] Ibid., p. 267.

as other organizationally based occupations striving for professional recognition. Such a concept might be termed "bureaucratic professionalization," which implicitly recognizes the difference between the old free professions and the newer organizationally based professions. By redefining their goals to eliminate the pursuit of the impossible, semiprofessionals will eliminate the frustration of trying to be like doctors and lawyers.

17. The career patterns of semiprofessionals are characterized by training programs which have some resemblance to those of established professions, little upward mobility, and a good deal of horizontal mobility.

Training programs. Although semiprofessional training programs are not nearly as complete as those of the established professions, there are many similarities. For example, many of the same processes found informally in medical school are also manifest in semiprofessional training schools. Simpson, for example, feels that the socialization of nurses[79] in particular, and professionals in general, takes place in three stages, "each involving some learning of the cultural content of the role and some self-identification with it."[80] In the first stage the student must learn to become proficient in the required tasks. Second, out of the number of reference groups available, she selects the one which will serve as her major reference group. Finally, she comes to internalize the basic values of the profession and adopts the proper modes of behavior.

a) Examining nurses in detail, Simpson finds they enter professional school with a variety of preconceptions about nursing, most of which are idealistic notions of the nurse's role in society. The first stage of nursing school focuses on "the mastery of technical skills and knowledge," which helps to bring the idealistic view more in line with occupational reality. Nursing students, like medical students, enter school with notions of helping the sick, but this goal is quickly thwarted. Emphasis is on classroom work and learning such skills as the "21 consecutive steps" needed to properly make a bed. They soon learn that their status as nurses is based not on "nurturant relationships with patients," but on how well they perform their daily chores. In time this emphasis leads to a basic change in the view of the nursing role: "the primary concern of the student shifted from helping a patient to playing the role of a nurse."[81] b) In the second stage there is a shift away from the patient as the major significant other. Gradually, coworkers who prize technical skill become the student nurse's major reference group. By the middle of the sophomore year, the student begins working in the hos-

[79] Ida Harper Simpson, "Patterns of Socialization into Professions: The Case of Student Nurses," *Sociological Inquiry* 37 (1967), 47–54.
[80] Ibid., p. 47.
[81] Ibid., p. 50.

pital and the views of doctors and established nurses become important. As these significant others come to recognize and approve of the student nurse, she comes to view herself as a "real" nurse. c) In the third stage she becomes truly "professional" as she comes to believe that it is only the view of fellow "professional" nurses which is important. It is this last stage of socialization which proves difficult for nursing schools to accomplish. Not many nurses accept this third stage, as exemplified by the fact that one hears much more about the "doctor's nurse" than the "nurse's nurse." Simpson concludes that this is not unusual, since few if any professionals ever achieve this third stage. Although the process of socialization of nurses is an important contribution, Simpson's conclusion is weak. Most established professions are marked by a vast majority of individuals who are primarily responsive to other members of the profession. Indeed, this is one of the basic aspects of professional status. The nurse is unable to achieve this third stage because she interacts with doctors, who are professionals of higher status. The doctor can generally be responsive solely to other doctors because there are fewer occupations with higher status.

Many other similarities between the socialization of professionals and semiprofessionals might be pointed out here, but space limitations restrict us to one more example. Psathas has studied the fate of idealism in nursing school in much the same way Becker and Geer analyzed the same phenomenon in medical school.[82] He compared the perceptions of groups of freshmen and senior nursing students on a series of projective tests and found student nurses to be similar to medical-school students. That is, the freshmen nurses were much more idealistic and optimistic than their senior counterparts. In their attitudes toward patients seniors tended to be technique-oriented while the freshmen were more patient-centered. Although they were confident of the outcome, freshmen nurses were much more uneasy about handling new or unstructured situations. Seniors had a clearer idea of the status system in the hospital and, interestingly, were less likely to see themselves "as a valuable contributor to the physician in providing better patient care."[83] In general entering student nurses had idealized images of the significant others in the hospital, while seniors had a much more realistic view of what significant others do and what they could expect them to do. This change occurred because of the student's involvement in the socialization process. A naive, idealistic view was gradually replaced by a view of the hospital social system as it really is and a view of self and other which was congruent with the views of self and other held by significant others. Thus the socialization of nurses is in this sense, and many others, similar to the socialization of professionals.

---

[82] George Psathas, "The Fate of Idealism in Nursing School," *Journal of Health and Social Behavior* 9 (1968), 52–65.

[83] Ibid., p. 62.

Upward mobility. The semiprofessions are like the free professions in that once out of school and in the occupation, there is little left for the semiprofessional in terms of upward mobility. The only alternative open to him is an administrative position and there are few of these for the many teachers, social workers, and nurses. Further, not many semiprofessionals see such movement as a meaningful goal, for it is a nonprofessional goal, and in effect a move out of the occupation. Movement down, in any formal sense, is also a very remote possibility for the semiprofessional. His most viable mobility route is through horizontal moves. This is shown in Becker's study of the schoolteacher, although the same ideas apply to the other semiprofessions.

Horizontal mobility. As Becker points out, horizontal mobility has been an ignored dimension in the study of career patterns. There are clearly important differences between occupations which are on the same level. Becker writes,

all positions at one level of a work hierarchy, while theoretically identical, may not be equally easy or rewarding places in which to work. Given this fact, people tend to move in patterned ways among the possible positions, seeking that situation which affords the most desirable setting in which to meet and grapple with the basic problems of their work.[84]

The schoolteacher's major problem at work is the student, and his career pattern typically consists of moving from school to school until the "right" kind of student is found. Becker found that the teachers he studied in Chicago placed students in three categories: a) Lower-class and Negro students who were viewed as "difficult to teach, uncontrollable and violent in the sphere of discipline, and morally unacceptable on all scores." b) Middle-class students, who were viewed as "hard-working but also slow to learn, extremely easy to control, and most acceptable on the moral level." c) Upper-class students, who "were felt to be quick learners and easy to teach, but somewhat 'spoiled' and difficult to control and lacking in the important moral traits of politeness and respect for elders."[85]

In addition to the right kind of students, there were the "right" kind of principals, colleagues, and parents.

A desirable position is one in which are found the desired types in each of the four categories. Lower-class slum schools were least desirable on all counts. Therefore, there are many requests to transfer out of these schools and few requests to transfer into them. Slum schools are typically staffed by new teachers, who generally transfer out as soon as they can. How quickly this is done is based on a number of career contingencies. For one thing, the teacher must have enough information to judge what is in fact a good school.

---

[84] Howard S. Becker, "The Career of the Chicago Public Schoolteacher," *American Journal of Sociology* 57 (1952), 470.

[85] Ibid., pp. 470–477.

Second, if she is black, or is labelled as a troublemaker, she will find it diffi-cult to move to a "better" school. Finally, patience is required to wait for the "right" opening, rather than accepting the first available change of location.

A second type of career pattern exists for those teachers who adjust to the lesser school in which they began. They learn to live in that school, to be satisfied with lesser accomplishments, and to understand the behavior of the students they once found repugnant. A number of factors serve to keep them in the lower-class schools: acquisition of status among colleagues, a reputation as a disciplinarian which helps to keep the students from misbehaving, and stable relationships with the parents. These adjustments help to commit the teacher to her school and make her afraid to move because of what she would lose.

Through either of these adjustments the teacher achieves a relatively stable worklife, but this stability is continually threatened by external changes. If the social-class composition of the students should change, desir-able locations would become undesirable. The age distribution in a commu-nity might change, leaving fewer children and a smaller need for public school teachers. Finally, a new, unsympathetic principal might upset the teacher's stable worklife.

18. The semiprofessions offer relatively comfortable havens for fe-males, but males find themselves the minority group faced with status problems.

Male nurses; a minority group. Since the semiprofessions are "femi-nine" occupations, females are comfortable working in them. Each of the three semiprofessions discussed in this section is oriented toward helping someone. This is very compatible with the female sex role as it is defined in the United States. Males are the minority group in the semiprofessions and face a variety of peculiar problems. They must be able to work in an occupa-tion which is defined as feminine and dominated by females. Segal's study of male nurses focuses on both aspects of this problem.[86] He studied a 250-bed private psychiatric hospital in Boston which had 103 nurses, 22 of whom were males. Segal points out that this percentage of male nurses is high be-cause the school attached to the hospital is coeducational and it has been a major source of trained male nurses. The male nurses were likely to be placed in wards which had male or senile patients. This removed the sexual element from their relationship with patients. The male nurses were also likely to be in higher administrative positions within the hospital. This did not alleviate the status tensions of male nurses since they continued to feel that they did not receive the prestige and respect they deserved. Unlike female nurses, they "compared themselves to the doctors and aspired to decrease the social distance

[86] Bernard Segal, "Male Nurses: A Case Study in Status Contradiction and Prestige Loss," *Social Forces* 41 (1962), 31–38.

between the doctors and themselves."[87] However, they were rebuffed in their efforts to identify with doctors. On the other hand, they tried to dissociate themselves from the male aides below them in the hospital hierarchy, whom they considered to be blue-collar workers, while viewing themselves as "professional men." They wanted a clear line drawn between themselves and the aides, but this was impossible because they frequently performed work very similar to the aides' work. There was also considerable strain in the relationship between male and female nurses. The males were likely to see themselves as at least as capable as female nurses, while female nurses were rather derogatory in their comments about male nurses.[88] The female nurses were more likely to see a role for male nurses in the aspects of nursing the females found difficult or distasteful. In effect the females wanted to relegate the males to hospital chores which were traditionally performed by the aides. The male nurses resisted this definition because they would soon have found themselves being supervised by female nurses. This continuing threat of female supervision causes a great deal of status anxiety among male nurses, for males in our society are not supposed to be supervised by females. Another aspect of the male nurses' problem is that society does not define the occupation as an acceptable mobility step for males. That this view is also accepted by the male nurses is evidenced by Segal's finding that "40 percent of the men and only 10 percent of the women located themselves in a stratum below the middle class."[89]

In the case of male nurses there is a reversal of the discussion of minority groups in occupational life. Most frequently females find themselves in male occupations, and hence confronted with a host of problems. The female doctor who succeeds in her position in spite of the difficulties is likely to be praised by society. However, the male nurse who succeeds is more likely to be looked down upon. America is dominated by male values, and the female who succeeds in the male world has accomplished something in terms of our values, while the male who succeeds in the female world is not conforming to major values and is therefore unlikely to receive favorable recognition for his accomplishments. This is true not only of male nurses, but also of successful male hairdressers, clothes designers, etc. In effect, male nurses "are involved in a status contradiction between characteristics ascribed to men in our society and characteristics that are supposed to inhere among members of the nursing profession."[90] In many ways the male in a female occupation is in a far more uncomfortable situation than the female in a male occupation.

19. Blacks in the semiprofessions face fewer problems than in many other types of occupations.

[87] Ibid., p. 34.
[88] Ibid., p. 35.
[89] Ibid., p. 37.
[90] Ibid.

One reason is that they are able, in many cases, to work almost exclusively with black clients. The black teacher in a predominantly black school is in a relatively comfortable position, as are the social worker and nurse in comparable situations. When the clients are predominantly white there are problems, but these problems seem to be far less severe than in other occupations. Perhaps the reason is the femininity of the occupations—femininity calls for passivity, and this is congruent with the passive role accorded the black in our society. The semiprofessional is not seen as a decision maker, but as a helper. White society finds it difficult to accept a black decision maker, but it is more comfortable with a black helper. This is congruent with the historical place accorded the American black. This is not to say that he has no problems in the semiprofessions. He clearly has problems with white patients, peers, and superiors as well as the public. However, the passive image of the semiprofessions serves to mitigate these problems.

5

Low-Status Occupations

The sociological study of occupations had its origin in the study of low-status occupations. The pivotal figure in occupational sociology generally and the study of low-status occupations specifically is Everett Hughes. In 1928, when Hughes wrote his dissertation on realtors, there was by his own account, "really no occupational sociology."[1] There had been, of course, intellectual interest in the world of work. Hughes notes those who had influenced his early interest in occupational sociology:

Of course, people have always, in the western world at any rate, been interested in work. With the coming of the industrial revolution there began to be writings on the relations of workers to their work. The assumption was that since the worker no longer owned his tools his work would go down. The main trouble with that is that there is no evidence that it ever was up. At any rate, there was a good deal of writing on the subject moving toward the later work on alienation. Marx had already started along this line; a Belgian, LeMan, continued, Max Weber had already, before 1910, done a monograph on modern industrial work, and Sombart had done some similar work in his book on capitalism. Both of them talk of the great change of habit and attitude required to turn the handworker into a clock-bound machine worker. You are aware, of course, of the scientific management movement which set out to create a theory of how to get the most out of a workman. Veblen and Hoxie, an economist at the University of Chicago, began to study trade unions and factory work from an essentially sociological point of view. Along in the 1920s and 1930s there was a big surge of study of human behavior in industries with some experimenting and a good deal of attention to informal organization.

But by this time Park (1915) and others . . . Carr-Saunders and Wilson, *The Professions* (1933) had already noticed the tremendous upward swing in the number of people in these occupations in modern urban industrial settings. It was only after this, however, that there began to be special courses and a good deal of graduate work on the nature of occupations and organizations and their social relationships. . . . Around 1938 or 1939 I gave a course at the University of Chicago

[1] Everett C. Hughes, *Men and Their Work* (Glencoe, Ill.: Free Press, 1958).

on the professions and later broadened the title and simplified it . . . to the sociology of work.[2]

The major direct intellectual influence on Everett Hughes was Robert Park. Faris confirms this in his book on the Chicago School of sociology, in which he notes that Hughes and his wife were closest to Park and most influenced by him.[3] Hughes again:

Since I belonged to no interesting minority and had no special social cause on my mind when I went to graduate school, no thesis topic was built into my system. I was what one might call a footloose soul. Robert Park and the sociological view of the world rescued me. I wrote a paper on policemen in Burgess' course on crime. In Park's course on the newspaper and public opinion . . . I had great fun learning about the press agent. . . . It was the press agent as a budding profession that interested me. I got interested in the marvellous propaganda which real estate men made for the "good guys" in real estate—about how they were truly experts on land value and brokers: in short, professionals, not businessmen. Since I had already read and heard a good deal about cities as the places where many services and occupations took on an abstract, disinterested professional quality, I was soon taken with the thought that here was a wonderful case where the professional attitude was fostered by some in the same market (for land and houses). . . .[4]

Although Hughes began with this interest in professionalism he soon shifted to an interest in low-status occupations. The major force behind this change was Park, whose interest in low-status occupations in the city is exemplified by the following:

The effects of the division of labor as a discipline, e.g., as means of molding character, may therefore be best studied in the vocational types it has produced. Among the types which it would be interesting to study are: the shopgirl, the policeman, the peddlar, the cab-man, the night-watchman, the clairvoyant, the vaudeville performer, the labor agitator, the quack doctor, the bartender, the ward boss, the strikebreaker, the school teacher, the reporter, the stockbroker, the pawnbroker: all of these are characteristic products of the conditions of city life; each, with its special experience, insight, and point of view determines for each vocational group and for the city as a whole its individuality.[5]

Hughes, taking off from this lead, felt that the best place to study the dynamics of occupational life was in low-status occupations. These offered an excellent laboratory for the study of occupational life because there was less distortion than in high-status occupations. In all types of work men strive to make their work more tolerable to themselves and important to others. Hughes contends that there is less effort to disguise the true nature of work in low-status occupations. Because it is easier to see work processes in them,

[2] Everett C. Hughes, personal communication to the author.
[3] Robert E. L. Faris, *Chicago Sociology: 1920–1932* (San Francisco: Chandler, 1967).
[4] Hughes, personal communication to the author.
[5] Robert Park et al., *The City* (Chicago: University of Chicago Press, 1925), p. 14.

he urged his students to begin with them. When one studies low-status occupations insights are gained "about work behavior in any and all occupations."[6] Behind this contention is the basic premise that "the essential problems of men at work are the same whether they do their work in some famous
laboratory or in the messiest vat room of a pickle factory."[7] In order to study
these occupations Hughes encouraged his students to be participant observers.
Donald Roy, an occupational sociologist who was one of Hughes' students,
says of him: "Many years ago, in a course on methods of field research, he
taught us that it was fun to sally forth with pencil and notebook, like newspaper reporters, to observe and to question."[8] The result was numerous rich
descriptive studies of particular occupations, which, however, lacked any theoretical base. This chapter is devoted to an effort to cull from the many descriptive studies of low-status occupations generalizations which may be developed into hypotheses to be tested in future research on such occupations.

    1.   Low-status occupations which exist within formal organizations
    tend to be highly alienating.

As Hughes has pointed out, alienation was one of the early concerns of
theorists interested in work. Karl Marx was concerned primarily with the
alienation of factory workers, while Max Weber expanded the concept to include other occupational levels. Despite Weber's work, the literature has focused on the alienation of low-status occupations within formal organizations.

    Robert Blauner's definition of alienation, which breaks it down into four
components, is utilized here.[9] The first element is powerlessness or the domination of an individual by another person or object, and the inability of the
individual to reduce or eliminate that control. Meaninglessness is the second
aspect of alienation, and results from the individual's inability to see his role
in relation to other roles and his purpose in the organization. Third, the
alienated individual suffers from isolation: he lacks a feeling of belonging to
the work situation and identification with the workplace. Finally, alienation
involves a feeling of self-estrangement, which manifests itself in a lack of involvement in one's work. The self-estranged worker is unable to express his
"unique abilities, potentialities, or personality." "Further consequences of
self-estranged work may be boredom and monotony, the absence of personal
growth, and a threat to a self-approved occupational identity."[10]

    Assembly-line workers. The occupation which epitomizes these charac-
teristics of alienation is assembly-line work, where the major source of alien-

<hr />

[6] Hughes, *Men and Their Work,* p. 49.
[7] Ibid., p. 48.
[8] Donald Roy, "The Union-Organizing Campaign as a Problem of Social Distance: Three Crucial Dimensions of Affiliation-Disaffiliation," in Howard S. Becker,
et al., *Institutions and the Person* (Chicago: Aldine, 1968), p. 49.
[9] Robert Blauner, *Alienation and Freedom* (Chicago: University of Chicago Press,
1964).
[10] Ibid., p. 26.

ation is the omnipresent assembly line. The assembly-line worker performs his assigned tasks (e.g., tightening a bolt, fastening a fender) at set intervals and no variation is allowed. For eight hours every work day he performs the same task at set intervals. Respite comes when the line breaks down, an event many workers hope for and sometimes contribute to by sabotaging the machinery. Walker and Guest have said that the assembly-line worker is "the classic symbol of the subjection of man to the machine in our industrial age."[11] In Blauner's estimation, it is the automobile assembly-line industry in which "technological, organizational and economic factors" combine to produce the most alienating work environment.[12]

The assembly-line worker is almost totally powerless. He is unable to control the pace of the line, his superiors, and top management. The machine pace is set by the organization's time and motion specialists and is designed to get the maximum productivity from each employee. Once the speed of the line is set there is little the worker can do to affect it and consequently he is unable to control his own workpace. This is perhaps the most demoralizing aspect of his job, and differentiates his work from virtually all other occupations: both his rate of work and kind of work are invariable and uncontrollable. There is some degree of powerlessness in virtually all occupations, but most workers are able to have some control over the pace and kind of work. Even the lowliest clerk can generally vary his own workpace and make his work more interesting by changing the tasks he performs.

The assembly-line worker is also characterized by an inability to control his immediate supervisor. For one thing, it is difficult for him to interact with his foreman. The combination of noise, job pressure, and need for continual attention to the line make it almost impossible to communicate with anyone. Even if an assembly-line worker could communicate with his supervisor, he would have little chance of affecting his behavior. In fact, he has few resources which he can use to gain something from his superior, for he has few skills and is easily replaceable. His almost total unimportance to the organization further increases the assembly-line worker's sense of powerlessness. He lacks even the power to withdraw occasionally, because his absence would be noticed immediately. It is also hard for him to quit, because he has few skills and would find it extremely difficult to get another position.

For a variety of reasons, the assembly-line worker finds his job meaningless. He is unable to see what his very specialized task has to do with the work of others on the line or of those who work at other levels in the organization. He also is unable to see what tightening his bolt has to do with the finished product (and in many cases does not even know what the finished product is). Finally, the intrinsic nature of the job contributes to a feeling of meaninglessness. It is so specialized, uninteresting, and unimportant that it is difficult for anyone to derive any satisfaction from his work.

[11] Charles R. Walker and Robert Guest, *Man on the Assembly Line* (Cambridge: Harvard University Press, 1952), p. 9.
[12] Blauner, *Alienation and Freedom*, p. 182.

The assembly-line worker's problems are compounded by his isolation. The noise and demands of the line prevent interaction on the job, making it difficult for an informal work group to develop. The worker is also isolated from all levels of management because of the nature of his work and the desire of management to maintain what it considers to be proper distance. Assembly-line work is frequently found in large plants, and their size also serves to inhibit the development of personal relationships. Huge cafeterias, parking lots, and rest rooms are scarcely designed to encourage social interaction.

Finally, those on the assembly line are particularly prone to self-estrangement. The work is boring and monotonous, requiring continual attention but little real involvement in the task or the organization. Hence, the worker spends a good part of his time daydreaming. No real skills or abilities are needed and he is unable to express himself in his work.

Telephone operators. Although alienation is perhaps most extreme in assembly-line occupations, it is also found in most other low-status occupations in organizations. Let us examine another such occupation, telephone-switchboard operation. Most of the operators are females who must sit in front of a row of switchboards.[13] The operator is powerless to control her workpace, which is set by the volume of calls. When a light flashes, indicating an incoming call, she must complete it and write out the required ticket. The work requires discipline because an incoming call must not be missed. The operator is subjected to extremely close supervision and is isolated because of the incessant demands of the job and the necessity of staying at her workplace so she is sure to receive all incoming calls. The work is rather meaningless in the sense that she fails to see the importance of what she is doing. It is self-estranging as well, because few skills are needed and few opportunities for self-expression are offered. A number of other characteristics of the job make it alienating. For example, someone must be on duty at all times, which necessitates "night work, Sunday and holiday work, and split shifts."[14] The telephone company recognizes the lack of intrinsic job satisfaction and seeks to compensate by emphasizing such extrinsic factors as "attractive lounges and lunchrooms and . . . recreational facilities in the company buildings. The companies provide medical assistance to employees, along with limited legal and financial advice. There is a high degree of paternalism in the telephone company."[15] Because of these extrinsic factors many operators express contentment at working for the phone company. They like working for such a large and important organization and the pensions, other side benefits, and the steady employment. However, the work itself is alienating and few can find any intrinsic satisfaction in it.

Thus it is contended here that low-status workers in organizations are

[13] Joel Siedman et al., "Telephone Workers," in Sigmund Nosow and William H. Form, eds., *Man, Work and Society* (New York: Basic Books, 1962), pp. 493–504.

[14] Ibid., p. 494.

[15] Ibid., p. 495.

likely to be more highly alienated than workers in any other type of occupation. This is *not* to say that workers in other occupations are not alienated, for studies have demonstrated that even high-status professionals[16] and semi-professionals[17] can also be alienated. Nevertheless, the bulk of the evidence indicates that low-status workers are more likely to be alienated and more likely to exhibit a high degree of alienation. This has been shown most recently in a study by Bonjean and Grimes which compares the degree of alienation among managers, businessmen, and blue-collar (low-status) workers.[18] Their scale of alienation includes three of the four dimensions used here as well as three additional ones: normlessness, general alienation, and anomie. Normlessness is defined as a perception of unclear or conflicting norms, general alienation as a feeling of alienation from society, while anomie is "a generalized pervasive sense of self-to-other alienation."[19] Thus Bonjean and Grimes compared managers, businessmen, and workers on the six sub-dimensions of alienation: general, isolation, normlessness, powerlessness, anomie, and self-estrangement. Table 5-1 summarizes the results;

TABLE 5-1

Alienation Scores by Occupational Status

Percent Scoring in
1st Quarter (Low)

Alienation Scale	Managers N=108	Businessmen N=104	Workers N=120	Significant Differences*
1. General	38.9	22.1	16.7	M-W, M-B
2. Isolation	37.0	22.1	19.2	M-W, M-B
3. Normlessness	48.1	21.2	22.5	M-W, M-B
4. Powerlessness	31.5	25.9	13.3	M-W, B-W
5. Anomie (percent scoring low, o on scale)	51.9	26.9	23.3	M-W, M-B
6. Self-estrangement	37.0	27.9	17.5	M-W

* Significant at the .05 level or beyond.
Charles M. Bonjean and Michael D. Grimes, "Bureaucracy and Alienation: A Dimensional Approach," *Social Forces* 48 (1970), 369.

On all six subdimensions significantly more managers scored low (in the first quarter) than workers. Although also in the predicted direction on five of the six subdimensions, the differences between businessmen and workers are statistically significant on only one subdimension, powerlessness. Thus, in this

[16] George Miller, "Professionals in Bureaucracy: Alienation Among Industrial Scientists," *American Sociological Review* 32 (1967), 755–768.
[17] Leonard Pearlin, "Alienation From Work: A Study of Nursing Personnel," *American Sociological Review* 27 (1962), 314–326.
[18] Charles M. Bonjean and Michael D. Grimes, "Bureaucracy and Alienation: A Dimensional Approach," *Social Forces* 48 (1970), 365–373.
[19] Ibid., p. 367.

comparative study managers are significantly more likely to score low in alienation than workers, while businessmen are also more likely to score low in alienation, but the differences in the latter case are not statistically significant. These and other studies tend to support the generalization made here: low-status workers in organizations are more likely to experience a high degree of alienation.

    2. The degree of alienation of those in low-status occupations in formal organizations depends primarily on the nature of the technology.

Blauner's previously cited study examines alienation in four types of industries and points out the effect of technology on alienation. The assembly-line worker's alienation is attributed primarily to the technology of the automobile industry. The machine controls the pace of work; the speed is set by external forces and is invariable; the line requires constant attention; interaction is made impossible because of the nature of assembly-line work; the contribution of each individual is small and no one knows how he contributes to the final product; and few skills or abilities are needed to perform the work. Blauner compares three other industries (printing, textiles, and chemicals) in an effort to determine the relationship between technology and alienation.

Printers. Printing, a skilled occupation, is the least alienating of the four occupations Blauner studied. Perhaps the major reason is that printing has been virtually untouched by technological change. Much of the work is still done by hand or by traditional machine methods. Other factors have also contributed to the relative lack of alienation among printers. Printing plants are comparatively small; management, generally, is by traditional rather than bureaucratic means; there is high job security; and labor unions in printing are quite powerful. Above all, however, is the fact that the machine has not taken over the printing industry and the printer retains his traditional skills and control over the means of production. The printer's job is complex and requires the mastery of a series of diverse skills. An apprenticeship period of from four to six years is necessary before one can be considered a journeyman printer. The complexity and diversity of the work militates against its standardization and mechanization. The skill required enables the printer to set his own pace and determine his own techniques, tools, and the sequence in which he will perform his tasks. Each occupation in printing is different and this gives the printer great latitude in terms of decision making, initiative, and judgment. Further, he is relatively free to try out new ideas, move about the plant, and work without supervisory control. Because of these factors printing is by far the most meaningful occupation in the Blauner study. It allows those in the occupation the opportunity for self-actualization. As a result printers are highly pleased with the intrinsic aspects of their work. Blauner neatly summarized the position of the printer:

In some ways, the printer is almost an anachronism in the age of large-scale industrial organizations. His relation to his work is reminiscent of our picture of the independent craftsman of preindustrial times. Craft technology, favorable economic conditions, and powerful work organizations and traditions result in the highest level of freedom and control in the work process among all industrial workers today.[20]

Textile workers. Blauner finds textile workers more alienated than printers, but less alienated than automobile assembly-line workers. This is because textiles, technologically, is a throwback to the early days of industrialization. The basic job in this industry is tending a number of machines which do most of the production. The jobs themselves require little skill because most of the necessary skill has been built into the machines. Because textiles is a machine industry the workers are faced with unvarying work pressure, an inability to control that pressure, and an inability to choose techniques or to move around freely. Further, the technology which forces each worker to handle several machines also has the need, built in, for close supervision. In a craft technology close supervision is not needed and is even resented, because of the strong sense of craftsmanship among skilled workers. In the assembly-line technology close supervision is not needed because the machines control the work pace and the quality. In textiles, however, neither the machines nor the norms of craftsmanship insure quality or quantity production. Further the textile industry is composed mainly of small, marginal firms which must get maximum productivity in order to stay in business. Despite these alienating aspects of textile work, it is not as alienating as the automobile assembly line. Blauner accounts for this in several ways, citing the traditional, more personalized nature of the organization; the social cohesion of the workers resulting from their life in small southern towns; the small size of the plants, which allows for considerable interaction; and the fact that most textile workers (almost half of whom are females) have few ambitions. Above all, however, is the fact that the machine-tending technology allows the worker more freedom than his counterpart on the assembly line.

Workers in continuous-process industries. Most theorists have accepted the notion that as technology advances work will become increasingly alienating, but Blauner found that in the technologically advanced continuous-process industry there is, in fact, a decline in alienation. In continuous-process industries such as chemicals

the flow of materials; the combination of different chemicals; and the temperature pressure, and speed of the process are regulated by automatic control devices. The automatic controls make possible a continuous flow in which raw materials are introduced at the beginning of the process and a large volume of the product continually emerges at the end stage.[21]

[20] Blauner, *Alienation and Freedom*, p. 56.
[21] Ibid., p. 125.

Few employees are needed in such industries, and these are generally thinly spread throughout the numerous buildings which make up a particular plant. Because the number of employees is already minimal and because amount of production is determined by the machine, not the individual, there is a high degree of job security in continuous-process industries. The employee does little physical work; instead, "the work of the chemical operator is to monitor these automatic processes: his tasks include observing dials and gauges; taking readings of temperatures, pressures, and rates of flow; and writing down these readings. . . ."[22] The employee has a great deal of responsibility for the maintenance of the smooth operations and for the care of expensive machinery. In performing these tasks he works in small groups of from three to seven men. There is little standardized work and most of the time is spent in waiting for, or trying to prevent, a breakdown and trying to repair it when it occurs. Because of the nature of his job the chemical worker has considerable freedom in terms of time and movement. There is no continuous pressure; rather, the work routine is highly erratic. The work environment is relaxed and the employee can set his own pace except in the case of an emergency. He is also free to determine the quality of his work and the methods he will employ. There is much free time and few employees and this provides the basis for the development of highly cohesive work groups. There is ample chance for advancement in the organization for those who are deserving. All of these factors, which stem primarily from the nature of the continuous-process technology, enable the chemical worker to be less alienated than the assembly-line or textile worker.

3.   The degree of alienation of those in low-status occupations in formal organizations also depends on the structure of the organization.

The effect of the structure of the organization on alienation in low-status occupations has already been alluded to in the preceding generalization. We have seen that in the textile industry the nonbureaucratic, traditional structure of the organization helps to reduce alienation. On the other hand, the highly bureaucratized automobile industry contributes to the alienation of the assembly-line worker. In general it may be hypothesized that the more bureaucratic the organization, the more alienated are its lower-status employees. This alienation stems from some of the basic principles of bureaucratic structure. For example, a bureaucracy is characterized by a clear division of labor and a high degree of specialization. This specialization pervades the organization, but is especially acute at the lower levels. Individuals at this level find themselves performing highly specialized tasks in which it is extremely difficult to become involved. The hierarchical pyramid which characterizes highly bureaucratic organizations necessitates a wide gap be-

[22] Ibid., p. 133.

tween leaders and followers and decreases the power of the lower-status employee to affect decisions made at the top. The formal system of rules which is typical of bureaucracy further reduces the lower-status employee's ability to affect decision making. The size of the organization and its impersonality make it difficult for such an individual to see the meaningfulness of his work. Finally, he is alienated in the Marxian sense because he does not own the means of production.

Alienation and bureaucracy. A caveat is in order here before we discuss some examples of the effect of organizational structure on low-status workers. The relationship between the structure of an organization and alienation is far more complex than has been contended in Generalization 3, because neither alienation nor bureaucracy is a unidimensional concept. We have already pointed out that Blauner feels that alienation is composed of four subdimensions. In measuring the degree of bureaucratization Bonjean and Grimes employ a general measure of bureaucracy as well as measures of five subdimensions of bureaucracy: authority, procedures, specialization, written rules, and impersonality. All of these subdimensions, by the way, are drawn from Weber's ideal-typical bureaucracy. Since both alienation and bureaucracy are multidimensional, it is highly unlikely that there is a simple direct relationship between them. Bonjean and Grimes have provided some important insights on this point by correlating each of the measures of alienation with each of the measures of bureaucracy for the managers, businessmen, and workers they studied. In most cases the results are in the predicted direction since there is a positive correlation between the subdimensions of bureaucracy and alienation. However, there are also a number of negative correlations, although none of these is statistically significant. Most of the positive corrrelations between the dimensions of alienation and bureaucracy are *not* statistically significant even though they are in the predicted direction. Based on these correlations we can see that the relationship between alienation and bureaucracy is far from clear-cut. Must we then reject our hypothesis that the more bureaucratic the organization, the more alienated are its low-status employees? Although the findings of Bonjean and Grimes indicate that this is an oversimplification, they also present results which tend to support our hypothesis. For each of the three occupations studied by Bonjean and Grimes, 36 correlations were computed (the six alienation dimensions times the six dimensions of bureaucracy). For the managers only 1 of these 36 correlations was statistically significant, while for businessmen only 5 were statistically significant. In contrast, 12 of the 36 correlations computed for workers were statistically significant. Although this is far from conclusive, it certainly implies that bureaucracy and alienation are more likely to be correlated significantly among blue-collar workers. But again, the relationship is not generalized. For example, none of the correlations between written rules and the six dimensions of alienation are statistically significant for workers, while five of the six correlations between authority and alienation are statistically significant. The implication is that authority is a more important factor than written rules in the alienation of blue-collar workers. In effect workers respond to a high degree of bureaucratic authority with feelings of powerlessness, anomie, self-estrangement, normlessness, and general alienation (but not social isolation). Thus we may conclude that it is not bureaucratization per se, but certain aspects of a bureaucratic structure which lead to alienation among low-status blue-collar workers.

Total institutions. Perhaps the most alienating organizational structure in terms of powerlessness is what Goffman has termed the "total institution." He defines this as a place "of residence and work where a large number of like situated individuals, cut off from the wider society for an appreciable period of time, together lead an enclosed, formally administered round of life."[23] Total institutions are characterized by all aspects of life taking place in the same location under one authority; all working together doing the same things and treated alike; all activities tightly scheduled by a single plan; a large gap between superiors and subordinates with little mobility between their positions; members having information about themselves restricted; work on a 24-hour-a-day basis; and a gulf between the total institution and the rest of society.

Sailors. Zurcher has examined the ship as a total institution and the plight of the sailor in such a situation.[24] Once at sea the sailor is totally controlled by the ship's organization and in some ways is even worse off than the assembly-line worker. If he is dissatisfied he cannot even quit, at least until the ship docks, and even his off-hours are rigidly determined and controlled by the ship's authority structure. On the other hand, he is not isolated, since there is much interaction among the small number of sailors on board and a very cohesive group frequently develops. Nor is his work meaningless, because he knows that he plays a central role in the successful completion of the voyage. Also, the skill required of him makes him less likely to be self-estranged than the assembly-line worker. Thus the sailor's work is less meaningless, self-estranging, and isolated than that of the assembly-line employee, but he has a greater sense of powerlessness, since his whole life, not just his worklife, is determined by the ship.

Military recruits. The recruit in a military academy also exists in a total institution. The first stage of the socialization process in the United States Coast Guard Academy involves a two-month period during which he is cut off from his previous life as well as all outside life by being restricted to the base.[25] He is taught unquestioning acceptance of authority and the

[23] Erving Goffman, *Asylums* (Garden City, N.Y.: Anchor Books, 1961), p. xiii.

[24] Louis A. Zurcher Jr., "The Sailor Aboard Ship: A Study of Role Behavior in a Total Institution," *Social Forces* 43 (1965), 389–400.

[25] Sanford M. Dornbusch, "The Military Academy as an Assimilating Institution," *Social Forces* 33 (1955), 316–321.

customs of the Coast Guard. Like the sailor, he is almost totally powerless. Also like the sailor, the recruit does not suffer much from meaninglessness, isolation, and self-estrangement. He knows what his role is and how it relates to other roles in the organization. Further, he knows that he will ultimately be able to find a measure of self-actualization in a career in the Coast Guard. Most important, the recruit is not isolated. The whole structure of socialization is designed to develop a cohesive group. Isolation from external life is designed to mute differences in social status and permit the development of a united group of "swabs." The hazing of swabs by upperclassmen further increases the recruits' solidarity. Although they do the hazing, the upperclassmen also seek to be close to the recruits. These "informal contacts serve to unite the classes and spread a 'we feeling' through the academy."[26] This overall unity is enhanced by hostility to such outsiders as the reserves and the enlisted men. Security and status are also acquired in the military academy. Since the behavior of everyone in the academy is predictable, the swab feels quite secure. In addition, as he identifies with the Coast Guard he begins to recognize that this will yield him high status in the outside world. This assurance of status serves to increase his sense of security. In sum, the total institution is most alienating in terms of powerlessness. When it is viewed from the perspective of inmates in a mental institution or a prison it is also the most alienating type of organization in terms of the other three dimensions of alienation. However, in the case of the sailor aboard ship or the Coast Guard academy recruit, the structure of the organization seems to reduce meaninglessness, isolation, and self-estrangement.

Division of labor and economic structure

Two other variables are, in Blauner's view, related to the degree of alienation; the nature of the division of labor and the economic structure of the organization. In general, the greater the division of labor, the more alienating the job. This is another reason why work on the assembly line is so highly alienating, for it is here that we find perhaps the most minute specialization. In fact, one of Henry Ford's basic ideas about the automobile assembly line was "a breakdown of operations into their simple constituent motions."[27] Take for example the work of one man on the automobile assembly-line: "I put in the two different toe plates. They cover the holes where the brake and clutch pedals are. I am inside the car and have to be down on the seat to do my work. On one kind of car I put in the shift lever while another man puts in the toe plates."[28] Or the description of a man who works on a subassembly

[26] Ibid., p. 318.
[27] Charles Walker and Robert Guest, "The Man on the Assembly Line," in William Faunce, ed., Readings in Industrial Sociology (New York: Appleton-Century-Crofts, 1967), p. 245.
[28] Ibid., p. 246.

line: "The only operation I do is work the clip gun. It takes a couple of seconds to shoot six or eight clips into the spring, and I do it as I walk a few steps. Then I start right over again."[29] Thus specialization has reached its ultimate expression on the assembly line. Other jobs in automobile plants and in other industries are not as specialized. Work in the machine-tending industries is specialized, but not to the degree that it is on the assembly line. One of the major reasons for the lack of alienation in the skilled crafts is the fact that there is not much specialization. In fact, the nature of skilled work almost makes it impossible to break it down into specialized subprocesses. One of the reasons why alienation seems to decline in automated plants is that the trend there toward specialized work has been reversed to some degree.

Economic structure of the organization seems to be the least important factor discussed by Blauner. He contends that "when an industry is economically profitable and progressive, workers are less likely to be subjected to intense pressure, more likely to be free from fears of unemployment and to have opportunities to advance. Economic prosperity therefore furthers a social climate in which the worker becomes more integrated in the company."[30] Although this may be generally true, the exceptions to it are numerous. For example, few companies are as economically prosperous as the automobile companies, where alienation is at its peak. Although economic factors are an important consideration, technology, organization, and division of labor are far more closely related to alienation.

4. In the face of these alienating tendencies, low-status workers in organizations develop a variety of informal practices to make their worklife more meaningful.

Sailors. There is a rich literature in occupational sociology on the efforts of individuals in low-status occupations in organizations to flesh out their worklives. For example, in Zurcher's study of the sailor aboard ship, there is a description of the "underlife" which develops there to make his life more palatable. Some of the informal practices are recognized by the authorities on board, while others persist although they often conflict with the smooth running of the ship. Examples of the first type are bypassing chains of command to cut red tape, use of the grapevine for information, and the use of "unofficial, pirated, or homemade parts to maintain machinery in full operation."[31] All of these function to help in the operation of the ship and grant a measure of individuality to the sailor. But there are also what Goffman calls "secondary adjustments," which seem to be dysfunctional for the ship while they are functional for the sailor in retaining some individuality within a total institution. Examples of such secondary adjustments are deals

---

[29] Ibid., p. 247.
[30] Blauner, *Alienation and Freedom*, p. 10.
[31] Zurcher, "The Sailor Aboard Ship," p. 394.

to get a better bunk, snacks, haircuts, first priority on leaves, private use of the ship's property, and deviations from the prescribed mode of dress.

Letter carriers. The letter carrier is another example of an individual in an occupation who seeks to make his worklife more meaningful through a variety of informal practices.[32] "The official job of the letter carrier is to sort incoming mail for those on his route, to deliver it, to collect mail deposited in collection boxes along his route, and to perform various duties associated with these activities."[33] There are a number of rules which determine in part his work activities, and such things as his route, sequence of delivery, and how mail is to be delivered are subject to the rules of the post office. In addition, his work is circumscribed by his supervisor and by inspectors' performance checks.

Despite the formal rules and supervision, the actual work behavior of the letter carrier is quite different from his formal job description. Because he is on his own most of the time he has little difficulty reorganizing his work routine to suit him better. For example, the work route is designed to take eight hours to complete, but the carrier is normally able to complete his work in much less time. When the route is being timed he is careful to follow the rules of the post office exactly, but once the route has been set he utilizes a variety of shortcuts which may violate formal rules, but which enable him to complete his route sooner. Such "illegal" shortcuts as criss-crossing streets, using his automobile, walking on lawns, and failing to deliver all of the mail enable the letter carrier to have an hour or more of free time each day.

A threat to these informal practices is the substitute carrier, who may not know the informal norms of mail delivery and therefore may do the work more efficiently than the regular carrier without breaking the rules of the post office. In order to protect themselves from this, carriers have instituted a norm, which is known to the substitutes, that substitutes must take longer than regulars to do the job. If the substitute violates this norm the regular carriers have a number of sanctions at their disposal. They may not tell him how to work his route, or they might "forget" to tell him of some vicious dogs to be wary of, or they might actively interfere with his work by placing the sacks of mail he needs in the wrong pick-up box.

This is similar in many ways to restriction of output in industry. The production worker restricts his output because he fears that his pay rate will be cut or his job expectations increased, and when under observation, the letter carrier restricts his productivity, for essentially the same reasons. If he shows his supervisor that he can complete an eight-hour job in seven hours, his route might be lengthened without a corresponding increase in pay. In addition, he fears that if his route is expanded there will be fewer routes and

[32] Dean Harper and Frederick Emmert, "Work Behavior in a Service Industry," *Social Forces* 42 (1963), 216–225.
[33] Ibid., p. 217.

hence fewer jobs for letter carriers. Unlike the industrial worker, the letter carrier has an additional incentive to restrict output. When the factory worker finishes work early he has no place to go and must remain on the job until quitting time. The letter carrier is normally free of direct observation by his superior and is free of the workplace. If he can finish his work early he is free to go home.

Restriction of output. The richest descriptions of informal practices designed to restrict production come from a number of industrial studies. The famous Hawthorne studies first brought these informal practices to the attention of the social scientist.[34] In the bank wiring room portion of the Hawthorne studies there was a complicated incentive system which was based on both group and individual productivity. The individual incentive system was designed to get high productivity from each worker by tying his earnings to his productivity. By also tying earnings to group productivity it was felt that the group as a whole would prevent slacking by any of its members. However, both of these techniques failed to maximize productivity. An informal group norm developed which defined what was a "proper day's work." The individuals chosen for the bank wiring room had been from the same department, but they had not been friendly previously. As soon as they were put into the room friendships, and two cliques, developed. Despite the cliques all of the workers shared the norm of how much should be produced. Those who turned out too much work were called "rate busters" and those who turned out too little were "chiselers." No one was supposed to "squeal" on anyone else, nor were they supposed to act "officiously." The group had a variety of sanctions at its disposal. If an individual deviated from the norm he would be "binged" by a fellow worker. (Binging was a sharp punch on the arm.) The group also used less direct means of sanctioning, such as name calling. "If a person turned out too much work, he was called names, such as 'Speed King' or 'The Slave.' "[35] In his analysis of the bank wiring room, Homans feels that the workers' restriction of output was not a logical response to the threat of the reduction of piece rates if they produced more. Although they claimed that this was the reason for restricting output, none had ever been so threatened. Restriction of output is rather viewed as a reflection of the "conflict between the technical organization of the plant and its social organization."[36] In the face of technical norms and orders from the top, "the industrial worker develops his own ways of doing his job, his own traditions of skill, his own satisfactions in living up to his standards."[37] He also develops subgroups to

[34] Fritz Roethlisberger and William J. Dickson, *Management and the Worker* (New York: John Wiley, 1964).

[35] George C. Homans, "The Western Electric Researches," in Amitai Etzioni, ed., *Readings on Modern Organizations* (Englewood Cliffs, N.J.: Prentice-Hall, 1969), p. 110.

[36] Ibid., p. 111.

[37] Ibid., p. 113.

protect himself from these technical norms and especially from technological changes which might disrupt his work routine or the routine of the informal group. The sentiments of the informal organization and its protective practices serve to make the worklife of the industrial worker more meaningful.

Beating the system. In addition to protection, the informal group in industry develops cohesiveness by "beating the system." This desire to beat the system indicates again the conflict between the technical and social organizations of the plant. Roy's study of a machine shop shows that much cheating was done in order to make the quota and that a great deal of loafing, swindling, and conniving also existed.[38] Roy was a participant observer and noted that "we machine operators did 'figure the angles,' we developed an impressive repetoire of angles to play and devoted ourselves to crossing the expectations of formal organization with perseverance, artistry, and organizing ability of our own."[39] For example, the workers would take longer to do a job when it was being timed in order to set piecework rates. They would run the machines at slower speeds or utilize extra movements such as "little reachings, liftings, adjustings, dustings, and other special attentions of conscientious machine operation and good housekeeping that could be dropped instantly with the departure of the time-study man."[40] When the time-study man made a job difficult, the workers revised it to make it easier. The set process was streamlined even though it might be harder on tools or reduce the quality of production. A variety of devices were needed to keep these practices from supervisors and inspectors. Finally, there were collusive arrangements with other groups in the plant to beat the system. All of these activities may be viewed as protective devices. Although protection cannot be minimized, the pre-eminent function of these activities is to enhance the meaningfulness of work for low-status workers. The informal group, its norms, its cohesiveness, and its efforts to beat the system all serve to make work more fun.

All of the informal practices discussed in this section are functional both for the worker and management. Even though some of the informal mechanisms may be contrary to the immediate goals of management, they do enhance job satisfaction and reduce turnover rates. Without such informal practices management might find itself confronted with a disgruntled group of workers who quit at the first opportunity. Given this it may be that management should encourage the development of such groups rather than act to prevent their development. If it did encourage informal group development it might well find that these groups work more often with the organization rather than against it.

[38] Donald Roy, "Efficiency and 'the Fix': Informal Intergroup Relations in a Piecework Machine Shop," *American Journal of Sociology* 60 (1954), 255–266.
[39] Ibid., p. 257.
[40] Ibid.

Games workers play. In another study Roy examines informal group processes which are not aimed against management but do nevertheless serve to make the worklife more meaningful.[41] Roy himself admits that in this study he is interested in how machine operators prevent themselves from "going nuts." He was a participant observer in a group of machine operators who were engaged in work which was repetitious and very simple and which required long hours and a six-day week. This is Roy's description of the work he and his group performed:

Standing all day in one spot beside three old codgers in a dingy room looking out through barred windows at the bare walls of a brick warehouse, leg movements largely restricted to the shifting of body weight from one foot to the other, hand and arm movements confined, for the most part, to a simple repetitive sequence of place the die,—punch the clicker,—place the die,—punch the clicker, and intellectual activity reduced to computing the hours to quitting time.[42]

(Blauner and others, by the way, have pointed out that clock watching is an excellent index into how alienating an occupation is.) Roy is concerned with devices these operators used to find some meaning in this essentially meaningless occupation. First they found that they could make a little game out of their work: they varied their activity by changing the colors of the material or die shapes used or engaging in some maintenance work on the machinery. These little games, however, were of secondary importance to the informal group activities which took place on the job. Roy observed a variety of minor group processes which served to pass the day more pleasantly and interestingly. During the morning "peach time" was announced, at which time one worker took out two peaches and divided them among the four workers. Then there was "banana time." The same man who brought the peaches also brought one banana, which was for his own consumption. However, regularly each morning one of the workers would steal the banana and consume it gleefully while yelling "banana time!" The person who brought the banana would regularly protest and just as regularly another worker would admonish him for protesting so vociferously. As the day progressed there was "window time," "lunch time," "pickup time," "fish time," and "coke time." The reader is referred to Roy's study if he is interested in a detailed description of the events which transpired during each of these times. Suffice it to say that through these rather pathetic little devices workers on an essentially meaningless job endeavored to make their worklife more interesting.

5. In the face of these alienating tendencies individuals in low-status occupations in organizations also develop a variety of psychological mechanisms to make their worklife more meaningful.

[41] Donald Roy, " 'Banana Time': Job Satisfaction and Informal Interaction," *Human Organization* 18 (1959–1960), 158–168.
[42] Ibid., p. 160.

Assembly-line workers.   Early in this chapter it was made abundantly clear that the automobile assembly-line worker is highly alienated. Many just wallow in their alienation, while others seek, psychologically, to flesh out their worklives. Although the work routine itself offers little hope, many assembly-line workers rationalize their plight by focusing on extrinsic job factors such as the high pay and job security: the job is a means to an end and not an end in itself, since the activity of work is fundamentally unrewarding.[43] Real advancement is virtually impossible for most assembly-line workers, so advancement becomes "the search for security, the pursuit of small goals in the factory, and the constant accumulation of personal possessions."[44] Another major psychological "out" for this worker is the projection of "[his] unfulfilled ambitions upon [his] children."[45] He cannot improve his own worklife, so he concentrates on his children, seeking to prevent them from working in a factory and encouraging them to go to college. As one assembly-line worker put it: "I never had a chance, but I want my kids to go to college and do something better than factory work."[46] However these psychological resolutions and the resulting actions are only marginally successful. Many children, despite their fathers' aspirations, do finally go into factory work. More important, for our purposes, the de-emphasizing of the job and focusing on other factors only serves to increase the assembly-line worker's alienation. Work becomes little more than "a necessary evil to be endured because of the weekly pay check."[47]

Hashers.   The hasher is a college student who works in a sorority or fraternity house performing menial tasks.[48] In a sorority his major tasks include setting tables, doing dishes, cleaning, disposing of garbage, carrying the girls' luggage, and general subservience to the coeds. These expectations clearly conflict with the self-image of most college men: sophisticated, conqueror of women, fun-loving, and a potential white-collar or professional worker. "The hasher then finds himself in the unique situation of having middle-class definitions and expectations of work, but performing tasks and conforming to expectations which clearly are representative of a lower class job."[49] The actions he takes to ease the burden of his menial job are not of focal interest here, but they include withdrawing into the kitchen, horseplay and ingroup jokes, mimicking the girls, spilling food on them, and doctoring the food with such things as blood. Psychologically, the hasher employs a va-

---

[43] Ely Chinoy, *Automobile Workers and the American Dream* (Boston: Beacon Press, 1955).
[44] Ibid., p. 124.
[45] Ibid., p. 126.
[46] Ibid., p. 127.
[47] Ibid., p. 130.
[48] Louis A. Zurcher, Jr., David W. Sonenschein, and Eric L. Metzner, "The Hasher: a Study of Role Conflict," *Social Forces* 44 (1966), 505–514.
[49] Ibid., p. 509.

riety of means to make his worklife more tolerable. He might contend that being a hasher is merely a means to an end, and that he is just doing it until something else comes up. He might rationalize by claiming that it is the only job which does not interfere with classes. Or he might claim that he stays because he wants to get close to the girls. Some emphasize the "good kid," who is a coed who does not look down on the hasher. Finally, there are those who concentrate on the good old days when the life of the hasher was much better. Whatever the rationalization, they all serve to make an essentially demeaning and meaningless job more palatable.

Telephone operators. Another favorite device of individuals in low-status occupations is to overemphasize the status or importance of their job. For example the work of telephone operators is similar in many ways to assembly-line work, yet most operators consider themselves white-collar employees.[50] Ignoring the intrinsic similarities to blue-collar jobs, they emphasize the cleanliness of the work, their better manners, and superior dress. One operator contends: "It's not like manual labor, it's more like office work."[51] Another states: "It is the same as any business office. In fact, I think they [telephone operators] should be called communication secretaries because they do a great deal of work for business firms."[52] Others in the telephone company have a more realistic appraisal: "I tell you I simply can't see that they [operators] are classified as white collar people . . . it's just like an assembly-line. . . . But if you say that they all resent it—they don't want to admit it because it degrades them. . . ."[53]

Psychiatric attendants. Another psychological mechanism employed in low-status occupations is generally called a mythical occupational image. Low-status workers may "seize upon some aspect of their work which is highly valued, either throughout society or in the work subculture, and build a self-image around it."[54] Simpson and Simpson's study of the psychiatric attendant is perhaps the best example of the utilization of this device.[55] Most of the psychiatric attendants gave extrinsic reasons (salary, not qualified for anything else, etc.) for taking their jobs, but gave intrinsic reasons (interest in patients, etc.) for staying on the job. When the activities the attendants say are most important are compared to the activities they say are most time-consuming, some interesting differences appear, as shown in Table 5-2.

[50] Seidman et al., "Telephone Workers," in Nosow and Form, *Man, Work and Society*, pp. 493–504.

[51] Ibid., p. 498.

[52] Ibid.

[53] Ibid., pp. 498–99.

[54] Richard L. Simpson and Ida Harper Simpson, "The Psychiatric Attendant: Development of an Occupational Self-Image in a Low-Status Occupation," *American Sociological Review* 24 (1959), 389.

[55] Ibid., pp. 389–393.

TABLE 5-2

*A Comparison of Activities Considered Most Important by Psychiatric
Attendants and Those Which Are Most Time-Consuming*

Activity	% of Attendants Mentioning Activity as Most Important	% of Attendants Mentioning Activity as Most Time-Consuming
Interaction with patients	28.4	4.9
Physical care of patients	45.4	29.9
Supervision and observation of patients' behavior	18.4	13.2
Housekeeping and miscellaneous	7.8	52.0
Total	100.0	100.0

Adapted from Richard L. Simpson and Ida Harper Simpson, "The Psychiatric Attendant: Development of an Occupational Self-Image in a Low-Status Occupation," *American Sociological Review* 24 (1959), 389.

It is clear that the attendants stress their activities which relate to the care of the patient while they spend the majority of their worktime on housekeeping and miscellaneous chores. By focusing on the highly valued aspect of patient care the psychiatric attendants are able to maintain a highly favorable self-image. Although all attendants are not satisfied with their work, this exaggerated self-image serves to make the job more tolerable.

Night watchmen. Trice's study of the night watchman also presents evidence that those in low-status occupations emphasize a minor, but highly valued, aspect of their work.[56] The night watchman is required to move around his location in order to be sure that there is no trouble. This however tends to be dull and routine, since there is rarely anything wrong. To enhance their occupational self-image the watchmen chose to focus on several aspects of their job which were regarded by society as being very important. For example, almost all of them felt that fire prevention was their most important task, despite the fact that for years there had been no fire at the location Trice studied. They also emphasized that they were management surrogates, "representing the company to anyone who came or went in the building."[57] This image was held despite the fact that rarely, if ever, did anyone come into the building during the hours that they were on duty. In sum, an occupational self-image which emphasizes highly valued aspects of the job makes work in low-status occupations more satisfying to the individuals in these occupations.

It is interesting to ponder whether this emphasis on a highly valued aspect of the job is really accepted by individuals in the occupation, or whether

[56] Harrison M. Trice, "Night Watchman: A Study of an Isolated Occupation," *ILR Research* 10 (1964), 3–8.

[57] Ibid., p. 7.

it is merely for public consumption. If they truly believe it, they are confronted with an enormous task of self-deception. They must hold this belief although most of the things they do and are expected to do contradict it. Further, if they do believe in their mythical occupational image they will be confronted with much status inconsistency, for they will think they have high status while virtually everyone else in the organization has a more realistic view of their position. This is exemplified by the individual in the telephone company who said that he could not see how operators could classify themselves as white-collar workers when their work more closely resembles that of the assembly line. If the individuals in low-status occupations hold their image merely for public relations purposes, they are faced with other problems. They can not enhance their own job satisfaction if they do not really believe in the occupational image they are trying to project. Further, they are unlikely to convince anyone else if they do not believe it themselves. One must question whether occupational myths can ever be truly successful. How can one convince himself that his self-image is true when he is constantly faced with evidence to the contrary? How can he convince others when they clearly see that the image does not reflect reality? We need only think of the janitors who want us to call them sanitation engineers to realize how unsuccessful are such efforts. The lack of success of such mythical occupational images points up the frustration of those in low-status occupations. Despite the difficulties inherent in them, mythical occupational images are an important part of the life of individuals in low-status occupations in organizations. As Dubin notes, these occupational myths (or fictions as he calls them) "are necessary in order that action within the formal organization may proceed."[58] Everyone knows they are untrue, but "the truth, however, is disturbing, so by a kind of silent agreement among members of the organization, this truth is clothed in fiction."[59]

6. Unions, theoretically at least, constitute an important structure which low-status workers may use to reduce their alienation.

Reducing powerlessness. Approximately 17 million Americans belong to labor unions and most of them are what would be considered low-status employees. A low-status worker (when he has a choice—and if there is a union shop agreement a worker has no choice) can utilize labor unions to compensate for and reduce the alienating tendencies of his worklife. As an individual the low-status worker was, historically, powerless vis-à-vis management. As a matter of fact, the most important reason for the development of unions was the total control of management over the worker. Once a union enters the picture management is no longer able to fire, promote, demote, or punish a worker at will, and if it acts without just cause the worker can bring

[58] Robert Dubin, "Organization Fictions," in Robert Dubin, ed., *Human Relations in Administration,"* 3rd ed. (Englewood Cliffs, N.J.: Prentice-Hall, 1968), p. 494.
[59] Ibid., p. 496.

a grievance against it which the union will generally actively support. The mere existence of the possibility of the expensive grievance process has reduced managerial dictatorial power. As a group, through the collective bargaining process, union members also have a good deal of power over management, which can no longer arbitrarily set wages, hours, and working conditions. Instead, these conditions must be agreed upon by both parties during labor negotiations. If management does not present a reasonable proposal, the union can call a strike which, in most organizations, would severely cripple or totally halt production. It is not only the strike, but also the mere threat of one which gives the union a good deal of leverage in its dealings with management.

Reducing other aspects of alienation.   Besides lessening feelings of powerlessness, the union may help to reduce the other three dimensions of alienation: meaninglessness, isolation, and self-estrangement. If the low-status worker seeks some meaning in his worklife, he may turn to the union. By being active there he can see his role in relation to other roles within the union structure. Further, he can get a clear idea of what the purpose of the union is and what is his part in the attainment of its objectives. This is especially true in small local unions. The union can also help alleviate the low-status worker's feelings of isolation. If he does not feel as if he belongs in the work setting, he can get a feeling of belonging within the union, where he finds himself in an organization with his peers and where all strive for a mutual goal. In sociological terms the union, in particular the local union, is a *Gemeinschaft* (communal-like) structure within a *Gesellschaft* (corporate-like) society. The low-status worker who cannot identify with his workplace can, in many instances, identify with the union and its objectives.

Finally the worker may be able to alleviate some of his feelings of self-estrangement by becoming involved in the union. It has been pointed out before that he is frequently unable to express his abilities, his potential, or his personality on the job. The union offers an alternative: frequently the capable worker who was barred from a managerial position has been able to utilize his administrative skills and fulfill his desire for leadership within the union. At the local level there are low-level administrative positions available and above this are such positions as union secretary, treasurer, vice president, and president. For those who demonstrate exceptional administrative ability there is the possibility, at least, of high-level positions within the national union or even within the AFL-CIO. The success of such men as the former plumber George Meany (currently president of the AFL-CIO) and former auto worker Walter Reuther (recently deceased president of the United Automobile Workers) indicates that there is administrative ability within the ranks of low-status employees which management has been unwilling or unable to utilize. The union constitutes one of the last remaining sources of upward mobility for talented blue-collar workers.

Union dysfunctions. The preceding discussion indicates some of the ways in which a union can serve to reduce the alienation of low-status employees. In all fairness we should point out that in many cases unions fail to fulfill this function, and that occasionally they have instead increased alienation. Some unions have developed their own hierarchies, which have not been responsive to the needs and demands of the membership. In these unions it is not unusual to find leaders who have remained in power for thirty or even forty years. They have retained their power by systematically excluding members from a say in how the union should be run and by making deals with management which serve their own ends without serving the members' needs. Sociologists who have studied unions have often explained this phenomenon in terms of Michels' Iron Law of Oligarchy. That is, once in power a leader becomes more concerned with maintaining his position than in pursuing the goals he had promised to attain. This problem is especially acute in unions because of the huge gap between the pay of a union leader and the pay that he received as a worker, or would receive again if he should fail to be reelected. Once in power the union leader has a number of devices within his control to solidify his position. He has patronage to dole out, union funds to support his reelection campaigns, and control of the union press with which he can extol his virtues and downgrade those of his opponent. Lipset et al.'s study of the Typographers has indicated that the Iron Law of Oligarchy is neither iron, nor a law.[60] They found that in the ITU there was a substantial turnover of leadership, but were quick to point out that there were a number of historical peculiarities and differences in the nature of printers which account for this. These peculiar conditions exist in few other unions, and therefore many unions are typified by an oligarchical structure.

In those unions which are oligarchical and not responsive to the needs of the members, alienation is increased rather than decreased. Hence many workers who turn to the union to reduce alienation find to their dismay that alienation has increased. A good example is the recent unionization of taxi drivers in New York City. With physical and monetary support from the electrical workers' local, a union of taxi drivers fought hard for the union because of what they considered to be management abuses. They were frequently hired, laid off, or fired rather arbitrarily. They felt that the union would right these wrongs and also give some of them a chance to display their administrative abilities within the union organization. Soon after victory many of these hopes were dashed, for important union positions went to members of the electrical union, not to the taxi drivers who had fought for its formation. In addition, a series of contracts were signed which failed to eliminate many of the abuses. More discouraging to many drivers was the fact that they found themselves even more powerless than before: now they

---

[60] Seymour M. Lipset, Martin Trow, and James Coleman, *Union Democracy* (Garden City, N.Y.: Anchor Books, 1962).

were not only powerless at work, but they also had no power within the union.

In general it may be concluded that when unions are run with the focus on the needs of the members they may serve to reduce the alienation of low-status workers. However, alienation may be increased when they are designed to serve the interests of the leaders. Most unions probably fall between these extremes and hence serve to reduce the alienation of low-status workers to some degree.

7.   There are a number of ways in which the formal organization can reduce the alienation of its low-status employees.

Alienation is costly to the employer of low-status workers. The question management has always had to deal with is: Is the cost of the solution greater than the cost of the problem? In human terms reducing alienation is certainly a worthwhile investment, but unfortunately management tends to think more in terms of profit margins than in terms of human work satisfaction. Even looking at the problem of alienation from a dollars and cents perspective indicates that alienation is economically costly. Walker and Guest, among others, found that turnover and absenteeism are highly related to the repetitiveness of work on the assembly line.[61] Sabotage of the assembly line, and glee when the machine breaks down accidentally, are not uncommon in mass production factories. Many of the workers are careless and this results in low quality, even where the quality is ostensibly set by the machine. An alienated worklife is also likely to lead to hostility toward management which might take the form of involvement in the union or even wildcat strikes. Given these and other costs, some organizations have sought to reduce the alienation of their low-status employees.

Managerial manipulation.   Unfortunately many of these efforts have been more manipulative than sincere. The most blatant example of managerial manipulation was developed by the Human Relations School of management theory. This approach was a reaction to the scientific management theory of F. W. Taylor, who felt that the needs of the laborer and the needs of the organization could be united if pay was tied to productivity. Since the worker was supposedly motivated by economic desires he would produce more under such an arrangement and the company would be more profitable. In the original human relations study at Hawthorne it became quite clear that men were not driven solely, or even primarily, by economic motives. The findings that the group acted to restrict productivity indicated that social needs were as important, if not more important. This led to the conclusion that if the group was content, and understood what management was trying to do, it would produce up to its maximum capabilities. An offshoot of this conclusion was the development of a variety of techniques to make the group

[61] Walker and Guest, *Man on Assembly Line.*

happier and therefore more productive. Communication was deemed of the utmost importance. The emphasis however was on communicating what management wanted rather than on the needs of the workers. It was also felt that if the worker could participate in decision making he would be more productive, but this participation most often took the form of asking what the worker wanted and then ignoring his desires in the ultimate decision, which remained in the hands of top management. At its extreme the human relations approach came to be known as "cow sociology": as long as the worker was content he would be productive. In order to make him content management piped in music, painted walls brightly, and provided comfortable rest rooms. But all of these devices were extrinsic to the job, and the job was the basic source of the worker's alienation. The basic assumption of the Human Relations School (and scientific management) was that there was no irreconcilability between the goals of management and the goals of the worker. However, management's goal of highest possible profit is in most cases contrary to the needs of the workers. In opposition to the "harmony" view of the Human Relations School has grown the Structural School in the sociology of organizations. The structuralists recognize "the inevitable strains—which can be reduced but not eliminated—between organizational needs and personal needs; between formal and informal relations; between management and workers, or, more generically, between ranks and divisions."[62] There is inevitable conflict between the worker and the organization which can never be eliminated, but it can be reduced to manageable proportions. In the next paragraph some specific ways in which the alienation of blue-collar workers can be reduced are discussed, but it should be kept in mind that these can only reduce the conflict and the alienation. Because of the nature of blue-collar work, alienation can never be eliminated short of a restructuring of the entire organization. Such a reorganization would also be necessary to eliminate the conflict between management and the worker.

Job enlargement and job rotation. One of the most alienating aspects of the work of the low-status employee, especially the assembly-line worker, is its minute specialization. In many jobs only one action is required. A solution to this problem is what has been called "job enlargement." This, in effect, is an effort to reverse the trend in modern industry to greater specialization. On a simple level job enlargement could be accomplished by simply giving a worker several tasks to perform. On a more sophisticated level a group of workers could be assigned to the line and they could decide who will do what tasks and could even change job assignments from day to day. Another device management has employed is "job rotation": on a periodic basis workers could be shifted from one job to another. "This practice provides variety, lets the employee see more of the total operation, and gives

[62] Amitai Etzioni, *Modern Organizations* (Englewood Cliffs, N.J.: Prentice-Hall, 1964), p. 41.

workers a chance to learn additional skills. The company also benefits, since the workers become able to perform a number of different jobs in the event of an emergency."[63]

Other devices. Related mechanisms suggested by Sayles and Strauss include enabling the worker to change his pace by, for example, building up a bank of work so that he can slack off at times, and the strategic use of rest pauses. They devote a good deal of attention to ways in which management can give the workers a feeling of accomplishment, and one means they suggest is giving the workers more autonomy. This may be accomplished by letting them decide how the work should be done or by giving them meaningful participation in decisions which affect their work. If there is a quota of production it should be attainable. Further, when a worker has made his quota he might be allowed to leave for the day. The work should be in meaningful units. Jobs which are too small should be expanded to make a meaningful whole, while jobs which are too large should be broken down into a cohesive group of tasks. While they are in the middle of a task, workers should not be interrupted. "Secretaries object to be being asked to do something else when they are in the middle of a letter. . . . Similarly, workers object to starting a new job just before quitting time. . . ."[64] Employees can get some feedback on how they are doing when management utilizes some sort of counter or graph to show the worker how much he has done and how much more he needs to do. The company can also enhance the workers' sense of importance by showing each man his place in the production process and his role in it. Alienation can be reduced by better selection of low-status employees. From a white-collar perspective all blue-collar jobs may seem intrinsically meaningless, but there are some people who thrive on this kind of work. For example, in his study of the night watchman Trice has shown that there are certain personality types who can better handle the temperamental demands of this isolated occupation.[65] The organization can also allow its low-status employees some chance for upward mobility. Alienation will be reduced if they feel that they can be rewarded for outstanding performance. Finally, the organization can encourage, rather than discourage, the development of informal workgroups, for these yield a good deal of social satisfaction to low-status employees.

Informal workgroups. Blau has contended that if it encourages the development of informal workgroups, management may find that these groups work more with it, rather than opposing its goals.[66] Organizations cannot develop cohesive informal workgroups, but they can contribute to their devel-

---

[63] Leonard R. Sayles and George Strauss, *Human Behavior in Organizations* (Englewood Cliffs, N.J.: Prentice-Hall, 1966), p. 48.

[64] Ibid., p. 52.

[65] Trice, "Night Watchman," 3–8.

[66] Peter M. Blau, *Bureaucracy in Modern Society* (New York: Random House, 1956).

opment. For example, management can seek to reduce transfer and turnover rates. This leads to the development of a stable informal group and reduces the fear of transfer or firing which often leads to competition between members of the workgroup. Such competition operates against the development of a cohesive informal group. Management can also make explicit its standards of performance, so that an employee will know what reasons might cause him to be fired as well as the reasons for promotion. Clear standards also lead to worker security and enhance the likelihood of the development of a cohesive work group.

In conclusion several points must be reiterated. First, even if management utilized all of the above-mentioned devices, it would not eliminate alienation in low-status occupations but would merely reduce the level of alienation to more manageable proportions. Second, the use of these devices can easily become insincere and manipulative. When they are used merely to increase production they are more likely to fail. Management needs to be sincerely interested in reducing the level of alienation of its low-status employees. It must realize that the institution of some of these techniques may in fact reduce productivity and profit. In recognizing this we return to management's basic dilemma: Is there room for humanity within our profit and productivity-minded organizations? If there is, alienation can be reduced. If there is not, efforts to reduce alienation will be severely crippled.

8. The basic problem of those in low-status occupations which do not exist in formal organizations, or are relatively unconstrained by the organizations in which they exist, concerns relations with customers.

The individual in such a low-status occupation faces many of the same problems that confront the free professional. The free professional's problems center on his clients, while the individual in a "free" low-status occupation must deal with his customers. The problems of the latter are much greater, however, since he does not possess the authority that professionals have in dealing with clients. The individual in a low-status occupation must be able to handle his customers without this authority.

Taxi drivers. The problem of dealing with customers is perhaps greatest for taxi drivers. As Davis points out, the relationship between the driver and his customer is "fleeting."[67] It is this characteristic which differentiates the taxi driver-customer relationship from most other service relationships, where there usually are a series of constraints which keep interaction within certain boundaries. However, most of these constraints are lacking in the driver-passenger relationship. In general, "the cab driver's day consists of a long series of brief contacts with unrelated persons of whom he has no foreknowledge, just as they have none of him, and whom he is not likely to en-

[67] Fred Davis, "The Cabdriver and His Fare: Facets of a Fleeting Relationship," *American Journal of Sociology* 65 (1959), 158–165.

counter again."[68] The cab driver is never confronted with the same role-set—it varies from day to day. For this reason he does not deal with a well-defined group as do most other workers; rather, he deals with a series of unrelated persons. Control of interaction is in the hands of the customers and thus the driver is subject to such things as "stick-ups, belligerent drunks, women in labor, psychopaths, counterfeiters, and fare-jumpers."[69]

The cab driver's inability to control his customers is also tied to his lack of esoteric skill. Most people who ride in cabs also can drive and also know their way around the city. Therefore he is subject to much second guessing about his driving ability as well as the routes he selects.

Cab drivers are, in Goffman's terms, frequently treated as if they were "non-persons." That is, customers behave as if the driver were not even present. The frequent necking by young couples in cabs reflects the driver's non-person status. Because he is at times treated like a nonperson, he is unable to control interaction. On other occasions, because of the fleeting nature of the relationship, he becomes a confidant on extremely personal matters. He is one "to whom intimacies can be revealed and opinions forthrightly expressed with little fear of rebuttal, retaliation, or disparagement."[70]

The tip represents an important source of income for the driver, as well as a symbol of success. Given his inability to control his customers, he is also unable to control this important source of economic and symbolic reward.

Janitors. The apartment-building janitor also faces problems in dealing with his tenants.[71] Job security is one of the janitor's major goals. One source of security is the steady income the job provides. In order to gain this security he must focus on gaining technical and social skills. The technical aspects of the job are relatively easy to master and present no real problem—his major source of anxiety is the attainment of the social skills he needs to control the building's tenants. The janitor seeks to gain respect and recognition from the tenants and a good deal of his time is spent in "training" the tenants to give him respect. Gaining respect from tenants depends to a large extent on their social class. Upper-class tenants seem to be easier to get along with because they do not perceive the janitor as a status threat. On the other hand, tenants who are in occupations as marginal as janitorial work are often regarded as troublemakers. If the janitor's building is composed of such marginal people, it is more difficult for him to achieve his goal of status and security. Another factor affecting the janitor's ability to handle his tenants is the nature of the owner of the building or the real estate agent. If these individuals grant the janitor autonomy he will be better able to train recalcitrant tenants. If he is not granted this authority his task is much more difficult. Finally, janitors vary in their ability to achieve security on the job. Those who

[68] Ibid., p. 159.
[69] Ibid.
[70] Ibid., p. 160.
[71] Raymond L. Gold, "In the Basement—the Apartment-Building Janitor," in Peter L. Berger, ed., *The Human Shape of Work* (New York: Macmillan, 1964), pp. 1–49.

lack ability will be unable to effectively control the tenants, thereby making the job much more difficult.

Policemen. The police patrolman's major source of stress is the public. In trying to maintain order he is thrust into circumstances where there is unpredictable danger. He knows what might happen when he is chasing a robber, but such tasks are not a major portion of his job. More time is spent in dealing with such things as family squabbles, where he is never sure what to expect. He is generally not welcomed under such conditions and must use his own discretion in a situation that is "one of conflict and in an environment that is apprehensive and perhaps hostile."[72] In such situations he is dealing with an area in which the law is ambiguous (e.g., disorderly conduct, disturbing the peace) and therefore does not provide him with firm guidelines. He frequently must depend on the cooperation of the injured party, but the injured party is often unwilling to cooperate, regarding it as a personal matter or feeling unwilling to get involved with the law over such an issue. Thus the patrolman is expected to do something, but the victims are unwilling to help. In such crises he is supposed to handle the situation in a routine manner, but such impersonal behavior often exasperates the participants.

The policeman is thus frequently in the position of being unable to satisfy the public's needs. This is extremely frustrating to the public because it occurs in a situation which is both important and emotionally charged. The frustration of citizens is increased when they see patrolmen just standing around and not helping them with their problems. When the patrolman is dealing with the lower class he tends to judge beforehand that their complaints are not legitimate, and this further increases their hostility. In sum, the patrolman deals with the public in an environment which he feels is charged with suspicion, emotion, hostility, and uncooperativeness.

The patrolman sees himself as continually called upon to make quick judgments about the public by "making quick decisions about what their behavior has been in the past or is likely to be in the future."[73] He must rapidly evaluate such factors as social class, race, appearance, status, and influence. He must be ever alert to danger signals. This constant possibility of danger may make him nervous and likely to overreact when there is some danger.

Spurred on by student and racial unrest, many books which deal with the police have recently appeared. Included are Banton's *The Policeman in the Community*, Skolnick's *Justice Without Trial*, Niederhoffer's *Behind the Shield*, Bouma's *Kids and Cops*, Chevigny's *Police Power*.[74] Each focuses on

[72] James Q. Wilson, *Varieties of Police Behavior* (Cambridge: Harvard University Press, 1968), p. 21.
[73] Ibid., p. 38.
[74] Michael Banton, *The Policeman in the Community* (New York: Basic Books, 1965); Jerome Skolnick, *Justice Without Trial* (New York: John Wiley, Inc., 1966); Arthur Niederhoffer, *Behind the Shield* (Garden City, N.Y.: Anchor Books, 1969); Donald Bouma, *Kids and Cops* (Grand Rapids, Michigan: William B. Eerdmans, 1969); and Paul Chevigny, *Police Power* (New York: Vintage Books, 1969.)

a number of areas of police attitudes and behavior, but what unifies them is a concern with the stress between the police and the public and the ways in which this stress is dealt with. Bouma, for example, finds that while young people tend to have negative attitudes toward the police, the police felt that young people were far more negative toward them than they actually were. Thus the police are right in feeling stress between themselves and youth, but at least in this study, they overestimate the degree of hostility levelled at them. This misperception may have serious repercussions, such as police overreaction to the slightest affront. While police react to the real or presumed danger posed by the public, they also react to threats to their authority. Chevigny defines the "police character" in the following way: "a man, suspicious of outsiders, who is concerned with order, reacts aggressively to threats to his authority, and regards every attempt to control that authority with cynicism."[75] Thus anyone (blacks, hippies) who acts or looks as if he were a threat to the authority of the policeman is dealt with aggressively. At times, the patrolman even finds it necessary to engage in police abuses (distortion of facts, clubbing a hippie) in order to put this threat to his authority behind bars. But by acting in this way he is defeating his own purpose. He wants the public to respect his authority, but by employing such abuses he is undermining that authority, at least in the eyes of some segments of the public. Thus he faces real danger and real threats to his authority, but because he overestimates these threats he overreacts and this leads to still greater threats to himself and his authority.

It is impossible to summarize here the mass of literature on police, but it would be useful to examine in detail one excellent study.[76] Egon Bittner spent a year studying the police in two American cities and the way they operate on skid row. He is primarily concerned with the peacekeeping function of the police rather than their role in law enforcement. Bittner outlines five types of circumstances that do not involve law enforcement:

1. The supervision of traffic and a variety of licensed services. Although traffic regulation appears to imply at least some degree of law enforcement (e.g., issuing tickets), the police are urged not to be legalistic in their approach to traffic violations. Since most people have no contact with the police except on traffic matters, the police are urged to view these as public relations rather than legal matters.

2. In some situations in which arrest is possible the police do not make arrests if the violations are minor. Instead a policeman may, for example, warn a juvenile offender not to repeat his act.

3. The public frequently demands that police become involved in matters in which no law has been broken. Intervening in family squabbles and

[75] Chevigny, Police Power, p. 278.

[76] Egon Bittner, "The Police on Skid Row," American Sociological Review 32 (1967), 699–716.

helping an individual in trouble are examples of this type of police behavior.

4. Control of regular or spontaneous mass demonstrations by monitoring the
activities of the crowd.

5. Special attention to certain minority groups such as the very young, the
mentally ill, ethnic and racial minorities, bohemians, etc. These groups
"are perceived by the police as producing a special problem that necessitates continuous attention and the use of special procedures."[77]

In some of the above circumstances arrest may ultimately occur, but this
is rather unusual. If an arrest is made there are clear norms to determine
whether the policeman had to make it and whether it was proper. However
when the police are merely involved in peacekeeping, as they are in each of
the circumstances described above, there are no such clear guidelines in terms
of proper behavior. In such circumstances there are few departmental rules
and the policeman is essentially on his own. Thus, he must decide for himself whether he should be involved in a peacekeeping matter, how he should
handle it, and whether it should end in arrest. Peacekeeping is more stressful
for the police than law enforcement despite the fact that law enforcement entails greater danger, for in a law enforcement matter the policeman has guidelines to determine his behavior.

Much of the police activity on skid row is of the peacekeeping variety
since many of the residents are members of a minority group which does not
conform to what society deems a "normal" way of life. Many policemen are
assigned on a permanent basis to patrol skid row and they are given free rein
in their work. The police have a stereotyped view of skid row which defines
it as different from the rest of the society: they see life there as characterized
by untrustworthiness, momentary rather than long-term concerns, irresponsi-
bility, lack of accountability, and reduced visibility of the inhabitants. Since
skid-row residents are viewed as having little stake in anything, "nothing is
thought safe from them."[78] The policeman's major task is to keep the peace
in skid row rather than to protect society from the derelict, and so his main
job becomes "the protection of putative predators from one another."[79] How
he does this is shown later in this chapter in the discussion of ways in which
the police resolve their conflicts with the public.

9. In dealing with customers, individuals in low-status occupations which do not exist in formal organizations, or are relatively
unconstrained by the organizations in which they exist, frequently
employ typologies in order to gain some control and stability in the
relationship.

[77] Ibid., p. 704.
[78] Ibid., p. 706.
[79] Ibid., p. 707.

Taxi drivers. In the discussion of the taxi driver, the symbolic and economic importance of the tip was pointed out. Despite its importance the driver has no control over whether he will get a tip or how large it will be. In order to reduce this uncertainty he develops a typology of passengers on the basis of the size and likelihood of a tip: *The Sport* is generally a local celebrity who will treat the driver well and is likely to give a large tip. *The Blowhard* is a phony sport who talks big, but does not tip as well as the sport. *The Businessman* is the staple of the taxi business since he is the most frequent user of a cab. Although he is not a big tipper, he is generally a fair one. *The Lady Shopper* also frequently uses the taxi, but she is a notoriously low tipper. *The Live One* is generally an out-of-towner who is, at least potentially, the source of the largest tip.

By placing the passenger in one of these types the driver does nothing to increase the size of his tip, but he at least knows what to expect from each passenger.

Policemen. The policeman has developed a number of types of individuals who are likely to be potential sources of difficulties. He is likely to be suspicious of the following types: "a badly dressed, rough-talking person, especially one accompanied by friends and in his own neighborhood"; "a teenager hanging out on a street corner late at night, especially one dressed in an eccentric manner"; "a Negro wearing a 'conk rag'"; short-skirted girls; long-haired boys; and interracial couples.[80]

Again, this typology does not help in terms of actual control, but it does remove some of the uncertainty from dealing with the public.

Boxers. The professional boxer's customer/client may be considered his opponent in the ring. Like other individuals in low-status, free occupations, the boxer tries to bring some certainty into an anxiety-producing situation by placing opponents into types.[81] The "puncher" or the "mauler" is a fighter who is strong but not stylish; a "boxer" is noted for his style; the "cream puff" is unable to punch; a "miller" swings all of the time without pacing himself; a "butcher" hits hard and is ruthless even when his opponent has been reduced to helplessness; the "tanker" is knocked out easily and is very prone to fix a fight; and the "mechanical" fighter is not innovative in his fighting techniques, while the "smart" fighter is. Again these types do not help the boxer win the fight, but they reduce uncertainty by enabling him to know what to expect when he enters the ring.

Janitors. The apartment-building janitors simply divide tenants into two "ideal types," "good" and "bad." Bad tenants unnecessarily disturb the janitor at home and in his work routine; ask for immediate service or service

[80] Wilson, *Varieties of Police Behavior,* p. 39.
[81] S. Kirson Weinberg and Henry Arond, "The Occupational Culture of the Boxer," *American Journal of Sociology* 57 (1952), 460–469.

the janitor is not supposed to supply; ask him to do several things when they had called him to do one thing; are uncooperative in following building rules; do not appreciate what he does; will not recognize that he is the owner's representative; and are lazy, argumentative, and conniving. In short, they are inconsiderate of the janitor. The "good" tenant, on the other hand, is exactly the opposite of the bad tenant. He has none of the above characteristics.

10.   In dealing with customers, individuals in low-status occupations which do not exist in formal organizations or are relatively unconstrained by the organization in which they exist also employ more direct means of controlling the customer's behavior.

Janitors.   As Gold has pointed out, the janitor is not satisfied to passively categorize his tenants as either good or bad. He actively tries to change bad tenants into good ones and to keep the good tenants in line, and employs a number of ways of "training" them. The ability to train tenants comes with janitorial experience. If a tenant makes unreasonable demands the janitor may respond by stalling. If the tenant is disrespectful in making a demand, the janitor may refuse to do anything until he is asked in a "proper" manner. He tries to prevent tenant carelessness by threatening to force them to pay for the needed repairs. He may seek to train the tenant to tip him for services rendered. As with the taxi driver, the tip signifies respect for his position and his abilities. The janitor dislikes being bothered in his off hours and he seeks through a variety of responses to prevent such interference, which he regards as unnecessary and unwarranted. He may try to bring a bad tenant into line by refusing to receive packages for him. No matter what devices he uses, the janitor will find that some tenants are untrainable. When this occurs he tries to rationalize his failure by contending that there is something "wrong" with the tenant. He may also deal with the untrainables by making small concessions which keep them from complaining, or he may act as if they did not exist. If all of these fail, the janitor may resign himself to the fact he has some untrainable tenants and accommodate himself to them.

Taxi drivers.   The taxi driver cannot, because of his fleeting relationships with his customers, train them. In order to be able to train, there must be continual interaction. However, he has developed a number of techniques which help to increase the size or likelihood of a tip, such as fumbling with change or making change in such denominations that the passenger is forced to tip. Such devices as telling hard luck stories, opening doors, fancy driving, or calling the passenger "sir" or "madam" may also enhance the tip. Making up fictitious charges for services rendered is the most direct, and dishonest, means employed to increase income. Davis concludes, however, that these devices and the typing of passengers do not in the end give the driver a great deal of control over the tipping behavior of the passengers.

Henslin also analyzes the relationship between cab driver and fare, but he focuses on the "trust" between the two.[82] His analysis is an effort to apply Goffman's dramaturgical approach to the study of the driver-passenger relationship. Thus, trust is defined by Henslin in this way: *"Where an actor has offered a definition of himself and the audience is willing to interact with the actor on the basis of that definition, we are saying trust exists."*[83] Henslin asks what determines whether a driver will accept a passenger, and answers that a potential passenger is accepted if he wants a destination or service which the driver is able and willing to provide, if he will reimburse the driver adequately for the service, and if the risks involved are not too high. If the potential passenger does not meet these criteria he will not be accepted. Because a passenger may be a potential threat to the driver, the driver expends much effort evaluating potential passengers. He is acutely aware of words or actions which seem to indicate that the potential passenger is up to no good. In Goffman's terms, the driver pays close attention to the passenger's front behavior. He analyzes the setting in which the passenger presents himself (e.g., a taxi stand, in the ghetto), his appearance, and his manner. If these three aspects of the passenger's front behavior (setting, manner, appearance) are not coherent, he becomes wary of the individual as a possible passenger. Thus by paying close attention to certain symbols, the driver can be sure he only admits to his cab those passengers he can trust.

A number of factors help him define a trustworthy passenger. A driver is much more likely to trust a passenger who has phoned the company for a cab. The nature of the neighborhood is another important factor—the better the neighborhood where the passenger is picked up or going, the more likely the driver is to trust him. Passengers picked up during the day are more likely to be trusted than those picked up at night. This accounts for why many taxi drivers prefer to work during the day despite the fact that they generally can earn more at night. During the day the driver has a better chance to look over the passenger and assess his trustworthiness. Females are perceived as being more trustworthy than males, obviously because of the lesser physical threat they pose. Thus drivers will pick up females in situations in which they would never pick up a male. Drivers also consider the variable of age important: the very old and the very young are considered less threatening and are therefore more likely to be trusted. Finally, there are a number of more subtle factors (e.g., sobriety, the way the passenger sits, etc.) which the driver examines in an effort to determine whether a passenger is worthy of trust.

Policemen. In addition to typologies, policemen employ a wide variety of devices in order to control the public. In cases of law enforcement the

---

[82] James Henslin, "Trust and the Cabdriver," in Marcello Truzzi, ed., *Sociology and Everyday Life* (Englewood Cliffs, N.J.: Prentice-Hall, 1968), pp. 138–158.
[83] Ibid., p. 140.

policeman perceives himself to be in danger and acts to eliminate that danger as expeditiously as possible. He seeks to arrest the lawbreaker as quickly as he can, thereby reducing the risk to himself. He may even engage in a variety of police abuses (e.g., distorting the facts to expedite arrest and conviction) in order to successfully complete his mission. In all of this he is equipped with rather clear guidelines in terms of how he is supposed to act in dealing with someone who breaks the law. According to Chevigny, even police abuses are normative when lawbreakers are being dealt with:

Distortion of the facts becomes the most pervasive and the most significant of abuses. The police ethic justifies any action which is intended to maintain order or to convict any wrongdoer (i.e., anyone actually or potentially guilty of crime). In studying search and seizure, for example, we found that the police tend to justify a search made in "good faith"—really looking for a crime—regardless of whether it is a lawful search or not. Once again, the facts are distorted so as to justify the search in the eyes of the courts, although there is less distortion in connection with house searches than with searches of persons on the street.[84]

Much more interesting theoretically is how the police cope with their peacekeeping function, where the norms of how to behave are not as well defined. In examining how the police handle those who have not violated the law we return to Bittner's study of the police on skid row. First, Bittner notes that the policeman endeavors to gain very particularized knowledge about people and places in skid row. Since things are so transient there he can assume little about the inhabitants. If he does not know them personally, he knows nothing about them. In this sense he is at more of a disadvantage than the average patrolman since the average patrolman can make some assumptions about those he does not know on the basis of a variety of cues. The skid-row patrolman must know the people, the places, and the past events of skid row. The personalization of relationships enables him to pry into many private areas of a derelict's life. In so doing he is obviously violating some civil rights, but his explanation is that having free access to information about the lives of skid-row residents is in line with overall freedom of life in skid row. Not only do the police use this access to gain information; they also use it to gain personal control over at least some of the activities of the residents of skid row. The skid-row patrolman also offers them a variety of services. In part, engaging in this form of exchange enhances his control over them, but it is also in line with norm of helping and the expectations of the public which exist in skid row:

Hotel clerks normally call policemen when someone gets so sick as to need attention; merchants expect to be taxed, in a manner of speaking, to meet the pressing needs of certain persons; and the inhabitants do not hesitate to accept, solicit, and demand every kind of aid. The domain of the patrolman's service activity is vir-

[84] Chevigny, *Police Power*, pp. 276–277.

tually limitless, and it is no exaggeration to say that the solution of every conceivable problem has at one time or another been attempted by a police officer.[85]

Frequently skid-row policemen make arrests not to enforce the law, but to keep the peace. Thus, a policeman may spot a skid-row bum who is drunk and who he knows will, when he is drunk, commit a crime. In the patrolman's view such an individual "needs" to be arrested. So, since he is publicly drunk, he is arrested on that charge, although the real reason is to keep the peace and not to enforce the law against public drunkenness. In addition, if a patrolman can informally handle a minor case of illegal behavior he will, since he sees this technique as preferable to arrest. In other instances patrolmen make preventive arrests. In one case cited by Bittner an officer made such an arrest because he felt he was being tested by a suspicious individual. Thus, the officer in making the preventive arrest demonstrated that he had the upper hand. All of the situations discussed in this paragraph represent what Bittner calls "the restricted relevance of culpability" in skid row. Patrolmen often enforce laws to help them keep the peace and not really to punish an individual for violating them. Or they may ignore a violation and handle it informally if it helps them keep the peace.

Skid-row patrolmen, like all patrolmen, also do make arrests for lawbreaking. In fact in making arrests, skid-row police seem to be much more cavalier than other policemen. There are a number of reasons why they feel free to make arrests which other patrolmen would be wary of due to lack of information. In the eyes of the skid-row police, law violators are much more dangerous in skid row than in the rest of society. For one thing, because they are often old or unintelligent, and because they are frequently involved in illegal activities themselves, skid-row residents are much more vulnerable. Second, the police are more concerned with preventing an escalation of the trouble than they are in the niceties of civil rights. Third, skid-row patrolmen feel entitled to make snap judgments because of their personal knowledge of the skid-row residents. Finding themselves in tense situations, officers feel compelled to act unhesitatingly, even if they make a wrong decision. At least in this way they have reduced the possibility of greater trouble. Once again we come back to the fact that police officers on skid row make arrests ". . . not in the interest of law enforcement but in the interest of producing relative tranquility and order on the street."[86] The skid-row cop can make very arbitrary arrests since he knows that being arrested is unlikely to be a hardship to any resident of skid row.

Although in the last few pages we have examined in depth the techniques employed by the skid-row policeman to gain control over the derelicts, many of the same techniques are used by patrolmen in other areas. However, it is clear that the techniques employed by the policeman for gaining control

[85] Ibid., p. 709.
[86] Ibid., p. 713.

will vary from one situation to another. Nevertheless the point is clear: patrolmen seek to wrest control of the work situation from the public.

11. Potential employers utilize extremely simple methods of recruiting, hiring, and training low-status employees.

The recruiting of low-status employees is an extremely simple process. Potential employees come constantly to most organizations in search of jobs. The organization may keep a list of such people and simply notify them when there are openings. If not enough people appear in this way the organization may advertise in the newspaper or simply hang out a sign that it is hiring. There are a number of reasons why organizations do not use complex recruiting procedures for low-status occupations. For one, there is generally, in our society, an ample number of unemployed people who are looking for work. In general the recent unemployment rate in the United States has run between 3 and 7 percent. In addition, it is not only easy to hire low-status employees, but it is also relatively easy to fire them. Even when there is a union present there is generally a period of grace during which the organization can fire an individual if his performance is deemed inadequate, and the organization knows that there is a store of individuals who can be hired in his place. Firing is also easy because jobs in low-status occupations require very little training. A new individual can be hired and almost immediately produce up to the standard. Further, it is easy to let people go because the organization has invested little, if anything, in training them. The recruiting process is also simple because mistakes are not terribly important. If the organization makes a bad choice in hiring a janitor it is not likely to have an important effect on the organization. In the automobile industry a poor choice for the assembly line is not serious, because productivity is largely determined by machines, not by individual abilities.

For many of the same reasons the actual hiring of low-status employees is also a simple process. If an organization needs five janitors it may merely hire the first five applicants who appear. Again there is little risk involved because of the ease of firing and the fact that they can do little real damage to the organization. Organizations might use slightly more complex procedures by insisting on, for example, a high-school diploma, an interview, or some sort of test of intelligence or skill. The utilization of these really depends upon the labor market: if it is glutted, the organization can insist on a high-school diploma and a certain test score. If however it is tight, the organization is then likely to lower its standards. In any case tests and interviews for low-status employees are hardly rigorous.

Finally, the training of low-status employees is very simple, if it is done at all. Most frequently work in such occupations requires little more than on-the-job training. Again, this can be done because of the little damage a low-status employee can cause. An organization might also have someone already on the job train the new man; it will almost never utilize sophisticated training programs with its low-status employees.

Policemen: an exception. The police represent an exception in terms of recruiting, training, and hiring, for police departments are becoming more and more involved in active and elaborate efforts to recruit new patrolmen. Patrolmen must be actively recruited because of the increasingly dangerous nature of their jobs. The recent rash of murders of policemen is likely to make recruiting even more difficult and push police departments into even more active recruitment. Even now departments such as the one in Washington, D.C. are involved in nationwide recruiting efforts. The requirements for being hired as a policeman are more rigorous than those for any other free low-status occupation. A written examination which is similar to an intelligence test is generally required.[87] Recruits in the New York City Police Academy over the last ten years have had an average IQ of about 105. Thus those who have a below-average IQ have little chance of passing the test. Niederhoffer points out the following tests or requirements a recruit must meet if he is to be accepted by the police department: "1. U.S. citizenship; 2. Minimum age of twenty-one years; 3. Finger-printing . . . ; 4. No record of felony offense connection; 5. Good moral character determined by a complete background-check investigation; 6. Education through 12th grade; 7. Good physical fitness as shown by a complete medical examination; 8. Successful passing of an oral interview examination by the hiring agency."[88] About 50 percent of those who pass the written examination are later eliminated because investigation reveals something in their background which calls their moral character into question, and the department believes that any doubt should be resolved in its favor and against hiring the questionable individual. Knowing this many recruits ". . . dispose of books that might be considered too radical and drop friends with unsavory reputations."[89] An applicant might be turned down because he performed a delinquent act at 13 or joined a liberal organization. In addition, some departments are using lie detector tests and various projective psychological tests (e.g., Rorschach or Minnesota Multiphasic) to weed out candidates. Because of the elaborate hiring practices of police departments, few applicants are accepted. Niederhoffer notes that in New York City 15 percent are accepted, in Tucson 6 percent, and in Los Angeles 4 percent.

Training for the policeman is also far more elaborate than for other free low-status occupations. Niederhoffer views the police academy as a total institution in which the recruit is stripped and mortified in much the same way as in other such training schools. The idea is to break the rookie of his past habits so that he can fit better into his new role. He is formally trained in

[87] Niederhoffer, *Behind the Shield.*
[88] Ibid., p. 35.
[89] Ibid., p. 36.

how to handle his equipment (gun, nightstick, etc.) and is offered courses in law, government, police procedures and techniques, and human relations. Informally, he is trained in how to recognize and defer to those above him in the police hierarchy. Also informally he acquires the "art" of police work; "an instinct for the proper time to be masterly or to genuflect, to be warm and sympathetic or cold and imperious toward his future clientele."[90] Like the medical student and the student nurse, the police academy student begins with idealism which is soon transformed into cynicism. In class he is led to believe that he is, or soon will be, a person of great power and responsibility. Yet "outside of class the department indicates in many ways that it does not trust the young probationer. It sets curfews for him; it declares stores where liquor is sold 'off limits.' The recruit measures this treatment against the frequent appeals to him to conduct himself like a professional. Doubts assail him."[91] More cynicism is created when in contact with established members of the force he is told that he will have to forget everything he has learned in training when he gets a regular position. Unlike medical students, the police recruit may not outgrow his cynicism.

12. The career patterns of those in low-status occupations offer little chance of upward mobility.

This generalization, supported by recent studies, contradicts the widely held notion that any individual with ability can rise to the top of his occupation or organization. Blau and Duncan, for example, conclude that "men who start their working lives in manual occupations experience relatively little intergenerational mobility."[92] It is not within the bounds of this book to become involved in a discussion of the literature on occupational mobility. Rather, the goal is to deal with the ethnographic studies of occupational career patterns in order to pinpoint some of the reasons for lower mobility in low-status occupations. It is enough, for our purposes, to note that the statistical data collected in mobility studies generally support our contention.

Automobile workers. Chinoy's study of the automobile worker emphasizes the small possibility of upward mobility in that industry. He focused on the semiskilled workers and found that once in the occupation, an individual found few places to which he could move. Quitting the automobile industry and moving into independent business is not a viable alternative for the automobile worker: for one thing, the small industries which formerly were independent of, and essential to, the major automobile companies have been swallowed up by the large firms. Further, few automobile workers possess the skills and capital needed for success as an independent small entre-

90 Ibid., pp. 45–46.
91 Ibid., p. 46.
92 Peter M. Blau and Otis Dudley Duncan, *The American Occupational Structure* (New York: John Wiley, 1967), p. 424.

preneur. While owning his own business has been virtually closed to the automobile worker, movement up the organization's hierarchy has also become highly unlikely. The automobile industry is composed of huge plants within enormous organizations and this makes it difficult for the low-status employee to get the recognition which would enable him to rise. Technical and managerial occupations have become increasingly unlikely possibilities for the blue-collar worker, for these positions increasingly require levels of education and expertise which are far beyond the level he can hope to attain. Such positions are increasingly likely to go to individuals with undergraduate or even graduate degrees in highly specialized areas. As college graduates become more and more common, management is able to fill still lower managerial and technical positions with them. Without the degree it is virtually impossible for a blue-collar worker to move up in the organization.

Even such positions as skilled tradesman and foreman are not realistic goals for the upwardly mobile automobile worker. Increasing mechanization has expanded the number of semiskilled positions and reduced the number of skilled positions. Hence there are a large number of semiskilled workers vying for a decreasing number of skilled positions. Few of these workers have the skill or desire to undertake the extensive program of apprenticeship training required before one can become a skilled worker. At one time promotion to foreman was a possibility for blue-collar workers, but many companies now fill these positions with college graduates to give them some experience with production problems before moving them to higher levels in the organization. However, as mentioned earlier, many blue-collar workers would not desire the position in any case, for the pay differential between foreman and blue-collar worker is relatively small, and many do not find it worth the greater responsibility they must carry as foremen. Further, many blue-collar workers do not want to be in the uncomfortable position of supervising former peers, whose resentment they are likely to incur if they accept the position. They are also faced with the problem of gaining enough "social distance" between themselves and their former coworkers.

With all sources of upward mobility virtually closed to the blue-collar automobile worker, one might expect him to seek "better" jobs within the blue-collar category. Chinoy reports, however, that this too offers little hope for the auto worker, who finds that the pay and status differences between semiskilled occupations are so slight that it is hardly worth the effort. Furthermore union seniority rules have ruled out even this possibility of mobility.

Textile workers. This lack of opportunity for upward mobility is true in virtually all low-status occupations. The low-status worker in the textile industry is also locked in. As in the automobile industry, managerial and technical positions are practically closed to him because of skill and educational requirements. Other unskilled positions are not viable alternatives because of only minor work and pay differentials between them. For example, "in 1954 about half of the workers in the southern part of the industry were earning between $1.00 and $1.20 per hour."[93] The fact that most textile workers are women further restricts their mobility. Women are typically placed in the lowest-status positions and traditional views about females forbid upward mobility.

Letter carriers.   To complete the discussion in this section let us re-examine a low-status occupation which is not found in an industrial setting. The mailman holds a low-level civil service position and as such has few career alternatives open to him. After passing the civil service examination, he is appointed as a substitute carrier. He works as a substitute for the regular carrier on his days off, when he is sick, or on vacation. He may also pick up some work in the evenings collecting mail or working as a distribution clerk. He is able to move up when the regular carrier moves, retires, or dies. In general it takes a substitute carrier from three months to three years to become a regular carrier. Once in this position there are few career alternatives open to him: he has no real skill, and whatever he learns on the job is not trans-ferable to other types of occupations. He may take a civil service test for a supervisory position in the postal system, but there are very few of these positions in comparison to the number of letter carriers.

Policemen: an exception.   Once again, the patrolman is an exception in terms of his career pattern. There is a greater likelihood of upward mobility for policemen than for virtually any other free low-status occupation. The rookie's regular career begins while he is still in training school, when he is given assignments in the field for which he is accompanied by a regular patrolman. This experience constitutes a "reality shock" since he sees clearly for the first time the gap between theory and reality. This shock may result in a greater sense of solidarity with the police, or it may well lead to disen-chantment with the police force and police work. Those who persist and graduate promptly begin their first real job. Imbued with a bookish approach to law enforcement and peacekeeping, the rookie comes face to face immedi-ately with precinct pressures to make arrests. This in turn leads to pressure to forget theory and employ the pragmatic approach utilized by the older members of the force. For the first years the new policeman is assigned to the lowest-status position on the force, foot patrolman. After a few years many become disillusioned with the patrolman's life and seek to move up the ladder. Many take classes to prepare for the civil service promotion test which will, if passed, entitle them to a position as sergeant, but comparatively few will pass. For those who do, still higher positions become available, but their numbers decline the higher one goes in the organization. Another career possibility is being appointed a detective, a position which is generally a re-

---

[93] Blauner, *Alienation and Freedom,* p. 85.

ward for meritorious service. Most however are not promoted and remain patrolmen for all of their twenty-year career (a policeman can generally retire after twenty years of service). Since he is generally still young upon retirement, the policeman can look forward to a second career. However the possible occupations open to him are generally of lower-status than he had as a policeman: bank guard, night watchman, clerk, or messenger. Faced with these bleak possibilities, many policemen continue in the force beyond the point when they can retire. Niederhoffer found that over 50 percent of one group of policemen were on the job beyond the year in which they were supposed to retire.

Although he has more career opportunities than do individuals in other free low-status occupations, the policeman does not really have a great deal of mobility available to him. What opportunities he does have are being reduced through the same processes which have reduced mobility in other occupations. That is, there is an increasing propensity to hire college-trained people for higher-level positions, thereby reducing the patrolmen's chances to gain these positions. "The influx of college men into police work during and after the Great Depression upset the established pattern of upward mobility within the ranks. Educated policemen were able to shorten by half the time required for promotion to sergeant."[94] In time it may well be that policemen will be like all other free low-status occupations in terms of career patterns.

13. The nature of the problems faced by blacks and females in low-status occupations depends upon whether the occupation is congruent with their race and sex roles.

FEMALES

Just as females are confronted with distinctive problems in high-status occupations, they face particular kinds of stress when they are employed in low-status occupations.

Females in male low-status occupations

In previous chapters we have witnessed the plight of females in such male high-status occupations as law and medicine. While the sex typing of occupations occurs throughout the occupational hierarchy, it is nowhere more prevalent than in low-status occupations. One finds very few female laborers, janitors, taxi drivers, and patrolmen, for these are male occupations and a variety of forces prevent the entrance of females in large numbers. Before I turn to a discussion of these factors, it is important to point out that there are situa-

[94] Niederhoffer, *Behind the Shield*, p. 86.

tions (such as wartime, when males are called to the armed forces) in which females do make inroads into male low-status occupations. There are also circumstances specific to a given occupation which increase the likelihood of female participation. When men own their own taxis it is not unusual for their wives to drive during the husbands' off hours. In horse racing the demands of the fans have helped a number of women become jockeys. (They have met with resistance from male jockeys, but the fact that the appearance of a female jockey increases attendance at tracks has led track managers to allow them to ride.) Thus under a variety of circumstances the barriers in male low-status occupations do fall. Yet for every one that falls, many remain.

Occupational segregation is one of the ways in which the barriers are kept intact. Females are reluctantly admitted, but they are given different titles and duties which are more in line with their sex roles. Many women have been admitted to the police force in this way: they are called policewomen, and many are assigned to clerical work in order to free males for the more important tasks of law and order, while others perform actual police work, but are likely to deal solely with female offenders or work in female prisons. A number of women have become meter maids in charge of issuing tickets for violations of the parking laws; this too frees males for more important (and masculine) activities.

Similar segregation is found in other low-status occupations. Wherever such segregation occurs males manage to maintain the superordinate position for themselves. Thus janitors stand somewhat higher on the prestige scale than janitresses. They have retained for themselves such higher-status chores as repair and delegated lesser tasks such as cleaning and polishing to females. There is a slightly different distinction between waiters and waitresses. The "better" restaurants are far more likely to employ waiters, and, in fact, a good way of evaluating a restaurant's quality is to determine the sex of those who wait on the tables. In janitorial work females are delegated lesser tasks; in waiting females are relegated to lesser restaurants.

Females, therefore, have made inroads in some male low-status occupations under certain circumstances. However in most of these occupations and in most circumstances females have failed to break down the barriers. Let us turn to some of the reasons for this overall failure.[95]

1. Physical factors. Females simply do not have the strength required in many of these occupations. Whether the reason is the female socialization process or genetic makeup (or both), the fact remains that males in our society are stronger than females. Since many low-status occupations require more brawn than brains, it is not surprising that we find few females in them. Thus few females are as good as males at swinging a sledgehammer, driving a truck, and digging ditches.

[95] Theodore Caplow, *The Sociology of Work* (New York: McGraw-Hill, 1964), pp. 230–247.

2. Many low-status occupations have a well-developed male subculture with its own argot. Whether on the job or off the men do certain things together and discuss various topics using terms which are frequently considered not for women's ears. What they do, what they talk about, and how they say it are frequently regarded as off limits to females. Thus even if a woman had the physical abilities she would not be welcomed by her male coworkers. Few male workers would be comfortable with a female colleague who joined them in a visit to a bar or a discussion of sex. The reverse is also true; few women would be comfortable in such settings and in discussing such topics. To preserve this world males erect and man barriers to female admission. By the same token, few females desire to try to tear these barriers down.

3. If females were admitted to these subcultures, it is highly likely that emotional and sexual relationships would develop. I think both sexes would prefer to keep these kinds of relationships out of the workworld, for they are seen as forces which might lead to conflict within the group and to its possible disintegration. We have already discussed how important these informal groups are to low-status workers, so it is not surprising that they would keep females out in order to keep the groups intact.

4. Males in low-status occupations are generally proud of the masculine image of their work. In order to retain that image, they block the admission of females.

5. The admission of females raises the possibility that they might ultimately come to occupy supervisory positions. As has been discussed earlier, males are reluctant to be supervised by females. To prevent this eventuality, they block the admission of females to low-status occupations.

Female laborers

The factors discussed above reduce the likelihood that females will gain entrance to male low-status occupations. When, despite these barriers, females do gain entrance these same factors serve to make their worklife highly stressful, as is illustrated by the case of the female laborer. The sheer physical requirements of such a job are likely to make the female's life difficult; she will find it extremely hard to perform as well as her more brawny male coworkers. Even if she could do the job well, her male colleagues are likely to make her worklife miserable. Her entrance has adversely affected their masculine image of their work and upset the structure of the informal work group. The males may find themselves in competition or conflict for the attention of the female and this constitutes a further threat to the structure of the group. For these reasons males are likely to be hostile to females on the job and may even sabotage their work in order to get them to leave. In addition to hostility from male coworkers, the female laborer must cope with the likely hostility of her male superiors, for her effect on the male workers has complicated the work of the supervisor. Resenting this, the male supervisor is likely to vent his hostility on the female. He is made even more hostile by the petty nuisances (e.g., the need for separate rest rooms) which the employment of females has caused. Few females would be able to cope with the physical requirements of the job as well as the hostility from male coworkers and superiors.

Females in female low-status occupations

Waitresses. William Foote Whyte's analysis of the waitress is a classic example of the kinds of problems females face in occupations which are regarded as female.[96] The waitress is under a good deal of pressure because she must take orders from customers and supervisors and also adjust to the people who accept, process, and dispense food requests. The interdependence of all of these actors is extremely complex and a breakdown anywhere in the chain leads to stress for the waitress. A major dimension of Whyte's analysis is "who originates action for whom and how often." He hypothesizes that "relations among individuals along the flow of work will run smoothly when those of higher status are in a position to originate for those of lower status in the organization." Conversely "frictions will be observed more often when lower status individuals seek to originate interaction for those of higher status."[97]

The waitress's basic problem occurs when she calls in her orders to the male workers in the kitchen. In this case she is in a lower-status occupation and is giving direct orders to a male who is in a higher-status position. This situation is fraught with tension and blowups are frequent. Many restaurants recognize this problem and seek to do something about it. One solution is to limit face-to-face interaction between the female waitress and the male counterman. Whyte describes the following procedure which is an effort to institute this approach:

On the main serving floor of restaurant B, waitresses wrote out slips which they placed on spindles on top of a warming compartment separating them from the countermen. The men picked off the order slips, filled them, and put the plates in the compartment where the waitresses picked them up. In most cases there was no direct, face-to-face interaction between waitresses and countermen, and indeed, the warming compartment was so high that only the taller waitresses could see over the top.[98]

Whyte found that seniority helped to reduce the waitress's tension. The longer she worked on the job, the better able she was to cope with the built-in

[96] William Foote Whyte, *Men at Work* (Homewood, Ill.: Dorsey Press and Richard D. Irwin, 1961), pp. 125–135.
[97] Ibid., pp. 126–127.
[98] Ibid., p. 128.

problems. For one thing, those who could not handle the pressure left very quickly. Thus there was a measure of self-selection, with those better able to handle the role expectations remaining on the job. Further, over the years the women picked up formal and informal skills which helped reduce some problems. Friendships developed between them and they tried to help each other out. They also learned that they could be more aggressive to male bartenders and pantrymen and this also made the worklife a bit easier. The waitresses also developed a set of steady customers, and knowing what they wanted and how they would behave also eased their job. As time passed they knew their job well enough so that they did not need close supervision. The reduction of supervision removed another of the waitress's problems: she was less likely to be subjected to the criticisms of supervisors.

The waitress's basic problem revolved around her relations with male employees. It is interesting to note that the major solution discussed by Whyte, the spindle, is a structural solution—implicit is the recognition that males can never take orders from females. Thus the solution really sidestepped the problem by placing a mechanism between the waitresses and countermen.

Although waitressing is a female occupation, its basic problems involve relations with male coworkers. Other female occupations have the same sort of problem, although it is not quite as serious as in the case of the waitress. Most other individuals in female occupations are not in a position to "initiate interaction" for male coworkers, for most are deeply embedded in a female subculture or highly segregated from male occupations. Beautician work is in most cases a female occupation and coworkers and customers are primarily female. A female customer has no difficulty in allowing a female beautician to decide how her hair is to look. (On the other hand, one finds few female barbers. The idea of leaving the style of his hair to a woman is anathema to most men.) However, it is possible to find males who work as beauticians. Because in our culture the male is supposed to be dominant, females have little trouble allowing male hairdressers authority over how their hair will look. The female hairdresser does not have as many problems as the waitress because she does not initiate interaction for males. Other female occupations such as modeling and interior decoration are more like beautician work than waitressing.

Other low-status female occupations exist in a male milieu, but those in them have fewer problems than the waitress because they are subordinate to men in male occupations. Maids are clearly subordinate to their bosses and thus pose no threat to the male supervisor—initiation of interaction is almost exclusively in his hands. Other women in primarily female occupations, such as janitoresses and cooks, find themselves in a position similar to the maid's. They work with males, but are rarely in a position to initiate interaction because men are likely to hold the supervisory positions.

Lack of mobility. Another distinctive problem of most low-status female occupations is their lack of possibilities for mobility. Many female occupations are terminal in career-pattern terms. A girl may graduate from high school or business school and immediately assume a position as a waitress, but there are few places for the ambitious waitress to go. She might look for a more desirable boss or a better location, but in terms of the organization's formal hierarchy she is at a dead end. The same holds true for nurse's aides, maids, janitoresses, dishwashers, etc. Even women in higher-status occupations, such as airline stewardesses or fashion models, have few opportunities for upward mobility.

Housewives. Perhaps the best example of a "low-status" female occupation which is a dead end in career-pattern terms is the major female occupation, that of the housewife. Lopata defines housewives as "women who are, or have been, married and who 'run' their own households. Girls go through little anticipatory socialization for their ultimate role as housewives. Teenage girls and society in general place little importance on training to be a housewife and for a potential or new bride the housewifely role is far from a focal concern. Rather, the major concerns in early marriage are outside the home in either job or school while in the home the major emphasis is on the "care and feeding" of the husband. Slowly but surely, however, the role of housewife assumes center stage for most married women. The coming of the first child completes the transition as most women are forced to quit school or job and become full-time housewives. Relationships with the husband change as a result of the birth of the first child; the couple relates more as father and mother than as husband and wife. The peak period of the occupation of housewife comes when all of the children are born and are still small and at home. This phase begins to end as the children enroll in school and spend an increasing amount of time outside the home. As the children mature some housewifely chores increase in importance while others decline. The housewife with school-age children devotes a good deal of her time to relations with playmate's parents and teachers and to PTA activities. With the marriage of the first child the "shrinking" stage of the housewife's role begins, and this decline in importance of housewifely duties is a serious problem to many women. If they do not have substitute areas in which to work and express themselves they tend to feel useless and functionless. This stage continues with the marriage of the last child and the death of the husband. The final stage, which Lopata calls the "minimal plateau," occurs when the housewife is the only member left in the house. This stage ends with her death or movement into an institution.[99]

The position of housewife is a terminal occupation, offering no oppor-

[99] Helena Znaniecki Lopata, "The Life Cycle and the Social Role of Housewife," in Truzzi, *Sociology and Everyday Life*, pp. 111–124. See also Helena Z. Lopata, *Occupation: Housewife* (New York: Oxford University Press, 1971).

tunity for upward or downward mobility. The career pattern described above is merely a cycle of activities that every housewife passes through. An outside career offers her the only hope of upward mobility, but in accepting such a career she wholly or partially disengages herself from her career as a housewife. As has been pointed out previously, however, females have few chances for upward mobility even if they choose to focus on an outside career.

Alienation. In addition to being a dead end and being in conflict with male occupations, low-status female occupations are also highly alienating. As has been discussed previously, alienation is characteristic of most low-status occupations in organizations. This point also exists in the case of low-status female occupations. Let us take the four dimensions of alienation and analyze some female occupations from this perspective. The nurse's aide is almost totally powerless. She is constantly supervised by her boss. The occupation is also meaningless in the sense that she is frequently unable to see the importance of emptying bed pans to the overall goals of the organization. She is also likely to be isolated from other nurse's aides. Finally, the tasks which she performs rarely offer her an opportunity to express her "unique abilities, potentialities, or personality." The maid is also alienated on all four of Blauner's dimensions. She is totally at the whim of her employer and powerless to control her own work destiny. Intrinsically the work is meaningless although a maid may take pride in keeping her mistress's house clean. She is isolated since she generally works alone. Aubert makes this point in his study of the maid: "she cannot satisfy her craving for companionship . . . and she does not have a role in a work group as a possible substitute for direct work satisfaction."[100] Finally, it is virtually impossible for the maid to achieve self-actualization in a work environment which requires little more than physical stamina. In addition to her other problems, she is now being threatened by the invasion of labor-saving devices which threaten whatever meaningful work she might have had.

Although the preceding discussion gives a rather dismal picture of female occupations, the situation may not be as bad as it first appears. The nature of female sex-role socialization enables the woman to occupy such alienating, conflictive, and terminal occupations with comparatively little difficulty. Childhood socialization stresses, for the female, the centrality of the wife and mother roles. An unsatisfying occupational experience is therefore not as catastrophic as it would be for a male, for whom the occupation is a central area in which to prove his abilities, competitiveness, etc. Further, females may indeed be well suited to some of the alienating occupations in which they find themselves. Trained to be passive, they may truly revel in the powerlessness of such occupations as secretary and maid. After all, they are being dominated by a male and this is supposed to be "natural" in our society.

[100] Vilhelm Aubert, "The Housemaid—an Occupational Role in Crisis," *Acta Sociologica* 1 (1956), 198.

BLACKS

When they have been employed blacks have been disproportionately represented in the low-status occupations.

TABLE 5-3

Comparison of White and Nonwhite Employment
in Low-Status Occupations—1968

	% of White	% of Nonwhite
Blue-collar operatives	17.7	23.7
Nonfarm laborers	4.0	10.7
Service workers	10.4	28.3
Total	32.1	63.1

Adapted from *The American Almanac: The U.S. Book of Facts, Statistics and Information for 1970* (New York: Grosset and Dunlap, 1970), p. 223.

The reasons for the overrepresentation of blacks in low-status occupations are manifold and lie deep within the racist structure of American society. Space limitations prevent delving into these reasons in depth, but it would be useful to at least list some of them.

1. The centuries of slavery, overt discrimination (e.g., Jim Crow laws), and covert discrimination have left a seemingly indelible mark on black Americans. Traits such as passivity and self-hatred have prevented many from even attempting to succeed occupationally.[101] The growth of such movements as black power and black nationalism promise to transform these traits into activism and pride with the likely result that more blacks will strive to move up the occupational hierarchy. However, changes within the black community will not make for great advances without a corresponding attack by whites on the racism which pervades their institutions.

2. The racism of America's educational institutions has prevented blacks from getting the education they need to rise occupationally.

3. Discrimination by employers has served to keep many blacks in low-status occupations or out of work altogether.

4. Unions have also contributed to the problem through their discriminatory activities.

5. Government legislation aimed at this institutional racism has not been very successful, mainly because the nation lacks the desire to really enforce the new laws.

6. For all of the reasons listed above a black youth is typically raised in a family in which there are no successful role models to emulate.

[101] See, for example, William H. Grier and Price M. Cobbs, *Black Rage* (New York: Bantam Books, 1968).

7. For those who try to rise occupationally despite all of the above, the likelihood of failure soon dampens the motivation of many.

I have only touched on a number of very important issues in the preceding list, but the focus here is on the problems of the black worker, not the institutional causes of those problems. A great paradox is here worth noting. Although blacks are overrepresented in the low-status occupations, they have had great difficulty in getting even these positions. This is reflected by the fact that their unemployment rate has consistently been double that for whites. Thus there are a greater percentage of blacks than whites who would like a low-status position but are unable to find one. Many who do find them only work on a part-time basis. Both black males and females are more likely to be underemployed than their white counterparts.[102] Thus the black is not only more likely to be employed in low-status occupations, but is also more likely to be without work or to work on a part-time basis.

Blacks in white low-status occupations

The black in a white low-status occupation is in a position similar to that of the female in a male occupation. His major problem is dealing with the disapprobation of his male colleagues and superiors. Faced with threats such as inflation, unemployment, and automation, the white low-status worker is unlikely to welcome the entrance of a new threat, a black coworker. A variety of external forces determine the intensity of his reaction: he is likely to be more hostile during periods of high inflation, high unemployment, and technological change, and his hostility is also likely to be higher when blacks first enter the workplace or threaten to become a majority. The following discussion of the black patrolman illustrates a number of the general problems faced by blacks in low-status occupations as well as some which are specific to that occupation.

Black policemen.   At this point, relying on a recent study by Nicholas Alex entitled Black in Blue,[103] it would be useful to take an in-depth look at the position of blacks in one low-status occupation, police work. Alex echoes the contention made in each of the sections in this book on blacks and females that the member of a minority group must cope with the general problems attached to the occupation as well as those which occur because he is a member of a minority group. "The Negro who enters into the police role is subject to all the tensions and conflicts that arise from police work. Moreover the conflict is compounded for the Negro. . . ."[104] Basically, the black policeman is a marginal man. He is generally not accepted by his white col-

---

[102] Arthur M. Ross, "The Negro in the American Economy," in Ross and Herbert Hill, eds., Employment, Race, and Poverty (New York: Harcourt, Brace, 1967), p. 28.
[103] Nicholas Alex, Black in Blue (New York: Appleton-Century-Crofts, 1969).
[104] Ibid., p. 13.

leagues, but this is not unusual. What is unusual for a low-status occupation is that the black policeman is often rejected by the black community. After all he represents, and is a guardian of, the white establishment and in this sense he is viewed as traitor by at least a segment of the black community, although despite this rejection he may well fight for his race and be active in civil rights causes. Because of this Alex argues that the black policeman is not merely a marginal man, but a man faced with "double marginality." Such marginality, and even double marginality, is much more typical of blacks in high-status occupations (e.g., professional, manager) than it is of those in low-status occupations. Perhaps the reason for this is explained by Alex's statement that although "the police job in society at large is a relatively low prestige job," it is of comparatively high prestige in the black community because more prestigious positions are closed to blacks.[105]

Blacks have been entering police work in increasing numbers. According to Alex between 1950 and 1960 in New York City the number of black professional, technical, and kindred workers increased by 27 percent while the increase in black policemen was 91 percent. What explains the growing number of black policemen? Police departments have been motivated to seek out and hire black police officers for several reasons:

1. The police have had, and continue to have, a negative image in the ghetto. By hiring black policemen the department hopes to improve its image.
2. Black policemen are a great help in peacekeeping and law enforcement in the black community.
3. Labor force changes such as the decline in interest in police work among the Irish and the decline in immigration have forced the police force to turn to the black community for recruits. This is related to the increasing number of blacks dwelling in urban areas throughout the country.
4. The increase in the numbers of blacks in the city has given them political power and the police force has found it necessary to be responsive to this political power by hiring them.
5. Finally, pressure from various civil rights groups has forced the police to hire more blacks.

On the other side of the ledger, a variety of factors have motivated blacks to seek police positions:

1. Police work is a civil-service occupation offering "a relatively high secure income, with no lay-off periods, the opportunity for advancement based on civil service examinations up to the rank of captain, and the opportunity of getting an education or continuing one's education either in police science or in some field outside police administration."[106]

[105] Ibid., p. 14.
[106] Ibid., p. 34.

2. As a civil service occupation police work offers the black an occupation which although not free of discriminatory practices, is less discriminatory than many other occupations.
3. Many other occupations offering similar remuneration and possibility of advancement are closed to blacks.
4. Compared to other available occupations, police work is a significant step up for many blacks.

For these reasons Alex found most of the black policemen he studied had joined for the kinds of rewards listed above rather than because they were interested in police work.

Three groups constitute the major sources of strain for the black policeman: white policemen, the white public, and the black public. Although white policemen seem to accept black policemen on the job, there is little or no intercourse off the job. Despite latent hostility white police officers accept their black colleagues because they need their cooperation in the face of common enemies. It is not surprising that white policemen express latent hostility toward black policemen in light of Niederhoffer's conclusion that the police system operates to produce officers who score high on authoritarianism.[107] In return, the black policeman tends to have a negative image of his white counterpart, viewing him "as brutal, incompetent, lazy, ultraconservative, and bigoted,"[108] and his position is made even more uncomfortable by racist comments made by white policemen about black policemen, blacks in general, and civil rights leaders. More discomfort is caused by the discrimination practiced by the police department. The black policeman believes the department discriminates against black applicants, puts them disproportionately in the black community, bars them from some specialized agencies, and is unlikely to put them in high-ranking positions. In sum, even though blacks have gained entry into the police force they remain second-class citizens in it.

Dealing with the white public clearly points up the status contradictions of the black policeman. He is an authority figure possessing all of the symbols of that authority, but he is also black, and in the eyes of the white public a black is not supposed to wield power, and certainly not over them. They sometimes see him "as inadequate for the job simply because he is black. The white feels uneasy about him—he is, after all, a member of a minority exercising authority—which in turn makes him uneasy."[109] Again, the black police officer is in a position analogous to that of the black professional, executive, or union official.

The final major source of strain for the black policeman is the black community. Even though he is black he is seen as an enemy in the black community because he is serving the white society. Since he generally works

[107] Niederhoffer, *Behind the Shield*, pp. 129–160.
[108] Ibid., p. 97.
[109] Ibid., p. 116.

in the black community and since he is also generally forced to live in that community, he is open to the disapprobation of the black community both on and off the job. He is alienated from the very community in which he lives. He also more frequently finds himself in the uncomfortable position of policing friends and neighbors. The black community is not monolithic and it is therefore not surprising that it is divided in terms of its attitude toward black policemen. Middle-class blacks are more likely to accept him because he has "made it," but the black lower classes are extremely hostile to him. In addition blacks who came from the south and young blacks are very hostile to black policemen as well as virtually all symbols of authority.

In dealing with black lawbreakers the black policeman has some interesting problems. The black lawbreaker is more likely to give the black policeman a hard time than the white. He is more likely to plead for special treatment because they are both black. More important, a black lawbreaker is more likely to challenge the authority of the black policeman than the white—he too is unaccustomed to seeing a black in a position of authority and likely to treat it as a joke. Faced with these threats to his authority the black policeman often must react strongly, thereby strengthening the view that he is a traitor to the black community. For all of the reasons discussed in the last few pages the black policeman is in a highly uncomfortable position. Added to the conflicts inherent in the occupation are those which occur simply because he is black. In this sense he is in a position no different from that of blacks in any occupation save the traditional low-status occupations of shoeshine boy, maid, or butler. However, of all low-status occupations police work is the most difficult for the black man.

Blacks in black low-status occupations

Just as males are less likely to be hostile to females in female occupations (except where females initiate interaction), whites are less likely to be hostile to blacks in black low-status occupations. There are a number of low-status occupations which are congruent with the black race role, including maid, porter, shoeshine boy, busboy, and elevator operator. Such occupations have a number of characteristics in common, but two are of utmost importance. First, they rank at, or near, the absolute bottom of the occupational prestige hierarchy. (Whites typically regard blacks as inferior and it is therefore "natural" for them to accept blacks in inferior occupations.) Second, all of these occupations are rather passive, requiring service to whites. The black problem in these occupations is clearly not white hostility; it is extreme alienation. Few occupations are as powerless, meaningless, isolated, or self-estranging as the black low-status occupations. Treated as nonpersons, performing meaningless tasks, the blacks in these occupations must somehow manage to gain a measure of self-respect from their work. This task is clearly not an easy one.

6

Deviant Occupations and Occupational Deviance

This chapter is divided into two sections. The first deals with deviant occupations, employing the same framework used for analyzing the other, more traditional occupational levels. It is of central importance in this section that deviant occupations can be analyzed using this same framework. Further, the study of abnormal occupations can lead to a greater understanding of straight ones. This is in line with Hughes' idea that occupational processes are essentially the same throughout the occupational structure. In the second section the focus shifts to deviance in "straight" occupational life, deviance in deviant occupations, and nonoccupational life. At every occupational level workers engage in a variety of deviant activities, and a large number of studies in occupational sociology have dealt directly or indirectly with this topic. These studies, however, have remained uncodified. The goal in the second section is to analyze a number of them, using aspects of the functional model developed by Robert Merton. In this way I hope to demonstrate the utility of wedding general sociological theory and occupational sociology. This theme of bringing general theory into occupational sociology takes up much of the final chapter of this book.

Following Robert Park's call for the sociological study of occupations, many students at Chicago sallied forth to observe occupational life. Much of this early work focused on what might be called deviant occupations, and included Anderson's study of the hobo,[1] Cressy's study of the taxi dance hall girl,[2] and Sutherland's work on the professional thief.[3] As a matter of fact, as Berger points out, it was not until the publication of Cottrell's study of the railroaders in 1940 that occupational sociology moved away from the study of

[1] Nels Anderson, *The Hobo* (Chicago: University of Chicago Press, 1923).
[2] Paul Cressy, *The Taxi-Dance Hall* (Chicago: University of Chicago Press, 1932).
[3] Edwin H. Sutherland, *The Professional Thief* (Chicago: University of Chicago Press, 1937).

deviant occupations and into an analysis of the more "respectable" ones.[4, 5] One of Everett Hughes' continuing interests was in what he termed "dirty work" and "mistakes at work." In analyzing the "clean" work of the professionals and the "dirty" work of the deviant occupation, one gets a picture of the diversity of occupational life and the impact of different situations on its nature. It is clear that just as the interaction between professional and client is affected by the structure of the professions, so is the interaction between the individual in a deviant occupation and his "mark" affected by the structure of the deviant occupations. It is as meaningful to analyze the structure of deviant occupations as it is to analyze the structure of the professions. Hughes was also interested in "dirty work" in legitimate occupations, the focus of the second half of this chapter, and makes it quite clear that virtually all occupations have elements which might be considered under that heading. Thus the study of deviant occupations and occupational deviancy has been a central focus throughout the history of the sociological study of occupational life.

An occupation will be classified as deviant if it fulfills any one of the following criteria:

1. If it is illegal.
2. If it violates "what is considered morally correct behavior toward one's fellow man."
3. If it is not considered "a proper or fitting occupation" by society.[6]

DEVIANT OCCUPATIONS

1. Those in free deviant occupations are primarily confronted with problems with customer/clients and the police.

Problems with customer/clients

Most deviant occupations are free occupations; that is, they do not exist in formal organizations. The exceptions are those which exist within such organizations as the Cosa Nostra, whose employees have a number of particular problems, as well as some of the same problems faced by those in free deviant occupations. (Some time is spent discussing these deviant occupations in organizations later in this chapter.) One source of insecurity for those in free deviant occupations lies in their relationship with customer/clients; the other stems from the fact that they may perform illegal acts which make them subject to police action. Those in illegal deviant occupations must continually live under the threat of police apprehension and ultimate incarceration.

---

[4] W. F. Cottrell, *The Railroader* (Stanford: Stanford University Press, 1940).
[5] Peter Berger, "Some General Observations on the Problem of Work," in Peter Berger, ed., *The Human Shape of Work* (New York: Macmillan, 1964), pp. 211–241.
[6] Ned Polsky, *Hustlers, Beats and Others* (Garden City, N.Y.: Anchor Books, 1969), p. 32.

Poolroom hustlers.   Problems with clients and customers are what make the deviant occupations similar to every other free occupation. Polsky shows that the poolroom hustler has two groups with whom he must deal, the audience and the mark.[7] Winning bets constitutes the hustler's source of income and there are three types of betting on pool games: player versus player, player versus spectator, and spectator versus spectator. The first type is by far the most common. Pool playing has one structural characteristic which allows the hustler to hustle; "on each shot, the difference between success and failure is a matter of a small fraction of an inch. In pool or billiards it is peculiarly easy, even for the average player, to miss one's shot deliberately and still look good. . . ."[8] Since the hustler's major job is to get the potential competitor, as well as the spectators, to believe that he does not play as well as he actually can, he must be able to play well, but generally look worse than he actually is. Quite clearly this is an occupation which is loaded with insecurities. He must be able to get games with opponents on the basis of a false image he seeks to project, win without ruining that image, and continue to get and win games without revealing his true abilities. Once his real ability becomes clear he is "dead" at a particular pool hall and must move on to a different hall or even to a different city. He must constantly live with the fact that his opponents or the spectators will find out his real skill. Once he maneuvers himself into a game with big stakes he must not crack under the pressure. Later in this chapter some of the ways in which the poolroom hustler seeks to make his hustle more secure are discussed, but it must be pointed out that no matter how good he is, the hustler is always in an extremely insecure position vis à vis his customer/client/mark.

Prostitutes.   The prostitute's insecurity stems from her relationship with her major source of income, the male customer, frequently called the "square" or the "john."[9] The fact that the prime years of the occupation are very short makes it inherently insecure. If she is to make big money, the prostitute must do it during the few years in which she is physically most attractive; after this she will either have to find other work or be relegated to the dregs of prostitution, street walking. Even during her prime years the prostitute's relationship with her customers is fraught with insecurities. For one thing it is difficult to build up a clientele, let alone a steady, high-paying group of customers. The prostitute usually does not exist within an organization which institutionalizes her customer contacts, although one exception is the prostitute who works in a house of prostitution. In such a set-up the "madam" procures the customers, but they choose the prostitutes they wish and she must therefore concentrate on pleasing them. Whether working alone or in a

---

[7] Ibid., p. 36.
[8] Ibid., p. 41.
[9] James H. Bryan, "Apprenticeships in Prostitution," in Marcello Truzzi, ed., *Sociology and Everyday Life* (Englewood Cliffs, N.J.: Prentice-Hall, 1968), pp. 257–268.

brothel she is faced with a work situation in which the power lies with the customer. Some may "stiff her" (refuse to pay for her services), while some take up too much of her time, causing her to lose considerable income. Like the poolroom hustler, the prostitute is very insecure about her relationship with her marks and seeks through a variety of means to enhance her job security. The devices she employs are also discussed later in this chapter.

Jazz musicians. In discussing jazz music as a deviant occupation (because it is not considered as a proper occupation by society), Becker points out the basic problem of members of all deviant or service occupations:

He is a member of a service occupation and the culture he participates in gets its character from the problems common to service occupations. The service occupations are, in general, distinguished by the fact the worker in them comes into more or less direct contact and personal contact with the ultimate consumer of the product of his work, the client for whom he performs the service. Consequently, the client is able to direct or attempt to direct the worker at his task and to apply sanctions of various kinds, ranging from informal pressure to the withdrawal of his patronage and the conferring of it on some others of the many people who perform the service.[10]

The power in the relationship between the jazz musician and the audience (like the relationship between individuals in every service occupation and the consumers of their services) lies with the audience. The jazz musician is deeply committed to his work and generally feels that the audience, which he generally labels as squares, is incapable of assessing the quality of his performance, yet is in a position to exercise control over it. This is especially threatening since the "square is thought of as an ignorant, intolerant person who is to be feared, since he produces the pressures forcing the musician to play inartistically."[11] This situation is made almost intolerable because the squares have the ultimate power; if the jazz musician does not play what they like, they will not pay to hear it. Some jazzmen relent in the face of this pressure and "go commercial," playing what the audience wants to hear. Others do not conform and employ a variety of devices to mitigate the threat from the audience, which is viewed as essentially hostile.[12]

Racketeers. Sutherland's classic study, *The Professional Thief,* details a wide variety of deviant occupations and their insecure status in relation to

[10] Howard S. Becker, *Outsiders* (New York: Free Press, 1963), p. 82.
[11] Ibid., p. 89.
[12] A recent study has cast doubt on a number of Becker's findings on jazz musicians. Edward Harvey contends that things have changed in jazz and that there has been a decline in the amount of conflict between the musicians and their audiences. He feels that audiences have developed a greater understanding and appreciation of jazz. Further, there has been a growth in "jazz clubs," where only jazz is played and the musician is not under pressure from a naive audience to play commercial music. See Edward Harvey, "Social Change and the Jazz Musician," *Social Forces* 46 (1967), 33–42.

their marks as well as the law.[13] In particular, the deviant occupations included under the heading of "rackets" involve direct contact with the mark. "All of these rackets involve manipulation of suckers by nonviolent methods. For this purpose the skills required in the different rackets differ somewhat from one another. But in all of them the thief must be a good actor and a good salesman in order to manipulate the sucker."[14] The racketeer is always trying to outsmart his sucker, and this interaction is always fraught with danger for him. Let us examine a number of these rackets, focusing on the interaction between thief and mark, and the dangers inherent in each contact.

Cannons. In underworld parlance, the "cannon" is a pickpocket. He usually works in small groups, although he may also operate alone. His object is to lift money or a wallet from the pocket of a client. Pickpocketing occurs in a series of steps, each one of which always carries with it the possibility of detection by the individual being robbed. The first step is known as "fanning, or feeling the pockets to determine where the money or wallet is located."[15] This step is unnecessary under two conditions; when the sucker has been observed putting his wallet in his pocket, or when, because of a "Beware of Pickpockets" sign, he has been observed checking his pocket to be sure his money is there. The second step involves "pratting" or gently pushing or distracting him so that his money may be lifted more easily. The cannon is aided by the "stall" in this operation, since the stall's function is to distract the mark. The third step involves the actual stealing of the wallet. "When his hand goes into your pocket, you never feel it, partly because your attention is being distracted by the stalls and partly because of his manual dexterity."[16] During the actual theft the pickpocket's hand is generally concealed by a colleague or by the pickpocket himself. This is not necessary if he and his mark are in a milling crowd where there is considerable pushing going on. Obviously, all of the above activities are carried on with considerable risk that the pickpocket will be caught in the act by the sucker or by a bystander. The pickpocket must have both considerable dexterity and the temperamental ability to work under the constant threat of exposure.

Boosters, heels, and jug heels. The "booster" goes into a store, asks the salesman to see some items, and then steals those that he wants. The "heel" is similar, although he merely takes what he wants from the racks or shelves without involving the salesman. Here, too, there is a constant threat of detection by salesmen as well as store detectives. To succeed the booster and the heel rely on their acting ability as well as the reluctance of the store management to confront a shoplifter because of its fear of angering real custom-

13 Sutherland, *Professional Thief.*
14 Ibid., p. 43.
15 Ibid., p. 44.
16 Ibid., p. 45.

ers. An interesting variation on the above is the "jug heel," who specializes in stealing from banks. "One group of jug heels specializes in raising bundles of money from the counters inside the cages up over the glass partitions by means of a stick and string, with a hook or gum or other sticky substances at the end."[17] Others get behind the counter, dressed like tellers, and take money while acting as if they were regular employees. Obviously, whatever approach he uses, the jug heel is constantly faced with the anxiety of detection by bank employees.

Pennyweighters. The "pennyweighter" requires the same acting ability as all of these criminals, as well as some particular skills. He works jewelry stores and attempts to substitute fake jewels for the real ones shown him by the jeweler. He may work alone or have a cohort who diverts the jeweler's attention while the switch is made. The particular skills required are a knowledge of jewels and the ability to make or utilize substitutes which are not immediately recognizable. The insecurity here stems from the possibility that the jeweler will catch him making the switch or immediately recognize that the substituted jewelry is fake. The "hotel prowl" steals by finding unlocked hotel doors or by opening locked ones.

Confidence men. There are a large number of "confidence games," although the "central principle in all con rackets is to show a sucker how he can make some money by dishonest methods and then beat him in his attempted dishonesty." A good con man must be a "good actor, a good salesman, and have good manners and a good appearance."[18] There are two basic types of con games, one requiring the relatively long-term involvement of the con man and the other merely aimed at getting all of the money the sucker is carrying at a given moment. Let us examine each type, keeping in mind the constant insecurity caused by the ever-present possibility of exposure. The "wire racket" is an example of a long-term con game: a sucker is selected whom the mob is sure has the money needed and is likely to be willing to use illegal means to make more. With its victim selected, the mob begins the build-up. One approach is to have a member of the gang (the "steerer") engage the sucker in conversation and then point out a passerby (who is another member of the gang) as a professional gambler who can give tips on future horse races and who happens to be indebted to the steerer. Another approach is to have the steerer and the sucker find a wallet which belongs to the professional gambler. When returning the wallet the sucker is infomed that the gambler is in a position to give tips on horse races. Whatever means are used, the initial contact has been made. In the next step, known as the "convincer," the sucker is allowed to win a number of bets and even allowed to collect several hundred dollars. He is then introduced into a gambling club

---

[17] Ibid., p. 52.
[18] Ibid., p. 56.

in which he is told it will be safer to place his bets, still with tips from the professional gambler. Ultimately, he wins a big bet which he has placed with an IOU. The manager of the club tells him that he cannot collect until he has shown he has the cash he bet. The sucker goes to the bank, secure that he has made a big "killing." When he returns, he is convinced that he should deposit all of his money in the club. Then the con man is ready for the big step, relieving the sucker of all of the money he has just deposited. The usual technique is to give him a tip which is worded in such a way that he will lose, but due to his "misunderstanding" of the instructions. For example, he is told "to place everything on a certain horse." The gambler knows that the horse has already come in second, but words his instructions so that the sucker will bet all his money on the horse to win. After the sucker loses all his money he is told that it was his fault—he had been instructed to bet on the horse to "place," (come in second). Finally, the gambler tries to "cool the sucker out" so that he will not go to the police. Sometimes the sucker is cooled out so well that he never knows he has been taken and returns again and again to lose his money. This kind of crime is loaded with perhaps more insecurity than any of the others discussed thus far. It takes place over an extended period, so there are several opportunities for the sucker to discover the criminal's tricks. Further, this kind of crime requires the work of several men and the involvement of a number of people increases the likelihood of a slip up.

An example of the short-run confidence game is the "money-making machine." The con man tells the sucker that he has a machine that makes counterfeit money, and gives a demonstration in which the machine produces a real ten-dollar bill. To really convince him, the sucker is told to bring it to a bank to see if they will cash it. The bank does cash it, because it is a real bill. The sucker is then talked into buying the machine, renting it, investing money to develop it, or buying some counterfeit bills. Soon after the deal is completed, the con man disappears and the sucker learns that he has been taken. Again this is a risky operation, with the chance that the sucker will discover what is really happening.

Pasteposters. Marvin Scott discusses some of the deviant occupations found at and around horse racetracks.[19] One is called "pasteposting." Successful pasteposting requires a team operation: a man is stationed at the track and signals the results of a race to a second who is at a phone booth outside the track; a third man is at a phone booth near the bookie establishment; and a fourth is in the bookie joint.[20] Bookies receive information about the result of a race over a wire soon after the race is finished. However, there is a short time lag between the end of the race and the reception of the results. Many bookies allow betting up until the time they get the results. One group of

[19] Marvin B. Scott, *The Racing Game* (Chicago: Aldine, 1968).
[20] Ibid., p. 108.

pasteposters may work this way: as soon as the race is over the individual at the track signals the result (by, for example, walkie-talkie, since there are no phones at racetracks) to his colleague outside the track who is standing by the phone and already on the line with the third pasteposter outside the bookie joint. The fourth pasteposter is involved in a conversation with the bookie "telling him he can't make up his mind which horse to bet and whether or not he should drop his whole wad or quit for the day."[21] The third pasteposter enters and signals the winner of the race to the fourth conspirator. He turns to the bookie and acts as if he has finally made up his mind to bet all he has on the horse he already knows has won. If the bookie has not yet gotten the result, he allows the bet, and finds out moments later that the late bet has been placed on the winner. He generally pays off, but "is left wondering whether he has been taken by an outfit of pasteposters."[22] It is clear that if the pasteposters have slipped up in any way, the bookie's wondering is turned into certainty that he has been taken. Since bookies are generally linked to the underworld, a discovery of this kind is very dangerous to the pasteposters. Thus they, like most other individuals in deviant occupations, must always operate with a strong feeling of insecurity in terms of their relationship to their marks.

Pigeon passers. Another deviant occupation discussed by Scott is "pigeon passing." A pigeon passer attempts to cash counterfeit or discarded parimutuel tickets. One variation is to pick discarded losing tickets and attempt to get them cashed. This is most successful with inexperienced or easily cowed cashiers. The pigeon passer picks up losing tickets from early races and waits for that number to show up in a later race. The inexperienced cashier, faced with a long line of winners impatient to collect, is anxious to please them and thus only glances at the ticket presented to him to be sure it has the winning number. He may not notice that although it has the right number, it is from the wrong race. A variation on this approach is to present the cashier with a "pigeon" included among a number of legitimate winning tickets. Still another variation is to pass counterfeit tickets. This is the most risky of the approaches, although all are fraught with danger. There is always the possibility of detection by the cashier. In the first two approaches the pigeon passer can claim ignorance and probably get away with it, unless he has been caught doing the same thing a number of times before. The pigeon passer who passes counterfeit tickets is in greater danger because being caught involves not only the anger of the cashier, but the notification of the track police. Many cashiers have ultraviolet lights which help them determine whether a ticket is counterfeit. The discussion of the pigeon passer leads naturally into a discussion of the second major problem for those in deviant occupations, the police.

[21] Ibid.
[22] Ibid.

Problems with the police

Many deviant occupations, although certainly not all, are also illegal. Most of the ones just discussed fall into this category. For those that are illegal, apprehension by the law constitutes a second ever-present source of insecurity. One example is the racetrack tout discussed by Scott, who over a period of time makes a number of contacts with regular trackgoers. He then arranges with his marks that in exchange for "inside" information the mark will bet $20 to $50 for him on the horse. Next, he selects a race in which there are, for example, four serious contenders and gives a "tip" on each of them to a different mark. The chances are that one of them will win and another will be close. He collects from the mark who has the winner. Both the mark who had the winner and the one who had the horse that was close are likely to be satisfied enough to continue their relationship with the tout. He may also expand his operation using perhaps sixteen marks and dividing his four tips equally among them. In this case he is likely to collect four winners and keep eight of sixteen happy enough to try again. In the next race he will probably use sixteen different people and repeat the same process. He uses different marks in each race because they tend to become suspicious when they receive too much "inside information." Of course, one of the dangers for the tout is the possibility that in talking to one another the clients may discover what he is really doing. The possibility that the police will become involved occurs because of the large number of clients the tout deals with in the course of the day at the track. "To keep up with all his clients, the tout sometimes uses different color chalks to mark them. When players are spotted with chalk marks on their backs, one can be sure that a tout is operating at the track. It is one of the things the track police are on the lookout for."[23] The offtrack bookie is also in constant danger of being caught by the police. He is particularly insecure when a new policeman is on the beat or a new city administration takes office. The fact is that the location of bookies is well known to every interested party in the neighborhood, but they are secure most of the time because they pay off both the police and higher city officials.

Returning to members of the deviant occupations discussed by Sutherland, we find that most of them must deal with the possibility that the police will notice them. In our previous discussion of the "cannon," the first three steps in the process of picking pockets were outlined. In the third step, the actual lifting of the wallet, there is the danger of being observed by the police. However, the greatest danger in terms of the police occurs in the fourth stage before the pickpocket has a chance to get rid of the wallet. If he is stopped by the police at this point, he is caught with the evidence. The "heel" and the "boost" must also cope with the fact that they may be caught by the police either in the act of shoplifting or after the act with the goods on their

[23] Ibid., p. 112.

person. The "jug heel" engages in one of the most hazardous acts, for since there are always bank guards on duty, there is a high probability that he will be observed lifting the money or impersonating a cashier. The "pennyweighter" is unlikely to be caught directly by the police, although if the jeweler catches him he will almost undoubtedly call the police. Those who engage in the various con games have a relatively low risk of being directly observed and apprehended by the police. Thus, some illegal deviant occupations stand a better chance than others of remaining unnoticed by the police. For those in such occupations and in legal deviant occupations, the major occupational problem involves relations with marks. In the next section some of the very interesting ways in which individuals in deviant occupations seek to resolve or reduce these conflicts are discussed.

    2. It is primarily through dramaturgical manipulation that those in free deviant occupations attempt to reduce or eliminate their occupational insecurities.

To reduce problems with customer/clients

Let us focus first on dramaturgical means which those in deviant occupations employ to reduce the insecurity stemming from the customer/client, and later turn to means used to reduce or eliminate the possibility of police detection. It should be pointed out first that the resolutions attempted in some deviant occupations are not marked by a great deal of dramaturgical success. Lemert's study of the systematic check forger shows this quite clearly.[24] In examining the life histories of check forgers, Lemert found that they had spent more of their adult life in prison than on the outside. This seems to indicate dramaturgical failure on the part of the forger. Lemert discovered that instead of writing bad checks intermittently, the forgers were more inclined to go on "sprees" of bad check writing. Such an approach obviously enhances the possibility of detection both by marks and the police. They were found not to be "professional" thieves; rather, they were often irrational and their blunders frequently led to arrest. They rarely seemed to plan their activities carefully: "What stands out in the behavior of systematic check forgers is the rapid tempo—almost impulsiveness—with which they work."[25] One of the major dramaturgical demands occurred when the forger was forced to impersonate someone else in order to cash a check. Few, however, wanted to go through the elaborate staging procedures necessary. In the next few pages we will examine the dramaturgical techniques employed by those in deviant occupations to reduce insecurity stemming from both customer/clients and the police.

    [24] Edwin M. Lemert, "The Behavior of the Systematic Check Forger," *Social Problems* (1958), 141–148.
    [25] Ibid., p. 142.

Poolroom hustlers.   Much of Polsky's discussion of the hustler focuses on dramaturgical manipulation. Pool is structured in such a way that it is almost impossible to tell when a player has purposely missed a shot. As Polsky says, the cardinal dramaturgical rule for the poolroom hustler is, never show your real "speed." The hustler has a number of ways to miss shots without arousing suspicion: he may

strike his cue ball hard and with too much spin ("english"), so that the spin is transferred to the object ball and the object ball goes into the pocket but jumps out again; or he may scratch (losing a point and his turn), either by "accidentally" caroming his cue ball into a pocket or by hitting his cue ball hard and with too much top-spin so that it jumps off the table; or, most commonly, he pockets his shot but, by striking his cue ball just a wee bit too hard or too softly or with too much or too little english, he leaves himself "safe" (ends up with his cue ball out of position, so that he hasn't another shot).[26]

Hustlers also may manipulate their play dramaturgically by resisting the temptation to make the very difficult shots. As Polsky points out, the hustler may feel inclined to make these shots because of the approval he is likely to receive from the audience. However, he must remember that he is not playing for approval, but to win money from his opponent. Once he has hustled a game, he must also resist the urge to win by a big margin. After all, he may want to play the same individual again or hustle someone in the audience at a later date, and if he wins by too big a margin he will not be able to do either. Finally, he must allow his opponent to win occasionally. If he looks too good, future opponents will begin demanding large "spots" (advantages) in order to play him. In such cases it will be harder and harder for him to continue winning.

Before he can hustle an opponent, the poolroom hustler must first entice him into a game. This also requires considerable dramaturgical ability. He must be able to argue an opponent out of what the hustler considers to be an unreasonable spot and he must be able to resist playing in games in which such a spot is demanded. In addition to arguing opponents into games, the hustler also uses more dramaturgically direct ways of getting a game. For example, he may lure "opponents by the ancient device of pretending to be sloppy-drunk."[27] One hustler told Polsky of wearing a soldier's uniform when going to a new location, because local pool players are less likely to suspect a soldier of being a hustler. Further, local hustlers may see the soldier as someone to be hustled and, in the end, they find themselves outhustled. Another hustler reported sporting a wedding band and a wallet because hustlers are supposed to be unmarried and to carry money loose in their pockets. Finally, Polsky contends that the superior hustler is one who is able to break the dramaturgical rules when he encounters an atypical situation.

[26] Polsky, *Hustlers, Beats and Others,* p. 42.
[27] Ibid., p. 46.

The above discussion focuses on how the hustler reduces the insecurity stemming from opponents. Just as the poolroom hustler uses dramaturgical devices to gain control over opponents, he also uses the same types of techniques to gain control over the audience. Not only do players bet against each other, but members of the audience bet against the players. In such cases the players may form what Goffman calls a "team," and work together against the spectators. Polsky notes that "two hustlers sometimes will agree before their session that if, on any one game, there is a good disparity between the amounts of action that each gets from spectators, the player with the most to gain from side bets with spectators will win the game and the players will later share the profits."[28] It is clear that this is one of the most risky ventures for the hustler, since it involves outright cheating. Hence it requires the most precise dramaturgical manipulation. The hustler who is supposed to lose must "dump" the game with the greatest care and skill so that the audience will not become suspicious. In order to throw them off the track he may make some bets on himself to win, even though he knows he is going to lose. Or the hustlers may deceive the spectators in preceding games, setting them up for the hustle:

Hustler X played hustler Y for $20 per game. By pre-arrangement, both players refused to make side bets with spectators on the first three games and player Y deliberately lost the first three games. At the end of the third game Y became enraged, claiming that bad breaks had beat him, that X was just lucky, etc.; he raised his bet with X to $50 and also offered to bet spectators. Naturally he got lots of action from spectators—and just as naturally he won the fourth game.[29]

All of this duplicity requires perhaps the ultimate in dramaturgical skill. The hustler must lose without revealing his true ability, perform his act after losing the third game, and win the fourth game in such a way that the audience does not become suspicious. The teamwork between the two hustlers helps to reduce the insecurity stemming from the possibility of discovery by the audience. The poolroom hustler, like every other individual in a deviant occupation, "needs to be continually concerned about evaluation of him by other persons."[30] Through the various dramaturgical devices discussed above the hustler seeks to ensure a positive evaluation by his opponents and the audience.

Heels. All of the members of deviant occupations discussed by Sutherland seek dramaturgically to reduce their insecurity by reducing the possibility that their actions will be detected. The heel, or shoplifter, may use a variety of devices to fool department store greeters or salesmen. One approach is to walk boldly past the greeter

[28] Ibid., p. 48.
[29] Ibid.
[30] Ibid., p. 55.

as though he had the most important business of anyone in the store and as though he knew perfectly well where he was going and what he was going to do. . . . Another method would be to reach the department by elevator, inform the greeter that he has an appointment there with a friend who wants to buy a suit and, not finding him in the department, state that he will wait at the other end of the department near the window. After looking out of the window for a time, he seems to get restless and walks back and forth, occasionally stopping to look at a suit or overcoat. When the coast is clear, he may take an overcoat . . . return to the greeter and inform him that he will not be able to wait longer for his friend. . . . The greeter in one Chicago store likes to brag about the length of time he has been there, and the thief, with a stolen overcoat over his arm, may say to the greeter: "How do you do, Mr. Green. This makes your twenty-second year here, doesn't it?" . . . In another store the greeter has a hobby of leghorn chickens and the thief may start a conversation about leghorn chickens. This seems to make the greeter feel that the person cannot possibly be a sneak thief.[31]

Another technique is for the heel to start a disturbance in another area so that he may go about his business. "Fights have been started, women have apparently fainted, children have been knocked down, and other theatrical settings arranged for the purpose of distracting attention. . . ."[32] Still another device is engaging in "team" operations with employees of the store. Again the list of dramaturgical devices employed by those in deviant occupations is almost endless, but the goal is always the same: the reduction or elimination of the insecurity involved in dealing with customer/clients in a deviant way.

Prostitutes. The prostitute also engages in a variety of dramaturgical techniques to reduce the insecurity in her relationship to her customer. One problem for the prostitute is to attract enough customers, so some of the girls develop telephone "pitches" in which they try to get the man to visit them. A sob story over the phone is a typical device: "either it's the rent or she needs a car, or doctor's bills, or any number of things."[33] Other, lower-status prostitutes, must go out and actively recruit clients in such places as bars. Again the dramaturgical pitch employed is critical in determining whether the prostitute will successfully recruit customers. For the high-status prostitutes, call girls, the setting is extremely important, as is their appearance. "In the circle in which they move the girls have to make a good appearance. They must, for example, be able to walk in and out of the finest hotels without attracting undue attention because of dressing too poorly or too garishly. . . . Call girls' apartments are generally in expensive neighborhoods."[34] Since the

---

[31] Sutherland, *Professional Thief*, pp. 49–51.

[32] Ibid., p. 51.

[33] Bryan, "Apprenticeships in Prostitution," in Truzzi, *Sociology and Everyday Life*, p. 264.

[34] Harold Greenwald, "The Social and Professional Life of the Call Girl," in Simon Dinitz et al., eds., *Deviance* (New York: Oxford University Press, 1969), p. 401.

lower-status streetwalker caters to a different clientele, she sports a different appearance. For her an appearance and setting which attract men are important; virtually any type of man will do, as long as he can pay. Cleanliness of both body and working environment are emphasized, especially for call girls. Once involved sexually with the john, the prostitute generally follows a series of rules about what constitutes a proper performance. She is not supposed to drink or take drugs since this would prevent her from transacting her business as quickly as possible. She is also taught not to become too emotionally or sexually involved with customers since this might also inhibit her ability to expeditiously dispense with them and collect the fee. She also learns a variety of tricks to ensure payment. The prostitute employs many other dramaturgical devices, but these suffice to indicate the ways in which she seeks to provide herself customers and successful relations with them.

Jazz musicians. As has been pointed out previously, the jazz musician's basic problem is the demands of the audience. They desire "square" music and are in a position to enforce their demands, since they pay the money. One of the ways in which the jazz musician mitigates the effect of these demands is to manipulate the situation in which he plays. Fearing the customers, he seeks to isolate himself spatially from them. He frequently works on a platform which serves this purpose, and this physical isolation means, at least symbolically, that he is telling them that he will allow no interference in how and what he plays. It is very threatening, as one musician states, when he finds himself in a situation without the structural barrier: "Another thing about weddings, man. You're right down on the floor, right in the middle of the people. You can't get away from them . . . man, you're right in the middle of them."[35] In such situations musicians frequently construct barriers to protect themselves from the audience:

I had a Jewish wedding job for Sunday night. . . . We set up in a far corner of the hall. Jerry pulled the piano around so that it blocked off a small space, which was thus separated from the rest of the people. . . . I wanted to move the piano so that the boys could stand out in front of it and be next to the audience, but Jerry said, half-jokingly, "No, man. I have to have some protection from the squares." So we left things as they were . . . Jerry . . . had put two chairs in front of him. . . . Johnny said, "Man, why don't we sit on those chairs?" Jerry said, "No, man. Just leave them there. That's my barricade to protect me from the squares."[36]

The musicians try to avoid any type of contact with squares while they are working. This even goes as far as their desire not even to have their eyes meet those of a square for fear that he will request some square music.

[35] Becker, *Outsiders,* p. 96.
[36] Ibid., pp. 96–97.

To reduce problems with the police

Although those in virtually all deviant occupations must deal in some way with the insecurity stemming from relations with customer/clients, only those in illegal deviant occupations must contend with the insecurity born of the ever-present possibility of police detection. In reducing the latter type of uncertainty, members of deviant occupations utilize equally sophisticated dramaturgical techniques, as well as some more direct methods. Let us discuss the more direct means first since they are sociologically less interesting, although they are clearly widely employed.

Direct means. The most direct means employed is the payoff, and nearly all those employed in illegal deviant occupations pay off the police, the courts, and highly placed politicians. Payoffs are used at different levels for different purposes. The small-time operator may merely pay off the local cops on the beat, while bigger operators also give money to top police officials, who then unofficially declare them off limits to the local policeman. If the individual in an illegal occupation is caught by the police, then efforts are frequently made to buy off the courts so that he will not be convicted. At a still higher level, politicians are paid off to prevent the passage of unfavorable legislation or to influence them into persuading lower-level judges and policemen to leave certain individuals alone. Scott indicates the importance of the fix in his discussion of the bookie establishment commonly called a "horse room": "Obviously, then, horse rooms cannot operate unless a political 'fix' has been arranged. Whenever the police crack down or an anti-gambling reform administration takes office, the horse books are often the first and most obvious targets, since their operation and location is common knowledge in a community."[37] Scott's statement shows that although the fix is ubiquitous, it is rarely totally effective; there are always periodic police crackdowns or reform movements by idealistic new administrations. Perhaps more important, there are even some policemen who refuse to be bought. In his study *Street-corner Society,* Whyte notes the omnipresence of the police payoff, but also mentions a number of policemen who were labelled by the racketeers as "untouchables."[38] A racketeer discussed one of these, Captain O'Leary: "'When O'Leary was around here, we didn't make no money for six months. What a hell of a six months that was. No profits at all. We had to pay out all the profits to take care of the pinches.'"[39] Or there was the honest local cop, Sergeant Clancy: "'There's only one honest cop down here, one man they can't pay off. That's Sergeant Clancy, I know. They've offered him hun-

---

[37] Scott, *Racing Game,* p. 143.
[38] William F. Whyte, *Streetcorner Society* (Chicago: University of Chicago Press, 1967).
[39] Ibid., p. 132.

dreds, even thousands, and he won't take the money.' "[40] In addition to the honest cop, another threatening figure to the individual in an illegal deviant occupation is the rookie cop. "The racketeers fear the rookies. It is hard to do business with them. Their actions are unpredictable."[41] Thus, despite the success of the payoff, the individual in an illegal deviant occupation must employ other means of reducing the insecurity caused by the police.

Dramaturgical means. A good dramaturgical device is to get a "stand-in" to do the actual dirty work. The pigeon passer frequently uses this technique. He may "sober up a skid-row type and hire his services for the day to cash a series of doctored tickets,"[42] thus making himself far less likely to be apprehended by the police than if he tried to pass the tickets himself. Another possibility is to sell counterfeit tickets to people headed for the track the day after the race has been run. The pigeon passer tells the mark that he has tickets on the horse that won the preceding day, but claims he was not able to stay around for the race and cannot get to the track on this day, but is willing to sell the tickets for slightly less than they are worth. If the mark buys the tickets, he is the one who is likely to get arrested should there be any problem in passing them.

Individuals in deviant occupations also hasten to get rid of stolen merchandise so that there will be no evidence if they are stopped by the police. For example, after a cannon has lifted a wallet, he frequently passes it on to another member of the mob. If the pickpocket feels that he is under surveillance, "he makes every effort to get rid of the pocketbook; he may drop it, throw it away, or stick it in the hand or pocket of the sucker or of some other person near by."[43] He may drop it in any relatively deserted place, although a mailbox seems to be a favorite receptacle.

In the confidence rackets, "cooling out" is frequently employed to prevent the mark from going to the police. A good example of this is in the wire racket discussed previously. After the sucker has been informed that he has lost everything due to his own misunderstanding, the next step "is to cool him off so that he will not go to the police or make a fuss in other ways."[44] Goffman developed this concept in his seminal article, "On Cooling the Mark Out."[45]

After the blowoff has occurred, one of the operators stays with the mark and makes an effort to keep the anger of the mark within manageable and sensible proportions. The operator stays behind his teammates in the capacity of what may be called a cooler and exercises upon the mark the art of consolation. An attempt is made to

[40] Ibid., p. 133.
[41] Ibid., p. 132.
[42] Scott, *Racing Game*, p. 110.
[43] Sutherland, *Professional Thief*, p. 46.
[44] Ibid., p. 60.
[45] Erving Goffman, "On Cooling the Mark Out," *Psychiatry* 15 (1952), pp. 451–463.

define the situation for the mark in a way that makes it easy for him to accept the inevitable and quietly go home. The mark is given instruction in the philosophy of taking a loss.[46]

Another way is for the racketeer to tell the mark that he himself has also lost his own money in the same way and to promise to attempt to borrow more to win back both their losses.

Goffman notes that sometimes, however, a mark is not quite prepared to accept his loss as a gain in experience and to say and do nothing about his venture. He may feel moved to complain to the police or to chase after the operators.[47] It is especially in such situations, where an individual has involuntarily been deprived of a role under conditions in which he is likely to look bad, that it is necessary to cool him out, and this is why cooling out is essential in certain rackets in order to prevent the mark from going to the police.

3. Those in deviant occupations which exist within formal organizations face many of the same problems as faced by individuals in straight occupations in organizations.

The preceding discussion has focused on free deviant occupations, or those which do not exist within a formal organization. However there is some organization within the criminal world. It seems likely that those in deviant occupations within deviant organizations face the same kinds of problems as do individuals in all occupations within organizations. In this section the focus is on Cressey's analysis of the Mafia, the major example of organized crime.[48] Much of this section is an attempt to apply some of the ideas developed throughout this book to deviant occupations within organizations, and much is derived from Cressey's analysis, since there are no studies of the problems facing individuals in these occupations. However, it is true that there are deviant occupations within the Mafia which parallel the occupations discussed earlier in this book. Thus we will assume that, for example, an individual in a foreman-level occupation within the Mafia faces the same kinds of problems as an industrial foreman, or that the low-status employee in the Mafia is similar in many ways to the low-status worker in straight organizations. It is also clear that deviant occupations in deviant organizations have some rather distinctive problems. Two of these have been discussed above: problems with customer/clients and with the law. There are others which will be pointed out as the discussion proceeds.

Mafia occupations. At the top of the Mafia hierarchy is the "commission," which serves as the board of directors, legislature, supreme court, and arbitrator. The members of the commission are the leaders of the most powerful local "families." Below the commission, in some places, are "councils"

[46] Ibid., pp. 451–52.
[47] Ibid., p. 452.
[48] Donald R. Cressey, *Theft of the Nation* (New York: Harper & Row, 1969).

composed of the most experienced members of the families within that local-ity. Beneath these top levels are the 24 or so families, each of which has its own leader. According to Cressey, "the 'family' is the most significant level of organization and the largest unit of criminal organization in which allegiance is owed to one man, the boss."[49] The boss's function is to keep order and maximize profits and he is an absolute ruler in his location except in instances when he comes in conflict with the commission. In many families the boss has an assistant ("underboss") whom Cressey likens to an executive vice president or deputy director. On the same level as the underboss is a staff position, whose incumbent offers the boss counsel and advice. Like industrial staff officers, this Mafia advisor is not supposed to give orders, but only to advise. Also, like other staff officers we have discussed, he enjoys considerable influence and power. There is another staff position at this level, the "buffer." Its occupant is a link to subordinates as well as the police. Below these top-level positions is the "lieutenant," whom Cressey feels "is analogous to works manager or sales manager."[50] The lieutenant is the chief operating officer in the family structure. There is a position between the lieutenant and the next level, the "section chief" or "group leader." The lieutenant may, depending on the size of the family, have several section chiefs, each of whom handles a portion of his responsibilities, and five individuals, generally known as "soldiers," report to each section chief. This is the lowest level within the family, and all members at this level and above must be of Italian descent. Beneath the soldiers, but not actually members of the Mafia, "are large num-bers of employees, sharecroppers, franchise holders, and commission agents. . . . These are the persons carrying out most of the work 'on the street.' "[51] Many of the free illegal deviant occupations discussed earlier are at this level.

Cressey sees an increasing tendency for the Mafia to become more and more like legal bureaucracies. Its members are also becoming more like bu-reaucrats, and therefore the occupations which exist within the Mafia may be analyzed in the same way as other occupations in organizations have been examined. Those in these low-status occupations (employees, sharecroppers, etc.) are faced with the problems outlined previously: insecurity stemming from clients and the police. It is also reasonable to assume that they, like those in straight low-status occupations, are alienated. Of the four dimen-sions of alienation, low-status deviant occupations in the Mafia are probably plagued most with powerlessness, for they are not even considered to be within the Mafia, but external and subordinate to it. Thus it would be almost impossible for them to influence decisions made by middle- or top-ranking Mafia officials. All incumbents of the middle- and top-ranking managerial positions within the Mafia are likely, because of its structure, to face role con-flict. Individuals in each of these positions are certainly confronted with con-

[49] Ibid., p. 112.
[50] Ibid., p. 114.
[51] Ibid., p. 119.

flicting expectations from those above them, at their level, or below them in the hierarchy. The boss must balance the demands of the commission with the expectations of fellow bosses and the various officials who rank below him in the family. Similarly, all of those officials who rank below him (e.g., underboss, advisor, lieutenant) must handle conflicting demands from the various other officials within the family. There is also evidence that various professionals, such as lawyers, are attached to the Mafia. Like all professionals in nonprofessional organizations, they are likely to face the conflict between their professional norm of autonomy and the organization's demand for authority over their actions. In sum, individuals in deviant occupations within the Mafia face distinctive problems as well as the same kinds of problems faced by all other occupations which exist within organizations. It is also reasonable to assume, since the Mafia is similar in many ways to most organizations, that its resolutions of these conflicts are similar to those employed by persons in straight occupations in organizations.

4.   Since free deviant occupations are similar to low-status occupations, individuals in them have very restricted career patterns.

Most of the free deviant occupations require little, if any, specific education or training. Most individuals enter these occupations almost by accident, and then find few possibilities for mobility. Let us examine some specific occupations of this type in terms of their career patterns.

Strippers.   According to Skipper and McCaghy, "stripping qualifies as an unskilled occupation requiring little talent and almost no formal training."[52] Further, entry into stripping tends to be "adventitious," being "spontaneous, nonrational, fortuitous, and based on situational pressure and contingencies."[53] Very few of the women in the Skipper and McCaghy study planned to become strippers. There is little anticipatory socialization, prior contact with the occupation, or training. (As is discussed later, this is far more characteristic of stripping than of other deviant occupations.) Although there was no training for stripping, many of the girls held previous jobs which were similar in some ways; for example, they were dancers, singers, go-go girls, artists' models, hat check girls. Their main reason for becoming strippers was the economic rewards promised by friends, agents, etc. They have little hope of upward mobility, for according to Skipper and McCaghy, there are only three levels within the stripping career hierarchy. At the top are the stars, the headliners, who earn a median salary of about $450 per week. At the second level are the cofeatured girls, who earn between $275 and $350 per week. At the bottom are the vast majority of strippers, those who work

[52] James K. Skipper, Jr., and Charles H. McCaghy, "Stripteasers: the Anatomy and Career Contingencies of a Deviant Occupation," *Social Problems* 17 (1970), 398.
[53] Ibid.

in the line and earn between $200 and $250 per week. Upward mobility is highly restricted because there are far fewer positions at the top than at the bottom and because there are so few levels in the career hierarchy.[54]

Prostitutes. There is more stratification among prostitutes, although there does not seem to be significantly more upward mobility. At the bottom of the hierarchy are the streetwalkers, who literally walk the streets and are receptive to any man able to pay the price, which is comparatively small. These are generally lower-class girls who operate almost exclusively in lower-class areas. Near the bottom are the girls who work in houses of prostitution. There are several types of prostitutes who fall somewhere in the middle of the hierarchy, although their status is not exactly clear. One is the party girl, who goes out on no more than one date a night and never explicitly discusses the question of a fee. However, that there is a fee involved has been made clear by the person arranging the contact. Party girls are much more choosy than streetwalkers or house girls and frequently will refuse a customer if he is unappealing. Another category at this level is the kept woman, who "usually gives her favors to only one man at a time in return for financial security during the time that the arrangement is in effect."[55] At the top is the call girl "who operates on an appointment basis, maintaining her own residence, which may or may not serve as a place for entertaining clients."[56] In many cases it is unrealistic to differentiate between party girls, kept women, and call girls because the same girls may alternately occupy each of these positions at one time or another. By the same token the streetwalkers and house girls are also, in most cases, indistinguishable. Thus we are left with two basic levels and there is little possibility of mobility between them. Those who start at the bottom are unlikely to ever reach the top, while those at the top are unlikely to descend unless they fail or become too old. Thus, as in virtually all low-status occupations, prostitution offers little possibility of upward mobility.

[54] Like those in low-status occupations, individuals in deviant occupations also develop mythical occupational images. Strippers, for example, "try to upgrade their occupation in a definition of stripping that says that it is socially useful, constructive, good and generally all right to do." Thus they view their work as highly functional for men who without them "would be lonely and frustrated and lacking a sex outlet." They also seek to enhance their occupational image by having themselves called exotics or dancers in much the same way that the garbageman wants to be called a sanitation engineer. Some other rationalizations used by strippers are: a) They are only in stripping temporarily in order to get enough money to do something else. b) They are just like every other woman except for the fact that they are more honest about sex. c) They are sexually normal even though a high proportion are lesbians. d) Their special mission is to teach people about sex. e) What they do is good entertainment. f) If they did not exploit men sexually, men would exploit them. g) Theirs is just a job which is routinely performed.

Through these and other rationalizations they attempt to develop a more favorable occupational image. For a discussion of these points see Marilyn Salutin, "Stripper Morality," *Transaction* 8 (1971), 12–22.

[55] Greenwald, "Life of the Call Girl," in Dinitz et al., *Deviance*, p. 408.

[56] Ibid.

As was true of strippers, some types of prostitutes require little or no training. This seems to be particularly true of streetwalkers and house girls. On the other hand, the elite of prostitution, the call girl, goes through a rather rigorous training program. According to Bryan the vast majority of call girls enter the occupation on the basis of prior contacts with other call girls or their pimps, who in effect sponsor them. The sponsor also generally takes on the responsibility for training the new girl. In a number of cases although a pimp is the sponsor, he may delegate the training responsibility to an established call girl. The training of call girls is similar, in many ways, to the apprenticeship programs for skilled craftsmen. The major difference, however, is that the training of call girls is not concerned with the transmission of skills. Thus this is one of the few cases of an apprenticeship program for an occupation which is best characterized as being unskilled. While it is not concerned with transmitting skills, the apprenticeship program does focus on the transmission of values and rules for interpersonal behavior. Some of these are:

1. To maximize "gains while minimizing effort, even if this requires transgressions of either a legal or moral nature."
2. The belief that people in general and men in particular, "are corrupt or easily corruptible, . . . all social relationships are but a reflection of a 'con,' and . . . prostitution is simply a more honest or at least no more dishonest act than the everyday behavior of 'squares.'"
3. That customers "are, in some respects, stupid."
4. "Values such as fairness with other working girls, or fidelity to a pimp, may occasionally be taught."[57]

Although these values are communicated to the neophyte, they are frequently not really accepted. Bryan feels that this rejection is not terribly important since the apprenticeship program has the latent function, in terms of value communication, of creating in-group solidarity, alienating the prostitute from "square" society and serving both the trainer and the trainee economically, more than of allaying the anxieties of either.

Derived from the values discussed above are a series of rules which are communicated during the apprenticeship period:

1. Each customer is to be viewed as a mark.
2. A "pitch" is to be used in relating to the mark.
3. The prostitute is not to become emotionally involved with clients. (Unnecessary interaction with customers is frowned upon because it reduces income.)
4. Ways to size up particular customers and what to say and do during each step in the relationship.

[57] Bryan, "Apprenticeships in Prostitution," in Truzzi, *Sociology and Everyday Life,* pp. 262–263.

5. Rules on drug use, alcoholic consumption, and personal and sexual hygiene.

As was the case with values, the rules which are communicated during the apprenticeship period are frequently not followed by the call girl. "Some experience orgasms with the customer, some show considerable affection toward 'johns,' others remain drunk or 'high' throughout the contact."[58] Bryan explains the failure of both value and rule communication as due to the fact that the real reason for the apprenticeship period is to allow the new call girl to build up a clientele.

Male prostitutes. A recent study has outlined a heretofore ignored occupation, the male (homosexual) prostitute. His career is generally very short; few last more than three years in any house. A male prostitute may be recruited in three ways: through the recommendation of a current employee of the house, as a result of advertisements run in the underground press for "young, well-built and good-looking men," or through personal recruitment by the madam (a man) at a social gathering. Once recruited, the prostitute must have an interview with the madam, pass a physical, and prove himself physically attractive and capable of engaging in homosexual acts. In addition, he cannot have a morals record. Once accepted he is trained in techniques which will satisfy customers both physically and emotionally, taught how to dress and make up his body, and warned against affairs with coworkers and emotional involvement with customers.[59]

Poolroom hustlers. There is no formal hierarchy of positions in poolroom hustling. Rather, each individual player is ranked by his colleagues in terms of his skill in a particular type of game, his "heart," and a number of other variables. Thus there is an informal hierarchy ranging from the best hustler to the worst. Presumably, as one improves his hustling abilities he moves up in that hierarchy. The hustler must always take care that only his colleagues learn of his true abilities. Should marks or the audience learn his true "speed" he is likely to be left without a source of income. In a formal sense, however, he has little chance for upward mobility. At some point he may find that he can no longer earn a living at hustling and he may then "retire" to another line of work. Frequently, because his income is so highly variable, he is forced to moonlight. In career-pattern terms, then, the poolroom hustler, like almost all individuals in deviant occupations, has little opportunity for upward mobility.

Polsky sees poolroom hustling as a source of intergenerational mobility for people of lower-class origins. In fact, all the hustlers he studied came from lower-class or, at best, lower-middle-class backgrounds. Hustling is almost

[58] Ibid., p. 265.
[59] David J. Pittman, "The Male House of Prostitution," *Transaction* 8 (1971), 21–27.

totally open, except to blacks, to lower-class boys who can and do acquire the skills. In this occupation, unlike others we have discussed, whom you know is of little value—the only criterion for success is one's skill. For most pool-room hustlers that skill is acquired in high school while playing hooky:

Hustlers, even those who finished high school, played truant from school often, and in so doing found themselves in poolrooms much more frequently than either their classmates or their fellow-truants. Since the development of pool or billiard skill is, at least in the first several years of play, largely a matter of the number of hours one practices, they quickly developed superiority over their age-mates . . . they wanted to keep a good thing going, and in the process many dropped out of school entirely, while nearly all passed up job experience and training. . . . The transition from non-hustler to hustler status is smooth and almost imperceptible to the person involved. The transition never seems to involve a conscious decision to become a hustler. . . .[60]

Thus, unlike members of most occupations, the poolroom hustler never makes any real hard decisions, but merely seems to drift into his occupation. Further, there is no apprenticeship period or sponsorship pattern like those found in many occupations. Poolroom hustling is almost an ideal example of an achievement-oriented occupation.

Jazz musicians. Like the other members of deviant occupations dis-cussed in this chapter, the jazz musician has little chance of upward mobility if he remains a deviant. The basic difference between the jazz musician and individuals in other deviant occupations is that he has a chance to go straight within his occupation, and thereby greatly enhance his chances for upward movement. A basic dilemma confronts the jazz musician; to play pure jazz and remain in low-level jobs, or play what the audience wants and move up the hierarchy. The following informal hierarchy of occupations is open to the jazz musician, beginning with the lowest level:

1. The musicians "who [play] irregularly for small dances, wedding recep-tions, and similar affairs, and [are] lucky to make union wages."
2. The musicians "who have steady jobs in 'joints'—lower class taverns and night clubs, small 'strip joints,' etc.—where pay is low and community recognition is lower."
3. The musicians "who have steady jobs with local bands in neighborhood ballrooms and small, 'respectable' night clubs and cocktail lounges in better areas of the city." At about the same level are those musicians who play in second-ranking, nationally known bands.
4. The musicians "who work in 'class A name' bands, and in local orchestras that play the best night clubs and hotels, large conventions, etc."

[60] Polsky, *Hustlers, Beats and Others,* pp. 80–81.

5. The musicians "who hold staff positions in radio and television stations and legitimate theaters."[61] (The top position in the hierarchy.)

Only those jazz musicians who "sell out" and go commercial can aspire to the last position. The one who chooses artistic integrity finds himself mired in positions offering low pay and prestige, with as little chance at upward mobility as the stripper, the prostitute, the poolroom hustler, and members of virtually every other free deviant occupation.

Upward mobility among jazz musicians is determined by cliques. The musicians who prefer artistic integrity have chosen cliques which can reward them with little more than a pat on the back, while those who decide to play what the audience wants move up the hierarchy on the basis of contacts with those in the next higher clique. In a number of the cliques Becker found members from more than one level of the hierarchy; in this way lower-status jazzmen were able to interact with those at the next highest level. When a job becomes available at the next higher level, the jazzman may be sponsored by his contact in that higher clique. If he performs well at that level he is likely to become firmly rooted and will then be able to repeat the process with contacts at a still higher level. Thus, moving up for the jazzman requires both playing ability (although of a commercial nature) and contacts. Thus we return to the importance of contacts, after a brief excursion into the occupation of hustler, in which it was only skill that counted. We have seen here that the jazzman who chooses to play pure jazz is the real deviant and as such has virtually no chance of moving up in career-pattern terms.

5. Individuals in deviant occupations which exist within formal organizations have career patterns which are similar to those of individuals in straight occupations in organizations.

Those at the bottom of the hierarchy of the Mafia, a formal organization, probably have as little chance of moving to the top as do lower-level supervisors and managers in industry. However their chances are certainly greater than those of persons in low-status deviant occupations which exist outside the formal structure of the Mafia. Higher-level managers in the Mafia can move up its ladder in generally the same way as higher-level industrial managers ascend their hierarchy. Movement up for such individuals involves the possession of certain skills and contacts with those further up. There are even staff positions in the Mafia which have, like those in industry, high status, but offer little chance to move into the top positions. For example, Cressey points out that the Mafia is now hiring college graduates and those with advanced degrees for high-level staff positions, even though they may not be of Italian descent. Such people have little hope of moving up, but this is not much different from the situation faced by those in the plants studied by

[61] Becker, *Outsiders*, p. 104.

Collins, who had to be Yankees if they were to be promoted to the apex of the organization. Similarly, in Dalton's study those who aspired to top management positions had to be Anglo-Saxon or German, Masons, Republicans, and members of the yacht club.

Not only are the career patterns of those in the Mafia similar to those of persons in straight formal organizations, but the recruitment processes also have a number of similarities. Cressey contends that recruiting has continued although the "books are closed," and no new members have been recruited in the last ten years. The recruiting has been continued with the assumption that positions will open up in the future. The Mafia frequently actively seeks out and trains new recruits in much the same way as industry. Some of the recruits are youngsters who seem to have the kinds of abilities the Mafia feels it needs, while "other recruits, usually mature college graduates, are sought out because they possess the expert skills needed for modern large-scale business operations. One boss has financed the entire college education and law-school education of at least three white Anglo-Saxon Protestants who now serve him, even if they are not members of the Cosa Nostra."[62] Non-Italian college graduates are likely to serve in staff positions within the Mafia. The Mafia also recruits in the same informal way as industry: it seeks to inform young people that it offers a highly rewarding career. In some subgroups it is an honor to be recruited by the Mafia, just as in others it is an honor to be offered a job by the Ford Motor Company. Thus, although it seeks members from different subgroups than do establishment businesses, the Mafia seeks to instill in young people the desire to enter the organization. It even uses information checks on candidates' background, as well as sponsorship patterns.

There is still another interesting similarity between the Mafia and legal businesses. As has been pointed out in earlier chapters, those in industry have come to recognize the difficulty of starting at the bottom and moving up in the organization, and industrial workers now accept the fact that a college education is a prerequisite for top positions. Interestingly, the same thing seems to be happening in the Mafia. "Cosa Nostra members occupying the higher echelons of organized crime are orienting their sons to the value of education . . . they are sending their sons to college to learn business skills, on the assumption that these sons will soon be eligible for 'family' membership."[63] Overall, then, moving up in the Mafia requires the same two factors required to move up in any organization: competence and contacts.

6.   Minority groups have the same types of problems in deviant occupations as they have in similar straight occupations.

Females in deviant occupations are almost totally restricted to those which are congruent with their sex roles. We have already discussed two of

[62] Cressey, *Theft of the Nation,* p. 236.
[63] Ibid., p. 241.

these occupations, stripping and prostitution. The expectations attached to these occupations are perfectly congruent with the female sex role, for strippers and prostitutes are expected to do the same thing they are supposed to do as women; be passive and please men. When one moves out of the realm of deviant occupations which are congruent with the sex role, one finds few, if any, females. One would have to search hard to find a female bookie, poolroom hustler, or jazz musician. In their female deviant occupations, women have the same problems as all women in female occupations who must deal with customer/clients—the handling of male clientele and males in other occupations. The prostitute has problems with her male customers, and males in other occupations such as the pimp. The stripper must contend with a primarily male audience, a male manager, and a male owner of the theater or club in which she performs.

By the same token, blacks have the same kinds of problems in deviant occupations as in the rest of the workworld. They are restricted to certain low-status deviant occupations, primarily in the black community, and have little chance of moving up in the deviant occupational hierarchy. Similarly, they are excluded from other deviant occupations, just as they have been excluded, historically, from a number of straight occupations. Sutherland makes both of these points quite clearly: "Color places certain limitations. There is but one known professional Negro thief who operates with whites, but there are several well-known Negro thieves working in their own mobs."[64] Blacks have problems in poolroom hustling, but the situation there is similar to that of the black in professional baseball. The major source of resistance to black poolroom hustlers has been the poolhall owner. Polsky notes: "When I visited Cleveland in 1963, its public places were still so segregated that even in the action poolrooms on West 25th Street, the owners would pull the 'club members only' routine to keep Negroes out."[65] However, Polsky is quick to add that the situation is far better here than in the case of white industrial managers' attitudes toward black workers. However, black hustlers have not been discriminated against to any great extent by their white counterparts. There seem to be two reasons for this. In the first place, poolroom hustling, like professional baseball, is very achievement-oriented. Thus the talented black hustler is likely to be accepted by his peers in the same way the black baseball player is likely to be accepted by white players. The second reason is the cohesiveness of the subgroup of poolroom hustlers. Because they are all outcasts, "the social bonds uniting members of any deviant sub-culture tend to override race prejudice in large degree, and thus nearly every such sub-culture is more racially integrated than is 'respectable' society."[66] Thus in the case of the discrimination by Cleveland poolhall owners "the white

[64] Sutherland, *Professional Thief*, p. 24.
[65] Polsky, *Hustlers, Beats and Others*, p. 78.
[66] Ibid., p. 79.

hustlers objected strongly to this practice, and, moreover, would frequently travel to the Negro section for matches with the better Negro players. . . ."[67]

As in straight occupational life, there are deviant occupations which are the almost exclusive province of blacks. The black numbers man, as discussed by Roebuck, is an example of a person in one such occupation.[68] Playing the numbers is common in both white and black communities, but it seems to be more common in the black lower and middle classes. As a matter of fact, it has been "claimed that the numbers game has a certain integrative function for the Negro community, furnishing much of the content of casual conversation, imparting temporal structure to the day and offering a sense of participation in a community-wide institution."[69] Because of his importance to the black community and the money he earns, the black numbers man has come to hold a position of some status. This is an occupation in which white society allows the black to gain some status as long as he services only the black community. Few black numbers men are likely to work in white communities. Success at the local level does not enable the black numbers man to move up in the deviant occupational world. Although he may be very successful within his area, this does not give him access to the upper reaches of the underworld, as is made clear in Roebuck's finding that none of his respondents had any contact with other portions of the organized underworld. Thus in the world of deviant occupations, just as in the straight world of work, there are some low-status occupations in which blacks have been allowed by white society to succeed. However, it is almost impossible in both worlds for the successful black to move out of his comparatively low-level position.

DEVIANCE IN STRAIGHT OCCUPATIONAL LIFE

7. Deviant behavior occurs at all occupational levels and frequently is highly functional for one or more units within society.

In this section the focus is on deviant actions of those in straight occupations and some of the functions and dysfunctions of this behavior for various societal units.

Professionals

Although the professions are characterized by perhaps the ultimate in occupational rationality, there is also a considerable amount of deviant behavior among professionals. Such behavior, as is true of all occupational groups, ranges from legal to illegal deviant activities.

[67] Ibid., p. 78.
[68] Julian B. Roebuck, "The Numbers Man," in Dinitz et al., *Deviance*, pp. 74–82.
[69] Ibid., p. 75.

Physicians. Doctors, for example, perform both types. A fairly common form of legal deviant behavior among doctors is fee splitting, which occurs when a doctor refers a patient to another doctor (usually a specialist) and in return the specialist "kicks back" an agreed upon sum of money to the referring doctor. This is clearly very functional for both doctors—the referring doctor earns additional money and the specialist is guaranteed a continuous flow of patients. As with every form of behavior, there are dysfunctions as well. It may be highly dysfunctional for the patient if the specialist is not competent. It is also dysfunctional for other specialists who do not participate in the practice of splitting fees. On balance, the functions probably outweigh the dysfunctions, mainly because most doctors would be unwilling to engage in a fee-splitting relationship with an incompetent specialist. Physicians also engage in various forms of illegal deviant activities, as when they prescribe quack remedies. There is, for example, the following "cure" for cancer: "A Michigan physician developed some 'antitoxins' which he called Glyoxylide, Malonide and Benzoquinone. His therapy consisted of a dietary cleansing regimen, enemas, and injections. Glyoxylide, the chief method of therapy, contained one part of partially oxidized inositol (a vitamin) to a trillion parts of distilled water."[70] Nor is this an isolated incident, since it is estimated that about a billion dollars a year is spent on quack remedies.[71] Although physicians account for only a small part of this sum, that still amounts to a significant amount of quackery practiced by licensed physicians. Quack medicine is functional for some patients and highly dysfunctional for others. For patients who are suffering from a hopeless illness quack doctors offer at least a ray of hope, but for those who are curable, such treatment is highly dysfunctional since it keeps them from a real cure by responsible doctors. Quackery is clearly functional for those doctors who practice it, but it is dysfunctional for the vast majority of honest doctors since it gives them a bad public image.

One of the most common forms of illegal deviance practiced by physicians is illegal abortion. According to Schur, the police consider such abortions to be the third largest criminal activity in the United States, with only gambling and narcotics considered to be larger operations.[72] Most people who perform abortions are not even physicians, but a significant number of abortions are performed by trained doctors. Schur contends that several types of trained physicians perform abortions. One type is the physician who for one reason or another has lost his license; a second is the foreign-trained physician who cannot obtain a license in the United States. Some doctors seem to drift into performing abortions after first doing it for their own patients, while still

[70] *Changing Times,* "What the Health Hucksters Are Up To," in Gilbert Geis, ed., *White Collar Criminal* (New York: Atherton Press, 1968), p. 275.

[71] Ibid., p. 271.

[72] Edwin M. Schur, *Crimes Without Victims: Deviant Behavior and Public Policy—Abortion, Homosexuality and Drug Addiction* (Englewood Cliffs, N.J.: Prentice-Hall, 1965).

others perform them merely because it is highly lucrative. Schur leaves out a fifth type: there seems to be an increasing number of physicians in the United States who feel that laws against abortions must be disobeyed under certain circumstances. For example, the current vogue is the idea that the physician must treat the "whole person." Thus, he may feel compelled to end a pregnancy even though the patient is not in physical danger, but because the baby may present her with serious psychological problems. The trained physician who performs abortions in America is highly functional. At the very least he takes the business away from untrained, criminal abortionists who frequently injure or even kill the patient. He is also very valuable to women who, for a variety of reasons, may be endangered by the birth of an unwanted child. It is difficult to think of any dysfunctions, except perhaps for the professional damage done to the trained doctor who is caught by the police as an abortionist.

Lawyers. One also finds various forms of legal and illegal deviant behavior among lawyers. An example of a lawyer who commits illegal deviant acts is the one who is on the payroll of the Mafia. Such actions are of course highly functional for the underworld and lucrative for the lawyer involved, but dysfunctional to law enforcement efforts to wipe out organized crime. In his study of the ambulance-chasing lawyer, Reichstein shows a good example of legal deviant behavior in the legal profession.[73] He views the professions as segmental and sees the ambulance-chasing lawyer as one segment within the legal profession. The differentiation within the legal profession leads to "divergent attitudes toward professional norms"[74]—the norms accepted by the ambulance chaser are viewed as deviant by the bulk of the profession. Such a lawyer seeks out a party who has been injured and is able, because of his injury, to claim compensation. He attempts "to sign the injured party to a contingent-free contract entitling the lawyer to a fixed percentage of any amount paid to the injured party, in return for legal representation."[75] The profession considers this unethical behavior, but it is nevertheless continued because it is functional for certain types of lawyers and a certain segment of the client population. It is the low-status lawyer from small firms or individual practice, without an established clientele, who is most likely to practice ambulance chasing. Such lawyers are cut off from more traditional sources of income and are actually forced into ambulance chasing. Those lawyers who are members of the bar association and work in large established firms with a large number of high-status clients do not need to chase ambulances in order to make a reasonable income, and it is this group which is likely to disapprove of the ambulance chaser. Ambulance chasing

---

[73] Kenneth J. Reichstein, "Ambulance Chasing: A Case Study of Deviation and Control within the Legal Profession," *Social Problems* 13 (1965), 3–17.

[74] Ibid., p. 5.

[75] Ibid., p. 7.

is also very functional for that segment of the population which is unaware of legal services and does not avail itself of lawyers. If it were not for the ambulance chaser such individuals would have to deal personally with insurance companies and would, consequently, be at a severe disadvantage.

The lawyer's social setting and unethical behavior. By far the most rigorous study of deviant behavior among lawyers, indeed among all professionals, is Carlin's *Lawyers' Ethics.*[76] Carlin takes issue with traditional explanations of unethical behavior among lawyers, which explain unethical behavior in terms of a defect within the individual, the professional socialization process, the codes of ethics, and the mechanisms which enforce these codes. Carlin sees the social setting in which the lawyer works as at least as important an explanation of unethical behavior as the traditional explanatory variables. a) One of the most important aspects of the lawyer's social setting is the nature of his clientele. Quite simply, the lower the status of the clientele, the more likely the lawyer is to engage in unethical behavior. Forty-two percent of those with low-status clients engaged in unethical behavior, while only 15 percent of those in Carlin's study with high-status clients did so. A variety of forces push the former in the direction of unethical behavior. Low-status clients tend to be more unstable; thus, while a large corporation may enter into a long-term arrangement with a law firm, a small retailer may shop around for the lawyer who will give him the best deal and this deal may frequently involve unethical aspects. In addition, the lawyer who caters to low-status clients faces stiffer competition from other lawyers than is faced by those who deal with high-status clients. This competition also serves as a push toward violation of ethics. Faced with this competition and a transient clientele, the lawyer with low-status clients comes to believe that the ethical codes discriminate against him. After all, rules against client solicitation and advertising hurt him much more than the high-status lawyer.

Low-status clients are also easier to exploit than high-status ones. The neighborhood retailer, for example, is far more likely than a large corporation to be ignorant of the law. Even if a large corporation were ignorant of the law, the steadiness and size of its legal business would prevent the lawyer from taking advantage of the situation, while it is far less risky for a lawyer to exploit a transient retailer whose business does not constitute a significant portion of his income. The greater opportunity to exploit and the existence of expendable clients is a second reason why lawyers of low-status clients are more likely to violate professional ethics. A third reason is the fact that low-status clients are more likely to put pressure on their lawyers "to bribe or use improper influence with public officials, to press unfounded or fraudulent claims, or to break a promise to another lawyer."[77] Lawyers with such clients

[76] Jerome Carlin, *Lawyer's Ethics: A Survey of the New York City Bar* (New York: Russell Sage Foundation, 1966).

[77] Ibid., p. 73.

are almost twice as likely to have experienced such pressure as those with a high-status clientele. Yet even among low-status lawyers, there is a difference in ability to resist these pressures. Those lawyers who have an unstable clientele and who rely on one client for a major portion of their income are most prone to respond to this kind of pressure from clients. If these lawyers are involved in their client's businesses as a stockholder or officer, they are still more likely to respond to unethical demands. Also, the area of practice has an impact on unethical behavior, with it being more likely in personal injury, criminal, and divorce cases. These types of cases tend to be associated with low-status clients, but even when they are associated with high-status clients the lawyer is more likely to engage in unethical behavior.

b) A second important element in the lawyer's social system is the courts and government agencies. Here Carlin's findings parallel those on clients: the lower the level of the courts or governmental agencies the lawyer deals with, the more likely he is to violate professional ethics. Fifty percent of those who work with lower-level courts and agencies engage in unethical behavior, while only 15 percent who deal with upper-level courts and agencies are similarly inclined. Carlin offers a number of explanations for this phenomenon. In the first place, judges in lower-level courts are less well trained and have less experience. They are also, perhaps because of their lower status, more dependent on and beholden to political leaders. They are also subjected to fewer professional controls since they are less likely to be members of professional associations. Finally, they have more discretion in terms of their decisions for several reasons: those involved in cases in the lower courts do not have enough at stake, or sufficient resources, for a full-scale legal process; the cases involve areas which are not well developed legally and decisions therefore are not made with well-defined guidelines or rules; and the decisions of the judges in the lower-level courts are less likely to be reviewed by higher-level courts or fellow professionals. For all of these reasons lower-level judges are more likely to initiate, and be more receptive to, unethical behavior. Thus the lawyer who deals with such judges experiences more opportunity and more pressure to violate professional ethics. The subculture which is associated with lower-status courts also contributes to the development of unethical behavior, especially if the lawyer spends a great deal of time waiting for his case to be heard *and* talking with his colleagues about ethical questions. The converse is found to be true of lawyers associated with high-status courts.

c) Colleagues are the third important element in the lawyer's social system. Carlin differentiates law offices into three types in terms of the lawyers' attitudes toward professional ethics: permissive (reject most ethics and oppose strict enforcement); strict (accept most ethics and in favor of strict enforcement); and mixed. Predictably, lawyers in permissive offices are most likely to violate ethics, while those in strict offices are least likely, with those in mixed offices standing in the middle (41 percent of those in permissive offices violate ethics, but only 28 percent of the lawyers in mixed offices, and 15 percent of those in strict offices). The seniority of the lawyer is important here, for the longer one is in a permissive office, the more likely he is to be involved in unethical behavior. Conversely, the longer one is in a strict firm, the less likely he is to behave unethically. The amount of informal interaction is crucial in both of the extreme office types. "In offices characterized by a high degree of sociability, 52 percent of the lawyers exposed to an ethically permissive climate are violators. In offices with a low degree of sociability, on the other hand, violation rates are virtually unrelated to office climate."[78] Thus a consensus of opinion within an office on ethical questions is insufficient in itself; it must be supplemented by informal interaction, communication, and personal influence. The effect of these factors is most pronounced in offices composed of peers, while in stratified offices the size of the office and the position of the lawyer in the hierarchy are more important factors in unethical behavior. Those in small stratified offices who rank low in the hierarchy are more likely to engage in unethical behavior. Carlin's explanation is that low-ranking lawyers in small firms are more likely to deal with low-ranking courts and government agencies and are not as likely to be involved in the elite bar association.

d) The size of the firm is related to unethical behavior, although not directly. When lawyers in large and small firms practice under similar conditions, there is little difference in their rates of conformity or nonconformity to ethical codes. However, lawyers in these two settings rarely practice under similar conditions. The small firm lawyer or the lawyer in private practice is more likely to experience pressure from clients to violate ethics and to work in lower-level courts or with lower-level government agencies where both the pressure and opportunity to violate professional ethics are greater. Conversely, lawyers in large firms are more likely to be insulated from these pressures and inducements. Social background is also related to unethical behavior because certain backgrounds qualify one to work in large firms while other backgrounds restrict a lawyer to the smaller firms. Protestant lawyers are more likely to be accepted by the large firms; hence they are least likely to engage in unethical behavior. Catholics are less acceptable and hence more likely to behave unethically, while Jews are the least acceptable and therefore most likely to violate professional ethics. Thus the relationship between ethnicity and unethical behavior is not direct. The lower the status of the ethnic group, the more likely the lawyer is to be employed in small firms and therefore the more likely he is to be subjected to pressures toward, and opportunities for, unethical behavior. Conversely, under similar conditions lawyers from lower-status ethnic groups behave in essentially the same way as those from higher-status ethnic groups.

e) Finally, Carlin outlines the importance of personality, or "inner disposition" for unethical behavior. He finds lawyers with a low concern for

[78] Ibid., p. 100.

ethics most likely (54 percent) and those with a high concern least likely (10 percent) to behave unethically. Further, those with high personal ethics are very resistant to situational pressures. "Even when subjected to the combination of high client-related pressures and exposure to lower-level courts and agencies, only 20 percent of those with high ethical concern are violators, as against 77 percent of those with low concern."[79] Thus unethical behavior is a result of situational pressures and the inner disposition of the lawyer. But while the inner disposition to be ethical or unethical is spread evenly throughout the legal profession, the situational pressures to be unethical are greatest in its lower reaches.

Carlin's systematic analysis of unethical behavior among lawyers may be extended to all of the professions, indeed to all occupations. The focus must be on the social system of the worker and the situational pressures and opportunities he experiences to engage in deviant behavior. The clergyman in the university setting experiences more pressure and has more opportunity to behave in ways which might be considered in some quarters as deviant. The same would seem to be true of the physician who works in a slum, the professional military man in combat, or even the taxi driver who services the ghetto. But while the social system in which a man works is crucial, it is not the only factor in the development of deviant behavior. Also to be considered are characteristics of the individual, the nature of the occupational socialization process, the ethical codes within the occupation, and the ways in which these codes are enforced. For example, Carlin finds that the legal profession enforces its ethical codes in only a very few situations. How actively an occupation polices its members is obviously related to the amount of unethical behavior in it.

Managers and officials

Legal deviance. The literature abounds with examples of legal and illegal deviant behavior among managers and officials. There is a great deal of behavior in industry which while not illegal would certainly be considered unethical, even by business executives. Baumhart found that four out of five of his responding business managers admitted there was behavior in their industry which, while generally accepted, was also considered unethical.[80] The list of such actions is almost endless, but some common examples include the lavish entertainment of prospective clients; employment of women to "entertain" clients; gifts to employees of other companies, customers, or competitors in exchange for information or favors; underbidding competitors with the intention of using inferior workmanship or materials; and bank loans which grant customers more than they need or than is wise for them

[79] Ibid., p. 136.

[80] Raymond C. Baumhart, "How Ethical Are Businessmen?" *Harvard Business Review*, 39 (1961), 6-19, 156-176.

to borrow. The ubiquity of legal deviant behavior in commercial enterprises indicates that the practices are functional, at least for some parties. From a Machiavellian perspective such behavior, if it enhances the profit position of a firm, is highly functional for it. Such practices may also be viewed as functional, in many cases, for the customer or competitor who receives an advantage. On the other hand, legal deviant behavior is often very dysfunctional for other units in society. The honest competitor or customer is at an unfair disadvantage when his competition is in collusion with the firm with which they are both doing business. The public also frequently suffers from legal deviant behavior because prices may be higher or goods of inferior quality. Baumhart's study reveals an interesting duality on the part of businessmen on the question of unethical behavior. Five out of six of his respondents responded positively to the following statement: "For corporation executives to act in the interest of shareholders alone, and not also in the interest of employees and consumers, is unethical."[81] This seems to reveal a lofty sense of social responsibility on their part. There seems, however, to be a gap between what executives say and what they actually do. This is reflected in the fact that almost half of Baumhart's respondents agreed with the following statement: "The American business executive tends to ignore the great ethical laws as they apply immediately to his work. He is preoccupied chiefly with gain."[82] Further, four out of seven of the respondents believed that businessmen would violate ethical codes when they felt sure they would avoid detection.

Although the literature has been dominated by studies of legal deviant behavior in commercial enterprises, such behavior occurs in every type of organization. For example, the prison official is not supposed to inflict punishment on inmates, but to prepare them to fit into society when released. Nevertheless, much of prison life has been dominated by unnecessary punishment of inmates. As examples of unnecessary deprivation Sykes cites limitations on the amount prisoners can spend in the prison store, the sharp curtailment of hobbies, and unnecessary limits on letters and visits.[83] These do not even include the more sadistic practices employed by prison officials. Despite norms to the opposite, "the officials wish to punish the prisoner, but they cannot openly admit it."[84] The same idea would also apply to officials of mental institutions. Political leaders are also prone to violating norms concerning their behavior. One basic political norm is that an elected political official is to represent the needs and demands of his constituents. However, few norms are broken as frequently as this one, except when election time is near. To start at the top, Lyndon Johnson was elected president in 1964 over

[81] Ibid., p. 10.
[82] Ibid., p. 14.
[83] Gresham M. Sykes, *The Society of Captives* (New York: Atheneum Press, 1969).
[84] Ibid., p. 32.

Barry Goldwater because of Johnson's antiwar position. Yet almost immediately after his election, he chose to engage in almost full-scale warfare in Vietnam. Many high government officials seem to be far more responsive to the insistent demands of small organized lobbies than to the demands of their constituents—witness the success of the National Rifle Association in preventing significant antigun legislation in spite of strong public sentiment in favor of such laws. On another level, there is the example of Adam Clayton Powell and other Representatives who are supposed to represent their districts, but are infrequently on the job. The list, again, is endless, but the above examples suffice to emphasize the ubiquity of legal deviancy among managers and officials in virtually all types of organizations.

Illegal deviance. Illegal deviant behavior is also very common among managers and officials. Again, the bulk of the literature focused on illegal deviant behavior in commercial organizations. One of the main areas for such activity is in advertising. Sutherland discusses three basic types of misrepresentation in advertising.[85] The first is the advertising of "products which are physically dangerous, with the dangers denied, minimized, or unmentioned."[86] These abuses are most commonly found in the advertising of drugs and cosmetics, although they are not restricted to these fields. For example, such advertising exists in the toy industry, including the failure to mention that a toy stove heats to over six hundred degrees or that rusty nails hold a baby rattle together. The second type of illegal advertising involves exaggerated claims for a product. This, too, is most common in the drug field. One such drug was Krebiozen: "Krebiozen powder, according to the government, is mainly creatine, an amino acid derivative that is plentifully available from meat in an ordinary diet. The human body of itself produces in twenty-four hours 100,000 times as much creatine as the drug's label says there is in one Krebiozen ampule."[87] Despite the fact that most people get all the vitamins they need in their regular diet, millions are spent each year on vitamins and most of this sum spent by those who least need them. Similarly, millions are spent on quack cures for arthritis. Nor is this type of misrepresentation exclusive to the drug field. Sutherland talks of alligator shoes not made of alligator, Oriental rugs not from the Orient, and silk clothing made from cotton. The third type of misrepresentation is aimed at harming competitors rather than the consumer. An example of this type is the company which advertises that its product has features no other similar product has, when in fact it is exactly the same. In functional terms it is clear that these forms of misrepresentation are highly functional for the firm involved because of the boost they give sales. Some may even contend that it is functional for society as a whole since it keeps the American economy operating at a high level.

[85] Edwin H. Sutherland, "Crime of Corporations," in Geis, *White Collar Criminal*, pp. 57–70.
[86] Ibid., p. 61.
[87] *Changing Times*, "Health Hucksters," in Geis, *White Collar Criminal*, p. 275.

However, the dysfunctions to the consumer who is duped by such false advertising outweigh, on a moral basis at least, and certainly on a physical basis when injury occurs, the functions of misrepresentation in advertising.

Misrepresentation in advertising is far from the only form of illegal deviant behavior engaged in by industrial leaders. The list is long, but one other example will suffice: price fixing. Price fixing by large corporations is a restraint of trade and as such a violation of the Sherman Antitrust Act of 1890. A recent blatant example of price fixing involved the two giants of the electrical industry, Westinghouse and General Electric. The case began in 1959 when the Tennessee Valley Authority complained of getting identical bids from electrical companies despite the fact that the bids were sealed. The companies participating in this conspiracy agreed to divide the market on the basis of their past shares of it. Thus, if a company had 20 percent of the market, the conspirators agreed that it would in the future be guaranteed the same percentage. To do this the company was allowed to be low bidder on 20 percent of new contracts, with the others submitting bids which were slightly higher. On other occasions the conspirators drew lots on who should be allowed to submit the low bid, or they allocated the low bid on the basis of a rotating system. Convictions on these offenses led to heavy fines against a number of firms, with the heaviest fines levied against GE and Westinghouse. In addition, seven people including four vice presidents, two division managers, and one sales manager received thirty-day jail terms.

Geis' discussion of the explanations offered for this conspiracy does much to explain the pressure on managers to engage in illegal deviant behavior.[88] It is interesting to note that some of those involved sought to explain their actions in terms of the "functions" they performed. Basically they felt that price fixing was good for society because it "stabilized prices," good for the company and therefore for its employees, and not harmful to the consumer since he was not hurt by their actions. Beyond these rationalizations there were a number of structural reasons for the price fixers' behavior. These firms had a long history of "meeting with the competition." The new manager was generally taken to such meetings by his superior and introduced to the world of price fixing, and eventually price fixing came to be viewed as just part of the job, as is indicated in the following comments by some of those involved: "It had become so common and gone on for so many years that I think we lost sight of the fact that it was illegal." "Meeting with the competitors was just one of the many facets of responsibility that was delegated to me." "I thought it was part of my duty to do so."[89] There were also implicit but clear penalties involved for those who refused to go along. In 1946 General Electric issued a very strong directive against price fixing, but many executives believed that this was merely for public relations. One who did obey the

[88] Gilbert Geis, "The Heavy Electrical Equipment Antitrust Cases of 1961," in Geis, *White Collar Criminal*, pp. 103–118.
[89] Ibid., p. 109.

directive was viewed as troublesome and removed from his position. Those who refused to engage in price fixing knew the implications for their jobs.

There are myriad other examples of illegal deviant behavior in industry, but misrepresentation in advertising and price fixing will suffice for our purposes. Once again it must be pointed out that these forms of behavior are not restricted to commercial enterprises—there are other examples for virtually every type of manager and official. There is the police chief who is paid off by criminals so that he will ignore their illegal activities and force his subordinates to do the same. There is analogous behavior among political leaders. The cases of bribery of public officials are too numerous to mention, but include the case of the late Senator Dodd of Connecticut, who was involved in a scandal involving campaign funds which were used for personal expenses, and the recent case of the Mayor of Newark, New Jersey, who was accused of being involved with the Mafia. Governmental scandals of this type would require an entire book to summarize and analyze.

Proprietors

Legal deviance. Many of the same kinds of legal and illegal deviant behavior engaged in by managers and officials are also practiced by the independent entrepreneur. For legal examples one need only turn to the merchant, particularly in low income areas. Caplovitz found that the "lack of shopping sophistication and their vulnerability to 'easy credit' would suggest that many low-income families encounter serious difficulties as consumers."[90] The two most frequent legal but deviant activities of slum merchants include "bait" advertising and high-pressure salesmanship. Bait advertising is the use of very low-priced lead items to entice the customer into the store. Once he has entered, high-pressure salesmen take over. They show the inexpensive goods, but are quick to point out their failings and ultimately sell the customer a much higher-priced item. This process is neatly illustrated by one of the furniture salesmen quoted in Caplovitz's study: " 'I don't know how we do it. We advertise three rooms of furniture for $149 and the customers swarm in. They end up buying a $400 bedroom set for $600 and none of us can believe how easy it is to make these sales.' "[91] The customer can almost never afford to pay cash and is therefore forced to buy on time, at exorbitant prices. The landlord in slum areas engages in similar practices. The poor generally spend a much higher percentage of their income for rent than do more affluent citizens. Not only can a slumlord charge exorbitant rents, but he can also afford not to fix his apartments. He does not fear losing the tenants, since virtually all slum housing is in the same condition. Further, he has little desire to fix apartments since he could not possibly get any higher rent. Again,

[90] David Caplovitz, "The Merchant and the Low-Income Consumer," *Jewish Social Studies* 27 (1965), 48.
[91] Ibid., p. 49.

all of these types of practices may be viewed in functional terms. Caplovitz notes that in a society that emphasizes materialism, the practices of slum merchants allow those who ordinarily could not afford certain items the opportunity to obtain them. (This argument applies mainly to the easy credit policies of most slum merchants, for the kinds of poor risks they serve would not be able to obtain goods from more "respectable" merchants.) This is not to say that this system does not, as well, have a large number of dysfunctions for the slum consumer. On balance, however, it continues to exist because the slum consumer, in our materialistic society, cannot get the goods he desires elsewhere.

The focus above has been on legal deviant behavior by proprietors in slum areas, but similar practices occur elsewhere in society, although usually more subtly. Supermarkets frequently display meat with the good side up, concealing fat and bone; homes are constructed with low-priced materials which deteriorate soon after purchase; and used cars put into temporary running condition break down soon after the thirty-day warranty runs out. These and other practices may be functional for the proprietor, but it is difficult to find any functions for the consumer.

Illegal deviance. Proprietors are almost as likely to engage in illegal deviant behavior. Strodtbeck and Sussman's examination of watch repairmen[92] cites a study conducted by *Reader's Digest* in which people were sent to 462 watch repairmen throughout the United States. Parts of their watches were purposely loosened before they entered the jewelry store. The defect created was obvious and could be easily and quickly fixed. However, 226 of the 462 repairmen "lied, overcharged, gave phony diagnoses, or suggested extensive and unnecessary repairs."[93] Car dealers are among the proprietors most prone to illegal deviant behavior. They may sell used cars or demonstrator's models as new. Then there are such illegal abuses as turning back the odometers on used cars or lying about the number of previous owners. Butchers also seem particularly susceptible to illegal deviant behavior. One practice is "shortweighing," or labelling packaged meat as if it weighed more than it actually does. A related practice is the rather widespread use of the thumb on the scale while weighing a piece of meat. Then there is the substitution of inferior meat for quality meat after it has been purchased. Finally, there is the "doctoring" of hamburger to make it appear as if it is all meat when in fact it may be almost all fat. Again, there are almost innumerable other examples of such illegal behavior among merchants. All of them, however, are highly functional for the merchant and highly dysfunctional for the consumer.

[92] Fred L. Strodtbeck and Marvin B. Sussman, "Of Time, the City, and the 'One-Year Guarantee': The Relations Between Watchowners and Repairers," *American Journal of Sociology* 61 (1956), 602–609.

[93] Ibid., p. 606.

Quinney's study of prescription violation among retail pharmacists gives much insight into why proprietors engage in these kinds of illegal activities.[94] Quinney studied 20 retail pharmacists who were, according to state records, prescription violators and 60 additional pharmacists who were selected at random. He found that the retail pharmacist is torn between professional and business norms, and it is this conflict, and the way it is resolved, which accounts for prescription violation. By assessing orientation to business and/or professionalism, Quinney developed the following typology of pharmacists:

1. Professional pharmacists (16 percent of the sample), who were more oriented to the professional than the business role.
2. Business pharmacists (20 percent), who were more oriented to business than professionalism.
3. Professional-business pharmacists (45 percent), who were oriented to both business and professionalism.
4. Indifferent pharmacists (19 percent), who were not oriented to either business or professionalism.

Quinney found that business pharmacists were most likely to violate prescription rules, while the professional pharmacists were least likely to commit such offenses. In fact, none of those who were classified as professionals violated prescription rules. The two mixed types were in the middle, committing some violations, but far fewer than the business-oriented pharmacist. Laws are not enough in the case of the pharmacist; they must be supplemented by professional norms in order to prevent prescription violation. The same seems to be true of all proprietors—laws are not enough. Most proprietors, like the business-oriented pharmacist, violate the law because of the business norm of "anything for a buck." The materialism of our society is the basic cause of legal and illegal deviant behavior among proprietors. This is pointed out quite clearly in the case of the pharmacist. Those who accept the business norms are the ones who are most likely to violate the law, but those who eschew business for professional norms are highly unlikely to violate these norms.

Middle-level occupations

Foremen. Although there are few studies of deviance at this level, there are some data on the phenomenon in literature which focus on other questions. In his study *Men Who Manage*, Dalton uncovered a number of acts which officially might be viewed as deviant, but were in fact utilized in an elaborate system of informal rewards.[95] Many of these informal rewards were granted

[94] Earl R. Quinney, "Occupational Structure and Criminal Behavior: Prescription Violation by Retail Pharmacists," *Social Problems* 11 (1963), 179–185.
[95] Melville Dalton, *Men Who Manage* (New York: John Wiley, 1959).

when a promotion or a raise was not possible, or as a bonus for "dirty work" and "for great personal sacrifices."[96] The foremen were basic to this system of informal rewards, either as producers or recipients of them. A foreman who became a Mason and ceased being a Catholic (one had to be a Mason to move up in the plant studied by Dalton) was allowed to dispense "gravy jobs" and to build a machine shop in his home with company materials and with company consent. "He equipped his drill press, shaper and lathe with cutters and drills from Milo [one of the plants studied by Dalton]. He supplemented these with bench equipment, such as taps, reamers, dies, bolts and screws. Finally, piece by piece and day by day he removed an entire grinder from his shop."[97] Another foreman was an important cog in the company's unofficial reward system and therefore played a key role in the organization. He "spent a minimum of six hours daily making such things as baby beds, storm windows, garage windows, doll buggies, rocking horses, tables, meat boards and rolling pins. These objects were custom built for various managers."[98] Still another foreman

had a wood and steel archway for his rose garden prefabricated in the plant, and removed it piecemeal. Incentive-appliers estimated that exclusive of materials the time spent on this object would have made it cost at least $400, in terms of hourly charging rate. Also . . . fourteen storm windows made, and a set of wooden lawn sprinklers cut in the form of dancing girls and brightly painted . . . a stainless steel churn that cost over a hundred and fifty dollars . . . several cold-pack lifting pans—"worth their weight in gold."[99]

A general foreman "'carried out several hundred dollars worth' of bricks and cement and used Milo bricklayers on company time to build much, or most, of his house."[100] Dalton views all of these deviant activities in functional terms. In a formal system such as the Milo plant, such informal practices as these are essential for the smooth operation of the organization when formal practices are not, or cannot be, effective. Dalton contends that if one views these activities as either morally good or bad, he misses the point. They are neither good nor bad, but they are essential for the operation of the organization. Also, they are in line with, and reflect, the general value structure of the United States.

As with all other occupations, deviant behavior among foremen can take many forms, depending upon the nature of the position. The foreman is not in a position to practice many of the types of deviant behavior practiced by professionals or managers and officials, for he is not at as high a level and lacks as many occupational contacts with others outside the organization. Thus he is generally not in a position to bribe or be bribed by clients, to mis-

96 Ibid., p. 198.
97 Ibid., p. 199.
98 Ibid.
99 Ibid., p. 200.
100 Ibid., p. 201.

represent the firm, etc. When foremen do deviate, it is in terms of the expectations of significant others within the organization. One example occurs when foremen do not conform to the expectations of those above them in the organization that they maximize productivity within their department. Because of informal ties with subordinates, the foreman frequently sides with them in an effort to reduce pressure toward greater productivity. The union steward is in the same sort of position; he has few job-related contacts outside of the union and the company. His deviance is likely to take the form of lack of conformity to the expectations of significant others within the union. A good example, which also relates to deviance among foremen, is collusion with management. The steward is supposed to represent the interests of his constituents, but he frequently seeks to solidify his own position by making deals with the foreman. Both the foreman and the steward are in positions to make life miserable for each other. The steward can push every grievance actively and make life very difficult for the foreman, who must spend a good deal of his time handling difficult grievance cases. On the other hand, the foreman can make life hard for the steward by refusing to grant or process grievances or by punishing stewards for active grievance handling by giving them undesirable jobs. Because each has power over the other, they frequently find it best to enter into a collusive relationship. The steward agrees not to push too many grievances, if the foreman agrees to grant enough of them to keep the steward's constituents happy. In a sense this is deviant behavior for both parties, for the steward is supposed to press grievances on the basis of their merit while the foreman is supposed to grant only those grievances which are meritorious.

White-collar workers. Like foremen, white-collar workers have far fewer opportunities for deviant behavior. Again the reason lies in the nature of the occupation. Occupational life is almost totally within the organization and deviance takes the form of lack of conformity to the expectations of significant others within the organization. Because they are so closely supervised, it is difficult for white-collar workers to deviate. Some of their informal practices, discussed earlier, may also be categorized as deviant behavior. One example, which also applies to those in low-status occupations, is restriction of output. White-collar workers may be expected to produce at a certain level, but because of informal agreements among them they may peg their output below the expectations of management. Another form of behavior which may be viewed as deviant is the displacement of goals. White-collar workers are supposed to perform in such a way that the organization is helped to achieve its goals. Frequently, however, they concentrate instead on rigidly following the rules of the organization. This sort of behavior has been labelled by Merton as characteristic of the "bureaucratic personality."

The female semiprofessions. A similar form of deviance is found among the female semiprofessions. Each of them has a formal goal, or goals, but these are frequently replaced by a rigid adherence to the rules. The social worker is supposed to help those in need in the community, but frequently, she is so wrapped up in paper work and the following of rules that the helping of clients becomes at best secondary. Teachers are supposed to educate children, but this goal also tends in many cases to be displaced by others. Some teachers become so concerned with the problem of maintaining discipline that they forget about educating their students. Others make teaching techniques the ultimate goal and neglect the relevance of these techniques to the education of children. Still others become so involved in the making of reports and bookkeeping that they neglect education. Nurses, like the other semiprofessionals, are prone to the same sorts of behavior. Following the rules and making reports displaces patient care as the primary goal for many nurses.

An interesting form of deviance occurs in the relationship of teachers and social workers to black students or clients. Theoretically all students are supposed to be treated alike by the teacher and all clients are supposed to receive equal help from the social worker. However, the racism which pervades American society affects the behavior of teachers and social workers. Some teachers have a blatant prejudice toward blacks, but more insidious is the behavior of those teachers who believe that they are "liberal" on the race issue. There are some good examples of this type of behavior in Kozol's book on the Boston school system, *Death at an Early Age*.[101] In the school in which Kozol taught there was a reading teacher who professed to be a liberal, yet revealed her prejudice toward blacks in a variety of ways. She did occasional favors for white students, but Kozol "did not once observe her having offered to do anything of that sort for any child who was Negro . . . when I [Kozol] took it on my own initiative to do something similar for a couple of the Negro children in my class, she heard about it immediately and came up to advise me that it was not at all a good idea."[102] A more important way in which the reading teacher unconsciously discriminated against blacks was in her expectations for children. She expected far less from black students, and a basic sociological tenet is that if you expect less, you very frequently will get less. In addition to these more subtle forms of racism, there was a wide variety of more blatant discriminatory behavior in the Boston school system. Similar behavior is also true of many social workers. This process is described in many places, but no more succinctly than by Malcolm X in his autobiography: "I truly believe that if ever a state social agency destroyed a family, it destroyed ours. We wanted and tried to stay together. Our home didn't have to be destroyed. But the Welfare, the courts, and their doctor, gave us the one-two-three punch. And ours was not the only case of this kind."[103]

Skilled workers. Deviant behavior among skilled workers seems to be

[101] Jonathan Kozol, *Death at an Early Age* (New York: Bantam Books, 1967).
[102] Ibid., p. 24.
[103] Malcolm X with the assistance of Alex Haley, *The Autobiography of Malcolm X* (New York: Grove Press, 1964), p. 21.

relatively uncommon. One reason lies in the strong norms of craftsmanship which are internalized by skilled workers. Thus in most cases they do not deviate from external expectations, since their relevant expectations are internalized. A deviant, in this case, is the skilled worker who has not internalized these norms and hence does not turn out a quality product. Another factor here is the highly cohesive informal group among skilled workers, which serves to enforce the norms of the occupation. Deviation is obvious and sanctions are quick. Finally, there is little opportunity for the kinds of deviant behavior which characterize higher-status occupations. Skilled workers do not interact with clients or competitors and they are not in the kind of central position which would make them liable to bribes and other forms of inducements.

Salesmen. Of all those in middle-status occupations, the salesman is most prone to deviant behavior. Once again the explanation lies in the nature of the occupation. The salesman almost always works in organizations which emphasize, above all else, profit. He constantly deals with clients with this profit motive firmly in mind, and relationship with them is evaluated by superiors almost entirely on the basis of the number of sales. Thus the salesman who seeks to succeed is led to use any means available, even deviant ones, to make sales. The literature is replete with examples of such behavior employed to increase sales. Deviant behavior among salesmen is well known to everyone, so there is no need to go into a great deal of detail. However, some of the more common abuses include lying about a product, doctoring it to make it appear better than it is, and giving false or misleading information on financing. One example of the wide range of deviant behavior by used car salesmen deserves special note: "Used car dealers have allowed unscrupulous salesmen to use the classified columns of newspapers, particularly in weekend editions, to pose as private party sellers, under such intriguing headings as 'Lady must sell,' 'Low mileage car,' 'Urgent necessity compels sale.' "[104]

Low-status occupations

Those in low-status occupations in organizations, like most of those in the middle-level occupations, are restricted in the forms of deviant behavior they may practice. For one thing, they are closely supervised by their supervisors. For another, they have perhaps the least occupational contact with those outside the organization. Finally, they are in many ways the least central group within the organization and are therefore not good objects for such things as bribes. Deviant behavior in low-status occupations generally takes the form of going against the expectations of those in the workgroup or superiors. Among those

[104] President's Committee on Consumer Interests, "Automobiles," in Geis, *White Collar Criminal*, p. 258.

who deviate from the expectations of their peers are the rate buster, who produces more than is dictated by the group norm, and the chiseler, who produces less. Such deviants are highly functional for the group since they tend to reinstill a sense of cohesiveness in the members. That is, deviant behavior tends to unite the members of the workgroup in an effort to bring the deviate back into line. There are similar examples of deviant behavior in free low-status occupations where the opportunities are greater because individuals are relatively independent of organizational control. For example, policemen frequently engage in such deviant behaviors as taking bribes from criminals. On the other hand, there are a number of patrolmen and officers who may deviate from the norms of their occupational subgroup by refusing to sell out to criminal elements. Such a policeman performs the same kinds of functions for the group as the worker who produces above or below the norm. In addition, he is very functional in other ways. When the police force is under pressure from the community, it can unleash the honest cops in order to soothe public opinion. Such a policeman is also very functional for the community as a whole since his presence helps to keep some check on crime. Deviation from group norms by industrial workers and the police are only two examples of a process which occurs in virtually all low-status occupations.

Airplane factory workers. There are other forms of deviant behavior by those in low-status occupations, and a good example is found in Bensman and Gerver's study of deviance in an airplane factory.[105] This study is also interesting because it shows how various levels within the organization are implicated in the deviant behavior. In this factory there existed a tool called a "tap" which could be used on an airplane wing to bring a nut and bolt into alignment. The engineering requirements dictated that the alignment must be perfect. "The use of the tap is the most serious crime of workmanship conceivable in the plant. A worker can be summarily fined for merely possessing a tap."[106] Despite these stringent regulations Bensman and Gerver estimated that about half of the workers owned the instrument. Using it was an extreme offense because it was felt it weakened the wing structure and hid basic failings in the manufacturing process. Supervisory personnel were aware of its widespread utilization and had even trained some recruits in its use.

There were inspectors whose job it was, among other things, to prevent the use of the tap. Air Force inspectors were the supreme authority, but there were too few of them to police the entire plant, whose workers acted in collusion to prevent them from witnessing the tap in use. Plant inspectors were more numerous and were aware of the use of the tap. These inspectors, how-

---

[105] Joseph Bensman and Israel Gerver, "Crime and Punishment in the Factory: the Function of Deviancy in Maintaining the Social System," *American Sociological Review* 28 (1963), 588–598.
[106] Ibid., p. 590.

ever, were close to the workers and were reluctant to report them, and the workers generally agreed not to use the tap in their presence. There were occasional drives when the inspectors had to "get tough," but these lasted only a few days and then taps were returned to full use. If, during one of these periods, an inspector caught a worker using a tap he reported him to his foreman. The foreman "ceremoniously" reprimanded him and then returned the worker to the job. Since the foreman was judged by how productive his department was, he condoned the use of tap to keep production high.

The use of the tap "is a crime only in that there is an official ruling against its use, and that there are a wide range of ceremonial forms of law enforcement and punishment."[107] In fact, the use of the tap was as important to the smooth operation of the airplane factory as the white-collar "crimes" described above are to the operation of organizational life. In short, such offenses are highly functional for the individuals involved as well as for the entire organization. In Merton's terms, the functions of such deviance far outweigh the dysfunctions.

Policemen. A highly topical occupational crime is police violence. This problem has attracted considerable public attention because of the so-called "police riots" which accompanied the Democratic convention of 1968 in Chicago. Police lawbreaking was the subject of a study by a Hughes' student, William Westley, in 1953.[108] Although dated, the study is highly relevant to current police crimes. Westley acknowledges a clear debt to Hughes in focusing on occupational problems as they shed light on "the occupationally derived definitions of self and conduct which arise in the involvements of technical demands, social relationships between colleagues and with the public, status, and self-conception."[109] Westley contends that illegal violence is accepted morally by the police, that this "acceptance and justification arise through their occupational experience," and that the use of violence is functional for the collectivity of policemen.

Police monopolize the legitimate use of violence in American society. However, there seems to be an inevitable tendency for the police to extend the use of violence to illegal lengths. Advancement and prestige as a policeman are dependent on making what they call a "good pinch." Routine action brings little notoriety, but the dramatic apprehension of a dangerous criminal, whatever the means, attracts attention. Public outcry against sexual deviates and the difficulty in apprehending and convicting such offenders puts added pressure on the policemen to use violence. The police believe the use of violence against such criminals to be supported by their own subculture as well as by the public. There is a strong suggestion that in addition to personal

[107] Ibid., p. 597.
[108] William A. Westley, "Violence and the Police," *American Journal of Sociology* 59 (1953), 34–41.
[109] Ibid., p. 34.

gain, violence is used to gain public respect for the police occupation. Despite these pressures, police violence is not consistently used. Westley feels that "individual inclinations, the threat of detection, and a sensitivity to public reactions" keeps police violence down.[110]

Police violence is therefore viewed as an effort to enhance both individual and occupational status. Since individually and collectively police are of low status, violence within bounds is highly functional for them.

DEVIANCE IN DEVIANT OCCUPATIONS

It is interesting to note that deviance in deviant occupations is likely to be considered "normal" by some of the general population. A good example is the "stool pigeon," or individual in a deviant occupation who informs on the activities of his colleagues. Such activity is deviant in the sense that it violates the norms of the underworld. There are, however, some groups in straight society who are not likely to applaud the stool pigeon, and in fact, view him as bad for "squealing" on his colleagues. Another type of deviate from the point of view of the underworld is the young Italian who is raised in the slums but who refuses to enter the world of crime. Such action is almost incomprehensible to the underworld since it views itself as a normal route of upward mobility for such individuals. However, some of the general public are likely in this case to think such action normal and applaud it. In general, however, deviance by those in deviant occupations may be viewed in essentially the same way one views deviance in other low-status occupations: it generally takes two forms; lack of conformity to subgroup norms or lack of conformity to the expectations of those above one in the underworld hierarchy.

Deviance in deviant occupations is probably more functional for society as a whole than any other form of occupational deviancy. The informer constitutes a major tool in the war on organized crime. Without informers organized and unorganized crime would be even more widespread than it is. Similarly, the ability of many slum children to shun the world of crime and move into straight occupational life has also helped to keep crime within bounds. The deviating deviant is indeed very functional for American society.

NONEMPLOYMENT—A FORM OF OCCUPATIONAL DEVIANCY

An interesting form of deviance in the world of work is the absence of occupational life. Since most people in America are employed, those who are not may be viewed as deviants. Just as work causes problems for individuals, so

110 Ibid., p. 39.

does the lack of it. The absence of work takes a variety of forms and in the ensuing pages each form is briefly discussed along with the distinctive problems with it.

Unemployment. Unemployment, one of the forms of the absence of occupational life, has not been a popular topic for the sociological researcher. Nevertheless, a small but significant percentage of Americans are, and always have been, unemployed. Since 1954 the unemployment rate has generally ranged between 3 and 6 percent with a maximum of 6.1 percent in 1958. More important, certain segments of the population are far more likely to be unemployed. In general, all nonwhites have been twice as likely to be unemployed as whites (their highest unemployment rate was 12.6 percent in 1958). In addition, unemployment rates are higher for females and young people. An examination of unemployment rates tells only a small portion of the story. The unemployed individual's problem is that he must try to exist in an extremely wealthy society. This is made virtually impossible, since a concomitant of unemployment is poverty, and the poverty itself is made far more difficult by the fact that the unemployed individual is surrounded by affluence. He is forced to go through a series of demeaning experiences. When he is laid off from work, he generally must seek unemployment benefits from the government, and this is degrading to most people, especially in a society which emphasizes rugged individualism. If he succeeds in getting unemployment compensation, he finds that the payments are not nearly enough to cover his expenses and only last for a relatively short period. During this period he seeks work, but if he is typical of most unemployed, he has neither the education nor the skills to get another job. If the individual is black, female, or young, still other barriers must be overcome, and if the unemployed person has all three characteristics, it is virtually impossible to find work. The longer the period of unemployment, the deeper he plunges into the world of poverty. He may try to move to another area to find work, but his chances are generally not greatly improved. Further, he frequently is unable to move because of a series of commitments he has made. He may prefer to wait for work at his old location because of the numerous benefit plans in which he has an investment and which he would lose should he move. Other constraints may include a home he partially owns, his children's schools, and his and his wife's friends within the community. Thus most unemployed individuals remain in their communities and futilely seek work or hopefully wait for their old jobs to reopen. In the interim wives and children may be forced to seek employment, with sometimes disastrous effects on the family structure. The unemployed male may find himself in the demeaning position of cooking supper and doing dishes while his wife and/or children are out working. Such a situation cannot help but contribute to the possibility of the disintegration of the family. Unemployment, especially of the male head of the household, has enormous repercussions for everyone involved.

Underemployment. This includes those people who hold part-time, casual, or intermittent jobs. Again, the most common groups to suffer from this problem are blacks, females, and the young. The results are similar to although not quite as extreme as in the case of unemployment. An interesting case to consider here is the large number of people who work on farms. Technological change has had an enormous impact upon them. Technological advances led to mass migrations from the farms to the cities and to employment in industry. For those who remained, farming was transformed so that in general only the large farm could be economically successful. The farmers who work on these large farms and the small independent farmers are in the main hard pressed to eke out a living. But of all farm workers the migrant workers are "the most obvious victims of this triumphant agricultural technology; their plight has been created by progress."[111] Many large farming operations require migrant workers during the short period in which their product is ripe to pick produce "that is too delicate for machines and too dirty for any but the dispossessed."[112] (Migrant work is most common in the picking of grapes, oranges, and grapefruits.) Most typically the migrant worker is a southern black, Mexican, Mexican-American, or poor white.

For most migrants the remainder of the year is spent in unemployment, waiting for the next picking season to begin. During this time they must struggle to live on the meager amount they earned during the last season. They continue as migrant workers because they have neither the skills nor education needed for other, more steady employment. When they do work, the conditions are hard. The workday runs between 10 and 12 hours, usually under a hot sun. Drinking water is either nonexistent or in big communal barrels. The work is hazardous because the migrant worker must use ladders or dangerous machinery.

Harrington describes the situation in Stockton, California, one of the centers of migrant labor: "the workers 'shape up' at three o'clock in the morning. There is a milling mass of human beings down by skid row, and they are there to sell themselves in the market place."[113] Those who are lucky enough to get work are crammed into unsafe pick-up trucks and transported like cattle to the work site. Most frequently the migrant worker is forced to work on a piece-rate basis which means that he is guaranteed nothing in terms of income. If he is sick one day, he will earn nothing. For those who are capable, and who have a good day, the daily income is reasonable. But for those who are not so able, for women, and for children, the daily pay may be less than $5.00." Added to this are the additional problems caused by the conditions under which a migratory minority group are forced to live while they are working. On the job the migrant worker is probably

[111] Michael Harrington, *The Other America: Poverty in the United States* (Baltimore: Penguin Books, 1962), p. 43.
[112] Ibid.
[113] Ibid., p. 53.

far more alienated than the lowest-level industrial worker. However, his situation is made far more serious by the fact that he is underemployed. The alienated blue-collar worker, generally because of unions, is at least fairly sure of permanent work, while the migrant worker is both alienated while he works and unemployed for most of the year. These conditions have led to one of the few important unionization drives in recent years. A farm workers' union led by Cesar Chavez has made great progress in its efforts to organize, in particular, migrant farm workers.

Retirement. Another common form of the absence of occupational life is retirement. Two factors have made retirement a major problem: the trend toward lower retirement ages and increasing longevity. Thus the individual who retires is faced with a substantial number of years in which he must adjust to the absence of occupational life. In their analysis of the problem of retirement Friedmann and Havighurst point out that work performs five functions in terms of meaning to the individual; "income, regulating of life-activity, identification, association, and meaningful life-experience."[114] In terms of each of these meanings of work, the retired person faces problems. When he retires, in most cases he suffers a loss of income. Despite increasing retirement funds and social security, few people retire with the same income they received while working. Thus most must rather rapidly scale down their way of living. Because of his stage in the life cycle the retired person needs less to live on, but still the loss of income necessitates a significant readjustment. For some, such as the self-employed and migrant workers, there is no pension plan, and many must live exclusively on their savings and social security. The second problem for the retired individual centers around the regulation of his life activity. At work, one's daily activities are largely determined by the work routine. Up at seven, at work at nine, coffee at ten, lunch at twelve, another break at three, quit at five, home at six, dinner at seven, and asleep at eleven to be well rested to begin the cycle again. The workworld structures much of a man's life, and when he retires he must adjust to the lack of such external structuring. He must learn to regiment himself, something most people are not asked to do until they are 60 or 65.

For most people their work has been something with which they identify. For some, like professionals and skilled workers, the identification has been with the occupation. For others, such as managers and blue-collar workers, the identification is more likely to have been with the organization. When asked who they are, most people will say that they are doctors, or plumbers, or employees of General Motors. This sense of identification is broken when an individual retires. He is then, at an advanced age, faced with answering the question, Who am I? In addition, for almost all people, work has been a

---

[114] E. A. Friedmann and R. J. Havighurst, "Work and Retirement," in Sigmund Nosow and William H. Form, eds., *Man, Work and Society* (New York: Basic Books, 1962), p. 41.

place in which meaningful social contacts have been made. For the blue-collar assembly-line worker, the informal workgroup has been an important source of interpersonal satisfaction. The skilled worker's fellow tradesmen have frequently given him much satisfaction. The professional's colleagues and friends within professional associations have provided a great deal of work-related gratification. Upon retirement most of these personal contacts are severed. The individual is no longer in a position to associate with his work friends. Those who retire with him are very likely to die shortly or to move to other locations. The retired person must readjust by finding a whole new group of friends. This is difficult for a man of 65 and probably accounts for the proliferation of "golden-age" clubs.

Finally, some occupations also offer an opportunity to gain a meaningful life experience. As defined by Friedmann and Havighurst, this may include "purposeful activity," "self-expression," "new experience," and "service to others."[115] As is quite clear throughout this book, all occupations do not offer such opportunities; those occupations which are of middle status and above are most likely to offer them. Low-status occupations have few structural characteristics which might be considered meaningful by those in them. However, individual differences must be taken into account, and some types of individuals may well find assembly-line work meaningful. Nevertheless, those who have found their worklife meaningful have, perhaps, the most difficult adjustment problem after retirement. To many professionals, managers, skilled craftsmen, etc., their life is their work, and it is precisely in these groups that we find individuals who are most troubled by retirement. How is the doctor to compensate for the loss of the satisfaction of curing or helping patients? How is the college professor to compensate for the loss of contact with students? How is the manager to compensate for the loss of the thrill of competing and, at times, winning? How is the skilled craftsman to compensate for the loss of the pleasure of completing a very difficult task? The answer for most of these men is that such compensation is impossible, and this makes retirement very difficult.

Leisure time. Related to the question of retirement, and faced by everyone who is employed, is the problem of leisure time. DeGrazia defines such time as "a state of being free of everyday necessity, and the activities of leisure are those one would engage in for their own sake."[116] Although De-Grazia contends that most persons do not have leisure in this sense, an increasing proportion of time is being spent off the job. Workdays and work-weeks have grown shorter to the point, in some skilled trades, where a man works a four-day, thirty-hour, week. Man is increasingly faced with the problem of what to do with his spare time. In addition to spare hours during the

---

[115] Ibid., pp. 41–55.
[116] Sebastian De Grazia, *Of Time, Work, and Leisure* (Garden City, N.Y.: Anchor Books, 1964), p. 312.

workweek, there are vacations, which in some cases are as long as four weeks or more. The fact is, however, that in a society which is characterized by materialism, the Protestant Ethic, and rugged individualism, we do not know how to pass time idly. Americans spent a large part of their leisure time at work or in work-like activities. There are many trends in our society which support this contention. One should note, for example, the growing frequency of moonlighting—when a workweek is cut, many people, instead of enjoying their leisure, hurry off to find another job to take up the slack. Those who do not seek another job are very likely to engage in leisure-time activities which closely resemble work. Many men spend spare time working in the house to help their wives. Baby-sitting, washing dishes, and doing the wash are not leisure-time activities in DeGrazia's terms; they are merely a different type of work. Then there is the do-it-yourself craze, popular in many circles. Mowing the lawn, fixing the sink, repairing the car, or working in the shop are also not leisure activities—they are, again, different forms of work. There is also the question of what people do on their lengthening vacations, for another American practice is to take long automobile trips on which the man spends many hours driving, and in this he is much like the truck or taxi driver at work. When he gets to his destination, he is likely to pitch tents, build fires, cook food, and perform a variety of other activities which also sound alarmingly like work. Thus many Americans have resolved the problem of what to do with leisure time quite simply—they work!

The alienated nonoccupations

There is a final type of nonwork which, while defying a name, deserves some attention. Included here are members of nonoccupations, such as the skid-row bum, the mental patient, and the prisoner. All of these must attempt to gain some sort of meaning from daily existence despite the absence of any sort of occupational life. There are really two types included here: those who actively seek to avoid occupational life (the skid-row bum and the hippie) and those who are prevented from occupational life by the structure in which they find themselves (mental patients and prisoners). However, both types have one important factor in common; they are the most alienated groups discussed in this book. They are powerless in terms of affecting society, or in many cases, even in determining their own behavior. Their activities have no meaning in terms of relevance to the rest of society, from which they are almost totally isolated. Finally, their activities hardly offer an opportunity for self-actualization. (The hippies and skid-row bums are an exception here, as will be pointed out later.) For lack of a better name, we might call these types of groups the alienated nonoccupations.

Skid-row residents. The process of becoming alienated from society is well described in Wallace's study of the road to skid row.[117] He defines skid

[117] Samuel E. Wallace, "Road to Skid Row," *Social Problems* 16 (1968), 92–105.

row as "an isolated and deviant subcultural community expressing the features of a distinct and recognizable way of life. The skid rower may be viewed as one who shares this way of life."[118] He is an outcast and deviant from the normal community. The four-step process which Wallace outlines exemplifies the increasing alienation of the skid rower as he becomes progressively involved in the skid-row subculture. In the first stage, there is a dislocation from broader society. Such a dislocation may be caused by a type of work, by destitution, or by deviance (e.g., alcoholism), all of which cut him off from traditional ties. In the second stage, the dislocated individual is exposed to skid row, and this exposure leads to still greater alienation from the broader society. In the third stage, he becomes a regular participant in the skid-row subculture: he becomes committed to its way of life and ceases to hold on to whatever status he had left in the outside world. He is actively socialized by established skid rowers into the deviant subculture and his commitment is enhanced by external pressure. "Every day in his contact with the outside community the skid rower is told he is no good, a failure, a misfit, a bum, and this pressure of community condemnation forces the newcomer on skid row to make increasing use of skid row attitudes in an attempt to neutralize what the rest of the world is saying about him."[119] He comes to the point where he turns around and condemns the outside world while glorifying the skid-row way of life. In the fourth and final stage, he is integrated into the community and acculturated into skid-row existence. He masters its argot and is labelled as an insider by his peers. He is also labelled as a skid rower by larger society, and this increases his alienation from it. He is fully accepted by skid row and alienated from society when he accepts the strong skid-row norm of heavy drinking.

It is interesting to note that there is an elaborate stratification system in skid row with the top rung in the hierarchy going to the drunk, who is perhaps the least inclined to work and the most inclined to be loyal to his peers and share whatever drink he may acquire. The hobo is also looked up to, but he seems to be a dying breed. There are other skid-row types who try harder to make money, but because of the closer resemblance their efforts bear to normal work, these men rank lower in the stratification system. There is the beggar, whose "success depends on his abilities as an actor, psychologist, and tactician."[120] There is a subhierarchy among beggars, with those who beg on the streets at the top and those who pick through refuse for such things as bottles and rags at the bottom. Then there is the "tour director," who makes money by assisting tourists, journalists, or researchers. Low in the hierarchy are those who live off the local missions or who accept relief money from the government. Also low in the hierarchy is the alcoholic, who is differentiated from the drunk because he comes from a better background and has more contacts within society. It is precisely these linkages with society which give

118 Ibid., pp. 96–97.
119 Ibid., p. 100.
120 Ibid., p. 103.

the alcoholic his lowly status. In sum, the stratification system in skid row reflects its alienation from work and the broader society. Those at the top do things which least resemble work and are most nearly totally alienated from the larger society. Those who do things which look like traditional work (e.g., begging, guiding tours) or who have ties with the broader community are ranked lower in the skid-row stratification system.

Hippies. Like inhabitants of skid row, hippies are alienated from the broader society because they have both rejected and been rejected by it. In general they have rejected competitiveness, and in particular they have rejected the competitiveness of the workworld. Most are from the middle class and therefore have witnessed the spectacle of their parents vigorously competing in the workworld. If they are forced to work, they do so only for a short period, or until they have enough to live on for a while. They may form communes and live off what is given to them or what they can beg from straight society. They have also rejected the symbols of success for which straight society works so hard. Conspicuous consumption is replaced by conspicuous nonconsumption. Just as they have rejected society, they have come to be rejected by it. Middle-class America shuns their mode of dress, their supposed lack of cleanliness, their sexual norms, their drug use, and their lack of desire to work and compete.

Although the hippie and the skid-row bum are clearly alienated from the larger society, are they in fact as alienated as the assembly-line worker? The answer to this question really has two parts. In terms of the broader society, skid-row bums and hippies are clearly more alienated than assembly-line workers. But what about alienation from themselves, or self-estrangement? Here it would seem that the assembly-line worker is more alienated. He participates in the system, but the system operates to prevent him from self-actualization. On the other hand, the hippie and the skid rower reject the system and do not seek self-fulfillment within it. Thus the system does not act to estrange them from themselves, because they have chosen to withdraw from it. Instead, they seek self-actualization within a subculture whose norms are more in line with their own inclinations. Within this subculture, the hippie and the skid-row bum are likely to have more power, be less isolated, gain more meaning, and have a greater likelihood of self-actualization. Thus those in these nonoccupations are likely to be more alienated from society, but less alienated from their subculture and themselves.

Prisoners and mental patients. The second group included under the heading of the alienated nonoccupations consists of those who are prevented from participating in occupational life because of constraints imposed by the organizations in which they are found. In the main these are deviants who are incarcerated in what has been called total institutions: the prisoner and the institutionalized mentally ill are the major examples. Such persons face problems quite different from those of the skid rower or the hippie. They have not rejected society, but have been rejected by it. They have generally not rejected occupational life, but have been forcibly removed from it. The prisoner has been removed from a deviant occupation, while the mental patient has most likely been removed from a straight occupation. Nevertheless, both have been removed from the workworld and within the confines of their total institution must seek to compensate for this loss. Total institutions seem to recognize this need by providing worklike activities for inmates. Since these activities are not in most cases real work, they frequently do not provide an adequate substitute for the former occupation. The literature on total institutions has detailed the elaborate underlife or informal practices which develop within them. In part this underlife is an attempt to flesh out meaning in the highly restrictive confines of the total institution, and in part it is also an attempt to compensate for the loss of contact with family and friends. From our point of view, it is an attempt to compensate for the loss of occupational life as well. This is not an unreasonable assumption, since such a large part of the meaning of one's life is defined by his workworld. Such compensation is vital in the case of prisoners and mental patients, because they have not willingly surrendered their worklife. They cannot really perform meaningful work in the total institution, but they can attempt to compensate for its lack by active involvement in the institution's underlife. It is clear that such informal practices help to compensate for each of the five functions of work. Income per se is not possible, but incomelike rewards such as food, clothing, and cigarettes are obtainable by "working the system." Although life is rigidly regulated by the total institution, the involvement in the underlife offers the inmate the opportunity for more meaning within the regimentation. Informal groups within the institution offer the possibility of something to identify with and are as well a source of friends. Finally, in the generally meaningless atmosphere of a total institution, the underlife offers the inmate the opportunity to participate in a "meaningful life-experience."

Summary. The bulk of this book has focused on problems and their resolutions in occupational life. This chapter throws some interesting light on what has been said before. First, it is clear that those who engage in deviant occupations have many of the same kinds of problems as those in straight occupational life, as well as some rather distinctive problems. But then it is obvious throughout this book that individuals in each occupation have their own distinct problem or problems as well as a number of problems in common with those in other occupations. Second, those in straight occupations are very frequently involved in deviant activities and they are, therefore, very similar to members of deviant occupations in this sense. The basic difference between straight and deviant occupations is more quantitative than qualitative. Individuals in both types of occupations engage in deviant behavior; the basic difference is that it is more frequent among those in deviant occupations. Finally, it is clear that just as occupational life is laden with problems, the absence of occupational life brings many problems of its own. The answer, therefore, to problems in occupational life lies mainly in the efforts of individuals and organizations to reduce, eliminate, or learn to live with them. However, we must not blind ourselves to the fact that some people (hippies are the major example) can build themselves a meaningful life outside of our occupational system.

7

Conclusions

The sociology of occupations has been dominated by ethnographic studies of particular occupations. One of the goals of this book has been to codify this mass of studies by occupational level. In each chapter the focus has been on conflict and its resolution and on change, in particular change throughout an individual's career. A number of empirical generalizations have been drawn from the literature to illustrate the discussion of each occupational level, but these are often too broad to be used by the sociological researcher in future studies of occupations. Thus one of the goals in this chapter is to generate some testable propositions about occupational life, which will serve the dual functions of summarizing the book and of acting as guidelines for research into occupations. More generally, it is hoped that these propositions will aid in the development of a theory of occupations. The second half of this concluding chapter is devoted to a review of the variety of theoretical perspectives which have been employed in the sociological study of occupations. In various places throughout the preceding chapters there have been discussions of the application of role theory, dramaturgical theory, conflict and functional theory, etc., to the study of occupations, but this chapter presents a more systematic discussion of the applicability of various theoretical approaches to the study of occupations. This constitutes a second way in which the sociology of occupations can move away from mere description of occupational life. (The first is through the development and testing of propositions.) Some issues in occupational sociology are better examined from a particular theoretical perspective, and I hope this chapter will give the sociological researcher with a particular occupational question in mind both propositions to test and a theoretical perspective with which to examine the question. Descriptive studies have played, and no doubt will continue to play, a central role in occupational sociology, but now, after over forty years of studying occupations, sociology needs to stand back and examine what all of these studies have told us about occupational life. It is to this goal of assessing where occupational sociology stands theoretically that this chapter, and more generally this book, is devoted.

HYPOTHESES

Hypotheses are "tentative explanations . . . suggested to us by something in the subject matter and by our previous knowledge. . . . The function of a hypothesis is to *direct* our search for the order among facts."[1] Most of the hypotheses discussed in this chapter have been suggested by descriptive studies of a number of occupations and are derived from current knowledge of occupational life. As such they should not be taken as statements of fact, but rather as propositions which may be refuted or supported by future occupational research. They are meant to summarize where we now stand and to direct future research. As Sellitz et al. point out, there are several types of hypotheses. One type contends "that something is the case *in a given instance, that a particular object, person, situation, or event has a certain characteristic.*"[2] For example, an hypothesis that a profession is characterized by rationality represents this type of hypothesis. Another type is concerned with the frequency of occurrence in a given unit: it might be hypothesized, for example, that alienation is more likely to occur in low-status occupations than at any other occupational level. This is also a statement of the association between two variables, occupational level and alienation. Finally, a hypothesis may take the form of a statement of a causal relationship: for example, that the structure of low-status occupations is the major cause of the preeminence of alienation at this occupational level. It will become clear as we proceed that all these types of propositions will be employed in this chapter.

Before turning to the hypotheses concerning specific occupational levels, it would be useful to point out two general propositions which apply across all occupational levels.

    1. Although the specific forms vary, conflict and change are ubiquitous in all levels of occupational life.

This proposition is very much in line with more general postulates developed by Ralf Dahrendorf, that every society is subjected at every moment to change and social change is ubiquitous; and that every society experiences at every moment social conflict and social conflict is ubiquitous.[3] Like Dahrendorf, I do not contend this denies that all occupations are also characterized by peace and order. Rather, this proposition seeks to emphasize realities of occupational life which have been demonstrated in a large number of descriptive studies of the workworld. Each chapter in this book has pointed out the distinctive types of conflict and change at each occupational level.

---

[1] In Claire Selltiz, Marie Jahoda, Morton Deutsch, and Stuart Cook, *Research Methods in Social Relations* (New York: Holt, Rinehart and Winston, 1959), p. 35.

[2] Ibid., p. 35.

[3] Ralf Dahrendorf, *Class and Class Conflict in Industrial Society* (Stanford: Stanford University Press, 1959), p. 162.

The sum of all of this is the ubiquity of conflict and change at all levels in the occupational structure.

2. Efforts to resolve or reduce conflict are ubiquitous in all levels of occupational life.

In each chapter the efforts of individuals, groups, occupations, and organizations to reduce or eliminate conflict have been detailed. In general, these efforts are at best only partially successful. The failure of many of them should not necessarily be regarded as bad, for many forms of occupational conflict are highly functional for many of those involved, and the resolution of these conflicts would have negative effects on individuals, groups, occupations, and organizations. Nevertheless, whether the resolution of conflict would entail negative or positive results, there are efforts at all occupational levels to resolve or reduce conflict. In addition to these general propositions there are a large number which relate only to particular occupational levels. It is to these propositions that we now turn.

Professionals

3. All occupations may be ranked on their degree of professionalization.

One of the basic contentions in this book is that professional standing is not an either-or question; it is a matter of degree. Implicit in this is the notion that professionalization is a continuum ranging from the established professions on one end to the nonprofessions at the other.

4. The degree of professionalization of any occupation depends on how many of the following characteristics, and how much of each, it possesses:
   a) General, systematic knowledge.
   b) Authority over clients.
   c) Community rather than self-interest; symbolic rather than monetary rewards.
   d) Self-control.
   e) Recognition by the public and law of professional status.
   f) A distinctive culture.

An occupation which has all six of these characteristics, and in their ultimate degree, would be classified at the professional end of the continuum. Many occupations which fall in the middle of the continuum have all of these characteristics, but only to a moderate degree, while others in the middle have only some. At the nonprofessional end of the continuum are those occupations which have none of the six characteristics. Thus in assessing the degree of professionalization of an occupation one must be concerned with both the numbers of characteristics it possesses as well as the degree to which it possesses each.

5. The position of an occupation on the professional continuum is not fixed; instead, occupations are continually rising and falling.

Recent technological changes have pushed some occupations, in particular scientific ones, close to the professional end of the professional continuum. Other occupations have consciously sought professional standing because of the rewards associated with it (e.g., social work and teaching). Still others, such as the clergy, have declined in professional standing because of internal and external changes which have reduced their prestige. Thus professionalization is a two-lane highway, with occupations moving by in both directions.

6. Many occupations which aspire to a position on the professional end of the continuum face insurmountable barriers to such status.

The occupations which have in the past reached the professional end of the continuum have been those which were free from organizational control. Newer occupations striving for professional recognition are in a quite different situation, for their members are all employees of formal organizations. The existence of teachers, librarians, social workers, personnel managers, and the like in organizations makes movement to the professional end of the continuum unlikely. Employing organizations have, and will continue to have, far more power over individuals in these occupations than professional groups, for it is the employing organization, not the professional one, which pays salaries. This forces most individuals in these occupations to remain locals who owe their allegiance to the employer, rather than cosmopolitans who owe their allegiance to the occupation. Members of the old free professions of medicine and law could afford to be cosmopolitans, but those in the newly rising occupations seeking professional status cannot. Nor is existence in an organization the only barrier to professionalization for these occupations. To take one other example, they do not have general systematic knowledge of their own and they are unlikely to acquire it in the foreseeable future.

7. Just as occupations may be ordered on their degree of professionalization, individuals in any occupation may be ordered in terms of their degree of professionalism.

Heretofore, individual degrees of professionalism have been ignored by occupational sociologists. It is clear, however, that individuals as well as occupations vary in their degree of professionalism. Although medicine is an established profession some doctors are more professional than others. Similarly, although taxi driving is a nonprofession, some taxi drivers are more professional than others.

8. The position of an individual on the professional continuum depends on the number, and degree, of the following characteristics he possesses:

    a) General systematic knowledge.

    b) Authority over clients.

    c) Community rather than self-interest.

    d) Membership in professional (or occupational) organizations, training in professional (or occupational) schools, existence of a sponsor.

    e) Recognition by the public that he is a professional.

    f) Involvement in the professional (or occupational) culture.

The above are individual corollaries of the factors used in Proposition 4 to determine the degree of occupational professionalization. One may use essentially the same procedure to assess individual professionalism as is used in assessing occupational professionalization except that information is gathered about individuals rather than the occupation as a whole.

9. There is a strong but not perfect relationship between occupational professionalization and individual professionalism.

An occupation which is a profession is likely to have a higher percentage of individuals who rank high in individual professionalism. Conversely, an occupation on the nonprofessional end of the continuum is likely to have a lower percentage of such individuals. However, the relationship between occupational professionalization and individual professionalism is not perfect. Again, there are some nonprofessional physicians and some highly professional taxi drivers.

10. As do occupations, many individuals who aspire to professional recognition face insurmountable barriers.

This, too, varies to a great extent depending upon the degree of professionalization of the occupation. Those in the professions or near-professions face fewer barriers than those in the nonprofessions. Nevertheless, many of those at every occupational level who seek professional recognition face barriers to such status. The inept lawyer who wants to be recognized as a professional individual must overcome, for example, his lack of general, systematic knowledge. His existence in a professional occupation is a help, but not a guarantee, of such recognition. For those who are in the nonprofessions the entire structure of the occupation serves as a barrier to their recognition as professional individuals. Thus a taxi driver must exert almost superhuman effort to be viewed as a professional in his occupation, but some do achieve such recognition.

11. Every profession is composed of a number of competing segments which often conflict.

    a) The conflict of segments within a profession is a major source of internal social change.

There has been a tendency in the literature to view professions as monoliths, a trend which has been reversed by a number of recent studies of particular professional occupations. A profession, like any other social system, is made up of a number of subsystems. Spurred on by changes in demand, technology, etc., new segments arise. The established segments find them threatening and first oppose them. Out of this conflict between new and established segments comes a great deal of change within the occupation as a whole. Ultimately, each segment must adapt to the other's existence (assuming one cannot eliminate the other), and the result of this adaptation is a changed occupational structure. The process, however, is never complete because more new segments are constantly arising and the cycle of opposition, adaptation, and change is repeated again and again.

12. If a professional is employed in a nonprofessional organization, there is likely to be conflict between professional and organizational norms.

The professional is by definition a cosmopolitan who identifies with his occupation and accepts and internalizes its norms. When he is employed in a nonprofessional organization, and an increasing number of professionals are, he is confronted with an inherent conflict between the professional norms he has internalized and the norms of the organization. For example, the professional norm of autonomy stands in direct opposition to the bureaucratic norm of control from the top. The professional feels that only he, or fellow professionals, can evaluate his performance, while top managers in the organization, who usually are not professionals, feel that only they have the "big picture" and are able to evaluate and determine the work of professional employees. This disagreement gives rise to considerable conflict with which both the professional and the organization must cope.

13. Professions can ameliorate the conflict between organizational and professional norms by adapting their structures to recognize the fact that their members are likely to be increasingly employed in nonprofessional organizations.

One of the great changes within the professions has been the move among their members from work as free professionals to work as professionals employed in organizations. The professions have been slow to adapt to this change, and generally have continued to act as though their members were free professionals. Of late, however, the professions have begun to adapt their structures to take into account the likelihood that their members will work in organizations. Professional schools have begun to socialize their students into this reality by giving courses in the structure of organizations, and the informal structure in professional schools has also begun to prepare students for this eventuality. There is also a growing recognition that the professions should adjust their reward structure to this fact. Thus, professions are beginning to give recognition to those who make outstanding contributions to their organization rather than rewarding only those who contribute to the profession as a whole.

14. Individual professionals can also adapt to the conflict between professional and organizational norms by focusing on one or the other, fusing the two, or focusing on neither.

When confronted with normative conflict, the professional employed in a nonprofessional organization has four options. Perhaps the most frequently chosen is to attempt to compromise by conforming in part to both sets of norms. A professional choosing this course of action is neither a cosmopolitan nor a local, but a local-cosmopolitan. The professional can also choose to be a professional first, or he can "sell out" and become primarily a bureaucrat. Finally, at least theoretically, he can commit himself to neither his profession nor his employing organization. The choice depends on the nature of the profession, the employing organization, and the individual in question.

15. Employing organizations also can make structural adjustments which reduce the conflict between professional and organizational norms.

Like professional associations, organizations which employ professionals have come to recognize, and structurally adapt to, the conflict between professional and organizational norms. Some have made the professional suborganization virtually autonomous from the total organization. Others have appointed administrators of professional groups who are themselves professionals. A "dual ladder" is frequently employed with movement up in the organization possible (in terms of title and money, if not power) for those who make important contributions to professional knowledge. Finally, organizations have recognized the professionalism of their professional employees by allowing them time and facilities to work on pure rather than applied problems and have given them time off for involvement in professional activities.

16. The free professional must cope with problems emanating from his relationship with clients.

Since he is not employed in an organization, the free professional need not cope with the conflict between professional and organizational norms. However, like every other individual in an occupation, the free professional must deal with conflict in the workworld. His basic conflict stems from his relationship with clients, for his livelihood depends on a steady stream of them. In order to obtain and retain a clientele he must engage in a variety of behaviors, some of which may contradict professional norms. At the most innocuous level, he must dramaturgically manipulate clients so that they are satisfied with his service. Thus, he may prevent himself from saying or doing anything which may antagonize the client. But he may be forced into doing things which violate professional norms: the ambulance-chasing lawyer who seeks out clients and the doctor who prescribes placebos for hypochondriacal patients are two examples. The professional, however, is not as troubled by this problem as are persons in other service occupations. His clients have usually surrendered their judgment to him, but individuals in other service occupations must deal with customers who refuse to surrender their judgment, and are therefore far more troublesome. The salesman has greater problems with his customers than the professional has with his clients.

17. The socialization of new professionals is primarily based in formal professional schools.

a) The manifest focus of professional schools is the transmission of knowledge and skills.

b) Latently, professional schools transmit the values and norms of professional behavior.

One of the distinguishing characteristics of the professions is the existence of formal professional schools. No other occupational level has as elaborate a formal system of training recruits. This of course relates to the extensive body of systematic knowledge which differentiates the professions from all other occupations. The declared goal of professional schools is to transmit this knowledge as well as the requisite skills, but latently they also transmit norms and values. This is important because of the professional norms of autonomy and self-control—in order for the professions to be granted the right to autonomy and self-control they must be sure that trainees are firmly indoctrinated in the profession's norms and values. Such indoctrination is latent in many courses and formal contacts and is an important part of the informal sturcture of any professional training school.

18. The nature of the socialization process in professional training schools depends in part on the prior socialization of the student and the nature of his commitment to the profession.

The socialization of student physicians is far easier if their fathers were doctors. In graduate schools of physiology, the task is made difficult by the fact that students enter with a commitment to another field, medicine. The graduate school must therefore both communicate knowledge and instill in the student a commitment to physiology. Engineering schools have an easier task since they accept students who have both commitment and some expertise. Their problem is to retain students in the face of the strong pull from firms willing to pay large salaries to engineers with only one year of graduate training.

19. Professional schools vary in how completely they socialize students, but no matter how complete the socialization, much is left for initial jobs.

Medical schools seem to do a far better job of preparing students for professional life than, for example, law schools. A large portion of the socialization of law students occurs in their first jobs. No professional school can completely socialize students; socialization in the professions, as in general, is a lifelong process.

20. On the completion of their training, professionals are subjected to highly elaborate recruiting practices.

No members of other occupational levels, except perhaps for managers and officials, are recruited as actively as professionals. They have highly valued skills which continue to be in relatively short supply in American society. Further, they are usually placed in sensitive positions so that a poor choice would have serious effects. Because they are scarce professionals are also very difficult to fire, and this makes it still more essential that hiring mistakes be avoided.

21. The professions are characterized by the most variable career patterns of any occupational level.

These patterns run the gamut from almost total immobility to almost total mobility. Free professionals, such as the physician in private practice, have very little career mobility. Once out of medical school and in private practice, there are almost no further formal steps open to the doctor, although he does have informal steps open, such as movement into medicine's inner fraternity. Such informal steps are generally not included in a discussion of career patterns. The college professor has some, but not a great many, steps available when he leaves graduate school. In formal terms he can only move from instructor to assistant, associate, and full professorship, although some informal upward mobility is possible, such as becoming a "name" in his discipline or movement to so-called prestige universities. Other professionals have a great many formal steps open to them: the beginning Wall Street lawyer, for example, is faced with a long succession of positions leading to the top of the organization. He and some other professionals have career patterns which are very similar to those with the greatest career-pattern mobility, managers and officials. There is more diversity in terms of career patterns in the professions than at any other occupational level. Professionals even have far more employment opportunities on retirement than do those at any other occupational level.

22. Despite the norms of rationality blacks and females face discrimination in the professions, although less than at most other occupational levels.

The negative stereotypes of blacks and females which pervade American society have their impact on the professions too. Blacks and females find it harder to enter the professions because of the discriminatory policies of professional schools. If they are accepted by these schools, they must cope with discrimination from peers, administrators, and established professionals. If they succeed in graduating, they find it more difficult to get good positions. In whatever positions they do obtain, they must face the prejudice of colleagues who may refuse to refer clients, or clients who may refuse to become involved with them. Nevertheless, because of the emphasis on knowledge and skill, minority groups have fewer problems in the professions than at virtually any other occupational level.

Managers and officials

23. The most characteristic problem faced by managers and officials in their occupational life is role conflict.

Role conflict is most common among managers and officials, for they are always employed at strategic positions in formal organizations. Because they exist in organizations and their positions are important, managers and officials are inevitably subjected to conflicting expectations. These conflicting expectations generally emanate from significant others within the organization, although they may also come from outsiders who have an interest in the occupational activities of managers and officials. Within the organization hierarchy, there are always significant others above, below, and beside them who have different interests which are conveyed to the manager or official in the form of conflicting expectations. While role conflict occurs at other occupational levels, it is not as serious a problem. The only exception is the first-line supervisor, who is perhaps even more likely to be confronted with role conflict. This is not surprising, however, since the first-line supervisor is in reality the lowest-ranking manager or official. Some professionals are seriously troubled by role conflict, while others are almost unaffected. Professionals in organizations, in particular those who choose to occupy professional-administrator positions, are subject to role conflict although their professional norms make it a less serious problem. Free professionals are relatively free of conflicting expectations, and because of their independent status, the same is true of small proprietors. Those in low-status and white-collar occupations are unlikely to be severely troubled by it because of their lesser importance in the organization and because they usually have only one supervisor. The semiprofessionals are faced with role conflict because they have some status within their employing organization, but they are far more troubled by their status insecurities. Individuals in deviant occupations are generally of low status, and are therefore in the same position as those in other low-status occupations. They are far more plagued by problems other than role conflict.

Those in deviant occupations which exist in the Mafia hierarchy are hypothesized to be similar to other managers and officials and thus are likely to be forced to deal with the problem of role conflict. In sum, it is the structure of the occupation and its position in its employing organization (if it is in one) which determine the nature of the conflict it is most likely to face. The importance of the manager or official and his position within the organizational hierarchy account for the fact that role conflict is the most characteristic problem at this occupational level.

Role conflict takes a variety of forms, all of which are likely to affect the manager and official. a) Inter-sender role conflict occurs when the manager is subjected to conflicting expectations from two or more significant others. b) Intra-sender role conflict is characterized by conflicting expectations from one significant other. c) Person-role conflict occurs when there is a disparity between what the manager is expected to do and what he wants to do. d) Inter-role conflict is a problem when the manager occupies two or more roles which have conflicting expectations attached to them. e) The manager or official is faced with role overload when he must deal with more expectations than he can handle. f) Role ambiguity, although it is not a formal type of role conflict, is also a related problem. Under this condition the manager or official is unsure about what he is expected to do.

24. The manager or official resolves role conflict by conforming to one expectation or the other, compromising, withdrawing, or taking independent action.

Within each of these types of role conflict resolution a wide array of particular actions may be included. For example, dramaturgical manipulation is one way of taking independent action, while "passing the buck" is an example of withdrawal. (Although these modes of resolution have been applied to managers and officials, they are equally applicable to any individual confronted with role conflict.)

25. Managers and officials are recruited almost as actively and elaborately as professionals.

Highly trained managers are in almost as great demand as professionals and the supply, in terms of the demand, is almost as short. Thus the aspiring manager or official, especially if he has a degree from a business school, is wooed almost as ardently as the aspiring professional. The recruiting is also very elaborate. The reason lies in the nature of managerial and official occupations, whose members quickly find themselves in strategic positions within their employing organization. A recruiting mistake at this level would be very costly to the organization; hence the care in recruitment. Further, most managers and officials are subjected to rigorous and expensive training programs, and the time and expense involved here cause organizations to take great care in their recruitment. There are exceptions to this, as well as every other, proposition. For example, officials in voluntary organizations are not generally recruited, but instead seem to be the only ones really interested in the position. Despite the exceptions the proposition holds in most cases.

26. The career patterns of managers and officials offer more mobility than those of any other occupational level.

In the course of their careers managers and officials are the most likely to move up, down, or laterally. This relates to the structure of the occupation and the employing organization. Managers and officials tend most to have a high need for achievement and the skills necessary to satisfy this need. Further, they find themselves in organizations which have a multitude of positions which offer the possibility of moves in every conceivable direction. Starting near the bottom, they are faced with a long set of steps leading to the top. Most have the training and ability to aspire to the lofty heights—the vast majority make a series of moves up the ladder and then are faced with various alternatives. Some may be able to move up still further, others will be required to move laterally until positions open above them, and still others may be demoted, subtly or overtly, because of their high degree of incompetence. Finally, there are those who will stay where they are for the rest of their lives because they have displayed the required competence (or incompetence).[4] No other occupational level offers its people as many career alternatives. Professionals in organizations cannot ascend as high or descend as low, while free professionals are highly immobile. Proprietors are already at the top and can only rise in an informal sense as their organization becomes more important or profitable. The semiprofessionals find themselves in the same position as professionals in organizations with some, but not a great many, career alternatives open. Those in other occupations—foremen, union stewards, skilled workers, white-collar workers, low-status workers, and most in deviant occupations—have little chance of ever moving. Again the reasons lie in the nature of these occupations and their positions in their employing organizations. We shall discuss each of these more fully as this final chapter proceeds.

27. Blacks and females have comparatively few distinctive problems as managers and officials when they supervise subordinates of the same race or sex.

a) Blacks and females face extremely acute problems when they supervise whites or males.

When subordinates are black or female, black or female managers and officials face essentially the same problems as members of their race or sex do in other occupational levels. It is harder for them to get the necessary training, harder to find jobs, and there are conflicts with peers and superiors. But

---

[4] For a humorous discussion of the relationship between competence and mobility, see Lawrence J. Peter and Raymond Hull, *The Peter Principle* (New York: W. Morrow, 1969).

once the black or female manager and official supervises members of the opposite sex or race the problems are greatly increased. Many Americans feel that blacks and females are inferiors who should never be in a position superior to that of those of the majority group. Because of this belief, blacks or females are unlikely ever to gain such important positions, and if they do, they are faced with the severest of occupational conflicts.

Proprietors

28. Proprietors' most characteristic conflicts stem from their economic, and in some cases professional, marginality.

a) Proprietors who are confronted with economic marginality seek to resolve their problem through a variety of devices which make their economic position more secure.

b) Proprietors who are confronted with professional marginality typically resolve their conflict by attempting to fuse the professional and business roles, although they may also eschew one or the other of these roles.

The independent proprietor is typically in a position of economic marginality, basically caused by the proliferation of huge corporations with which he generally cannot compete. Supermarket chains have driven many grocers and butchers out of business and pushed most of the others to the brink of bankruptcy, the big three automobile manufacturers have forced almost all of the smaller ones out of business, restaurant chains have had a similar effect on the small restauranteur—the list of examples is almost endless. Those proprietors who have survived have done so because they found some way of bolstering their economic position. Some merchants succeeded by giving highly personalized service to a small number of steady customers, who were willing to pay higher prices in return for the attention they could not get from a large chain. Other proprietors have existed by taking in partners who bring with them much needed capital and permit survival, at least in the short run. Some have joined co-ops which allow them to remain independent, but also allow them to reap the benefits of the lower wholesale prices which come with mass buying. Mergers, small business loans, and a variety of other tactics have also permitted a number of proprietors to continue, but generally not very comfortably.

A similar problem is the professional marginality which confronts other types of proprietors. Some, such as the druggist, the optometrist, and the chiropractor, have gone through a process which may be considered professional socialization. Often viewing themselves as professionals, they frequently also find themselves being proprietors. These antithetical roles are extremely difficult to fill at the same time. For example, professional norms generally frown on advertising, but advertising is a norm among proprietors.

In coping with this conflict, the most frequently employed technique seems to be an attempt to fuse the two roles. In effect, this means downplaying one or both to some degree or accepting aspects of both. Thus the druggist may open his drug store in a small town where he does not have to engage in active competition, or he may accept the business norms of advertising while clinging to other professional norms. The proprietor confronted with this type of conflict also has the option of withdrawing from one role or the other. He can work for a pharmaceutical firm and thereby withdraw from his role as businessman, or he can become a complete businessman, even to the point of violating norms on prescriptions, and deny his professional position.

29. Proprietorship is a terminal occupation in career-pattern terms.

Like those in many other occupational groups, the proprietor is faced with a very constricted career pattern. Once in his position he is at the end of the line in that occupation. He can move out, as can individuals in any occupation, or he may fail, but then his career begins in another occupational level. Although lacking in formal steps, proprietorship offers a variety of informal career steps. A firm can grow bigger or merge, or its proprietor can be accepted as a leader of the business community.

30. Blacks and females have been notably unsuccessful in their efforts to become proprietors, outside of a few areas which are defined as black or female.

They have, however, succeeded in businesses which are congruent with their race or sex roles or which cater to a clientele of the same race or sex. Even in these areas, however, the majority of firms are owned by whites or males.

Members of middle-level occupations

31. First-line supervisors are particularly prone to role conflict.
32. They resolve their role conflict through conforming to one expectation or the other, compromise, withdrawal, or independent actions.
33. They have highly constricted career patterns.
34. Blacks and females find it extremely difficult to handle the position of first-line supervisor, especially when their subordinates are not from the same minority group.

These propositions require little additional discussion because the first-line supervisor is similar in many ways to the manager or official and his conflicts and modes of resolution are the same. The major difference between foremen and managers is in terms of their career patterns. Some foremen, especially college graduates who are in foremen positions for training purposes, even have the same career-pattern possibilities as managers and officials. Many however continue to be promoted from the ranks and lack the training and skill needed for higher-level positions.

35. White-collar workers are more likely to face status insecurities than workers at any other occupational level.
36. White-collar workers seek to handle their status insecurity by involvement in informal groups and through rigid adherence to the rules.
37. Despite their status insecurity, they are not likely to join unions because of the association of unionization with blue-collar work.
38. White-collar workers have highly constricted career patterns.
39. Blacks and females at the white-collar level have few problems other than those which are common to them at all occupational levels.
40. Since it is a service occupation, salesmanship is an exceptional white-collar occupation; its major problem is with customers and its major resolution is dramaturgical.
41. Blacks or female salesmen have particular problems if their customers are of the opposite race or sex.

Status insecurity or "status panic" among white-collar workers is caused by the social changes which have threatened their always tenuous claims to status. Although many of their jobs are dull and relatively unskilled, white-collar workers have always gotten a good deal of satisfaction from the fact that they were of higher status than blue-collar workers. However, a number of changes have upset this source of gratification. Offices have become increasingly like factories with a high division of labor and even some elements of the assembly line. Formerly taking pride in their proximity to top management, white-collar workers now find themselves almost as distant from the executives as are blue-collar workers. For example, in many offices the private secretary has been replaced by the secretarial pool. While the white-collar worker has become more like the blue-collar, other changes have altered the latter's position. Unionization has improved his wages, hours, and working conditions to the point where they rival or exceed those of white-collar workers, and automation has made some factories look like offices and the blue-collar workers in them more like white-collar workers in dress and activities. Thus changes at both occupational levels have substantially reduced the gap between them. The result has been the strong sense of status insecurity in the middle-level occupations, which has been exacerbated by the automation of the office which poses another important threat to the status of the white-collar worker. Despite these threats white-collar workers have not turned to labor unions, for they associate unions with blue-collar workers and the mere suggestion of unionization constitutes another threat to their status. Involvement in informal groups with other white-collar workers constitutes one method by which they try to resolve, or at least insulate themselves from, the status threats. Another means commonly employed is to become expert on the rules and rigidly apply them; such actions set them apart from blue-collar workers.

In terms of their career patterns, white-collar workers have little chance to move in any direction. There is more than one level of white-collar work, but the differences between these levels are usually so small that movement is not very important, except in a symbolic sense. White-collar workers do have more opportunities to move than, for example, foremen or blue-collar workers, but the number of steps open to them is so small that it is safe to classify their career pattern as constricted. They certainly have infinitely fewer possibilities for mobility than managers and officials.

Blacks and females face few distinctive problems at the white-collar level, but they share the problems faced by blacks at every occupational level: discrimination in hiring and difficulties with peers and superiors. Females find relative peace at the white-collar level mainly because many of the occupations are congruent with their sex roles and are, in fact, defined as female. Even blacks have a relatively easy time at this level because the occupations are often congruent with the stereotypes of their race. That is, many white-collar positions are passive rather than active and in subordinate rather than superior positions.

Salesmen, although classified as members of a white-collar occupation, have some rather distinctive occupational characteristics. Their major problem is control over customers, the major source of their income. This control is very difficult for the salesman to achieve, since the customer has the ultimate power—whether to buy or not to buy. The salesman typically seeks to gain control of the situation through dramaturgical manipulation. By using a variety of acts, props, and the cooling-out process, he enhances his control over the customer. As a service occupation, salesmanship presents particular difficulties to minority-group members, especially when they are in the position of selling to members of the majority group. Thus there is particularly great friction when black or female salesmen (or saleswomen) deal with white or male customers. Again the explanation lies in the inability of whites or males to accept blacks or females in positions of authority.

42. The major problem for the skilled worker is threats to his autonomy.
43. Skilled workers seek to reduce these threats through a strong union and through the actions of their informal groups.
44. The career patterns of skilled workers are very rigid and offer little possibility of movement.
45. Females have not even tried to enter the skilled trades since they are so antithetical to the female sex role.

46. Of all the occupational levels, the skilled trades have had the greatest number of formal and informal barriers to the admission of blacks.

As in the case of the professional, the skilled worker has a strong norm of autonomy which is threatened when he is employed in a formal organization. Many of the defenses of autonomy which professionals employ are not available to craftsmen, but they have compensated to some degree by developing powerful unions, which in large part exist to defend the craftsman's autonomy. In addition, skilled craftsmen seek to retain their autonomy through the actions of informal groups. One follows a prescribed sequence of moves to become a skilled tradesman, and there then are few further moves available, as well as little desire on the part of craftsmen, because of their commitment to their trade, to be anything more. Females have no problems in the skilled crafts because few have ever even tried to enter them. The disparity between work and sex roles is so great in this case that females are highly unlikely to seek such employment. Blacks, on the other hand, have tried to enter the skilled trades, but they have been systematically excluded by the unusually great formal and informal barriers.

47. The major problem confronting semiprofessionals is their marginal professional status and the barriers they face in their efforts to become true professionals.

48. In their efforts to become more professional semiprofessionals may either redouble their efforts or define a new, more realistic goal for themselves.

49. The career patterns of semiprofessionals are similar to those of professionals in most organizations.

50. Males are the minority group in the semiprofessions and face problems similar to those which females face in other occupations.

51. Blacks have fewer problems in the semiprofessions, especially when their clients are also black.

The major semiprofessions of teaching, social work, and nursing have all been striving hard to be recognized as professions. In the eyes of most observers, however, they have not achieved this status. Their inability to achieve professionalization, despite their constant efforts, constitutes the source of their major occupational difficulty; they are not treated as professionals on the job. They may try to resolve their problem by redoubling their efforts or by defining for themselves a new, more realistic goal. It was suggested, for example, that such occupations can never become professions in the traditional sense and might be better served by defining for themselves a new goal such as "bureaucratic-professional."

The semiprofessions have training programs which are similar to, but less complete than, the training of professionals. Almost all semiprofessionals are employed in organizations and their career patterns are similar to those of most professionals employed in organizations. They have few opportunities for upward mobility, although there is considerable opportunity for lateral movement. The semiprofessions are interesting in that they are one of the few occupational levels in which males constitute the minority group. Men here face the same kinds of problems faced by females in most other occupational levels. Blacks have the same problems of entry and relating to peers and superiors as they do at every occupational level. However, they have more serious difficulties when they deal with white clients, and often they deal almost exclusively with blacks, thereby eliminating this problem.

Members of low-status occupations

52. The basic problem for those in low-status occupations in organizations is alienation.

53. The degree of alienation of low-status employees depends on the nature of the organization's technology.

54. The degree of alienation of low-status employees depends on the structure of the organization.

55. On a group level, individuals in low-status occupations deal with their alienation through a variety of informal group practices.

56. On an individual level, those in low-status occupations in organizations employ a variety of psychological devices to deal with alienation.

57. Theoretically, unions provide a structure through which low-status workers may reduce their alienation.

58. Frequently, unions serve to increase rather than decrease the alienation of low-status employees.

59. Employing organizations have, if they wish, a number of means which they may employ to reduce the alienation of low-status workers.

Although, as Max Weber for one has pointed out, alienation is a problem for most occupations, it is particularly acute for those in low-status occupations employed in organizations. The reason that such occupations are particularly prone to isolation, self-estrangement, meaninglessness, and powerlessness lies primarily in the nature of the technology and the structure of the organization. The assembly-line technology is the most alienating because of its unmitigated control over the worker. Other technologies, such as the new automated factories, exert far less control and are therefore less alienating. One of the earliest technologies, craft technology, provides the worker with the greatest freedom and is therefore the least alienating technological form. In the middle is the machine-tending technology, which controls the worker, but not to the extent that he is controlled by the assembly line. The other important determinant of alienation in low-status occupations is the structure of the employing organization. Obviously the larger and more bureaucratic the organization, the greater the alienation. Ultimately, of course, those in low-status occupations are faced with alienation because of the structure of the occupation, which is characterized by little training, low skill, large supply, and easy replaceability. Informal group practices which seek to restrict the control of the technology and the organization are a prime means of dealing with alienation, and restriction of output constitutes the most common manifestation of this device. Individuals in low-status occupations may deal with the alienation psychologically by concentrating on extra-work activities, overemphasizing the importance of their work, etc. Unions are supposed to provide a structure through which they may reduce their alienation, but due to the oligarchical structure of most unions, individuals frequently find themselves alienated within them as well as in their employing organizations. The employing organization is capable of taking actions which would reduce alienation, but the perpetual question is whether it is willing to pay the price required to reduce it. In fact, most organizations are more willing to endure the alienation of the workers rather than to do what is needed to alleviate the problem.

60. The basic problem for those in free low-status occupations is control of customer/clients.
61. In their efforts to gain control over customer/clients, those in free low-status occupations employ typologies and a variety of dramaturgical techniques.

Most free low-status occupations may be classified as service occupations. As such their major problems revolve around relations with customer/clients. In dealing with their customers many of those in low-status occupations do not have the weapons of those in other service occupations. In particular, their lowly status makes it most unlikely that customers will surrender any judgment to them. In their efforts to cope with the customer/client they frequently place them into types. This does not enable them to control customer behavior, but it does help them to know what to expect. On a more direct level, they may seek to "train" customers so that they behave the way they want them to. Those in low-status occupations most frequently employ a variety of dramaturgical devices which help to give them some measure of control over the behavior of customer/clients.

62. Low-status occupations are characterized by highly constricted career patterns.

Whether in an organization or on his own, the individual in a low-status occupation has increasingly fewer chances of moving beyond his first position in the labor market. In the past some low-status workers have been able to ascend the occupational and/or organizational ladder, but with increasing

MAN AND HIS WORK: CONFLICT AND CHANGE

educational demands at these higher levels they most frequently find themselves mired in the occupation in which they began their careers. Many, of of course, move from job to job, but rarely are any of these positions out of the low-status level.

63. The degree of stress faced by blacks and females in a low-status occupation depends on whether the occupation is congruent with their race and sex roles.

There is a clearer line between male and female, and black and white, in low-status occupations than at any other occupational level. Blacks and females face few problems when in low-status occupations congruent with their race and sex roles; in occupations which are not congruent, problems abound.

Members of deviant occupations

64. Those in free legal deviant occupations are primarily confronted with problems with customer/clients.
65. In addition to problems with customer/clients, those in free illegal deviant occupations must also cope with the problem of police detection.
66. Dramaturgical manipulation constitutes the most important way in which those in legal and illegal deviant occupations cope with customer/client-centered problems.
67. In dealing with the police, those in illegal deviant occupations employ dramaturgical means as well as more direct approaches.

There are two basic types of deviant occupations, those that are legal and those that are illegal. For those in legal deviant occupations the basic problem is the customer/client. In trying to outwit him the individual in a deviant occupation most frequently utilizes a wide array of dramaturgical techniques. For those in illegal deviant occupations the police constitute a second important problem. Direct means such as bribery are used to reduce the insecurity which results from the constant possibility of police detection. Dramaturgical manipulation is also used in an effort to forestall the possibility of police detection and apprehension.

68. Those in deviant occupations in organizations face the same types of problems as are faced by those in straight occupations in organizations.

Based on Cressey's analysis of the Mafia, it has been concluded that deviant organizations are very similar to straight ones. It is therefore likely that persons engaged in the various types of occupations in deviant organizations face many of the same problems which confront individuals at the same occupational level in a straight organization. Thus the problems of the Mafia foreman are similar to those of the industrial foreman (role conflict), and low-status workers in the Mafia are alienated in the same way that low-status workers in any organization are alienated. It is also true that low-status Mafia workers face the same kinds of problems as those in free deviant occupations.

69. Free deviant occupations have highly constricted career patterns.

70. Those in deviant occupations in organizations have career patterns which are similar to those of their counterparts in straight organizations.

Because he is usually of low status, the individual in a free deviant occupation has a very constricted career pattern. Once an individual is a stripper or a poolroom hustler there are few if any additional steps open in the occupation. On the other hand, the career patterns of deviant occupations in organizations resemble those of occupations at a similar level in straight organizations. Mafia managers have a good many career possibilities open to them, while foremen have far fewer opportunities to move up the hierarchy.

71. Blacks and females have the same kinds of problems in deviant occupations as they do in low-status occupations.

There are deviant occupations which are congruent with race and sex roles; the black numbers man in the ghetto and the prostitute are examples. There are deviant occupations which are not congruent with these roles and when a black or female enters these occupations problems abound.

72. Deviant behavior occurs throughout the occupational structure, and in most cases it is highly functional for many of the units involved.

The professional on one end of the occupational continuum and the individual in a deviant occupation on the other engage in what is defined by society or some subgroups, as deviant activities. The pervasiveness of occupational deviance indicates that it is highly functional for most of the units involved in and around the workworld.

73. Just as work creates problems for individuals, so does the lack of it.

Nonwork such as unemployment, underemployment, leisure, retirement, and nonoccupations (such as that of the skid-row bum) creates a series of distinctive problems. Although work has its problems, nonwork has at least as many and probably more. It is clearly not the answer to the troubles of the workworld. The implication is that instead of withdrawing from the workworld, individuals at all occupational levels must work to reduce conflict to manageable proportions.

The preceding 73 propositions constitute one of the ways in which occupational sociology can move away from mere description and become more theoretical. By utilizing one or more of these propositions occupational sociologists will be able to focus on particular questions in occupational life. Some will be accepted after testing while others will be rejected or modified. In the process, what we know about the dynamics of occupational life will be greatly clarified. There is another way in which occupational sociology can become more theoretical, and that is through the increasing utilization of theoretical perspectives, developed primarily in general sociology. Instead of merely observing occupational life, the occupational sociologist will be better able to understand what he sees if he has a theoretical perspective in mind. (There are a number of theoretical perspectives in general sociology. However, the vast majority of ethnographic studies of occupations have merely entailed observation.) These were valuable, but it is now time for occupational sociology to become linked with the broader theoretical perspectives of general sociological theory. What is now needed is a series of studies of occupations done from particular theoretical perspectives. In this way the linkage between occupational life and the other aspects of social life studied by sociologists can be better understood. It is not argued here that one theoretical approach is superior to any other, for in fact there is no agreement in general sociological theory on this question. Each theoretical perspective is useful in analyzing one or more aspects of occupational life, and the rest of this chapter outlines a number of these theoretical approaches.

FOUR THEORETICAL PERSPECTIVES

The ensuing discussion focuses on what are considered to be four major theoretical perspectives: functional theory, conflict theory, exchange theory, and symbolic interactionism. It is also important to note that we call these theoretical perspectives, not theories. Zetterberg defines sociological theory as "systematically organized, law-like propositions about society that can be supported by evidence."[5] In terms of this definition none of the above four theoretical perspectives can be classified as theories; they are perspectives from which theorists have viewed the social world. My contention here is that they are also useful perspectives for viewing the workworld, and as such offer the student of occupations another way (the first is hypothesis testing) of moving away from gross descriptive analyses, as well as supplying linkages to findings in other areas of social life which have been studied from these perspectives. The testing and linking of the propositions outlined in the first part of this chapter will give us a "middle-range" theory of occupations. The examination

[5] Hans Zetterberg, *On Theory and Verification in Sociology*, 3rd Edition (Totowa, New Jersey: Bedminister Press, 1965), p. 22.

of occupational life from these theoretical perspectives will lead us to an understanding of the relationship between a middle-range theory of occupations and other middle-range theories. It is only when these middle-range theories are linked that we will be able to develop a "grand theory" of social life. Lacking such a grand theory or even a middle-range theory, the best we can do at this point is to discuss the applicability of the four theoretical perspectives to areas of occupational life.

Functional theory

Although functionalism encompasses a wide range of often conflicting positions, there are some commonalities. In general, functionalists believe that society is a social system composed of various subsystems. Of basic concern is the relationship between the subsystems and the larger social systems. Each subsystem is seen as having consequences for each of the other subsystems as well as for the social system as a whole, and these consequences may either be positive (functional) or negative (dysfunctional). To oversimplify an enormously complex perspective, functionalism attunes us to the relationship between social systems and the reciprocal consequences these systems have for each other.

The functional perspective has been infrequently employed in occupational sociology; perhaps its major utilization has been in the area of occupational deviancy. Dalton detailed a long list of industrial "crimes" which he contends are highly functional for the maintenance of a rigid bureaucratic system.[6] To him, the foreman who manufactured illegal items which served as rewards for deserving managers was the cement which held the organization together. Similarly, the use of the tap in the airplane factory studied by Bensman and Gerver was highly functional for both workers and foremen,[7] although probably dysfunctional for the company and the air force, not to mention the potential pilots, since it led to the production of defective planes. The use of illegal forms of violence by the police was highly functional for them, although highly dysfunctional for the individuals who were victims of the violence. The Chicago police riots accompanying the Democratic Convention of 1968 were highly dysfunctional for Hubert Humphrey in terms of his effort to become president of the United States. Even deviant occupations may be highly functional to the community. The case of the black numbers man and his functions in the black community is an excellent example.

In addition to the study of deviance, functionalism also offers us a way of looking at any occupation and its consequences for the social system in which it is found. An excellent example is Wilensky's study of the union in-

---

[6] Melville Dalton, *Men Who Manage* (New York: John Wiley, 1959).

[7] Joseph Bensman and Israel Gerver, "Crime and Punishment in the Factory: The Function of Deviancy in Maintaining the Social System," *American Sociological Review* 28 (1963), 588–598.

tellectual.[8] Although it has not been discussed before, it would be useful at this point to analyze this example of functional analysis in some detail. Wilensky differentiates the union expert into three types (the facts and figures man, the contact man, and the internal communications specialist) and discusses each from a functionalist perspective. Before analyzing the functions of each type he discusses the functions of all union experts:

a) As "window dressing." Unions often employ economists, editors, and lawyers just for show, for these experts make the union leader feel he is as good as management. Having a resident expert also makes the rank and file members feel the union is being progressive and doing a good job. Finally, when the union must deal with such agencies as the university or the government it feels on a par with them because each has its experts. b) For verbalization. The union needs someone who can speak and write well. "The union expert needs this word-processing skill to write speeches and resolutions, by-laws, and contracts, to give testimony, edit papers, articulate policy, prepare legal or economic briefs, deal with the rank and file, speak in conference or mass meeting, contact community groups, and more."[9] c) To "take the heat." That is, the union expert often acts as a "fall guy" who takes the blame for an error and relieves the union officer of his guilt.

Following the analysis of general functions Wilensky turns to a discussion of the three sub-types:

The facts and figures man. "They have a primary concern with, and skill in, manipulating facts, figures, documents, records and arguments . . . these are the men who furnish technical-economic-legal intelligence—the 'ammunition' to build the union's case."[10] Occupationally, facts and figures men are engaged in economics, research, law, statistics, engineering, etc. The facts and figures man performs the following functions: a) He builds a strong case for the union vis-à-vis the employer. The better the case presented by the expert, the more difficult it will be for the employer to keep public opinion on his side and the more willing he will be to settle. b) He may frame presentations so as to indicate the union's real intent without making it explicit. For example, if the union raises an issue, but offers no statistical support, the company may safely assume that the issue was raised to assuage the rank and file and was not a real goal of the union. c) He is able to talk to the increasing number of "quasi-judicial boards, arbitrators, government hearing officers" that unions must deal with. d) He reorients discussions to facts and increases the strength of the union on these issues. e) He enhances the control of the leader in the eyes of the rank and file while at the same time increasing the morale of the union as a whole. f) He has helped move the

[8] Harold Wilensky, *Intellectuals in Labor Unions: Organizational Pressures on Professional Roles* (Glencoe, Ill.: Free Press, 1956).

[9] Ibid., p. 37.

[10] Ibid., p. 39.

union from an older "table pounding stance" to a more reasonable stance vis-à-vis management. (In terms of dysfunctions, the facts and figures man tends to slow the union down and make it less ideological.)

The Contact Man.   He is the union expert who has "a primary concern and skill with facts about, and techniques of, manipulating the thoughts, feelings, and conduct of men." He is the expert who has contacts, is a trouble shooter, can "fix" things, and generally "knows the ropes."[11] Lawyers, lobbyists, and public-relations experts may serve as contact men. The contact man performs the following functions for the union: a) He helps to maintain a smooth-running relationship between the union and the outside world. That is, he can "fix" any problem or mediate any conflict. A dysfunction here is that he encourages "a beat-the-game" philosophy rather than a more rational approach. b) He interprets the union to the public and the public to the union. In so doing he builds up a public image of the union. (The dysfunction is that it makes the union leader "other-directed" and may hinder his activities in behalf of the membership.)

The internal communications specialist.   He is concerned with "manipulating the thoughts and feelings and conduct of union members. He is the specialist who furnishes political-ideological intelligence to buttress the union leader in his task of communications and control within the union."[12] He is primarily concerned with problems of internal control as well as with problems created by rival unions. Occupations included under this title include editors, auditors, "education and recreation directors, political action representatives, and anti-discrimination representatives."[13] The functions of this type of expert include: a) Building the prestige of the top union official within the union. b) Facilitating communication and thereby enhancing the control of the leader. c) Helping to keep up union morale in time of crisis. d) Dealing with the pressures from minority groups within the union when they threaten the union's stability. (As possible dysfunctions the internal communications specialist may educate members to the point where they become competitors for the leader's position. He may also divert the union from the achievement of its primary goal.)

Other functionalist concerns.   While Wilensky focuses on the consequences of an occupation for a broader social system (the union), functionalists are also concerned with the effect of the broader social system on the occupation. On one level we can examine the effect of the employing organization on occupations within it. This issue has been considered at several places throughout this book, albeit unsystematically. For example, the effect of different types of employing organizations on professionals was discussed in Chapter

[11] Ibid., p. 61.
[12] Ibid., p. 80.
[13] Ibid.

2 and in Chapter 5 there was a discussion of the relationship between the degree of bureaucratization of the employing organization and the alienation of low-status workers. On another level, we have been consistently concerned with the relationship between broad social changes and occupations. Such broad social changes as the increasing division of labor, technological advances, increasing educational levels, the black revolution, and women's liberation have all had an enormous impact on the entire occupational system as well as on particular occupations. One of the concerns of the functionalists has not been dealt with at all in this book: the relationship between the occupational system and other subsystems in American society. Although we have purposely ignored this question in order to focus on occupations per se, it is important to say at least something about subsystemic linkages at this point. Thus the next few paragraphs are concerned with the relationship between the occupational system and the familial, educational, and political systems in American society.

Subsystemic linkages. The family system obviously produces (both biologically and socially) the people needed to serve in the occupational system. Biological production of manpower need not detain us here; of interest is the social production (socialization) of potential workers. As a crucial socialization agent (along with peer groups and schools) the family must socialize its offspring so that they can fit into the occupational world. By emphasizing the value of money, material possessions, and hard work, the American family prepares its children to fit into the American occupational system. It also focuses on the importance of education, thereby interesting children in advanced education, which we have seen is fast becoming a prerequisite to occupational success. The typical American family structure (the nuclear family of husband, wife, and dependent children) also permits the male to leave the family and devote a large portion of his time to the workworld. In the past this has relegated the wife to the roles of wife and mother, but we have seen that females are increasingly moving from a sole concern with these roles and into the workworld. The implications of this for American family structure are difficult to predict, but it is at least possible that many of the child-rearing functions will be taken over by other agents. As of now a number of factors (including changing ideologies about the role of women, household labor-saving devices, and increased education of women) have reduced the importance and difficulty of various household chores. In addition to producing the crucial manpower inputs for the occupational system, the family unit is also an important consumer of its outputs. Many occupations would disappear were it not for the father's purchase of a car, the mother's electric dishwasher, and the children's long-playing records.

The educational system receives as inputs the children of the family system and continues the socialization process begun in the home. While family socialization is very broad, the socialization process in the educational system becomes increasingly narrow. In the early school years the focus continues to be on broad social values as well as rudimentary skills, but as the child progresses the educational system begins to channel him into a particular occupation. For those students who make it to college there are some majors which prepare them for specific careers, while others are broad enough to allow deferment of occupational choice. At the graduate level the focus is still narrower, with graduate schools and departments always concerned with producing individuals who will fit into a given occupation. In the end, the combination of the family and educational systems has produced, in most cases, an individual who has the values and skills needed to fit into a niche within our occupational system. It might be noted, however, that a significant number of our young people are eschewing traditional occupational goals, and this represents at least some degree of failure in the socialization process. The educational system also produces another essential input into the occupational system, knowledge. Colleges and universities, in fact, have the dual roles of producing people to man occupations and new knowledge. The protected and supported production of knowledge which goes on in the vast American educational system has produced thousands of new occupations and led to changes in virtually every established one. In addition to producing the needed workers and knowledge, this system is also an important consumer of occupational goods and services and an employer of those in certain occupations. The growth of this educational system has made school and college teaching and administration important occupations.

The political system provides the necessary inputs for the occupational system on a variety of levels. The stability of the American government has permitted a widespread expansion of the entire occupational system. Our colonial adventures and international treaties have provided the occupational system with many of the raw materials it needs. Tariffs negotiated by the government have allowed many occupations to survive in the face of stiff competition from foreigners, and government legislation has helped shape the occupational system by limiting the power of large corporations and large labor unions. The licensing of many occupations from the professions to taxi driving has enabled the public to have greater trust in its occupational servants. Perhaps most important has been the massive expenditure of government funds in such different areas as defense, urban renewal, antipoverty programs, and foreign aid, which has literally created many occupations and increased the number employed in others. The government is also an important consumer of the products of the occupational system. Finally, since the New Deal the government has become the employer of those in virtually every conceivable occupation. The scientist, soldier, politician, administrator, bureaucrat, and blue-collar worker all may share one thing in common, a government employer.

In the preceding examination of the familial, educational, and political systems, we have tended to trace a one-sided perspective; that is, the effect of each of these on the occupational system. But the functional perspective assumes a feedback mechanism which notes that all systems affect, and are affected by, all other systems. Thus just as the family, the polity, and the educational system help shape the occupational system, they, in turn, are shaped by it. Thus the nature of our occupational system has contributed to the growth of the nuclear family and the demise of the extended family, the proliferation of colleges and universities, and the expansion of the federal government. The impact of the occupational system is perhaps clearest in the case of the system of social stratification. Blau and Duncan trace the relationship quite clearly: "In the absence of hereditary castes or feudal estates, class differences come to rest primarily on occupational positions and the economic advantages and powers associated with them."[14] In fact, in our society, occupation is often used as a measure of social class. The other variables which might be used in social-class analysis, such as income or educational level, are intimately related to one's occupational status. Thus we conclude that the functionalist perspective is best suited for analyzing the relationship between occupations, occupations and their employing organizations, the occupational subsystem and other social subsystems, and the occupational system and the larger social system.

Conflict theory

Conflict theory is often viewed as antagonistic to functional theory. While functionalists tend to look at what holds systems together, conflict theorists focus on what pulls them apart. Put another way, functional theorists are interested in order, conflict theorists in disorder. Thus the conflict view is generally considered to be the ideological left, while the functional perspective is seen as conservative. Despite these and other differences, much recent literature has been devoted to efforts to reconcile the two theories. Dahrendorf, who is generally regarded as a conflict theorist, has argued that the two theories are not antagonistic, but complementary.[15] For him, functional theory is useful in examining order while conflict theory is to be used when one examines disorder. Van den Berghe is another who has tried to reconcile the two theories, but he takes issue with Dahrendorf's effort: "The most ambitious task that remains is to reach a synthesis between the two. The desirability of achieving a unitary approach seems obvious. It is not enough to say that two theories are complementary and can be used *ad hoc* for different purposes; one must also show that they are reconcilable."[16] Such a goal is certainly desirable, not just for these two theories, but for all sociological theories. How-

---

[14] Peter Blau and Otis Dudley Duncan, *The American Occupational Structure* (New York: Free Press, 1967), p. vii.

[15] Dahrendorf, *Class and Class Conflict*.

[16] Pierre L. van den Berghe, "Dialectic and Functionalism: Toward a Synthesis," *American Sociological Review* 28 (1963), 70.

ever, this objective is beyond current sociological thinking as van den Berghe readily admits: "Such an endeavor is beyond the scope of this paper."[17] The best he can do is to show some points of convergence and overlap between the two theories in the hope of showing the "promise" of reconciliation. For example, both theories share a holistic view of society and a concern with an interrelationship between the subsystems. For another, he notes that consensus can lead to conflict just as conflict can lead to consensus. Despite these and other similarities, conflict and functional theories remain different ways of looking at the same social system.

Quite clearly this book is dominated by the conflict perspective, both on the individual and systemic level. Systemic conflict is the concern of conflict theory while individual conflict will be discussed later under the heading of symbolic interactionism. It would be useful to reiterate some of the systemic conflicts discussed in the preceding chapters. The professional system and the bureaucratic system are typically at odds because they are basically antagonistic methods of organizing work. The bureaucratic system is based on control from the top while the professional system relies on internalized controls. When one of these systems is superimposed on the other, conflict generally results. A similar situation occurs in the relationship between the skilled trades system of work and the bureaucratic system. Although the skilled trades are not identical to the professions there are a number of similarities, of which the main one is the dependence of both on internal controls. Thus the skilled craftsman and the professional are in similar positions when they are employees of bureaucracies. Conflict also occurs between subgroups within occupations. The major example is the conflict between segments within any profession. Finally, there are innumerable conflicts between occupations. The almost universal conflict between staff and line occupations is perhaps the classic example, but we have also dealt with the conflict between physicians and nurses, schoolteachers and principals, big businessmen and small entrepreneurs, members of illegal deviant occupations and the police, and many others.

Conflicts between the occupational and other subsystems. While we have dealt with many conflicts within the occupational system, we have not addressed ourselves to conflict between the occupational system and other social systems. In the discussion of functionalism we have briefly looked at the points of congruence between the occupational system and other subsystems. In this section there will be a short discussion of the conflicts between these systems.

While in some ways the occupational system meshes well with the family system, in other ways there is conflict between them. Perhaps the major one is over the role of women, for while the family system pulls the female in the direction of the wife and mother roles, the occupational system is,

[17] Ibid.

with increasing frequency, pulling her into work roles. As has been made clear in each of the preceding chapters, it is extremely difficult for a woman to satisfy both sets of expectations. One of the basic causes of this strain lies in the nature of the family system in the United States. In less "modern" societies the norm is the extended family, in which we find a number of other relatives in addition to the mother, father, and dependent children. While this was functional in agricultural economies where a number of workers were needed to till the soil, it is fast disappearing in the United States. As a result the wife-mother is robbed of a number of helpers who could assist with the household responsibilities, thereby allowing her to devote more of her time to the workworld.

There is also conflict between the educational and occupational systems. For example, although advanced education is highly specialized, it rarely adequately prepares an individual for the workworld. In fact, the educational system often makes it difficult for a graduate to adjust to his occupation, for since it focuses on skills and knowledge, it ignores the realities of occupational life. Thus the graduate is frequently confronted with "reality shock" when he enters the workworld. The new lawyer who was led to believe that he would handle interesting and exciting cases is usually appalled to discover that he does the dirty work for the established lawyers or tasks which are ordinarily the province of clerks. To take one more example, there is the conflict between the liberality of most college campuses and the conservatism of most of our occupational settings. Trained in liberal institutions, the new graduate frequently finds it necessary to cope with ideological discontinuity when he moves into the workworld.

Finally, there is also conflict between the occupational and political systems. For example, the government frequently intervenes excessively in the workworld, at least as far as some of the participants are concerned. In the 1930s pro-union legislation led to conflict between the government and business leaders, and in the 1940s and 1950s anti-union legislation led to conflict between union officials and the government. Government intervention in strikes and internal business affairs is likely to earn the enmity of both business and labor leaders. In sum, the subsystems within our social system are in conflict in some areas and mesh in others.

Exchange theory

Exchange theory differs from functionalism and conflict theory in that it is generally used at a more microscopic level;[18] it is more concerned with the relationship between actors than between systems. Exchange theory is basically concerned with rewards, costs, and profits in social situations. (In gen-

[18] See, for example, George Homans, *Social Behavior: Its Elementary Forms* (New York: Harcourt, Brace, 1961) and Peter Blau, *Exchange and Power in Social Life* (New York: John Wiley, 1964).

eral, people will engage in activity which is profitable, calculated as rewards minus costs, and seek to avoid those activities in which costs exceed the rewards obtainable.) This general principle, and all of its derivatives, have a broad and untapped applicability to occupational life. For example, the alienation which is most characteristic of low-status workers in organizations, but occurs throughout the occupational hierarchy, may be viewed as a result of greater on-the-job costs than rewards. In an effort to increase his rewards the worker may engage in a variety of informal activities, and should these fail, he is likely to give up psychologically, if not physically, and withdraw from work, focusing on those activities which are rewarding. The position of the professional employed in an organization may also be interpreted from an exchange theory perspective. The profits of the professional are likely to be optimized in a moderately bureaucratic organization in which he can use the resources of the organization, but not be totally controlled by it. In the highly bureaucratic setting the resources are also available, but the oppressiveness of the organization makes the costs exceed the rewards. The free professional does not have the resources an organization can offer, although he is free of bureaucratic control. One can extend this type of analysis almost indefinitely; the clerk is in the throes of status panic because social changes have gradually reduced the rewards and increased the costs attached to the occupation, the nurse desires professional recognition because of the greater profit it offers, and so forth. The point is that exchange theory offers those interested in occupational sociology a tool for examining a wide range of microscopic questions.

Perhaps the greatest utility of exchange theory is as perspective for analyzing and understanding career patterns. Individuals choose a particular career because the rewards for them exceed the costs. Thus the child of a professional chooses to be a physician because the costs of the lengthy training involved are exceeded by the rewards he will derive at the end, while the child of a working-class family chooses to be an assembly-line worker because the immediate monetary rewards are important to him and he cannot afford to become involved in a lengthy training program for a higher-status occupation. This implies that occupational choice is a rational process, but much of the literature indicates that many people simply fall into a given occupation. When occupational choice is rational, exchange theory helps us understand why a particular choice is made. More important, it helps us to understand why an individual stays in a given occupation. The side-bet theory of commitment developed by Becker may be viewed as an example of exchange theory. (According to Becker an individual stays in his occupation because of the side-bets or investments he has made. Thus, the more the investments in a particular occupation, the greater the rewards for staying and the greater the costs if the individual decides to leave.[19]) In effect, when an

[19] Howard S. Becker, "Notes on the Concept of Commitment," *American Journal of Sociology* 66 (1960), 32–42.

individual has a choice, he will stay in an occupation when the rewards exceed the costs and leave when the reverse is true. Of course, in many cases, workers do not have a choice and in these cases exchange theory is not applicable. The blue-collar worker, for example, typically has no choice. He cannot choose a more rewarding occupation because he lacks the skills and education to be offered one.

Symbolic interactionism

Like exchange theory, symbolic interactionism is most applicable to the microscopic level. Blumer writes:

Symbolic interaction involves *interpretation,* or ascertaining the meaning of actions or remarks of the other person, and *definition,* or conveying indications to another person as to how he is to act. Human association consists of a process of such interpretation and definition. Through this process the participants fit their own acts to the ongoing acts of one another and guide others in doing so.[20]

In this view social life is an ongoing process in which the actors are continually acting and reacting to others in the social setting. It encompasses a wide range of relationships including conflict, competition, disagreement, and consensus. Its great utility is in understanding the relationship between individuals in the workworld.

Dramaturgy. Although symbolic interactionism as such has not been employed in this book, two of its offshoots, dramaturgy and role theory, have been used extensively. Dramaturgical analysis is most helpful in understanding the ways in which individuals in the workworld cope with their conflicts: through the employment of various dramaturgical devices the physician seeks to deal with his conflict with his patients, the used-car salesman with his customer, the local union president with his membership, and the prostitute with her john. Thus dramaturgy is employed throughout the occupational hierarchy and as means of coping with a wide variety of stresses. It is interesting to note that the "social drama of work" has always been a concern of Everett Hughes, but it was not until the pioneering work of Erving Goffman that it evolved into a distinct sociological perspective. Implicit in many of the early studies of occupations, dramaturgical analysis is fast becoming one of the major explicit theoretical tools of the occupational sociologist. Employing concepts such as "front behavior," "back behavior," "teams," and the "cooling-out process," the dramaturgical analyst has been able to cast much new light on occupational life, in particular on the ways in which those in the workworld cope with conflict.

[20] Herbert Blumer, "Sociological Implications of the Thought of George Herbert Mead," in Walter L. Wallace, ed., *Sociological Theory* (Chicago: Aldine, 1969), p. 237.

Role theory. In many ways role theory is indistinguishable from the dramaturgical approach. The similarity between the two approaches is best expressed in the following description of role theory, which resorts to a theatrical analogy:

When actors portray a character in a play, their performance is determined by the script, the director's instructions, the performances of fellow actors, and reactions of the audience as well as by the acting talents of the players. Apart from differences between actors in the interpretation of their parts, the performance of each actor is programmed by all of these external factors; consequently, there are significant similarities in the performances of actors taking the same part, no matter who the actors are.[21]

From this description of role theory it would be virtually impossible to differentiate it from dramaturgy. Yet there is one crucial difference between the two perspectives. The role theorist explains behavior in terms of the structure of the situation. Given the structure an actor can either *conform* to the structure or in some way *deviate* from it. Dramaturgical analysts, on the other hand, give the actor a much greater role. He does not merely blindly conform to the social structure; instead, his action is a result of his interpretation of that structure.

Role theory offers us structural concepts which can be used to analyze any occupation. We can learn much about occupational life by systematically analyzing the positions, roles, role pressures, and role-sets of any and every occupation. These and other role concepts greatly enhance our ability to describe and understand the nature of the position of every individual in occupational life. Use of these concepts is clearly an advance over the descriptive studies of the past—at least the researcher has in mind a series of concepts with which he can orient his observations. Further it makes for greater uniformity in observation. Instead of observers aimlessly looking at occupations until something strikes their fancy, they will have these concepts to organize their observations. This does not mean, by the way, that the concepts should blind the observer to unforeseen circumstances.

The implication in the preceding paragraph is that role theory is useful only in statically describing an occupation, but it also has dynamic qualities. This is especially true in the areas of role conflict and role conflict resolution, where role theorists have provided us with a series of types. We know that in any occupation an individual is likely to be faced with inter-sender role conflict, inter-role conflict, intra-sender role conflict, person-role conflict, and role overload. We also know the general types of action a worker may take in a role conflict situation; conformance to expectation A, conformance to expectation B, compromise, withdrawal, and independent action. In addition, the literature has provided us with variables to help us predict which resolution

[21] Bruce J. Biddle and Edwin J. Thomas, *Role Theory: Concepts and Research* (New York: John Wiley, 1966), p. 4.

an individual will choose. For example, the power, legitimacy, and visibility of significant others must be considered as well as the personality of the actor in question.

Summation

What we have, then, are four theoretical perspectives which are useful in analyzing occupations from the sociological perspective. Again, these are not the only theories of utility to the study of occupations, but they are the major ones. Two of the perspectives, conflict and functional theories, seem to have greater utility at the macroscopic level, or for analysis of the relationship between occupations, between occupations and their employing organizations, and between the occupational system and other social systems. On the other hand, exchange theory and symbolic interactionism offer us the most help in understanding microscopic questions. We can use them to analyze the position of an individual in occupational life, the nature of his conflicts, and the ways in which he seeks to cope with his conflicts.

The goal of this book has been to systematically present the current state of sociological knowledge of occupational life. It is safe to conclude that a great deal is known about specific occupations and occupational processes. Despite the wealth of information, little of it has been generalized beyond a particular occupation or process. This last chapter is an effort to move toward generalizing these findings. Thus, based on studies of particular occupations, propositions have been derived which apply to each of the major occupational types. The empirical testing of these propositions will lead to a greater refinement of our knowledge of broad occupational types. Second, we have attempted to demonstrate the applicability of sociological theory to the study of occupations. Using the theoretical perspectives discussed in this chapter, occupational sociology can develop many new insights into occupational life. More important, the utilization of these perspectives will enable us to relate the developing theory of occupations to many other middle-range theories which are currently being developed. In conclusion, it is important to point out that although we know much about occupational life, a great deal more remains to be learned.

Bibliography

Abel-Smith, B. *A History of the Nursing Profession.* London: William Heine-mann, Ltd., 1960.

Abrahamson, Mark, ed. *The Professional in the Organization.* Chicago: Rand Mc-Nally, 1967.

Adams, S. N. "Origins of American Occupational Elites." *American Journal of Sociology* 62 (1957), 360–368.

Alex, Nicholas. *Black in Blue: A Study of the Negro Policeman.* New York: Appleton-Century-Crofts, 1969.

Allen, Philip J. "Childhood Backgrounds of Success in a Profession." *American Sociological Review* 20 (1955), 186–190.

Anderson, Nels. *The Hobo.* Chicago: University of Chicago Press, 1923.

———. *Dimensions of Work: The Sociology of a Work Culture.* New York: David McKay, 1964.

Antonovsky, Aaron, and Lerner, Melvin. "Occupational Aspirations of Lower Class Negro and White Youth." *Social Problems* 7 (1959), 132–144.

Argyris, Chris. *Executive Leadership: An Appraisal of a Manager in Action.* New York: Harper & Row, 1953.

———. "Explorations in Consulting-Client Relationships." *Human Organization* 20 (1961), 121–133.

Armor, David J. *The American School Counselor: A Case Study in the Sociology of Professions.* New York: Russell Sage Foundation, 1969.

Astin, Alexander. "The Functional Autonomy of Psychotherapy." *American Psychologist* 16 (1961), 75–78.

Aubert, V. "The Housemaid—An Occupational Role in Crisis." *Acta Sociologica* 1 (1956), 149–158.

Ausubel, David. "Relationships Between Psychology and Psychiatry: The Hidden Issues." *American Psychologist* 11 (1956), 99–105.

Axelson, Leonard. "The Working Wife: Differences in Perception Among Negro and White Males." *Journal of Marriage and the Family* 32 (1970), 457–464.

Babchuk, Nicholas, and Bates, Alan P. "Professor or Producer: The Two Faces of Academic Man." *Social Forces* 40 (1962), 341–348.

———, and Goode, William. "Work Incentives in a Self-Determined Group." *American Sociological Review* 16 (1951), 679–687.

Babcock, Charlotte. "Social Work as Work." *Social Casework* 34 (1953), 415–422.

Back, Kurt et al. "Public Health as a Career of Medicine: Secondary Choice Within a Profession." *American Sociological Review* 23 (1958), 533–541.

————, and Simpson, Ida Harper. "The Dilemma of the Negro Professional." *Journal of Social Issues* 20 (1964), 60–70.

Bakke, E. W. *The Unemployed Worker.* New Haven: Yale University Press, 1940.

Balma, M. et al. "The Role of Foreman in Modern Industry: I. The Development of a Measurement of Management Identification; II. Foreman Identification with Management, Work Group, Productivity, and Employee Attitude Toward Foreman; III. Some Correlates of Foreman Identification with Management." *Personnel Psychology* 11 (1958), 195–205, 367–378, 535–544.

Banton, Michael. *The Policeman in the Community.* New York: Basic Books, 1964.

Barber, Bernard. "Is American Business Becoming Professionalized? Analysis of an Ideology." In E. A. Tiryakian, ed., *Sociocultural Theory, Values, and Sociocultural Change: Essays in Honor of Pitirim A. Sorokin.* New York: Harper Torchbooks, 1967, pp. 121–145.

————. "Some Problems in the Sociology of the Professions." In Kenneth S. Lynn, ed., *The Professions in America.* Boston: Beacon Press, 1967, pp. 15–34.

————. "Some Problems in the Sociology of Professions." In Mark Abrahamson, ed., *The Professional in the Organization.* Chicago: Rand McNally, 1967, pp. 133–136.

Barber, J. *The Lawmakers: Recruitment and Adaptation to Legislative Life.* New Haven: Yale University Press, 1965.

Barnard, Chester. *The Functions of the Executive.* Cambridge, Massachusetts: Harvard University Press, 1945.

Barthuli, E. "Occupational Attitudes of Dentists." *Sociology and Social Research* 20 (1936), 548–551.

Barzun, Jacques. *Teacher in America.* Boston: Little, Brown, 1945.

Bates, Alan. *The Sociological Enterprise.* Boston: Houghton Mifflin, 1967.

Bayley, Daniel, and Mendelson, Harold. *Minorities and the Police: Confrontation in America.* New York: Free Press, 1969.

Becker, Gary. *The Economics of Discrimination.* Chicago: University of Chicago Press, 1957.

————. "Discrimination and the Occupational Progress of Negroes: A Comment." *Review of Economics and Statistics* 44 (1962), 214–215.

Becker, Howard. "The Professional Dance Musician and his Audience." *American Journal of Sociology* 57 (1951), 136–144.

————. "The Career of the Chicago Public School Teacher." *American Journal of Sociology* 57 (1952), 470–477.

————. "Some Contingencies of the Professional Dance Musician's Career." *Human Organization* 12 (1953), 22–26.

————. "The Teacher in the Authority System of the Public School." *Journal of Educational Sociology* 27 (1953), 128–141.

————. "Notes on the Concept of Commitment." *American Journal of Sociology* 66 (1960), 32–42.

————. "The Nature of a Profession." In *Education for the Professions.* Chicago: University of Chicago Press, 1962, pp. 27–46.

————. *Outsiders.* New York: Free Press, 1963.

————, and Carper, James. "The Development of Identification with an Occupation." *American Journal of Sociology* 61 (1956), 289–298.

————. "The Elements of Identification with an Occupation." *American Sociological Review* 21 (1956), 341–348.

————, and Geer, Blanche. "The Fate of Idealism in Medical School." *American Sociological Review* 23 (1958), 50–56.

————. "Student Culture in Medical School." *Harvard Educational Review* 28 (1958), 70–80.

————. "Medical Education." In Howard Freeman et al., eds. *Handbook of Medical Sociology*. Englewood Cliffs, N.J.: Prentice-Hall, 1963, pp. 169–184.

————, and Strauss, Anselm. "Careers, Personality, and Adult Socialization." *American Journal of Sociology* 62 (1956), 253–263.

———— et al. *Boys in White: Student Culture in Medical School.* Chicago: University of Chicago Press, 1961.

———— et al. *Institutions and the Person.* Chicago: Aldine, 1968.

Bell, Daniel. "Adjusting Men to Machines." *Commentary* 3 (1947), 79–88.

————. "Crime as an American Way of Life." *Antioch Review* 13 (1953), 131–154.

Ben-David, Joseph. "Professional Role of the Physician in Bureaucratized Medicine: A Study in Role Conflict." *Human Relations* 11 (1958), 255–274.

————. "Role and Innovation in Medicine." *American Journal of Sociology* 65 (1960), 557–568.

Benewitz, Maurice. "Migrant and Non-Migrant Occupational Patterns." *Industrial and Labor Relations Review* 9 (1956), 235–240.

Bennis, Warren. "The Social Scientist as a Research Entrepreneur: A Case Study." *Social Problems* 3 (1955), 44–49.

Bensman, Joseph, and Gerver, Israel. "Crime and Punishment in the Factory: The Function of Deviancy in Maintaining the Social System." *American Sociological Review* 28 (1963), 588–598.

Bereday, George, and Lanwerys, Joseph, eds. *The Education and Training of Teachers.* London: Evans Brothers, 1963.

Berenda, Carlton. "Is Clinical Psychology a Science?" *American Psychologist* 12 (1957), 725–729.

Berkowitz, David. *Inequality of Opportunity in Higher Education: A Study of Minority Groups and Related Barriers to College Admission.* Albany, New York: State of New York, 1948.

Berle, A. A. "Legal Profession and Legal Education: The Modern Legal Profession." *Encyclopedia of the Social Sciences.* New York: MacMillan, 1933, vol. 9, pp. 340–345.

Berlew, David, and Hall, Douglas T. "The Socialization of Managers." *Administrative Science Quarterly* 11 (1966), 207–223.

Bernard, Jesse. *Academic Women.* University Park: Pennsylvania State University Press, 1964.

Bidwell, Charles. "The Administrative Role and Satisfaction in Teaching." *Journal of Educational Sociology* 29 (1955), 41–47.

————. "The Young Professional in the Army: A Study of Occupational Identity." *American Sociological Review* 26 (1961), 360–372.

Bittner, Egon. "Police Discretion in Emergency Apprehension of Mentally Ill Persons." *Social Problems* 14 (1967), 278–292.

———. "The Police on Skid Row." *American Sociological Review* 32 (1967), 699–716.

Black, Gordon. "A Theory of Professionalization in Politics." *American Political Science Review* 64 (1970), 865–878.

Blalock, Hubert. "Occupational Discrimination: Some Theoretical Propositions." *Social Problems* 9 (1962), 240–247.

Blau, Peter. *Bureaucracy in Modern Society.* New York: Random House, 1956.

———. "Orientation Toward Clients in a Public Welfare Agency." *Administrative Science Quarterly* 5 (1960), 341–361.

———. *The Dynamics of Bureaucracy.* Chicago: University of Chicago Press, 1963.

———, and Duncan, Otis Dudley. *The American Occupational Structure.* New York: John Wiley, 1967.

———, and Scott, W. Richard. *Formal Organizations: A Comparative Approach.* San Francisco: Chandler, 1962.

Blauner, Robert. *Alienation and Freedom.* Chicago: University of Chicago Press, 1964.

Blizzard, Samuel. "The Roles of the Rural Parish Minister, the Protestant Seminaries, and the Sciences of Social Behavior." *Religious Education* 50 (1955), 383–392.

———. "The Minister's Dilemma." *Christian Century* 73 (1956), 508–510.

———. "The Parish Minister's Self-Image and his Master Role." *Pastoral Psychology* 9 (1958), 25–32.

———. "The Protestant Parish Minister's Integrating Roles." *Religious Education* 53 (1958), 374–380.

———. "The Parish Minister's Self-Image and Variability in Human Culture." *Pastoral Psychology* 9 (1959), 27–36.

Bloch, Herman. "Craft Unions and the Negro in Historical Perspective." *Journal of Negro History* 43 (1958), 10–33.

———. "Negroes and Organized Labor." *Journal of Human Relations* 10 (1962), 357–374.

Blum, Albert A. et al. *White Collar Workers.* New York: Random House, 1971.

Blum, Fred. *Toward a Democratic Work Process: The Hormel Packinghouse Workers' Experiment.* New York: Harper & Row, 1953.

Blumberg, Abraham. "The Practice of Law as Confidence Game: Organizational Co-optation of a Profession." *Law and Society Review* 1 (1967), 15–39.

Bock, E. Wilbur. "The Female Clergy: A Case of Professional Marginality." *American Journal of Sociology* 72 (1967), 531–539.

Boehm, Werner. "The Nature of Social Work." *Social Work* 3 (1958), 10–18.

Bonjean, Charles. "Mass, Class, and the Industrial Community." *American Journal of Sociology* 72 (1966), 149–162.

Booth, David. "Are Elected Mayors a Threat to Managers?" *Administrative Science Quarterly* 12 (1968), 572–589.

Bordua, David, ed. *The Police: Six Sociological Essays.* New York: John Wiley, 1967.

Borgatta, Edgar et al. *Social Workers' Perceptions of Clients: A Study of the Case-load of a Social Agency.* New York: Russell Sage Foundation, 1960.

Bouma, Donald. *Kids and Cops: A Study in Mutual Hostility.* Grand Rapids, Michigan: William B. Eerdmans, 1969.

Braude, Lee. "Professional Autonomy and the Role of the Layman." *Social Forces* 39 (1961), 297–301.

Braybrooke, David. "The Mystery of Executive Success Re-examined." *Administrative Science Quarterly* 8 (1964), 533–560.

Breed, Warren. "Social Control in the Newsroom: A Functional Analysis." *Social Forces* 33 (1955), 326–335.

Bridgman, Margaret. *Collegiate Education for Nursing.* New York: Russell Sage Foundation, 1953.

Broderson, Arvid. *The Soviet Worker: Labor and Government in Soviet Society.* New York: Random House, 1966.

Brody, Eugene. "Interprofessional Relations, or Psychologists and Psychiatrists are Human Too, Only More So." *American Psychologist* 11 (1956), 105–111.

Brooks, Earl. "What Successful Executives Do." *Personnel* 32 (1955), 210–225.

Brown, Esther. *Nursing as a Profession.* New York: Russell Sage Foundation, 1936.

———. *Social Work as a Profession.* New York: Russell Sage Foundation, 1936.

Brown, J. H. U. "The Science Administrator: A New Profession." *Journal of Medical Education* 43 (1968), 33–35.

Brown, Morgan. "The Status of Jobs and Occupations as Evaluated by an Urban Negro Sample." *American Sociological Review* 20 (1955), 561–566.

Browne, C. "Study of Executive Leadership in Business. II. Social Group Patterns." *Journal of Applied Psychology* 34 (1950), 12–15.

Bruner, Dick. "Why White Collar Workers Can't Be Organized." *Harpers Magazine* 215 (1957), 44–50.

Bruno, Frank. *Trends in Social Work, 1874–1956.* New York: Columbia University Press, 1957.

Bryan, Alice. *The Public Librarian.* New York: Columbia University Press, 1952.

Bryan, James. "Apprenticeships in Prostitution." *Social Problems* 12 (1965), 287–297.

Bucher, Rue. "Pathology: A Study of Social Movements Within a Profession." *Social Problems* 10 (1962), 40–51.

———, and Stellings, Joan. "Characteristics of Professional Organizations." *Journal of Health and Social Behavior* 10 (1969), 3–15.

———, and Strauss, Anselm. "Professions in Process." *American Journal of Sociology* 66 (1961), 325–334.

Bullock, Henry Allen. "Racial Attitudes and the Employment of Negroes." *American Journal of Sociology* 56 (1951), 448–457.

Burchard, Waldo. "Role Conflicts of Military Chaplains." *American Sociological Review* 19 (1954), 528–535.

Butler, John, and O'Hern, Edna. "Medical Education and Research in Catholic Medical Schools and Hospitals." *American Catholic Sociological Review* 19 (1958), 224–237.

Butler, Pierce. "Librarianship as a Profession." *Library Quarterly* 21 (1951), 235–247.

Cameron, Mary. *The Booster and the Snitch*. New York: Free Press, 1964.

Cameron, W. B. "Sociological Notes on the Jam Session." In W. B. Cameron, *Informal Sociology*. New York: Random House, 1963, pp. 118–130.

Campbell, Ernest, and Pettigrew, Thomas. "Racial and Moral Crisis: The Role of Little Rock Ministers." *American Journal of Sociology* 64 (1959), 509–516.

Caplovitz, David. *The Poor Pay More*. New York: Free Press, 1967.

Caplow, Theodore. *The Sociology of Work*. New York: McGraw-Hill, 1963.

———, and McGee, Reece J. *The Academic Marketplace*. New York: Basic Books, 1958.

Carlin, Jerome. *Lawyers on Their Own*. New Brunswick, N.J.: Rutgers University Press, 1962.

——— et al. *Civil Justice and the Poor: Issues for Sociological Research*. New York: Russell Sage Foundation, 1967.

Carlson, Richard. "Succession and Performance Among School Superintendents." *Administrative Science Quarterly* 6 (1961), 210–227.

Carper, James, and Becker, Howard S. "Adjustment to Conflicting Expectations in the Development of Identification with an Occupation." *Social Forces* 36 (1957), 51–56.

Carr-Saunders, Alexander, and Wilson, P. A. *The Professions*. Oxford: Clarendon Press, 1941.

Carter, Reginald. "The Myth of Increasing Non-Work Vs. Work Activities." *Social Problems* 18 (1970), 52–67.

Carter, Richard. *The Doctor Business*. New York: Doubleday, 1958.

Champion, Dean. "Some Impacts of Office Automation upon Status, Role Change, and Depersonalization." *Sociological Quarterly* 8 (1967), 71–84.

Chapman, Stanley. "The Minister: Professional Man of the Church." *Social Forces* 23 (1944), 202–206.

Chase, F., and Guba, E. "Administrative Roles and Behavior." *Review of Educational Research* 25 (1955), 281–298.

Cheek, Neil. "The Social Role of the Professional." In Mark Abrahamson, ed., *The Professional in the Organization*. Chicago: Rand McNally, 1967, pp. 9–16.

Chevigny, Paul. *Police Power: Police Abuses in New York City*. New York: Vintage Books, 1969.

Chinoy, Ely. "The Tradition of Opportunity and the Aspirations of Automobile Workers." *American Journal of Sociology* 57 (1952), 453–459.

———. "Manning the Machines—The Assembly-Line Worker." In Peter Berger, ed., *The Human Shape of Work*. New York: MacMillan, 1964, pp. 51–81.

———. *Automobile Workers and the American Dream*. Boston: Beacon Press, 1965.

Cicourel, Aaron. "The Front and Back of Organizational Leadership: A Case Study." *Pacific Sociological Review* 1 (1958), 54–58.

Coates, Charles, and Pellegrin, Roland R. "Executives and Supervisors: Contrasting Self Conceptions and Conceptions of Each Other." *American Sociological Review* 22 (1957), 217–220.

Cogan, Morris. "Toward a Definition of Profession." *Harvard Educational Review* 23 (1953), 33–50.

———. "The Problem of Defining a Profession." *The Annals* 297 (1955), 105–111.

Cohen, Michael. "The Emergence of Private Practice in Social Work." *Social Problems* 14 (1966), 84–93.

Cohen, Nathan. "Social Work as a Profession." *Social Work Yearbook* (1957), 553–562.

Cole, Robert E. *Japanese Blue Collar: The Changing Tradition.* Berkeley: University of California Press, 1970.

Cole, Stephen, and Cole, Jonathan R. "Scientific Output and Recognition: A Study in the Operation of the Reward System in Science." *American Sociological Review* 32 (1966), 377–390.

Coleman, James et al. "The Diffusion of an Innovation Among Physicians." *Sociometry* 20 (1957), 253–270.

Collins, Orvis. "Ethnic Behavior in Industry: Sponsorship and Rejection in a New England Factory." *American Journal of Sociology* 51 (1946), 293–298.

———, and Moore, David G. *The Enterprising Man.* Bureau of Business Administration, Michigan State University, East Lansing, Michigan, 1964.

——— et al. "Reduction of Output and Social Cleavage in Industry." *Applied Anthropology* 5 (1946), 1–14.

Colvard, Richard. "Foundations and Professions: The Organizational Defense of Autonomy." *Administrative Science Quarterly* 6 (1961), 167–184.

Conant, James. *The Education of American Teachers.* New York: McGraw-Hill, 1963.

Cook, Stuart. "The Psychologist of the Future: Scientist, Professional, or Both?" *American Psychologist* 13 (1958), 635–644.

Copeland, Melvin. *The Executive at Work.* Cambridge: Harvard University Press, 1951.

Corin, Genevieve. "Une Profession Feminine: L'Assistance Social." *Bulletin de L'Institut de Researches Economiques et Sociales* 19 (1953), 749–783.

Corwin, Ronald. "Role Conception and Career Aspiration: A Study of Identity in Nursing." *Sociological Quarterly* 2 (1961), 69–86.

———. "The Professional Employee: A Study of Conflict in Nursing Roles." *American Journal of Sociology* 66 (1961), 604–615.

———. *Militant Professionalism.* New York: Appleton-Century Crofts, 1970.

———, and Taves, Marvin J. "Nursing and Other Health Professions." In Howard E. Freeman et al., *Handbook of Medical Sociology.* Englewood Cliffs, N.J.: Prentice-Hall, 1963, pp. 187–212.

Coser, Rose Laub. "Authority and Decision-Making in a Hospital: A Comparative Analysis." *American Sociological Review* 23 (1958), 56–63.

Cottrell, W. F. "Of Time and the Railroader." *American Sociological Review* 4 (1939), 190–198.

———. *The Railroader.* Stanford: Stanford University Press, 1940.

Crane, Diana. "Scientists at Major and Minor Universities: A Study of Productivity and Recognition." *American Sociological Review* 30 (1965), 699–714.

———. "Social Structure in a Group of Scientists: A Test of the 'Invisible College' Hypothesis." *American Sociological Review* 34 (1969), 335–352.

———. "The Academic Marketplace Revisited: A Study of Faculty Mobility Using the Cartter Ratings." *American Journal of Sociology* 75 (1970), 953–964.

Cressey, Donald. *Theft of the Nation.* New York: Harper & Row, 1969.

Cressy, Paul. *The Taxi-Dance Hall.* Chicago: University of Chicago Press, 1932.

Crozier, Michael. *The Bureaucratic Phenomenon.* Chicago: University of Chicago Press, 1964.

Cumming, Elaine et al. "Policeman as Philosopher, Guide and Friend," *Social Problems* 12 (1965), 276–286.

Cummings, Larry, and ElSalmi, Aly. "The Impact of Role Diversity, Job Level, and Organizational Size on Managerial Satisfaction." *Administrative Science Quarterly* 15 (1970), 1–11.

Cussler, Margaret. *The Woman Executive.* New York: Harcourt Brace, 1958.

Dalton, Melville. "The Industrial 'Rate Buster': A Characterization." *Applied Anthropology* 7 (1948), 5–18.

———. "Conflicts Between Staff and Line Managerial Officers." *American Sociological Review* 15 (1950), 342–351.

———. "Unofficial Union-Management Relations." *American Sociological Review* 15 (1950), 611–619.

———. *Men Who Manage.* New York: John Wiley, 1959.

Daniels, Arlene. "The Captive Professional: Bureaucratic Limitations in the Practice of Military Psychiatry." *Journal of Health and Social Behavior* 10 (1969), 255–265.

Daniels, Morris. "Affect and Its Control in the Medical Intern." *American Journal of Sociology* 66 (1960), 259–267.

———. "Levels of Organization in the Role Position of the Staff Nurse." *Social Forces* 40 (1962), 242–248.

Davis, A. K. "Bureaucratic Patterns in the Navy Officer Corps." *Social Forces* 27 (1948), 143–153.

Davis, F. "Conceptions of Official Leader Roles in the Air Force." *Social Forces* 32 (1954), 253–258.

——— et al. "Scaling Problems in a Study of Conceptions of Air Force Leader Roles." *Public Opinion Quarterly* 18 (1954), 279–286.

Davis, Fred. "The Cabdriver and His Fare: Facets of a Fleeting Relationship." *American Journal of Sociology* 65 (1959), 158–165.

———, ed. *The Nursing Profession.* New York: John Wiley, 1966.

———, and Olesen, Virginia. "Initiation into a Woman's Profession: Identity Problems in the Status Transition of Coed to Student Nurse." *Sociometry* 26 (1963), 89–101.

Davis, Hazel, and Samuelson, Agnes. "Women in Education. *Journal of Social Issues* 6:3 (1950), 25–37.

Davis, Kingsley. "The Sociology of Prostitution. *American Sociological Review* 2 (1937), 744–755.

Davis, Milton. "Variations in Patients' Compliance with Doctors' Orders." *Journal of Medical Examination* 41 (1966), 1037–1048.

Davis, Stanley. "Entrepreneurial Succession." *Administrative Science Quarterly* 13 (1968), 402–416.

Dearborn, D., and Simon, H. "Selective Perception: A Note on the Departmental Identification of Executives." *Sociometry* 21 (1958), 140–144.

De Grazia, Sebastian, *Of Time, Work and Leisure.* Garden City, N.Y.: Anchor Books, 1964.

Delany, William, and Finegold, Alan. "Wall Street Lawyer in the Provinces." *Administrative Science Quarterly* 15 (1970), 191–201.

Denzin, Norman, and Mettlin, Curtis. "Incomplete Professionalization: The Case of Pharmacy." *Social Forces* 46 (1968), 375–382.

Desenberg, B. N. "Occupational Attitudes of Taxi-Dancers." *Sociology and Social Research* 25 (1941), 258–263.

Deutscher, Irwin. *Public Images of the Nurses.* Kansas City, Mo.: Community Studies, Inc., 1955.

Devereux, George, and Weiner, Florence R. "The Occupational Status of Nurses." *American Sociological Review* 15 (1950), 628–634.

Dewey, Donald. "Southern Poverty and The Racial Division of Labor." *New South* 17 (1962), 11–13.

Dexter, L. "The Representative and his District." *Human Organization* 16 (1957), 2–13.

Dictionary of Occupational Titles. 3rd Edition. Washington, D.C.: U. S. Department of Labor, 1965.

Doerschuk, Beatrice. *Women in the Law: An Analysis of Training, Practice and Salaried Positions.* New York: The Bureau of Vocational Information, 1920.

Doherty, Robert E. "Education for Professional Responsibility." *Journal of Engineering Education* 39 (1948), 76–80.

———. "Value Judgments in Professional Education." *Journal of Engineering Education* 40 (1949), 401–405.

Donovan, Frances. *The Woman Who Waits.* Boston: R. G. Badger, 1920.

———. *The Saleslady.* Chicago: University of Chicago Press, 1929.

———. *The School Ma'am.* Frederick A. Stokes, 1938.

Dornbusch, Sanford. "The Military Academy as an Assimilating Institution." *Social Forces* 33 (1955), 316–321.

Drexel Institute of Technology. *An Analysis of the Little Businessman in Philadelphia.* Vol. 1. Drexel Institute: Philadelphia, 1964.

Drucker, Peter. *The Practice of Management.* New York: Harper & Row, 1954.

Dubin, Robert. "Industrial Workers' Worlds: A Study of the Central Life Interests of Industrial Workers." *Social Problems* 3 (1956), 131–142.

———. "Organizational Fictions." In Robert Dubin, ed., *Human Relations in Administration.* 3rd Edition. Englewood Cliffs, N.J.: Prentice-Hall, 1964, pp. 493–498.

Dummett, Clifton. *The Growth and Development of the Negro in Dentistry in the United States.* Chicago: Stanek Press, 1952.

Duncan, Otis Dudley. "Social Origins of Salaried and Self-Employed Professional Workers." *Social Forces* 44 (1965), 186–189.

Dvorak, Eldon. "Will Engineers Unionize?" *Industrial Relations* 2:3 (1963), 45–65.

Dwyer, Robert. "The Negro in the U.S. Army." *Sociology and Social Research* 38 (1953), 103–112.

Eaton, Joseph. "Whence and Whither Social Work? A Sociological Analysis." *Social Work* 1 (1956), 11–26.

Ebaugh, Franklin, and Barnes, Robert H. "Psychiatric Education." *American Journal of Psychiatry* 112 (1956), 561–564.

Eby, Kermit. "The Expert in the Labor Movement." *American Journal of Sociology* 57 (1951), 27–32.

Edwards, Alba M. *Comparative Occupation Statistics for the United States, 1870–1940.* Washington, D.C.: Government Printing Office, 1943.

Edwards, G. Franklin. *The Negro Professional Class*. New York: Free Press, 1959.

Einstadter, Werner. "The Social Organization of Armed Robbery." *Social Problems* 17 (1969), 64–83.

Engel, Gloria. "The Effect of Bureaucracy on the Professional Authority of Physicians." *Journal of Health and Social Behavior* 10 (1969), 30–41.

———. "Professional Autonomy and Bureaucratic Organization." *Administrative Science Quarterly* 15 (1970), 12–21.

Epstein, Cynthia. *Woman's Place: Options and Limits in Professional Careers*. Berkeley: University of California Press, 1970.

———. "Encountering the Male Establishment: Sex-Status Limits on Women's Careers in the Professions." *American Journal of Sociology* 75 (1970), 965–982.

Eron, Leonard. "Effect of Medical Education on Medical Students." *Journal of Medical Education* 10 (1955), 559–566.

Etzioni, Amitai. *A Comparative Analysis of Complex Organizations*. New York: Free Press, 1961.

———. *Modern Organizations*. Englewood Cliffs, N.J.: Prentice-Hall, 1966.

———, ed. *The Semi-Professions and Their Organization*. New York: Free Press, 1969.

Eulau, H. et al. "The Role of the Representative: Some Empirical Observations on the Theory of Edmund Burke." *American Political Science Review* 53 (1959), 742–756.

Evan, William, and Levin, E. G. "Status-Set and Role-Set Conflicts of the Stockbroker: A Problem in the Sociology of Law." *Social Forces* 45 (1966), 73–83.

Faris, Robert E. L. *Chicago Sociology: 1920–1932*. San Francisco: Chandler, 1967.

Faulkner, Robert. *Hollywood Studio Musicians, Their Work and Careers in the Recording Industry*. Chicago: Aldine-Atherton, 1971.

Faunce, William. "Automation and the Automobile Worker." *Social Problems* 6 (1958), 68–77.

———. "Automation in the Automobile Industry: Some Consequences for In-Plant Social Structure." *American Sociological Review* 23 (1958), 401–407.

———. "The Automobile Industry: A Case Study in Alienation." In Howard Boone Jacobson and Joseph Roebuck, eds., *Automation and Society*. New York: Philosophical Library, 1959, pp. 44–53.

———. "Automation and the Division of Labor." *Social Problems* 13 (1965), 149–160.

———, ed. *Readings in Industrial Sociology*. New York: Appleton-Century-Crofts, 1967.

———. *Problems of an Industrial Society*. New York: McGraw-Hill, 1968.

——— et al. "Automation and the Employee." *The Annals* 340 (1962), 60–68.

Fava, Sylvia. "The Status of Women in Professional Sociology." *American Sociological Review* 25 (1960), 271–276.

Ferguson, R. S. "The Doctor-Patient Relationship and 'Functional' Illness." In E. Gartley Jaco, ed., *Patients, Physicians and Illness*. New York: Free Press, 1958, pp. 433–439.

Fichter, Joseph. *Religion as an Occupation*. South Bend, Indiana: University of Notre Dame Press, 1961.

Field, Mark. "Structured Strain and the Role of the Soviet Physician." *American Journal of Sociology* 58 (1953), 493–502.

———. *Doctor and Patient in Soviet Russia*. Cambridge, Mass.: Harvard University Press, 1957.

———. "The Doctor-Patient Relationship in the Perspective of 'Fee for Service' and 'Third Party Medicine.' " *Journal of Health and Human Behavior* 2 (1961), 252–262.

———. "Doctors and Patients." In Alex Inkeles and Kent Geiger, eds., *Soviet Sociology*. Boston: Houghton Mifflin, 1961, pp. 361–381.

Flexner, Abraham. "Is Social Work a Profession?" *School and Society* 1 (1915), 901–911.

Floro, G. "Continuity in City Managers' Careers." *American Journal of Sociology* 61 (1955), 240–248.

Foley, Albert. "The Status and Role of the Negro Priest in the American Catholic Clergy." *American Catholic Sociological Review* 16 (1955), 83–93.

Foley, Eugene. "The Negro Businessman: In Search of a Tradition." *Daedalus* 95 (1966), 107–144.

Foote, Nelson. "The Professionalization of Labor in Detroit." *American Journal of Sociology* 58 (1953), 371–380.

Ford, James L. C. "Women who 'Arrive' in Journalism." In George F. Mott ed., *New Survey of Journalism*. New York: Barnes and Noble, 1950, pp. 133–137.

Form, William, and Geschwender, James. "Social References Basis of Job Satisfaction: The Case of Manual Workers." *American Sociological Review* 27 (1962), 228–237.

Fortune, Editors of. *The Executive Life*. Garden City, N.Y.: Doubleday, 1956.

Fox, Renee. "Training for Uncertainty." In Robert Merton et al., eds., *The Student Physician*. Cambridge: Harvard University Press, 1957, pp. 207–241.

———. "Physicians on the Drug Industry Side of the Prescription Blank: The Dual Commitment to Medical Science and Business." *Journal of Health and Human Behavior* 2 (1961), 3–16.

Freidson, Eliot. "Client Control and Medical Practice." *American Journal of Sociology* 65 (1960), 374–382.

———. "The Organization of Medical Practice and Patient Behavior." *American Journal of Public Health* 51 (1961), 43–52.

———. "Knowledge and Judgment in Professional Evaluation." *Administrative Science Quarterly* 10 (1965), 107–124.

———. "The Impurity of Professional Authority." In Howard S. Becker et al., eds., *Institutions and the Person*. Chicago: Aldine, 1968, pp. 25–34.

———. *Profession of Medicine: A Study of the Sociology of Applied Knowledge*. New York: Dodd, Mead, 1970.

———. *Professional Dominance: The Social Structure of Medical Care*. New York: Atherton Press, 1970.

———, and Rhea, Buford. "Processes of Control in a Company of Equals." *Social Problems* 11 (1963), 119–131.

Friedland, William. "Labor Waste in New York: Rural Exploitation and Migrant Workers." *Trans-action* 6 (1969), 48–53.

Friedman, Norman. "Career Stages and Organizational Role Decisions of Teachers in Two Public Junior Colleges." *Sociology of Education* 40 (1967), 231–245.

Friedmann, Georges. "Outline for a Psycho-Sociology of the Assembly-Line." *Human Organization* 12 (1954), 15–20.

————. *The Anatomy of Work*. New York: Free Press of Glencoe, 1961.

Fullan, Michael. "Industrial Technology and Worker Integration in the Organization." *American Sociological Review* 35 (1970), 1028–1039.

Fulton, Robert. "The Clergyman and the Funeral Director: A Study in Role Conflict." *Social Forces* 39 (1961), 317–323.

Garbin, A. P., and Ballweg, John. "Intra-Plant Mobility of Negro and White Workers." *American Journal of Sociology* 71 (1965), 315–319.

Gardner, B. B., and Whyte, William Foote. "The Man in the Middle: Position and Problems of the Foreman." *Applied Anthropology* 4 (1945), 1–28.

Gaston, Jerry. "The Reward System in British Science." *American Sociological Review* 35 (1970), 718–732.

Geis, Gilbert, ed. *White Collar Criminal*. New York: Atherton Press, 1968.

Gersuny, Carl. "Punishment and Redress in a Modern Factory." *Sociological Quarterly* 8 (1967), 63–70.

Getzels, Jacob. "A Psycho-Sociological Framework for the Study of Educational Administration." *Harvard Educational Review* 22 (1952), 235–246.

————, and Csikzentmihalyi, M. "On the Roles, Values, and Performance of Future Artists: A Conceptual and Empirical Exploration." *Sociological Quarterly* 9 (1969), 516–530.

————, and Guba, Egon G. "The Structure of Roles and Role Conflict in the Teaching Situation." *Journal of Educational Sociology* 29 (1955), 30–40.

Ghiselli, E., and Barthel, R. T. "Role Perceptions of Successful and Unsuccessful Supervisors." *Journal of Applied Psychology* 40 (1956), 241–244.

Gilmore, Harlan. *The Beggar*. Chapel Hill, N.C.: University of North Carolina Press, 1940.

Ginzberg, Eli. *The Labor Leader*. New York: MacMillan, 1948.

————. "Segregation and Manpower Waste." *Phylon* 21 (1960), 311–316.

————, ed. *What Makes an Executive*. New York: Columbia University Press, 1955.

————, ed. *The Negro Challenge to the Business Community*. New York: McGraw-Hill, 1964.

———— et al. *Occupational Choice: An Approach to a General Theory*. New York: Columbia University Press, 1951.

Glaser, Barney. "The Local-Cosmopolitan Scientist." *American Journal of Sociology* 69 (1963), 249–259.

————. *Organizational Scientists: Their Professional Careers*. Indianapolis: Bobbs-Merrill, 1964.

————. *Organizational Careers: A Sourcebook For Theory*. Chicago: Aldine, 1968.

Glaser, William. "Internship Appointments of Medical Students." *Administrative Science Quarterly* 4 (1959), 337–356.

Glenn, Norval. "Occupational Benefits to Whites from Subordination of Negroes." *American Sociological Review* 28 (1963), 443–448.

Goffman, Erving. "On Cooling the Mark Out: Some Aspects of Adaptation to Failure." *Psychiatry* 15 (1952), 451–463.

————. *Asylums*. Garden City, N.Y.: Anchor Books, 1961.

Gold, Raymond. "Janitors Versus Tenants: A Status-Income Dilemma." *American Journal of Sociology* 57 (1952), 486–493.

————. "In the Basement—the Apartment-Building Janitor." In Peter Berger, ed., *The Human Shape of Work*. New York: MacMillan, 1964, pp. 1–49.

Goldner, Fred. "Demotion in Industrial Management." *American Sociological Review* 30 (1965), 714–724.

————, and Ritti, R. R. "Professionalization as Career Immobility." *American Journal of Sociology* 72 (1967), 489–502.

Goldstein, Bernard. "Some Aspects of the Nature of Unionism Among Salaried Professionals in Industry." *American Sociological Review* 20 (1955), 199–205.

————. "The Perspective of Unionized Professionals." *Social Forces* 37 (1959), 323–327.

Goldstein, Sidney. "The Roles of an American Rabbi." *Sociology and Social Research* 38 (1953), 32–37.

Goode, William. "Community Within a Community: The Professions." *American Sociological Review* 22 (1957), 194–200.

————. "Encroachment, Charlatanism, and the Emerging Profession: Psychology, Sociology, and Medicine." *American Sociological Review* 25 (1960), 902–914.

————, and Fowler, Irving. "Incentive Factors in a Low Morale Plant." *American Sociological Review* 14 (1949), 618–624.

Gordon, Gerald et al. "Freedom and Control in Four Types of Scientific Settings." *American Behavioral Scientist* 6 (1962), 39–43.

Goss, Mary. "Influence and Authority Among Physicians in an Out-patient Clinic." *American Sociological Review* 26 (1961), 39–50.

————. "Administration and the Physician." *American Journal of Public Health* 52 (1962), 183–191.

Gottlieb, David. "Processes of Socialization in American Graduate Schools." *Social Forces* 40 (1961), 124–131.

Gouldner, Alvin. "Attitudes of 'Progressive' Trade-Union Leaders." *American Journal of Sociology* 52 (1947), 389–392.

————. *Patterns of Industrial Bureaucracy*. Glencoe, Ill.: Free Press, 1954.

————. "Cosmopolitans and Locals: Toward an Analysis of Latent Social Roles." *Administrative Science Quarterly* 2 (1957), 281–306; and 2 (1958), 444–480.

Granick, David. *The Red Executive: A Study of the Organization Man in Russian Industry*. Garden City, N.Y.: Doubleday, 1961.

Graves, Bennie. "Particularism, Exchange and Organizational Efficiency: A Case Study of a Construction Industry." *Social Forces* 49 (1970), 72–81.

Greenwald, Harold. *The Call Girl: A Social and Psychoanalytic Study*. New York: Ballantine Books, 1958.

————. "The Social and Professional Life of the Call Girl." In Simon Dinitz et al., eds., *Deviance*. New York: Oxford University Press, 1969.

Greenwood, Ernest. "Attributes of a Profession." *Social Work* 2 (1957), 45–55.

Greer, Scott. "Situational Pressures and Functional Role of the Labor Leader." *Social Forces* 32 (1953), 41–45.

————. *Last Man In: Racial Access to Union Power*. Glencoe, Ill.: Free Press, 1959.

Grimes, Andrew J., and Berger, Philip. "Cosmopolitan-Local: Evaluation of the Construct." *Administrative Science Quarterly* 15 (1970), 407–416.

Groff, Patrick. "Social Status of Teachers." *Journal of Educational Sociology* 36 (1962), 20–25.

Gross, Edward. "Some Functional Consequences of Primary Controls in Formal Work Organizations." *American Sociological Review* 18 (1953), 368–373.

———. *Work and Society*. New York: Crowell, 1958.

———. "The Occupational Variable as a Research Category." *American Sociological Review* 24 (1959), 640–649.

———. "Social Integration and the Control of Competition." *American Journal of Sociology* 67 (1961), 270–277.

———. "Industrial Relations." In Robert E. L. Faris, ed., *Handbook of Modern Sociology*. Chicago: Rand McNally, 1964, pp. 619–679.

———. "Cliques in Office Organizations." In Neil Smelser, ed., *Readings on Economic Sociology*. Englewood Cliffs, N.J.: Prentice-Hall, 1965, pp. 96–100.

———. "When Occupations Meet: Professions in Trouble." *Hospital Administration* 12 (1967), 40–59.

———. "Plus Ca Change . . ."? The Sexual Structure of Occupations Over Time." *Social Problems* 16 (1968), 198–208.

Gross, Neal, Mason, Ward, and McEachern, Alexander. *Explorations in Role Analysis: Studies of the School Superintendency Role*. New York: John Wiley, 1958.

Grusky, Oscar. "Role Conflict in Organizations: A Study of Prison Camp Officials." *Administrative Science Quarterly* 3 (1959), 452–472.

———. "Administrative Succession in Formal Organizations." *Social Forces* 39 (1960), 105–115.

———. "Corporate Size, Bureaucratization, and Managerial Succession." *American Journal of Sociology* 67 (1961), 261–269.

———. "Managerial Succession and Organizational Effectiveness." *American Journal of Sociology* 69 (1963), 21–31.

———. "Succession with an Ally." *Administration Science Quarterly* 14 (1969), 155–170.

Guest, Robert. "Work Careers and Aspirations of Automobile Workers." *American Sociological Review* 19 (1954), 155–163.

———. *Organizational Change: The Effect of Successful Leadership*. Homewood, Ill.: Irwin-Dorsey, 1962.

Gustafson, James, "An Analysis of the Problem of the Role of the Minister." *Journal of Religion* 34 (1954), 187–191.

Guzzardi, Walter Jr. *The Young Executives*. New York: New American Library, 1964.

Habenstein, Robert. "Critique of 'Profession' as a Sociological Category." *Sociological Quarterly* 4 (1963), 291–300.

———, and Christ, Edwin A. *Professionalizer, Traditionalizer, and Utilizer*. Columbia, Mo.: University of Missouri Press, 1966.

Hagstrom, Warren. *The Scientific Community*. New York: Basic Books, 1965.

Hall, Douglas T., and Lawler, Edward E. "Job Characteristics and Pressures and the Organizational Integration of Professionals." *Administrative Science Quarterly* 15 (1970), 271–281.

Hall, Oswald. "The Informal Organization of the Medical Profession." *Canadian Journal of Economics and Political Science* 22 (1946), 30–44.

———. "The Stages of a Medical Career." *American Journal of Sociology* 53 (1948), 327–336.

———. "Types of Medical Careers." *American Journal of Sociology* 55 (1949), 243–253.

———. "Half Medical Man, Half Administrator: A Medical Dilemma." *Canadian Public Administration* 2 (1959), 185–194.

Hall, Richard. "Some Organizational Considerations in the Professional-Organizational Relationship." *Administrative Science Quarterly* 12 (1967), 461–478.

———. "Professionalization and Bureaucratization." *American Sociological Review* 33 (1968), 92–104.

———. *Occupations and the Social Structure.* Englewood Cliffs, N.J.: Prentice-Hall, 1969.

Hammond, Phillip, and Mitchell, Robert. "Segmentation of Radicalism—The Case of the Protestant Campus Minister." *American Journal of Sociology* 71 (1965), 133–143.

Harding, J. and Rogrefe, R. "Attitudes of White Department Store Employees Toward Negro Co-Workers." *Journal of Social Issues* 8:1 (1952), 18–28.

Hare, Nathan. "Recent Trends in the Occupational Mobility of Negroes, 1930–1960: An Intracohort Analysis." *Social Forces* 44 (1965), 166–173.

Harmon, Lindsey R. "High School Backgrounds of Science Doctorates." *Science* 133 (March 10, 1961), 670–688.

Harper, Dean, and Emmert, Frederick. "Work Behavior in a Service Industry." *Social Forces* 42 (1963), 216–225.

Harper, Robert A. "Should Marriage Counseling Become a Full Fledged Specialty." *Marriage and Family Living* 15 (1953), 338–340.

Harrington, Michael. *The Other America: Poverty in the United States.* Baltimore: Penguin Books, 1962.

Harris, Richard. "The Effects of Political Change on the Role Set of the Senior Bureaucrats in Ghana and Nigeria." *Administrative Science Quarterly* 13 (1968), 386–401.

Harvey, Edward. "Social Change and the Jazz Musician." *Social Forces* 46 (1967), 34–42.

Hathaway, Starke. "A Study of Human Behavior: The Clinical Psychologist." *American Psychologist* 13 (1958), 257–265.

Haug, Marie, and Sussman, Marvin. "Professionalism and the Public." *Sociological Inquiry* 39 (1969), 57–67.

———. "Professional Autonomy and the Revolt of the Client." *Social Problems* 17 (1969), 153–161.

Hauser, Philip. "The Labor Force as a Field of Interest for the Sociologist." *American Sociological Review* 16 (1951), 530–538.

———. "Labor Force," in Robert E. L. Faris, ed., *Handbook of Modern Sociology.* Chicago: Rand McNally, 1964, pp. 160–190.

Hawkes, Robert. "The Role of the Psychiatric Administrator." *Administrative Science Quarterly* 6 (1961), 89–106.

Hayner, N. S. "Taming the Lumberjack." *American Sociological Review* 10 (1945), 217–225.

Hendersen, L. J. "Physician and Patient as a Social System." *New England Journal of Medicine* 212 (1935), 819–823.

Henning, Dale, and Moseley, Roger. "Authority Role of a Functional Manager: The Controller." *Administrative Science Quarterly* 15 (1970), 482–489.

Henry, William. "The Business Executive: Psychodynamics of a Social Role." *Social Forces* 54 (1949), 286–291.

Henslin, James. "Trust and the Cabdriver." In Marcello Truzzi, ed., *Sociology and Everyday Life*. Englewood Cliffs, N.J.: Prentice-Hall, 1968, pp. 138–158.

Hentoff, Nat. "Race Prejudice in Jazz." *Harper's Magazine* 218 (1959), 72–77.

Herzberg, Frederick et al. *The Motivation to Work*. 2nd Ed. New York: John Wiley, 1959.

Hetsler, S. "Variations in Role Playing Patterns Among Different Echelons of Bureaucratic Leaders." *American Sociological Review* 20 (1955), 700–706.

Hirsch, Walter. *Scientists in American Industry*. New York: Random House, 1968.

Hirschi, Travis. "The Professional Prostitute." *Berkeley Journal of Sociology* 7 (1962), 33–49.

Hodge, Robert, and Hodge, Patricia. "Occupational Assimilation as a Competitive Process." *American Journal of Sociology* 71 (1965), 249–264.

Hodge, Robert, and Treiman, Donald. "Occupational Mobility and Attitudes Toward Negroes." *American Sociological Review* 31 (1966), 93–102.

Hodge, Robert et al. "Occupational Prestige in the United States: 1925–1963." In Reinhard Bendix and Seymour Martin Lipset, eds., *Class, Status, and Power: Social Stratification in Comparative Perspective*. 2nd Edition. New York: Free Press, 1966, pp. 322–333.

Hollingshead, August. "Ingroup Membership and Academic Selection." *American Sociological Review* 3 (1938), 826–833.

Homans, George. "Status Among Clerical Workers." *Human Organization* 12 (1953), 5–10.

———. "The Western Electric Researches." In Amitai Etzioni, ed., *Readings on Modern Organizations*. Englewood Cliffs, N.J.: Prentice-Hall, 1969, pp. 99–114.

Hoos, Ida. "When the Computer Takes Over the Office." *Harvard Business Review* 38 (1960), 102–112.

———. *Automation in the Office*. Washington, D.C.: Public Affairs Press, 1961.

Hope, John, II, and Shelton, E. "The Negro in the Federal Government." *Journal of Negro Education* 32 (1963), 367–374.

Hornum, Finn. "The Executioner." In Marcello Truzzi, ed., *Sociology and Everyday Life*. Englewood Cliffs, N.J.: Prentice-Hall, 1968, pp. 125–137.

Howard, David. "An Exploratory Study of Attitudes of Negro Professionals Toward Competition with Whites." *Social Forces* 45 (1966), 20–27.

Howton, F. William. *Functionaries*. Chicago: Quandrangle Books, 1969.

———, and Rosenberg, Bernard. "The Salesman: Ideology and Self-Imagery in a Protoypic Occupation." *Social Research* 32 (1965), 277–298.

Hughes, Everett C. "Institutional Office and the Person." *American Journal of Sociology* 43 (1937), 404–413.

———. "The Knitting of Racial Groups in Industry." *American Sociological Review* 11 (1946), 512–519.

———. "Queries Concerning Industry and Society Growing Out of Study of Ethnic Relations in Industry." *American Sociological Review* 14 (1949), 211–220.

———. "The Sociological Study of Work: An Editorial Foreword." *American Journal of Sociology* 57 (1952), 423–426.

———. "The Making of a Physician: General Statement of Ideas and Problems." *Human Organization* 14 (1956), 21–25.

———. *Men and Their Work*. Glencoe, Ill.: Free Press, 1958.

———. "Stress and Strain in Professional Education." *Harvard Educational Review* 29 (1959), 319–329.

———. "Education for a Profession." *Library Quarterly* 31 (1961), 336–343.

———. "Professions." In Kenneth S. Lynn, ed., *The Professions in America*. Boston: Beacon Press, 1967, pp. 1–14.

———. "The Humble and the Proud: The Comparative Study of Occupations." *Sociological Quarterly* 11 (1970), 147–156.

———, and Hughes, Helen. *Where Peoples Meet: Racial and Ethnic Frontiers*. Glencoe, Ill.: Free Press, 1952.

——— et al. *Twenty Thousand Nurses Tell Their Story*. Philadelphia: Lippincott, 1958.

Huntington, Mary Jean. "The Development of a Professional Self-Image." In Robert Merton, George Reader, and Patricia Kendall, eds., *The Student Physician: Introductory Studies in the Sociology of Medical Education*. Cambridge, Mass.: Harvard University Press, 1957, pp. 176–187.

Inkeles, Alex. "Industrial Man: The Relation of Status to Experience, Perception, and Value." *American Journal of Sociology* 66 (1960), 1–31.

———, and Rossi, Peter. "National Comparisons of Occupational Prestige." *American Journal of Sociology* 61 (1956), 329–339.

Jackman, Norman et al. "The Self-Image of the Prostitute." *Sociological Quarterly* 4 (1963), 150–161.

Jaco, E. Gartley, ed. *Patients, Physicians and Illness*. Glencoe, Ill.: Free Press, 1958.

Jacobson, Eugene et al. "Employee Attitudes Toward Technological Change in a Medium Sized Insurance Company." *Journal of Applied Psychology* 43 (1959), 349–354.

Jacobson, Julius, ed. *The Negro and the American Labor Movement*. Garden City, N.Y.: Anchor Books, 1968.

Jahoda, Marie. "A Social Psychologist Views Nursing as a Profession." *American Journal of Nursing* 61 (1961), 52–56.

Janowitz, Morris. *The Professional Soldier: A Social and Political Portrait*. New York: Free Press, 1960.

———, and Delany, William. "The Bureaucrat and the Public: A Study of Informative Perspectives." *Administrative Science Quarterly* 2 (1957), 141–162.

Jefferson, Miles. "The Negro on Broadway, 1954–55: More Space Than Substance." *Phylon* 16 (1955), 303–312.

———. "The Negro on Broadway, 1955–56: Pits and Peaks in an Active Season." *Phylon* 17:3 (1956), 227–237.

Johnson, Charles. *The Negro College Graduate*. Chapel Hill, N.C.: University of North Carolina Press, 1938.

Johnson, Elmer. "The Professional in Correction: Status and Prospects." *Social Forces* 40 (1961), 168–176.

Johnstone, Quintin, and Hopson, Dan Jr. *Lawyers and Their Work.* Indianapolis: Bobbs-Merrill, 1967.

Jones, Jean. "The Social Role of the Priest." *American Catholic Sociological Review* 16 (1955), 94–103.

Joseph, Myron. "The Role of the Field Staff Representative." *Industrial and Labor Relations Review* 12 (1959), 353–369.

Kadushin, Charles. "The Professional Self-Concept of Music Students." *American Journal of Sociology* 66 (1961), 389–404.

———. "Social Distance Between Client and Professional." *American Journal of Sociology* 67 (1962), 517–531.

Kahl, Joseph. "Some Social Concomitants of Industrialization and Urbanization." In William Faunce, ed., *Readings in Industrial Sociology.* New York: Appleton-Century-Crofts, 1967, pp. 28–67.

Kahn, Alfred, ed. *Issues in American Social Work.* New York: Columbia University Press, 1959.

Kahn, Robert et al. *Organizational Stress: Studies in Role Conflict and Ambiguity.* New York: John Wiley, 1964.

Kammerer, Gladys. "Role Diversity of City Managers." *Administrative Science Quarterly* 8 (1964), 421–442.

Kaplan, Norman. "Role of the Research Administrator." *Administrative Science Quarterly* 4 (1959), 20–42.

Karsh, Bernard et al. "The Union Organizer and His Tactics: A Case Study." *American Journal of Sociology* 59 (1953), 113–122.

———, and Jack Siegman. "Functions of Ignorance in Introducing Automation." *Social Problems* 12 (1964), 141–150.

Katz, Daniel et al. *Productivity, Supervision and Morale Among Railroad Workers.* Institute for Social Research, Ann Arbor, Michigan: University of Michigan Press, 1951.

Katz, Fred E. "Occupational Contact Networks." *Social Forces* 37 (1958), 52–55.

———, and Martin, Harry W. "Career Choice Processes." *Social Forces* 41 (1962), 149–154.

Kendall, Katherine A. "Social Work Education: A Responsibility of the Total Profession." *Social Casework* 34 (1953), 17–23.

Kendall, Patricia. "Impact of Training Programs on the Young Physician's Attitudes and Experiences." *The Journal of the American Medical Association* 176 (June 24, 1961), 992–997.

———. *The Relationship Between Medical Educators and Medical Practitioners: Sources of Strain and Occasions for Cooperation.* Evanston, Ill.: Association of American Medical Colleges, 1965.

———, and Merton, Robert. "Medical Education as a Social Process." In E. Gartley Jaco, ed., *Patients, Physicians and Illness.* Glencoe, Ill.: Free Press, 1958, pp. 321–350.

———, and Selvin, Hanan. "Tendencies Toward Specialization in Medical Training." In Robert Merton et al., *The Student Physician.* Cambridge, Mass: Harvard University Press, 1957, pp. 153–174.

Kerckhoff, Richard K. "The Profession of Marriage Counseling as Viewed by Members of Four Allied Professions: A Study in the Sociology of Occupations." *Marriage and Family Living* 15 (1953), 340–344.

Kidneigh, John C. "Social Work as a Profession." In Russell H. Kurtz, ed., *Social Work Yearbook*. New York: National Association of Social Workers, 1957, pp. 553–562.

Kiehl, Robert. "Negro Engineers and Students Report on Their Profession." *Journal of Negro Education* 27 (1958), 189–194.

Killian, Lewis. "The Effects of Southern White Workers on Race Relations in Northern Plants." *American Sociological Review* 17 (1952), 327–331.

Kimbrough, Emory. "The Role of the Banker in a Small City." *Social Forces* 36 (1958), 316–322.

Kisch, Arnold, and Reeder, Leo G. "Client Evaluation and Physician Performance." *Journal of Health and Social Behavior* 10 (1969), 51–59.

Kitchen, Helen, ed. *The Educated African*. New York: Praeger, 1962.

Knudsen, Dean D. "The Declining Status of Women: Popular Myths and the Failure of Functionalist Thought." *Social Forces* 48 (1969), 183–193.

Koenig, S. "Ethnic Groups in Connecticut Industry." *Social Forces* 20 (1941), 96–105.

Koerner, James. *The Miseducation of American Teachers*. Boston: Houghton Mifflin, 1963.

Kornhauser, Arthur. *Mental Health of the Industrial Worker: A Detroit Study*. New York: John Wiley, 1965.

Kornhauser, William. "The Negro Union Official: A Study of Sponsorship and Control." *American Journal of Sociology* 57 (1952), 443–453.

———. *Scientists in Industry*. Berkeley: University of California Press, 1963.

Kosa, John, and Coker, Robert Jr. "The Female Physician in Public Health: Conflict and Reconciliation of the Sex and Professional Roles." *Sociology and Social Research* 49 (1965), 294–305.

Kriesberg, Louis. "The Retail Furrier: Concepts of Security and Success." *American Journal of Sociology* 57 (1952), 478–485.

———. "Careers, Organization Size, and Succession." *American Journal of Sociology* 68 (1962), 335–359.

———. "The Bases of Occupational Prestige: The Case of Dentists." *American Sociological Review* 27 (1962), 238–244.

Kutner, Bernard. "Surgeons and Their Patients: A Study in Social Perception." In E. Gartley Jaco, ed., *Patients, Physicians and Illness*. Glencoe, Ill.: Free Press, 1958, pp. 384–397.

Kuvlevsky, William, and Bealer, Robert C. "A Clarification of the Concept 'Occupational Choice.'" *Rural Sociology* 31 (1966), 265–276.

Ladinsky, Jack. "Careers of Lawyers, Law Practice and Legal Institutions." *American Sociological Review* 28 (1963), 47–54.

———. "Higher Education and Work Achievement Among Lawyers." *Sociological Quarterly* 8 (1967), 222–232.

Lancour, Harold. "The Librarian's Search for Status." *Library Quarterly* 31 (1961), 369–381.

Landsberger, Henry. "Interaction Process Analysis of Professional Behavior: A Study of Labor Mediators in Twelve Labor Management Disputes." *American Sociological Review* 20 (1955), 566–575.

LaPorte, Todd. "Conditions of Strain and Accommodation in Industrial Research Organizations." *Administrative Science Quarterly* 20 (1965), 21–38.

Larey, John, ed. *The Accounting Profession*. New York: American Institute of Certified Public Accountants, 1962.

Lazarsfeld, Paul, and Thielens, Wagner Jr. *The Academic Mind*. New York: Free Press, 1958.

Leggett, John C. *Class, Race, and Labor: Working Class Consciousness in Detroit*. London: Oxford University Press, 1968.

Lemert, Edwin. "The Behavior of the Systematic Check Forger." *Social Problems* 6 (1958), 141–148.

Leontief, Wassily. "Machines and Man." *Scientific American* 187 (1952), 150–160.

Levenson, Bernard. "Bureaucratic Succession." In Amitai Etzioni, ed., *Complex Organizations: A Sociological Reader*. New York: Holt, Rinehart and Winston, 1961, pp. 362–375.

Levinson, Harry. "The Psychologist in Industry," *Harvard Business Review* 37 (1959), pp. 93–99.

Lieberman, Myron. *Education as a Profession*. Englewood Cliffs, N.J.: Prentice-Hall, 1956.

Lieberson, Stanley. "Ethnic Groups and the Practice of Medicine." *American Sociological Review* 23 (1958), 542–549.

———, and Fuguitt, Glenn. "Negro-White Occupational Differences in the Absence of Discrimination." *American Journal of Sociology* 73 (1967), 188–200.

Lipset, Seymour Martin, and Bendix, Reinhard. *Social Mobility in Industrial Society*. Berkeley: University of California Press, 1959.

———, Trow, Martin, and Coleman, James. *Union Democracy*. Garden City, N.Y.: Anchor Books, 1962.

——— et al. "Job Plans and Entry into the Labor Market." *Social Forces* 33 (1955), 224–232.

Little, R. "The Sick Soldier and the Medical Ward Officer." *Human Organization* 15 (1956), 22–24.

Lopata, Helen Znaniecki. "The Life Cycle and Social Role of Housewife." In Marcello Truzzi, ed., *Sociology and Everyday Life*. Englewood Cliffs, N.J.: Prentice-Hall, 1968, pp. 111–124.

Lopate, Carol. *Women in Medicine*. Baltimore: Johns Hopkins Press, 1968.

Lortie, Dan C. "Anesthesia: From Nurse's Work to Medical Specialty." In E. Gartley Jaco, ed., *Patients, Physicians and Illness*. Glencoe, Ill.: Free Press, 1958, pp. 405–412.

———. "Laymen to Lawmen: Law School, Careers, and Professional Socialization." *Harvard Educational Review* 29 (1959), 352–369.

———. "The Balance of Control and Autonomy in Elementary School Teaching." In Amitai Etzioni, ed., *The Semi-Professions and Their Organization*. New York: Free Press, 1969, pp. 1–53.

Lupton, T. *On the Shop Floor: Two Studies of Workshop Organization and Output*. New York: MacMillan, 1963.

Lyman, Elizabeth. "Occupational Difference in the Value Attached to Work." *American Journal of Sociology* 61 (1955), 138–144.

Lynn, Kenneth S., ed. *The Professions in America*. Boston: Beacon Press, 1967.

MacIver, Robert. "Social Significance of Professional Ethics." *The Annals* 237 (1955), 118–124.

Mack, Raymond. "Ecological Patterns in an Industrial Shop." *Social Forces* 32 (1954), 351–356.

———. "Occupational Determinateness: A Problem and Hypothesis in Role Theory." *Social Forces* 35 (1956), 20–25.

MacRae, Duncan Jr. "The Role of the State Legislator in Massachusetts." *American Sociological Review* 19 (1954), 185–195.

Maddock, Charles. "The Corporation Law Department." *Harvard Business Review* 30 (1952), 119–136.

Magid, Alvin. "Dimensions of Administrative Role and Conflict Resolution Among Local Officials in Northern Nigeria." *Administrative Science Quarterly* 12 (1967), 321–328.

Magistretti, Frank. "Sociological Factors in the Structuring of Industrial Workers' Teams." *American Journal of Sociology* 60 (1955), 536–540.

Mann, Floyd, and Dent, J. "The Supervisor: Member of Two Organizational Families." *Harvard Business Review* 32 (1954), 103–112.

———, and Williams, L. K. "Organizational Impact of White Collar Automation." *Proceedings of the Eleventh Annual Meeting of the Industrial Relations Research Association.* Chicago: Industrial Relations Research Association, Publication No. 22, 1959, pp. 59–69.

———. "Observations on the Dynamics of a Change to Electronic Data Processing Equipment." *Administrative Science Quarterly* 5 (1960), 217–256.

———. "Some Effects of the Changing Work Environment in the Office." *Journal of Social Issues* 18 (1962), 90–101.

Marcson, Simon. *The Scientist in Industry.* Princeton, N.J.: Industrial Relations Section, Princeton University, 1960.

———. "Organization and Authority in Industrial Research." *Social Forces* 40 (1961), 72–80.

———. "Decision-Making in a University Physics Department." *American Behavioral Scientist* 6 (1962), 29–37.

Marcus, Philip. "Union Conventions and Executive Boards: A Formal Analysis of Organizational Structure." *American Sociological Review* 31 (1966), 61–70.

Margulies, Harold. "The Structure of Medical Education in Pakistan." *Journal of Medical Education* 38 (1963), 752–759.

Marshall, Ray. *The Negro and Organized Labor.* New York: John Wiley, 1965.

———. *The Negro Worker and the Trade Unions.* New York: John Wiley, 1965.

Mason, Ward, and Gross, Neal. "Intra-Occupational Prestige Differentiation: The School Superintendency." *American Sociological Review* 20 (1955), 326–331.

Mattfeld, Jacquelyn, and Van Aken, Carol, eds. *Women and the Scientific Professions.* Cambridge, Mass.: MIT Press, 1965.

Mauksch, Hans. "Becoming a Nurse: A Selective View." *The Annals* 346 (1963), 88–98.

Mayhew, Leon, and Reiss, Albert Jr. "The Social Organization of Legal Contacts." *American Sociological Review* 34 (1969), 309–318.

McCarty, Donald J., and Ramsey, Charles E. *The School Managers: Power and Conflict in American Public Education.* Westport, Conn.: Greenwood, 1971.

McCorkel, R. James. "Chicago and Ivy League Sociologies of Occupations: A Comparative Analysis of Assumptions, Theories, and Methods." Paper presented at the meetings of the Southern Sociological Society, 1969, New Orleans, La.

McCormack, Thelma. "The Druggist's Dilemma: Problems of a Marginal Occupation." *American Journal of Sociology* 61 (1956), 308–315.

McCormick, Mary J. "Professional Responsibility and the Professional Image." *Social Casework* 47 (1966), 635–641.

McDonald, Lois et al. *Leadership Dynamics and the Trade Union Leader.* New York: New York University Press, 1959.

McEwen, William. "Position Conflict and Professional Orientation in a Research Organization." *Administrative Science Quarterly* 1 (1956), 208–224.

McGregor, Douglas. *The Human Side of Enterprise.* New York: McGraw-Hill, 1960.

Melton, Marli Schenck. "Health Manpower and Negro Health: The Negro Physician." *Journal of Medical Education* 43 (1968), 788–814.

Meltzer, Leo, and Salter, James. "Organizational Structure and the Performance and Job Satisfaction of Physiologists." *American Sociological Review* 27 (1962), 351–362.

Menzel, Herbert. "Innovation, Integration, and Marginality: A Survey of Physicians." *American Sociological Review* 25 (1960), 704–713.

Merton, Robert. "Bureaucratic Structure and Personality." *Social Forces* 17 (1940), 560–568.

———. "The Search for Professional Status: Sources, Costs, and Consequences." *American Journal of Nursing* 60 (1960), 662–664.

———, Reader, George, and Kendall, Patricia, eds. *The Student Physician: Introductory Studies in the Sociology of Medical Education.* Cambridge, Mass.: Harvard University Press, 1957.

Methewson, Stanley. *Restriction of Output Among Unorganized Workers.* New York: Viking Press, 1931.

Meyer, Arthur. "Functions of the Mediator in Collective Bargaining." *Industrial and Labor Relations Review* 13 (1960), 159–165.

Michels, Robert. *Political Parties.* New York: Free Press, 1962.

Miller, Delbert. "Supervisor: Evolution of an Organizational Role." In Gerald Bell, ed., *Organizations and Human Behavior.* Englewood Cliffs, N.J.: Prentice-Hall, 1967, pp. 282–289.

———, and Form, William. *Industrial Sociology.* New York: Harper & Row, 1964.

———, and Shull, Fremont. "The Prediction of Administrative Role Conflict Resolution." *Administrative Science Quarterly* 7 (1962), 143–160.

Miller, Frank, and Coghill, M. "Sex and the Personnel Manager." *Industrial and Labor Relations Review* 18 (1964), 32–44.

Miller, George. "Professionals in Bureaucracy: Alienation Among Industrial Scientists and Engineers." *American Sociological Review* 32 (1967), 755–768.

Miller, Norman P. "Professional Education." *The Annals* 313 (1957), 58–67.

Miller, Robert et al. *The Practice of Local Union Leadership: A Study of Five Local Unions.* Columbus, Ohio: Ohio State University Press, 1965.

Miller, Stephen. "The Social Base of Sales Behavior." *Social Problems* 12 (1964), 15–24.

Mills, C. Wright. *The New Men of Power.* New York: Harcourt, Brace and World, 1948.

———. *White Collar.* New York: Oxford University Press, 1951.

————. *The Power Elite*. New York: Oxford University Press, 1957.

Minard, R. D. "Race Relationships in the Pocahontas Coal Field." *Journal of Social Issues* 8:1 (1952), 29–44.

Mitchell, William. "Occupational Role Strains: The American Elective Public Official." *Administrative Science Quarterly* 3 (1958), 211–228.

Moeller, Gerald. "Bureaucracy and Teachers' Sense of Power." *Administrator's Notebook* 11 (1962), 1–4.

Montagna, Paul. "Professionalization and Bureaucratization in Large Professional Organizations." *American Journal of Sociology* 74 (1968), 138–146.

Moore, David, and Renck, R. "The Professional Employee in Industry." *Journal of Business* 28 (1955), 58–66.

Moore, Wilbert. *Industrial Relations and the Social Order*. New York: MacMillan, 1951.

————. *The Conduct of the Corporation*. New York: Random House, 1962.

————. *The Professions: Roles and Rules*. New York: Russell Sage Foundation, 1970.

More, Douglas. "A Note on Occupational Origins of Health Service Professions." *American Sociological Review* 25 (1960), 403–404.

————. "Demotion." *Social Problems* 9 (1962), 213–221.

————, and Kohn, Nathan Jr. "Some Motives for Entering Dentistry." *American Journal of Sociology* 66 (1960), 48–53.

Morris, Charles. "Career Patterns of Teachers." In Lindley J. Stiles, ed., *The Teacher's Role in American Society*. New York: Harper & Row, 1957, pp. 247–263.

Morris, Richard, and Murphy, Raymond. "The Situs Dimension in Occupational Structure." *American Sociological Review* 24 (1959), 231–239.

Morse, Dean. *The Peripheral Worker*. New York: Columbia University Press, 1969.

Morse, Nancy. *Satisfactions in the White-Collar Job*. Ann Arbor, Michigan: Survey Research Center, University of Michigan, 1953.

————, and Weiss, Robert. "The Function and Meaning of Work and the Job." *American Sociological Review* 20 (1955), 191–198.

Moskos, Charles Jr. "Racial Integration in the Armed Forces." *American Journal of Sociology* 72 (1966), 132–148.

Mouzelis, Nicos. *Organization and Bureaucracy: An Analysis of Modern Theories*. London: Routledge and Kegan Paul, 1967.

Mowrer, O. Hobart. "Payment or Repayment? The Problem of Private Practice." *American Psychologist* 18 (1963), 577–580.

Myers, R. R. "Inter-Personal Relations in the Building Industry." *Human Organization* 5 (1946), 1–7.

Nash, Dennison. "The Socialization of an Artist: The American Composer." *Social Forces* 35 (1957), 307–313.

National Manpower Council. *Womanpower*. New York: Columbia University Press, 1957.

National Opinion Research Center. "Jobs and Occupations." In Reinhard Bendix and Seymour Martin Lipset, *Class Status and Power*. Glencoe, Ill.: Free Press, 1954.

Neal, Arthur, and Rettig, Solomon. "Dimensions of Alienation Among Manual and Non-Manual Workers." *American Sociological Review* 28 (1963), 599–608.

Nelkin, Dorothy. "A Response to Marginality: The Case of Migrant Farm Workers." *British Journal of Sociology* 20 (1969), 375–389.

————. "Unpredictability and Life Style in a Migrant Labor Camp." *Social Problems* 17 (1970), 472–487.

New, Peter K. "The Osteopathic Student: A Study in Dilemma." In E. Gartley Jaco, ed., *Patients, Physicians and Illness*. New York: Free Press, 1958, pp. 413–421.

Newcomer, Mable. "The Little Businessman: A Study of Business Proprietors in Poughkeepsie, New York." *Business History Review* 35 (1961), 477–531.

Nicholson, Lowell S. *The Law Schools of the United States*. Baltimore: Lord Baltimore Press, 1958.

Niederhoffer, Arthur. *Behind the Shield: The Police in Urban Society*. Garden City, N.Y.: Anchor Books, 1969.

Nosow, Sigmund, and Form, William. *Man, Work, and Society*. New York: Basic Books, 1962.

Nye, F. I., and Hoffman, Lois. *The Employed Mother in America*. Chicago: Rand McNally, 1963.

O'Donovan, Thomas, and Deegan, Arthur X. "Some Career Determinants of Church Executives." *Sociology and Social Research* 48 (1963), 58–68.

Opler, Marvin. "Industrial Societies and the Changing Roles of Doctors." *Journal of Occupational Medicine* 4 (1962), 237–241.

Orzack, Louis. "Work as a 'Central Life Interest' of Professionals." In Erwin Smigel, ed., *Work and Leisure*. New Haven, Conn.: College and University Press, 1963, pp. 73–84.

Park, Robert et al. *The City*. Chicago: University of Chicago Press, 1925.

Parsons, Talcott. "Remarks on Education and the Professions." *International Journal of Ethics* 47 (1937), 365–369.

————. "The Professions and Social Structure." *Social Forces* 17 (1939), 457–467.

————. "Illness and the Role of the Physician: A Sociological Perspective." *American Journal of Orthopsychiatry* 21 (1951), 452–460.

————. "Professional Training and the Role of the Professions in American Society." In *Scientific Manpower 1959*. Washington, D.C.: National Science Foundation, 1959, pp. 536–547.

————. "Some Trends of Change in American Society: Their Bearing on Medical Education." In Talcott Parsons, ed., *Structure and Process in Modern Societies*. New York: Free Press, 1960, pp. 280–294.

————. "Professions." In David Sills, ed., *International Encyclopedia of the Social Sciences*. New York: Free Press, 1968, vol. 12, pp. 536–547.

Pauling, N. G. "Some Neglected Areas of Research on the Effects of Automation and Other Technological Change on Workers." *Journal of Business* 37 (1964), 261–273.

Pearlin, Leonard. "Nurse-Patient Social Distance and the Structural Context of a Mental Hospital." *American Sociological Review* 27 (1962), 56–65.

Pease, John. "Faculty Influence and Professional Participation of Doctoral Students." *Sociological Inquiry* 37 (1967), 63–70.

Peck, Sidney. *The Rank and File Leader*. New Haven, Conn.: College and University Press, 1963.

Pelz, Donald. "Influence: A Key to Effective Leadership in the First-Line Supervisor." *Personnel* 29 (1952), 209–217.

———. "Interaction and Attitudes Between Scientists and Auxiliary Staff: I. Viewpoint of Staff; II. Viewpoint of Scientists." *Administrative Science Quarterly* 4 (1959), 321–336; and 4 (1960), 410–425.

———, and Andrews, Frank. *Scientists in Organizations: Productive Climates for Research and Development.* New York: John Wiley, 1966.

Pennings, J. M. "Work-Value Systems of White-Collar Workers." *Administrative Science Quarterly* 15 (1970), 397–405.

Perrucci, Carolyn Cummings. "Minority Status and the Pursuit of Professional Careers: Women in Science and Engineering." *Social Forces* 49 (1970), 245–259.

Perrucci, Robert, and Gerstl, Joel. *Profession Without Community: Engineers in American Society.* New York: Random House, 1969.

———, eds. *The Engineers and the Social System.* New York: John Wiley, 1969.

Perry, Cyrus C. "A Code of Ethics for Public School Teachers." *The Annals* 297 (1955), 76–82.

Phelps, Charles. "Women in American Medicine." *Journal of Medical Education* 43 (1968), 916–924.

Polsky, Ned. "The Hustler." *Social Problems* 12 (1964), 3–15.

———. *Hustlers, Beats, and Others.* Garden City, N.Y.: Anchor Books, 1969.

Powers, L., Parmelle, R. D., and Wiesenfeld, H. "Practice Patterns of Women and Men Physicians." *Journal of Medical Education* 44 (1969), 381–391.

Prandy, Kenneth. *Professional Employees: A Study of Scientists and Engineers.* London: Faber and Faber, 1965.

Pratt, Lois et al. "Physicians' Views on the Level of Information Among Patients." In E. Gartley Jaco, ed., *Patients, Physicians and Illness.* New York: Free Press, 1958, pp. 222–229.

Prewitt, Kenneth. *The Recruitment of Political Leaders.* Indianapolis: Bobbs-Merrill, 1970.

Price, Daniel O. "Occupational Changes Among Whites and Nonwhites, with Projections for 1970." *Social Science Quarterly* 49 (1968), 563–572.

Psatha, George. "Toward a Theory of Occupational Choice for Women." *Sociology and Social Research* 52 (1958), 254–268.

———. "The Fate of Idealism in Nursing School." *Journal of Health and Social Behavior* 9 (1968), 52–65.

———, and Henslin, James. "Dispatched Orders and the Cab Driver." *Social Problems* 15 (1967), 424–443.

Purcell, Theodore. *Blue-collar Man: Patterns of Dual Allegiance in Industry.* Cambridge, Mass.: Harvard University Press, 1960.

Quinney, Earl. "Occupational Structure and Criminal Behavior: Prescription Violation by Retail Pharmacists." *Social Problems* 11 (1963), 179–185.

———. "Adjustment to Occupational Role Strain; The Case of Retail Pharmacy." *Southwestern Social Science Quarterly* 44 (1964), 367–376.

Radom, Matthew. *The Social Scientist in American Industry: The Self-Perception of Role, Motivation, and Career.* New Brunswick, N.J.: Rutgers University Press, 1970.

Rapaport, Lydia. "In Defense of Social Work: An Examination of Stress in the Profession." *Social Science Review* 34 (1960), 62–74.

Raphael, Edna. "Power Structure and Membership Dispersion in Unions." *American Journal of Sociology* 71 (1965), 274–283.

Raulet, H. M. "The Health Professional and the Flouridation Issue: A Case of Role Conflict." *Journal of Social Issues* 17:4 (1961), 45–54.

Rayack, Elton. "Discrimination and the Occupational Progress of Negroes." *Review of Economics and Statistics* 43 (1961), 209–214.

Rayback, Joseph. *A History of American Labor*. New York: Free Press, 1966.

Reader, W. J. *Professional Men*. New York: Basic Books, 1966.

Record, Wilson. "Some Reflections on Bureaucratic Trends in Sociological Research." *American Sociological Review* 25 (1960), 411–414.

Reichstein, Kenneth. "Ambulance Chasing: A Case Study of Deviation and Control within the Legal Profession." *Social Problems* 13 (1965), 3–17.

Reif, Fred and Strauss, Anselm. "The Impact of Rapid Discovery Upon the Scientist's Career." *Social Problems* 12 (1965), 297–311.

Reiss, Albert J. Jr. "Occupational Mobility of Professional Workers." *American Sociological Review* 20 (1955), 693–700.

Reissman, Leonard. "A Study of Role Conceptions in Bureaucracy." *Social Forces* 27 (1949), 305–310.

———. "Life Careers, Power and the Professions: The Retired Army General." *American Sociological Review* 21 (1956), 215–222.

———, and Rohrer, John, eds. *Change and Dilemma in the Nursing Profession.* New York: Putnam's, 1957.

——— et al. "The Motivation and Socialization of Medical Students." *Journal of Health and Human Behavior* 1 (1960), 174–188.

Reitzes, Dietrick. *Negroes and Medicine*. Cambridge, Mass.: Harvard University Press, 1958.

Rettig, Solomon et al. "Status Overestimation, Objective Status, and Job Satisfaction Among Professions." *American Sociological Review* 23 (1958), 75–81.

Richard, Michael. "The Ideology of Negro Physicians: A Test of Mobility and Status Chrystallization Theory." *Social Problems* 17 (1969), 20–29.

———. "The Negro Physician: Babbitt or Revolutionary?" *Journal of Health and Social Behavior* 10 (1969), 265–275.

Ritzer, George. "Professionalism: An Ignored Dimension." Paper presented at the meetings of the American Sociological Association, September, 1970, Washington, D.C.

———, and Trice, Harrison. *An Occupation in Conflict: A Study of the Personnel Manager*. Ithaca, N.Y.: Cornell University, 1969.

———. "An Empirical Study of Howard Becker's Side-Bet Theory." *Social Forces* 47 (1969), 475–478.

———. "On the Problem of Clarifying Commitment Theory." *Social Forces* 48 (1970), 530–533.

———, and Gottesman, Susan. "Profile of a Professional." *The Personnel Administrator* 13 (1968), 1–7.

Robin, Stanley. "The Female in Engineering." In Robert Perrucci and Joel E. Gerstl, eds., *The Engineers and the Social System*. New York: John Wiley, 1969, pp. 203–219.

Rodehaver, Myles. "Ministers on the Move: A Study of Social Mobility in Church Leadership." *Rural Sociology* 13 (1948), 400–410.

Roe, Anne. *Psychology of Occupations*. New York: Harper & Brothers, 1957.

Roebuck, Julian. "The Numbers Man." In Simon Dinitz et al., eds., *Deviance: Studies in Process of Stigmatization and Societal Reaction.* New York: Oxford University Press, 1969, pp. 714–782.

Roethlisberger, Fritz. "The Foreman: Master and Victim of Double Talk." *Harvard Business Review* 23 (1945), 283–298.

———, and Dickson, William. *Management and the Worker.* New York: John Wiley, 1964.

Rogoff, Natalie. "The Decision to Study Medicine." In Robert Merton, George Reader, and Patricia Kendall, eds., *The Student Physician.* Cambridge, Mass.: Harvard University Press, 1957, pp. 109–128.

Rosen, Bernard, and Bates, Alan. "The Structure of Socialization in Graduate School." *Sociological Inquiry* 37 (1967), 71–84.

Rosen, Hjalmar, and Rosen, R. A. H. "Personality Variable and Role in a Union Business Agent." *Journal of Applied Psychology* 41 (1957), 131–136.

Ross, Arthur, and Hill, Herbert, eds. *Employment, Race, and Poverty.* New York: Harcourt, Brace and World, 1967.

Ross, Jack C., and Wheeler, Raymond H. *Black Belonging: A Study of the Social Correlates of Work Relations Among Negroes.* Westport, Conn.: Greenwood, 1971.

Rossi, Alice. "Characteristics of the Scientist and Implications for Women's Career Choices." In John Scanzoni, ed., *Readings in Social Problems.* Boston: Allyn and Bacon, 1967, pp. 248–258.

———. "Status of Women in Graduate Departments of Sociology: 1968–1969." *The American Sociologist* 5 (1970), 1–11.

Roth, Julius. "Hired Hand Research." *American Sociologist* 1 (1966), 190–196.

Rothman, Robert A., and Perrucci, Robert. "Organizational Careers and Professional Expertise." *Administrative Science Quarterly* 15 (1970), 282–293.

Rothstein, E. "Plant Relations and Discarded Workers." *Social Problems* 1 (1953), 28–31.

Roy, Donald. "Quota Restriction and Goldbricking in a Machine Shop." *American Journal of Sociology* 57 (1952), 427–442.

———. "Work Satisfaction and Social Reward in Quota Achievement: An Analysis of Piecework Incentive." *American Sociological Review* 18 (1953), 507–514.

———. "Efficiency and the 'Fix': Informal Intergroup Relations in a Piece-Work Machine Shop." *American Journal of Sociology* 60 (1954), 255–266.

———. " 'Banana Time' Job Satisfaction and Informal Interaction." *Human Organization* 18 (1959–1960), 158–168.

———. "The Union-Organizing Campaign as a Problem of Social Distance: Three Crucial Dimensions of Affiliation-Disaffiliation." In Howard S. Becker et al., *Institutions and the Person.* Chicago: Aldine, 1968, pp. 49–66.

Rueschmeyer, Dietrich. "Doctors and Lawyers: A Comment on the Theory of the Professions." *The Canadian Review of Sociology and Anthropology* 1 (1964), 17–30.

Rushing, William. "Social Influence and the Social Psychological Function of Deference: A Study of Psychiatric Nursing." *Social Forces* 41 (1962), 142–148.

———. *The Psychiatric Professions: Power, Conflict and Adaptation in a Psychiatric Hospital Staff.* Chapel Hill, N.C.: University of North Carolina Press, 1964.

————. "The Effect of Industry Size and Division of Labor on Administration." *Administrative Science Quarterly* 12 (1967), 273–295.

Sayles, Leonard. *Behavior of Industrial Work Groups.* New York: John Wiley, 1958.

————, and Strauss, George. *The Local Union: Its Place in the Industrial Plant.* New York: Harper & Row, 1953.

————. *Human Behavior in Organizations.* Englewood Cliffs, N.J.: Prentice-Hall, 1966.

Schmid, Calvin, and Giblin, Mildred. "Needs and Standards in Training Sociologists." *Sociology and Social Research* 39 (1955), 296–306.

Schneider, Eugene. *Industrial Sociology.* 2nd Edition. New York: McGraw-Hill, 1969.

Schur, Edwin. *Crimes Without Victims.* Englewood Cliffs, N.J.: Prentice-Hall, 1965.

Schwab, J. B. "Occupational Attitudes of Lawyers. *Sociology and Social Research* 24 (1939), 53–62.

Schwartz, Morris et al. *The Nurse and the Mental Patient: A Study in Interpersonal Relations.* New York: Russell Sage Foundation, 1956.

Scott, Marvin. *The Racing Game.* Chicago: Aldine, 1968.

Scott, W. Richard. "Reactions to Supervision in Heteronomous Professional Organizations." *Administrative Science Quarterly* 10 (1965), 65–81.

————. "Professionals in Organizations—Areas of Conflict." In Howard Vollmer and Donald Mills, eds., *Professionalization.* Englewood Cliffs, N.J.: Prentice-Hall, 1966, pp. 265–275.

————. "Professional Employees in a Bureaucratic Structure: Social Work." In Amitai Etzioni, ed., *The Semi Professions and Their Organization.* New York: Free Press, 1969, pp. 82–140.

————, and Volkart, Edmund, eds. *Medical Care: Readings in the Sociology of Medical Institutions.* New York: John Wiley, 1966.

Seashore, Stanley. *Group Cohesiveness in the Industrial Work Group.* Ann Arbor, Michigan: Survey Research Center, University of Michigan, 1954.

Seeman, Melvin. "On the Personal Consequences of Alienation in Work." *American Sociological Review* 32 (1967), 273–285.

Segal, Bernard. "Male Nurses: A Case Study in Status Contradiction and Prestige Loss." *Social Forces* 41 (1962), 31–38.

————. "Nurses and Patients: Time, Place, and Distance." *Social Problems* 9 (1962), 257–264.

Segal, David. "Selective Promotion in Officer Corps." *Sociological Quarterly* 8 (1967), 199–206.

Seidman, Joel et al. *The Worker Views His Union.* Chicago: University of Chicago Press, 1958.

————. "Telephone Workers." In Sigmund Nosow and William Form, eds., *Man, Work, and Society.* New York: Basic Books, 1962, pp. 493–504.

Selznick, Phillip. *Leadership in Administration.* New York: Harper & Row, 1957.

Shapiro, Carol et al. "Careers of Women Physicians: A Survey of Women Graduates from Seven Medical Schools, 1945–1951." *Journal of Medical Education* 43 (1968), 1033–1040.

Sharaf, Myron, and Levinson, Daniel. "The Quest for Omnipotence in Professional Training: The Case of the Psychiatric Resident." *Psychiatry* 27 (1964), 135–149.

Shepard, Herbert. "Nine Dilemmas in Industrial Research." *Administrative Science Quarterly* 1 (1956), 295–309.

Sherlock, Basil. "The Second Profession: Parallel Mobilities of the Dental Profession and its Recruits." *Journal of Health and Social Behavior* 10 (1969), 41–51.

————, and Cohen, Alan. "The Strategy of Occupational Choice: Recruitment to Dentistry." *Social Forces* 44 (1966), 303–314.

Sherwood, R. "The Bantu Clerk: A Study of Role Expectations." *Journal of Social Psychology* 47 (1958), 285–316.

Shortle, Caroll. *Occupational Information.* Englewood Cliffs, N.J.: Prentice-Hall, 1952.

Shostak, Arthur. *Blue Collar Life.* New York: Random House, 1969.

————, and Gomberg, William, eds. *Blue Collar World.* Englewood Cliffs, N.J.: Prentice-Hall, 1964.

Shuval, Judith. "Ethnic Stereotyping in Israeli Medical Bureaucracies." *Sociology and Social Research* 46 (1962), 455–465.

————. "Perceived Role Components of Nursing in Israel." *American Sociological Review* 28 (1963), 37–46.

————. "Sex Role Differentiation in the Professions: The Case of Israeli Dentists." *Journal of Health and Social Behavior* 11 (1970), 236–244.

Sibley, Eldridge. *The Education of Sociologists in the United States.* New York: Russell Sage Foundation, 1963.

Simon, Herbert. *Administrative Behavior.* 2nd Edition. New York: Free Press, 1957.

Simpson, Ida Harper. "Patterns of Socialization Into Professions: The Case of Student Nurses." *Sociological Inquiry* 37 (1967), 47–54.

Simpson, Richard, and Simpson, Ida Harper. "The Psychiatric Attendant: Development of an Occupational Self-Image in a Low Status Occupation." *American Sociological Review* 24 (1959), 389–393.

Skipper, James Jr., and McCaghy, Charles. "Stripteasers: The Anatomy and Career Contingencies of a Deviant Occupation." *Social Problems* 17 (1970), 391–405.

Skolnick, Jerome. *Justice Without Trial: Law Enforcement in a Democratic Society.* New York: John Wiley, 1966.

Slotkin, James Sydney. *From Field to Factory: New Industrial Employees.* New York: Free Press, 1960.

Small, Leonard. "Toward Professional Clinical Psychology." *American Psychologist* 18 (1963), 558–562.

Smigel, Erwin. "Trends in Occupational Sociology in the United States: A Survey of Postwar Research." *American Sociological Review* 19 (1954), 398–404.

————. "The Impact of Recruitment on the Organization of the Large Law Firm." *American Sociological Review* 25 (1960), 56–66.

————. *The Wall Street Lawyer: Professional Organization Man?* Bloomington, Indiana: Indiana University Press, 1969.

———— et al. "Occupational Sociology: A Re-examination." *Sociology and Social Research* 47 (1963), 472–477.

Smith, Harvey. "Contingencies of Professional Differentiation." *American Journal of Sociology* 63 (1958), 410–414.

Smith, James Otis, and Sjoberg, Gideon. "Origins and Career Patterns of Leading Protestant Clergymen." *Social Forces* 39 (1961), 290–296.

Smith, Joel, and Kornberg, Allan. "Self-concepts of American and Canadian Party Officials: Their Development and Consequences." *Social Forces* 49 (1970), 210–226.

Smith, Peter et al. "Relationships Between Managers and Their Work Associates." *Administrative Science Quarterly* 14 (1969), 338–345.

Smith, Verlie. "Role Conflicts in the Position of a Military Education Advisor." *Social Forces* 40 (1961), 176–178.

Sofer, Cyril. *Men in Mid-Career: A Study of British Managers and Technical Specialists.* London: Cambridge University Press, 1970.

Solomon, David. "Ethnic and Class Differences Among Hospitals as Contingencies in Medical Careers." *American Journal of Sociology* 66 (1961), 463–471.

———. "Sociological Perspectives on Occupations." In Howard S. Becker et al., *Institutions and the Person.* Chicago: Aldine, 1968, pp. 3–13.

Solzbacher, Regina. "Occupational Prestige in a Negro Community." *American Catholic Sociological Review* 22 (1961), 250–257.

Soni, B. D. "Sociological Analysis of Legal Profession: A Study of Mechanisms in Lawyer-Client Relationship." *Journal of Social Sciences* 1 (1958), 63–70.

Soule, James, and Clarke, James W. "Amateurs and Professionals." *American Political Science Review* 64 (1970), 888–898.

Spinrad, William. "Correlates of Trade Union Participation: A Summary of the Literature." *American Sociological Review* 25 (1960), 237–244.

Sprey, Jesse. "Sex Differences in Occupational Choice Patterns Among Negro Adolescents." *Social Problems* 10 (1962), 11–23.

Stebbins, Robert. "A Theory of the Jazz Community." *Sociological Quarterly* 9 (1968), 318–331.

———. "On Misunderstanding the Concept of Commitment: A Theoretical Clarification." *Social Forces* 48 (1970), 526–529.

———. "Career: The Subjective Approach." *Sociological Quarterly* 11 (1970), 32–49.

Steele, H. Ellsworth. "Jobs for Negroes: Some North-South Plant Studies." *Social Forces* 32 (1953), 152–162.

Stern, Bernard. "The Specialist and the General Practitioner." In E. Gartley Jaco, ed., *Patients, Physicians and Illness.* New York: Free Press, 1958, pp. 352–360.

Stiles, Lindley, ed. *The Teacher's Role in American Society.* New York: Harper & Row, 1957.

Stinchcombe, Arthur. "Bureaucratic and Craft Administration of Production: A Comparative Study." *Administrative Science Quarterly* 4 (1959), 168–187.

Stinett, T. M. "The Accreditation and Professionalization of Teaching." *Journal of Teacher Education* 3 (1952), 30–39.

Strauss, Anselm, and Rainwater, Lee, with Barbara Berger and Marc Swartz. *The Professional Scientist: A Study of American Chemists.* Chicago: Aldine, 1962.

Strauss, George. "The Set-Up Man: A Case Study of Organizational Change." *Human Organization* 13 (1954), 17–25.

————. "Control by Membership in Building Trade Unions." *American Journal of Sociology* 61 (1956), 527–535.

————. "The Changing Role of the Working Supervisor." *Journal of Business* 30 (1957), 202–211.

————. "Tactics of Lateral Relationships: The Purchasing Agent." *Administrative Science Quarterly* 7 (1962), 161–186.

————. "Professionalism and Occupational Associations." *Industrial Relations* 2:3 (1963), 7–31.

————, and Sayles, Leonard. "The Local Union Meeting." *Industrial and Labor Relations Review* 6 (1953), 206–219.

————, and Sayles, Risha. "Leadership Roles in Labor Unions." *Sociology and Social Research* 38 (1953), 96–102.

Street, David, and Leggett, John. "Economic Deprivation and Extremism: A Study of Unemployed Negroes." *American Journal of Sociology* 67 (1961), 53–57.

Strodtbeck, Fred, and Sussman, Marvin. "Of Time, the City, and the 'One-Year' Guarantee: The Relations Between Watchowners and Repairers." In Marcello Truzzi, ed., *Sociology and Everyday Life.* Englewood Cliffs, N.J.: Prentice-Hall, 1968, pp. 303–313.

Sturmthal, Adolph, ed. *White Collar Trade Unions.* Urbana, Illinois: University of Illinois Press, 1966.

Sultan, Paul. *The Disenchanted Unionist.* New York: Harper & Row, 1963.

Super, Donald. *The Psychology of Careers.* New York: Harper & Brothers, 1957.

Sutherland, Edwin. *The Professional Thief.* Chicago: University of Chicago Press, 1937.

————. *White Collar Crime.* New York: Dryden Press, 1949.

Swaine, Robert. "The Impact of Big Business on the Profession." *American Bar Association Journal* 35 (1949), 168–171.

Sykes, Gresham. *The Society of Captives.* New York: Atheneum, 1969.

Taeuber, Alma et al. "Occupational Assimilation as a Competitive Process: A Re-Analysis." *American Journal of Sociology* 72 (1966), 273–285.

Tagliacozzo, Daisy, and Seidman, Joel. "A Typology of Rank-and-File Union Members." *American Journal of Sociology* 61 (1956), 546–553.

Tannenbaum, Arnold, and Kahn, Robert. *Participation in Union Locals.* New York: Harper & Row, 1958.

Taub, Richard. *Bureaucrats Under Stress.* Berkeley: University of California Press, 1969.

Tausky, Curt, and Dubin, Robert. "Career Anchorage: Management Mobility Motivations." *American Sociological Review* 30 (1965), 725–735.

Taylor, Lee. *Occupational Sociology.* New York: Oxford University Press, 1968.

————, and Pellegrin, Roland. "Professionalization: Its Functions and Dysfunctions for the Life Insurance Occupation." *Social Forces* 38 (1959), 110–114.

Teitsworth, Clark. "Growing Role of the Company Economists." *Harvard Business Review* 37 (1959), 97–104.

Terris, Milton, and Monk, Mary. "Changes in Physicians' Careers: Relation of Time After Graduation to Specialization." In E. Gartley Jaco, ed., *Patients, Physicians and Illness.* Glencoe, Ill.: Free Press, 1958, pp. 361–365.

Thielens, Wagner. "Some Comparisons of Entrants to Medical and Law School."

In Robert Merton et al., *The Student Physician*. Cambridge, Mass.: Harvard University Press, 1957, pp. 131–152.

Thompson, Daniel. *The Negro Leadership Class*. Englewood Cliffs, N.J.: Prentice-Hall, 1963.

Thorne, Isidor. "Nursing: The Functional Significance of an Institutional Pattern." *American Sociological Review* 20 (1955), 531–538.

Thornton, Russell. "Organizational Involvement and Commitment to Organization and Profession." *Administrative Science Quarterly* 15 (1970), 417–426.

Toren, Nina. "Semi-Professionalism and Social Work: A Theoretical Perspective." In Amitai Etzioni, ed., *The Semi-Professions and Their Organization*. New York: Free Press, 1969, pp. 141–195.

Trice, Harrison. "Night Watchman: A Study of an Isolated Occupation." *Industrial and Labor Relations Research* 10 (1964), 3–8.

Trow, Donald. "Executive Succession in Small Companies." *Administrative Science Quarterly* 6 (1961), 228–235.

Tully, Judy Corder, Jackson, Elton F., and Curtis, Richard F. "Trends in Occupational Mobility in Indianapolis." *Social Forces* 49 (1970), 186–200.

Tunstall, J. *The Advertising Man in London Advertising Agencies*. London: Chapman and Hall, 1964.

Turner, Ralph. "Foci of Discrimination in the Employment of Non-whites." *American Journal of Sociology* 58 (1945), 247–256.

———. "The Navy Disbursing Officer as a Bureaucrat." *American Sociological Review* 12 (1947), 342–348.

———. "Some Aspects of Women's Ambition." *American Journal of Sociology* 70 (1964), 271–285.

Ujhely, Gertrude. "Servant? No! Service Professional? Yes!" *RN* 27 (1964), 56–60.

Viorst, J. "Negroes in Science." *Science News Letter* 87 (April 3, 1965), 218–219.

Vollmer, Howard, and Mills, Donald. *Professionalization*. Englewood Cliffs, N.J.: Prentice-Hall, 1966.

Vroom, Victor. *Motivation in Management*. New York: American Foundation for Management Research, 1965.

———, and MacCrimmon, Kenneth. "Toward a Stochastic Model of Managerial Careers." *Administrative Science Quarterly* 13 (1968), 26–46.

Wahlke, J. et al. "American State Legislators' Role Orientations Toward Pressure Groups." *Journal of Politics* 22 (1960), 203–227.

Walker, Charles. *Toward the Automatic Factory: A Case Study of Men and Machines*. New Haven, Conn.: Yale University Press, 1957.

———. "Life in the Automatic Factory." *Harvard Business Review* 36 (1958), 111–119.

———, and Guest, Robert. *The Man on the Assembly Line*. Cambridge, Mass.: Harvard University Press, 1952.

———, and Turner, A. N. *The Foreman on the Assembly-Line*. Cambridge, Mass.: Harvard University Press, 1956.

Walker, Helen. *The Negro in the Medical Profession*. Charlottesville, Va.: University of Virginia, Phelps Stokes Fellowship Papers No. 18, 1949.

Wallace, Samuel. *Skid Row as a Way of Life*. New York: Harper & Row, 1965.

———. "The Road to Skid Row." *Social Problems* 16 (1968), 92–106.

Wardwell, Walter. "A Marginal Professional Role: The Chiropractor." *Social Forces* 31 (1952), 339–348.

———. "Social Integration, Bureaucratization and the Professions." *Social Forces* 33 (1955), 356–359.

———. "The Reduction of Strain in a Marginal Social Role." *American Journal of Sociology* 61 (1955), 16–25.

———, and Wood, Arthur. "The Extra-Professional Role of the Lawyer." *American Journal of Sociology* 61 (1956), 304–307.

———. "Limited, Marginal, and Quasi-Practitioners." In Howard Freeman et al., eds., *Handbook of Medical Sociology*. Englewood Cliffs, N.J.: Prentice-Hall, 1963, Chapter 9.

Warkov, Seymour. *Lawyers in the Making*. Chicago: Aldine, 1965.

Warner, W. Lloyd. *The Social System of the Modern Factory*. New Haven, Conn.: Yale University Press, 1947.

———, and Abegglen, J. C. *Big Business Leaders in America*. New York: Harper & Row, 1955.

———. *Occupational Mobility in American Business and Industry: 1928–1952*. Minneapolis, Minn.: University of Minnesota Press, 1955.

Weil, Mildred. "An Analysis of the Factors Influencing Married Women's Actual or Planned Work Participation." *American Sociological Review* 26 (1961), 91–96.

Weinberg, S. Kirson, and Arond, Henry. "The Occupational Culture of the Boxer." *American Journal of Sociology* 57 (1952), 460–469.

Westley, William. "Violence and the Police." *American Journal of Sociology* 58 (1953), 34–41.

———. "Secrecy and the Police." *Social Forces* 45 (1956), 254–257.

Whyte, William Foote. *Human Relations in the Restaurant Industry*. New York: McGraw-Hill, 1948.

———. *Men at Work*. Homewood, Ill.: Dorsey Press, and Richard D. Irwin, 1961.

———. *Streetcorner Society*. Chicago: University of Chicago Press, 1967.

Whyte, William H. Jr. *The Organization Man*. New York: Anchor Books, 1957.

Wilensky, Harold. *Intellectuals in Labor Unions: Organizational Pressures on Professional Roles*. Glencoe, Ill.: Free Press, 1956.

———. "Work, Careers, and Social Integration." *International Social Science Journal* 12 (1960), 543–560.

———. "Orderly Careers and Social Participation: The Impact of Work History on Social Integration in the Middle Class." *American Sociological Review* 26 (1961), 521–539.

———. "The Professionalization of Everyone?" *American Journal of Sociology* 70 (1964), 137–158.

———, and Edwards, Hugh. "The Skidder: Ideological Adjustments of the Downward Mobile Worker." *American Sociological Review* 24 (1959), 215–231.

———, and Lebeaux, Charles N. *Industrial Society and Social Welfare*. New York: Russell Sage Foundation, 1958.

Williams, Josephine. "Patients and Prejudice: Lay Attitudes Toward Women Physicians." *American Journal of Sociology* 51 (1946), 283–287.

————. "The Woman Physician's Dilemma." *Journal of Social Issues* 6 (1950), 38–44.

Wilson, Bryan. "The Teacher's Role—A Sociological Analysis." *British Journal of Sociology* 13 (1962), 15–32.

Wilson, James Q. *Negro Politics*. New York: Free Press, 1960.

————. "Generational and Ethnic Differences Among Career Police Officers." *American Journal of Sociology* 69 (1964), 522–528.

————. *Varieties of Police Behavior*. Cambridge, Mass.: Harvard University Press, 1968.

Wilson, Logan. *The Academic Man: A Study in the Sociology of a Profession*. New York: Oxford University Press, 1948.

————. "Disjunctive Processes in the Academic Milieu." In E. A. Tiryakian, ed., *Sociocultural Theory, Values, and Sociocultural Change: Essays in Honor of Pitirim A. Sorokin*. New York: Free Press of Glencoe, 1963, pp. 283–294.

Wolfbein, Seymour. *Work in American Society*. Glenview, Ill.: Scott, Foresman, 1971.

Wood, Arthur. "Informal Relations in the Practice of Criminal Law." *American Journal of Sociology* 62 (1956), 48–55.

————. "Professional Ethics Among Criminal Lawyers." *Social Problems* 7 (1959), 70–83.

Woodson, Carter. *The Negro Professional Man and the Community*. Washington, D.C.: The Association for the Study of Negro Life and History, 1934.

Wooton, Barbara. "The Image of the Social Worker." *British Journal of Sociology* 11 (1960), 373–385.

Worthy, James. "Organizational Structure and Employee Morale." *American Sociological Review* 15 (1950), 169–179.

Wray, Donald. "Marginal Men of Industry: The Foremen." *American Journal of Sociology* 54 (1949), 298–301.

Wyle, Frederick. "The Soviet Lawyer: An Occupational Profile." In Alex Inkeles and Kent Geiger, eds., *Soviet Sociology*. Boston: Houghton Mifflin, 1961, pp. 210–218.

Young, Harding. "Negro Participation in American Business." *Journal of Negro Education* 32 (1963), 390–401.

Zald, Mayer. "The Power and Functions of Boards of Directors: A Theoretical Synthesis." *American Journal of Sociology* 75 (1969), 97–111.

Zapoleon, Marguerite. "Women in the Professions." *Journal of Social Issues* 6 (1950), 13–24.

Zelan, Joseph. "Social Origins and the Recruitment of American Lawyers." *British Journal of Sociology* 18 (1967), 45–54.

Zurcher, Louis. "The Sailor Aboard Ship: A Study of Role Behavior in a Total Institution." *Social Forces* 43 (1965), 389–401.

———— et al. "Value Orientation, Role Conflict, and Alienation From Work: A Cross Cultural Study." *American Sociological Review* 30 (1965), 539–548.

————. "The Hasher: A Study of Role Conflict." *Social Forces* 44 (1966), 505–514.

Name Index

Occupation Index

Subject Index